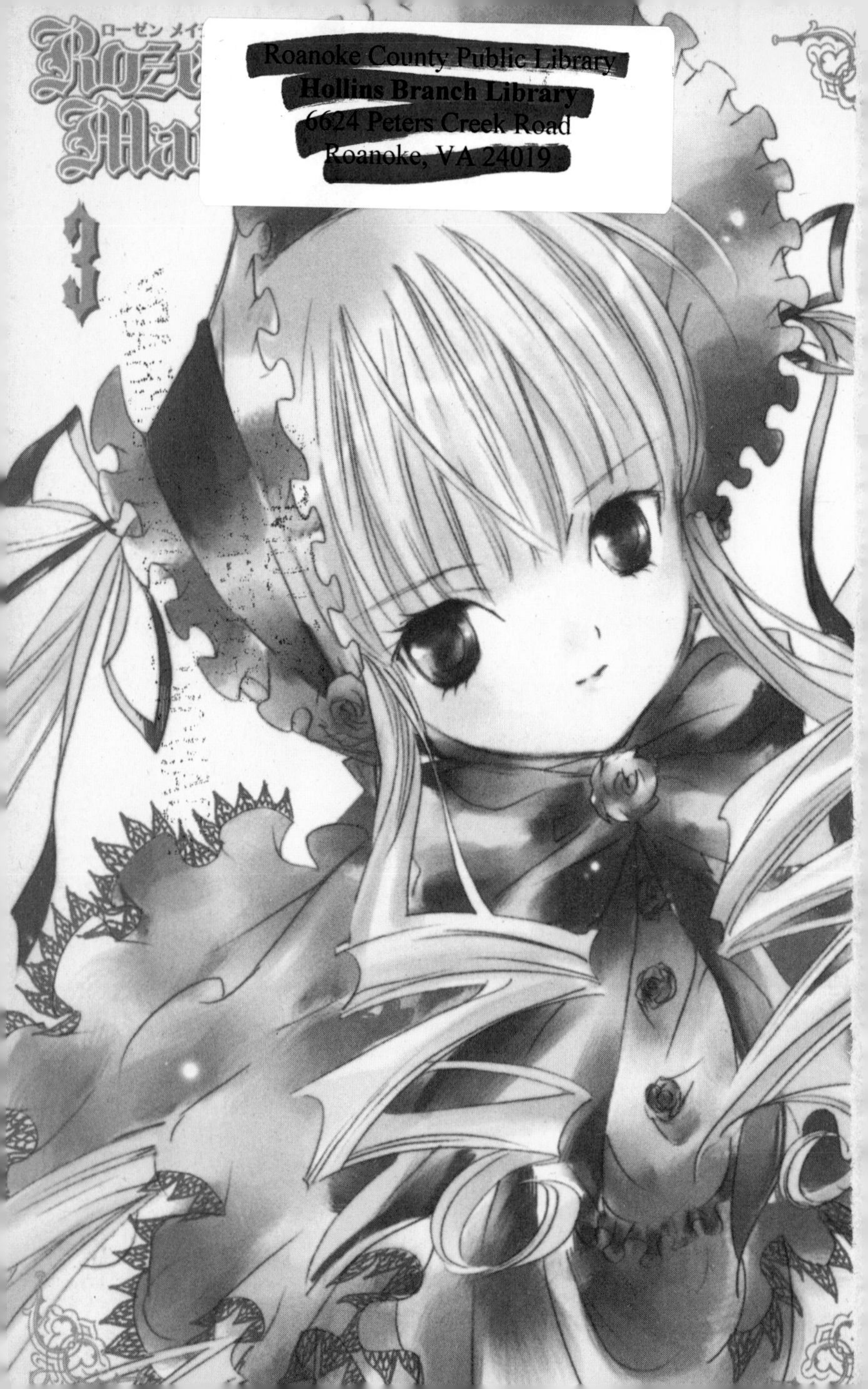
3

Rozen Maiden Vol. 3
Created by Peach-Pit

Translation - Yuko Fukami
English Adaptation - Rob Valois
Copy Editor - Stephanie Duchin
Retouch and Lettering - Michael Paolilli
Cover Design - Al-Insan Lashley

Editor - Luis Reyes
Digital Imaging Manager - Chris Buford
Production Manager - Elisabeth Brizzi
Editor-in-Chief - Rob Tokar
Managing Editor - Vy Nguyen
VP of Production - Ron Klamert
Publisher - Mike Kiley
President and C.O.O. - John Parker
C.E.O. and Chief Creative Officer - Stuart Levy

A  Manga

TOKYOPOP Inc.
5900 Wilshire Blvd. Suite 2000
Los Angeles, CA 90036

E-mail: info@TOKYOPOP.com
Come visit us online at www.TOKYOPOP.com

ISBN: 978-1-59816-314-8

First TOKYOPOP printing: January 2007

10 9 8 7 6 5 4 3 2 1

Printed in the USA

Rozen Maiden

PEACH-PIT

3

TOKYOPOP®

HAMBURG // LONDON // LOS ANGELES // TOKYO

The Story So Far...

In response to his parents' perpetual absence and an inability to connect with kids at school, Jun retreats bitterly from what he sees as a cruel world. He develops a strange internet buying habit that includes getting an online purchase in the mail, then returning it before the cool-down period ends. It is his way of playing with danger while remaining safe and secure in the confines of his house. All of this behavior worries his sister Nori, who adores school and people and who cares for her brother to no end.

Things begin to change in the Sakurada household, though, when Jun orders a doll online that turns out to be entirely sentient. Shinku is one of the Rozen Maidens, seven dolls created by Rozen the dollmaker and endowed with curious supernatural abilities, namely the ability to pass into the N-Field, a thrilling terrain of the unconscious. Each of the dolls is also tied to an artificial spirit—Shinku's is named Hollier. However, each of the dolls must rest, and when that happens, they must be wound up again.

Shinku is stern and severe with Jun, ostensibly bossing him around but actually getting him to realize the nature of his depression. Nori, of course, loves the companionship and serves Shinku anything she wants, much to the chagrin of Jun who just wants the doll out of the house.

So after defeating a stuffed bear that is sent to kill the two of them by Suigintoh—another one of the Rozen Maidens—Shinku drags Jun into the N-Field to face their attacker. It is in the N-Field that Jun comes face to face with the manifestation of his own insecurities, and the emotions he stirs in other people, namely Tomoe, a girl from his school.

Soon, several dolls end up taking residence at the Sakurada house: Hinaichigo, who belongs to Tomoe; Suiseiseki, who has come to get help finding her sister, Souseiseki; and Suigintoh, who continues to torment the whole lot of them through the passageway to the N-Field.

It seems now that Souseiseki has a mysterious new master who might not have the best of intentions for her or anybody else, a fate that Souseiseki, with the help of the rest of the Sakurada household, desperately wants to save her from.

Character Guide

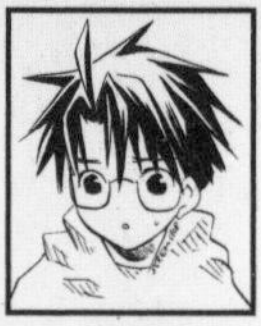

Jun Sakurada –
A social recluse who gets sucked into a world of bickering dolls. But it may be in the mystical realm they can occupy that he will discover the true nature of his depression and loneliness.

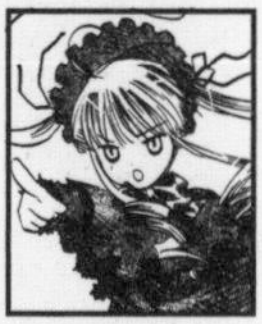

Shinku –
A doll that Jun ordered online who has now become a permanent fixture in his house. Though she seems bossy and rude, her commitment to restoring the unity of the Rozen Maidens seems unflagging.

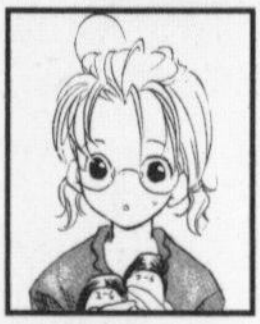

Nori Sakurada –
Jun's sister and a social butterfly who is ecstatic that the house is full again. She only has a tangential understanding of the mystical energies flowing through the house, but as long as she can serve tea, she's good.

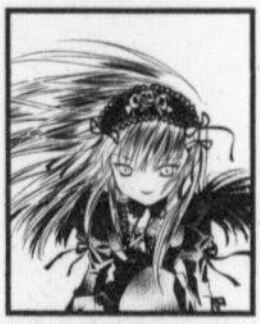

Suigintoh –
A sinister Rozen Maiden doll who for some reason wants Shinku dead.

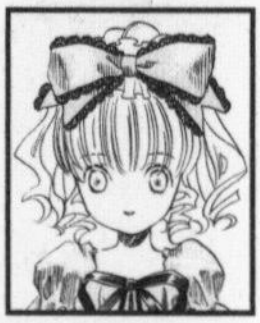

Hinaichigo –
A young Rozen Maiden doll who has an insatiable desire for companionship.

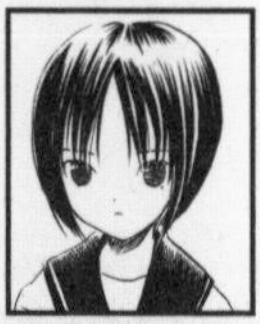

Tomoe –
Jun's classmate and Hinaichigo's master, though she is unable to handle her new ward and therefore lets the doll stay at the Sakurada house.

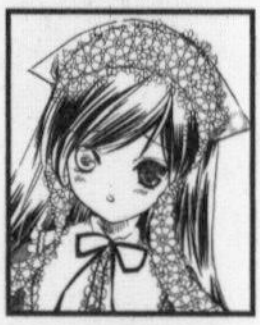

Suiseiseki –
Another of the Rozen Maidens who comes to Shinku for help finding her sister.

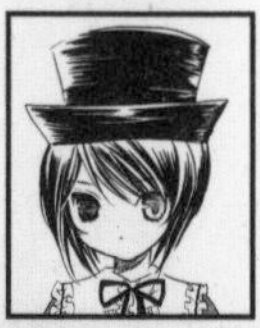

Souseiseki –
Suiseiseki's sister who has a mysterious master with seemingly sinister intentions.

Rozen Maiden

ローゼン メイデン

3

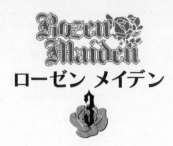

Contents

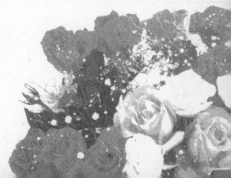

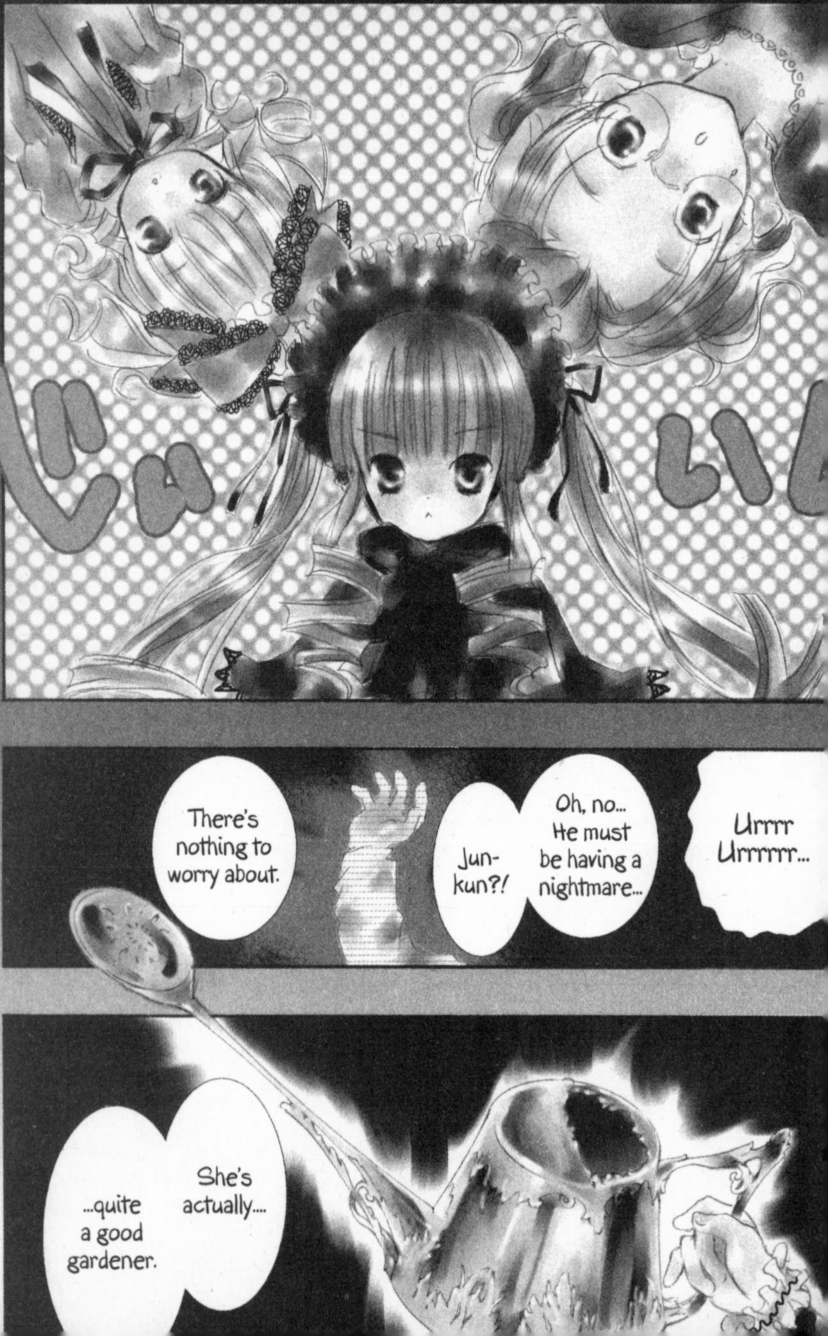
Urrrr Urrrrrr...
Oh, no... He must be having a nightmare...
Jun-kun?!
There's nothing to worry about.
She's actually....
...quite a good gardener.

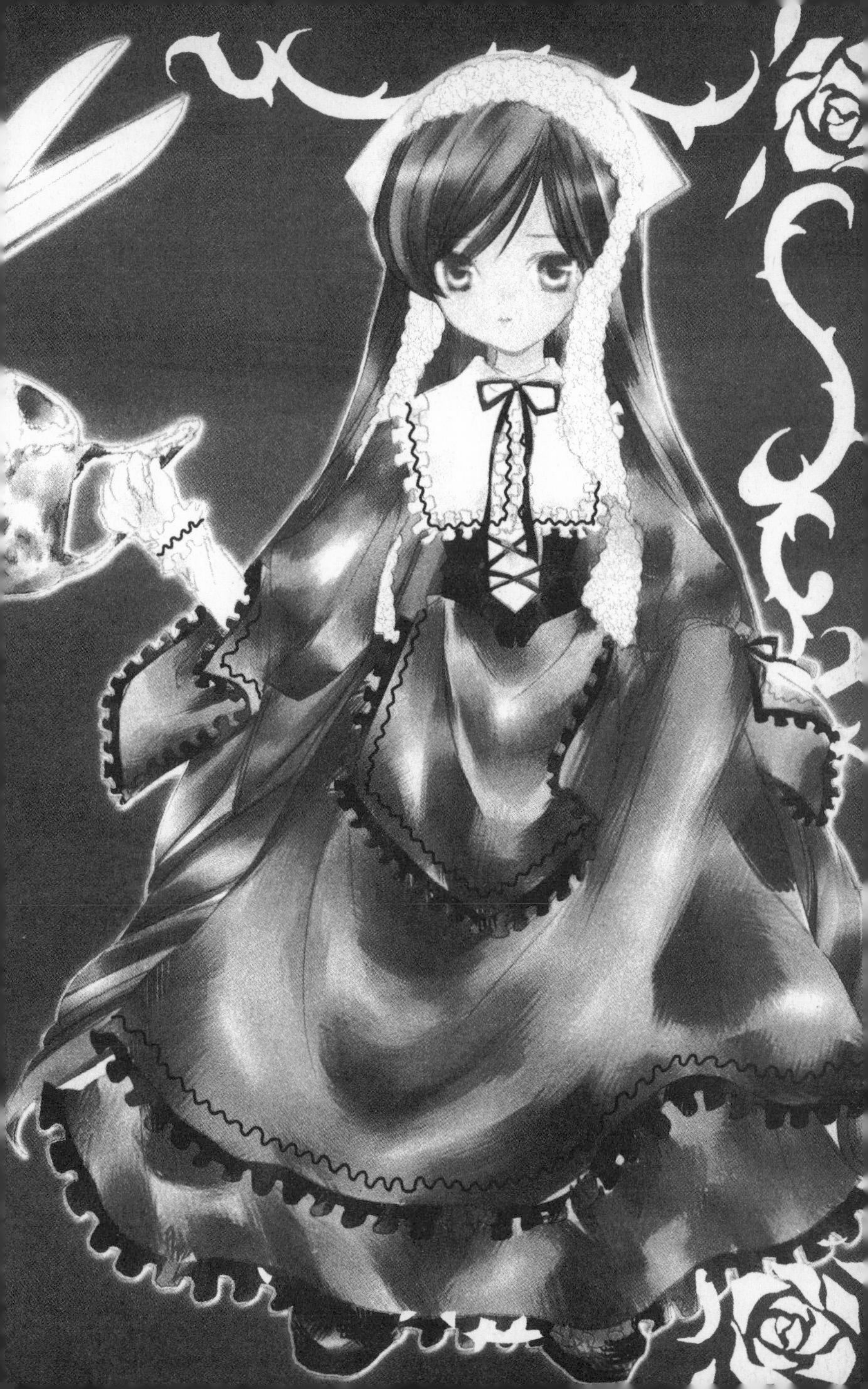

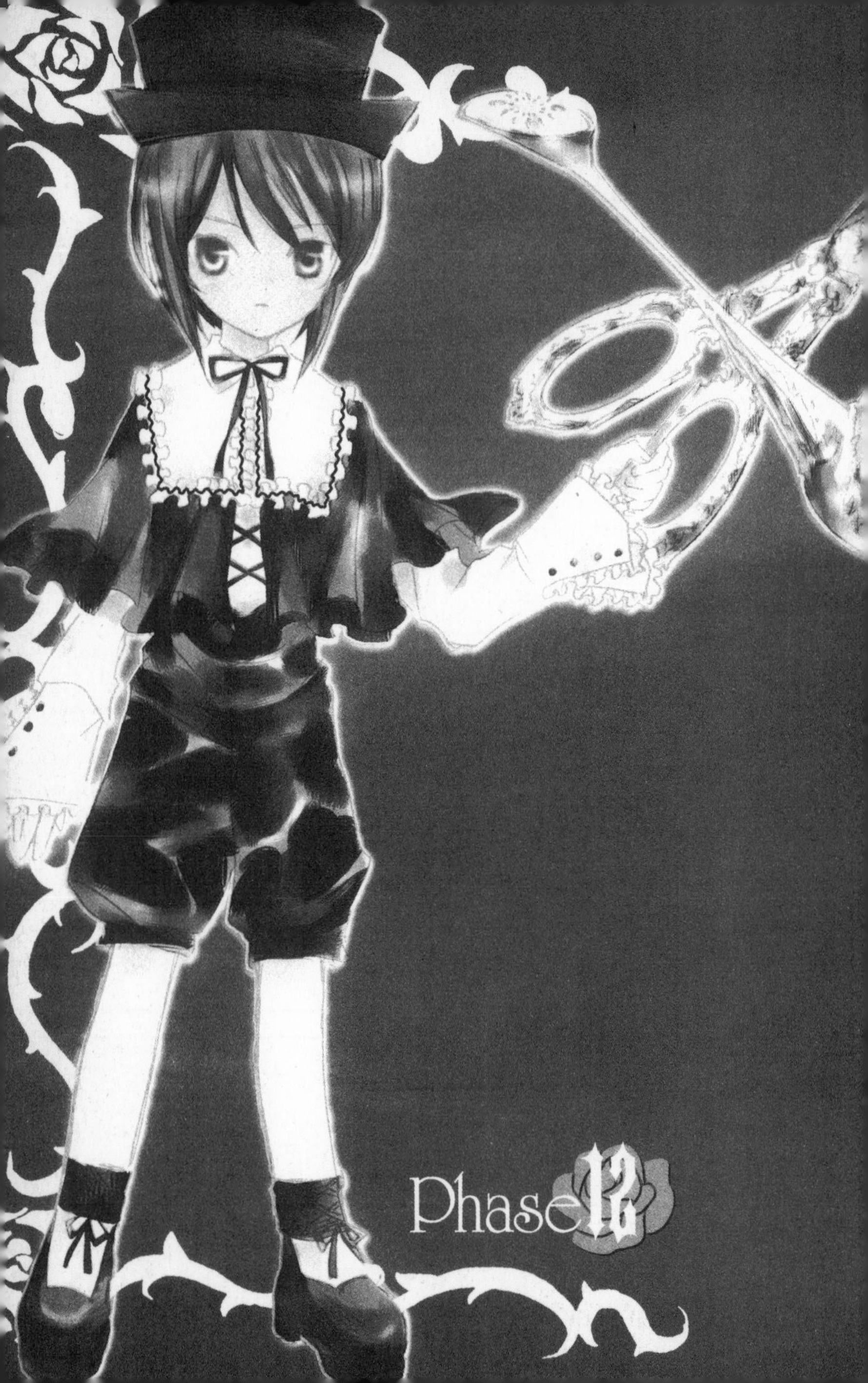
Phase 12

ローゼン メイデン
Rozen Maiden

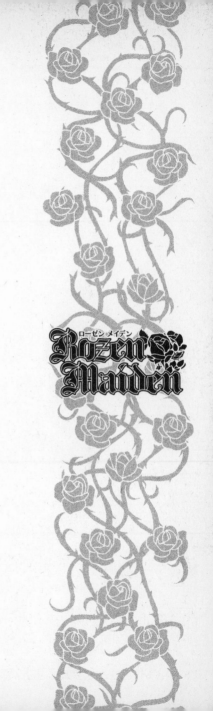

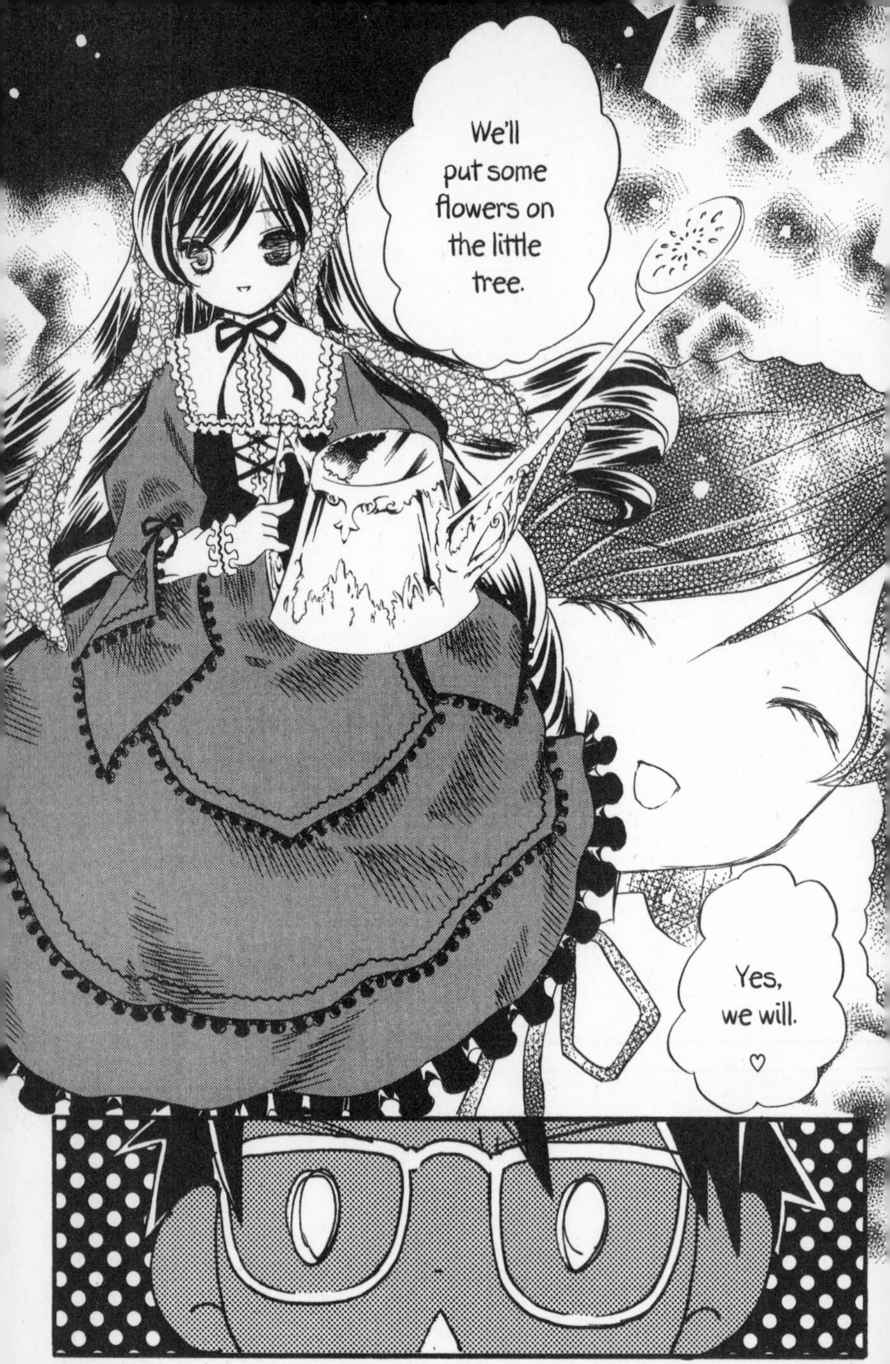
We'll put some flowers on the little tree.
Yes, we will. ♡

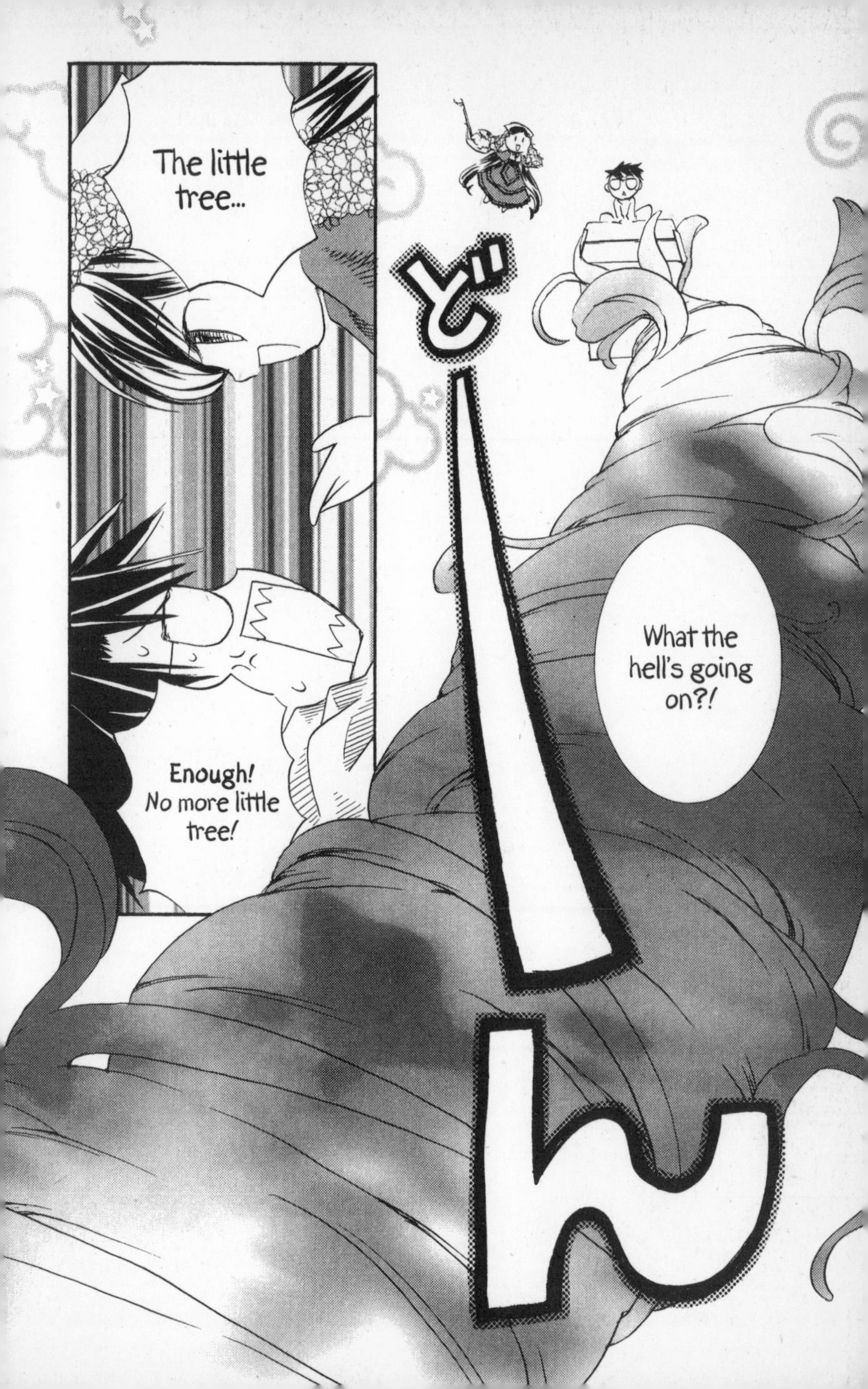

What the hell's going on?!
どーん
The little tree...
Enough! No more little tree!

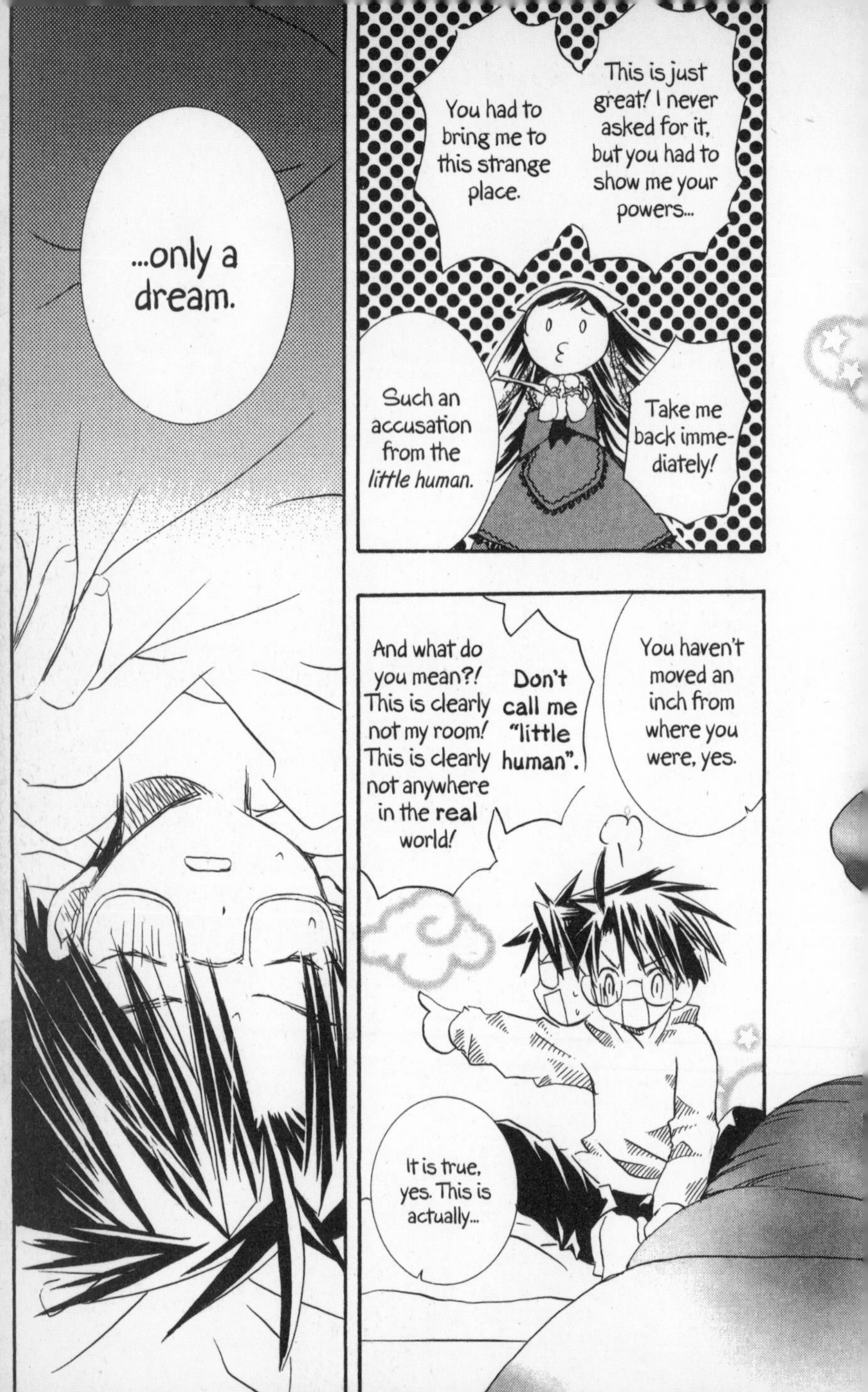
This is just great! I never asked for it, but you had to show me your powers...
You had to bring me to this strange place.
Take me back imme-diately!
Such an accusation from the *little human*.
You haven't moved an inch from where you were, yes.
Don't call me "little human".
And what do you mean?! This is clearly not my room! This is clearly not anywhere in the **real** world!
It is true, yes. This is actually...
...only a dream.

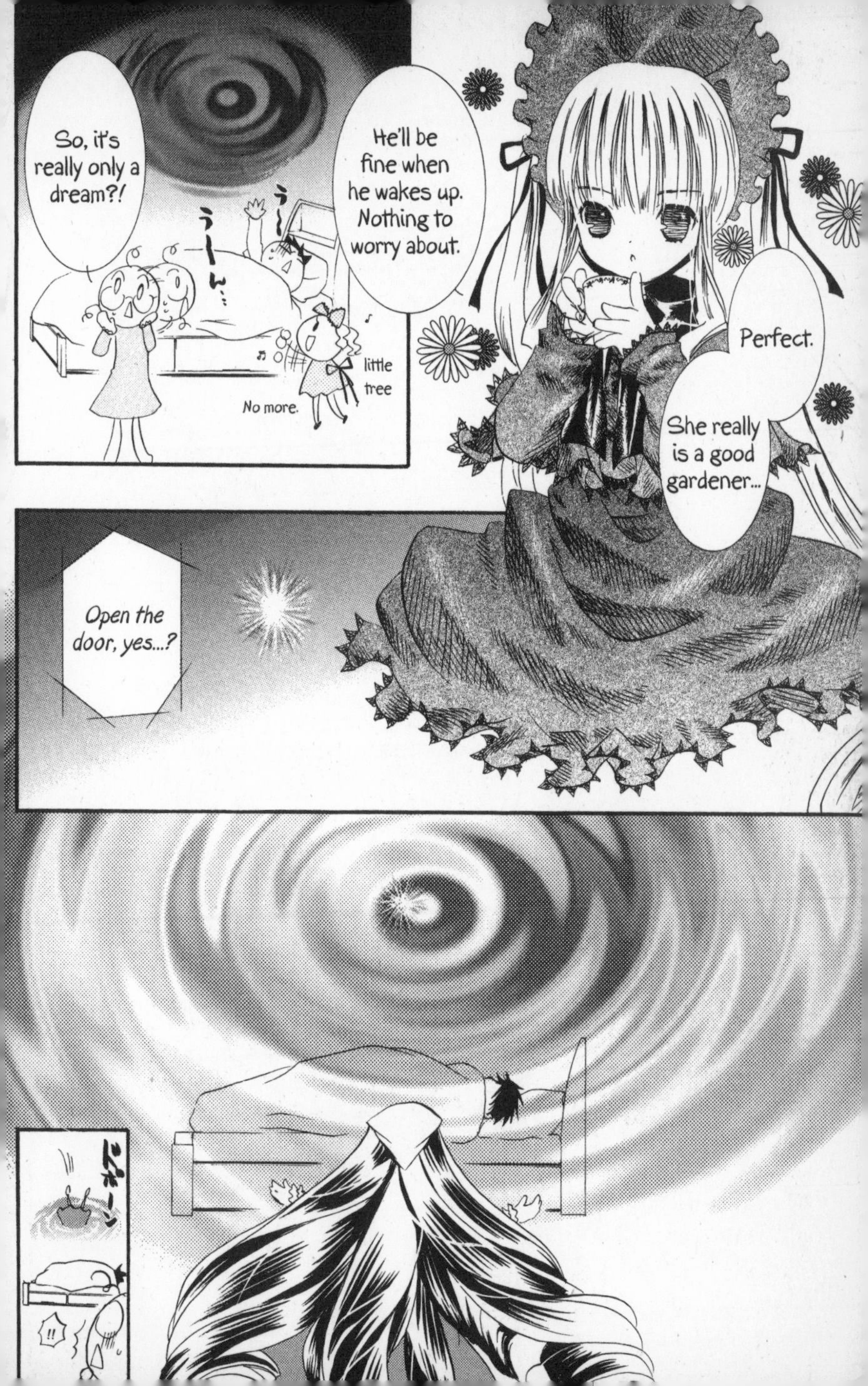
Perfect.
She really is a good gardener...
He'll be fine when he wakes up. Nothing to worry about.
So, it's really only a dream?!
う～
うーん‥
little tree
No more.
Open the door, yes...?
!!

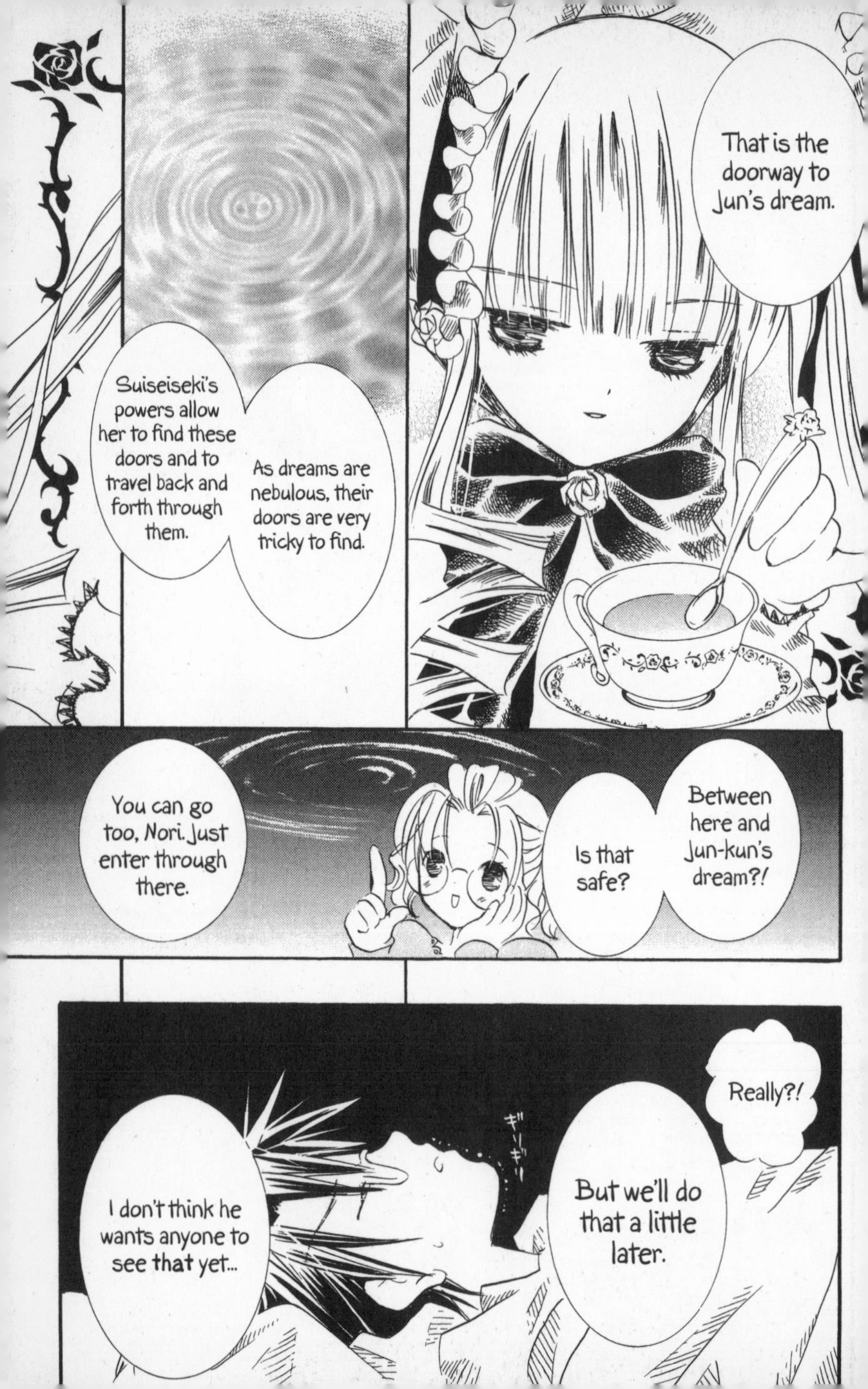
That is the doorway to Jun's dream.
As dreams are nebulous, their doors are very tricky to find.
Suiseiseki's powers allow her to find these doors and to travel back and forth through them.
Between here and Jun-kun's dream?!
Is that safe?
You can go too, Nori. Just enter through there.
Really?!
But we'll do that a little later.
ギリギリ
I don't think he wants anyone to see that yet...

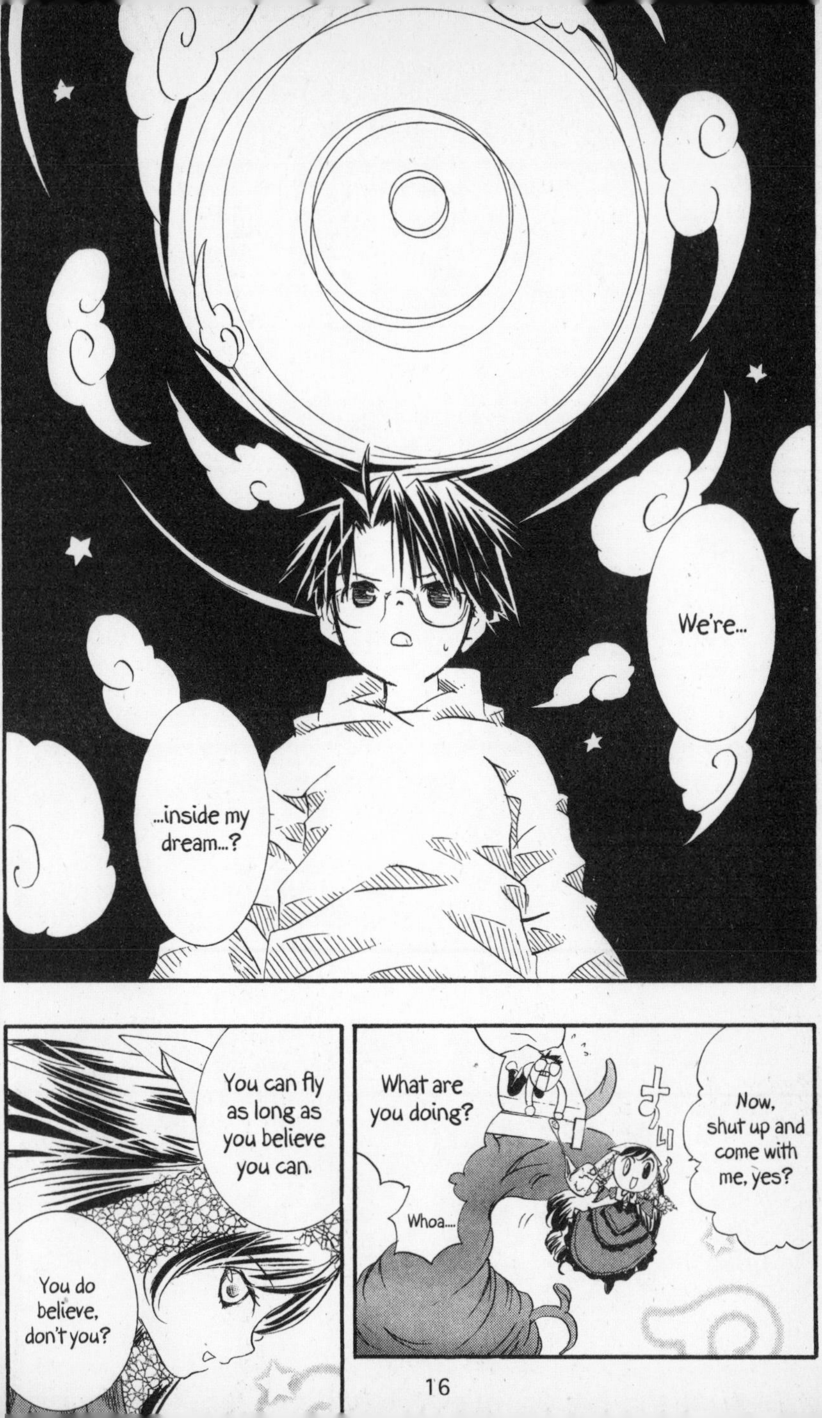
We're...
...inside my dream...?
Now, shut up and come with me, yes?
What are you doing?
Whoa....
You can fly as long as you believe you can.
You do believe, don't you?

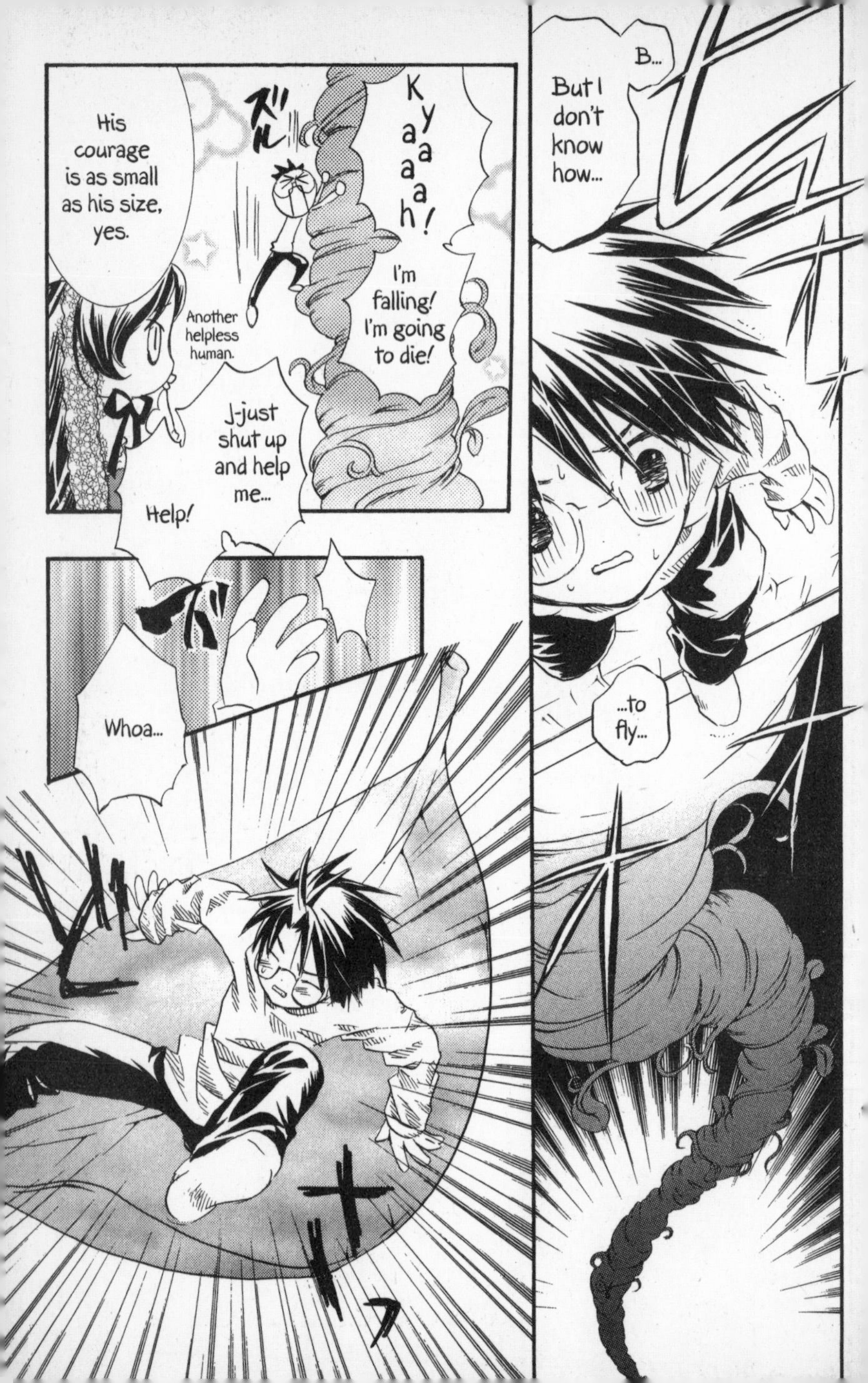
B...
But I don't know how...
...to fly...
Kyaaaah!
ズル
His courage is as small as his size, yes.
I'm falling! I'm going to die!
Another helpless human.
J-just shut up and help me...
Help!
Whoa...

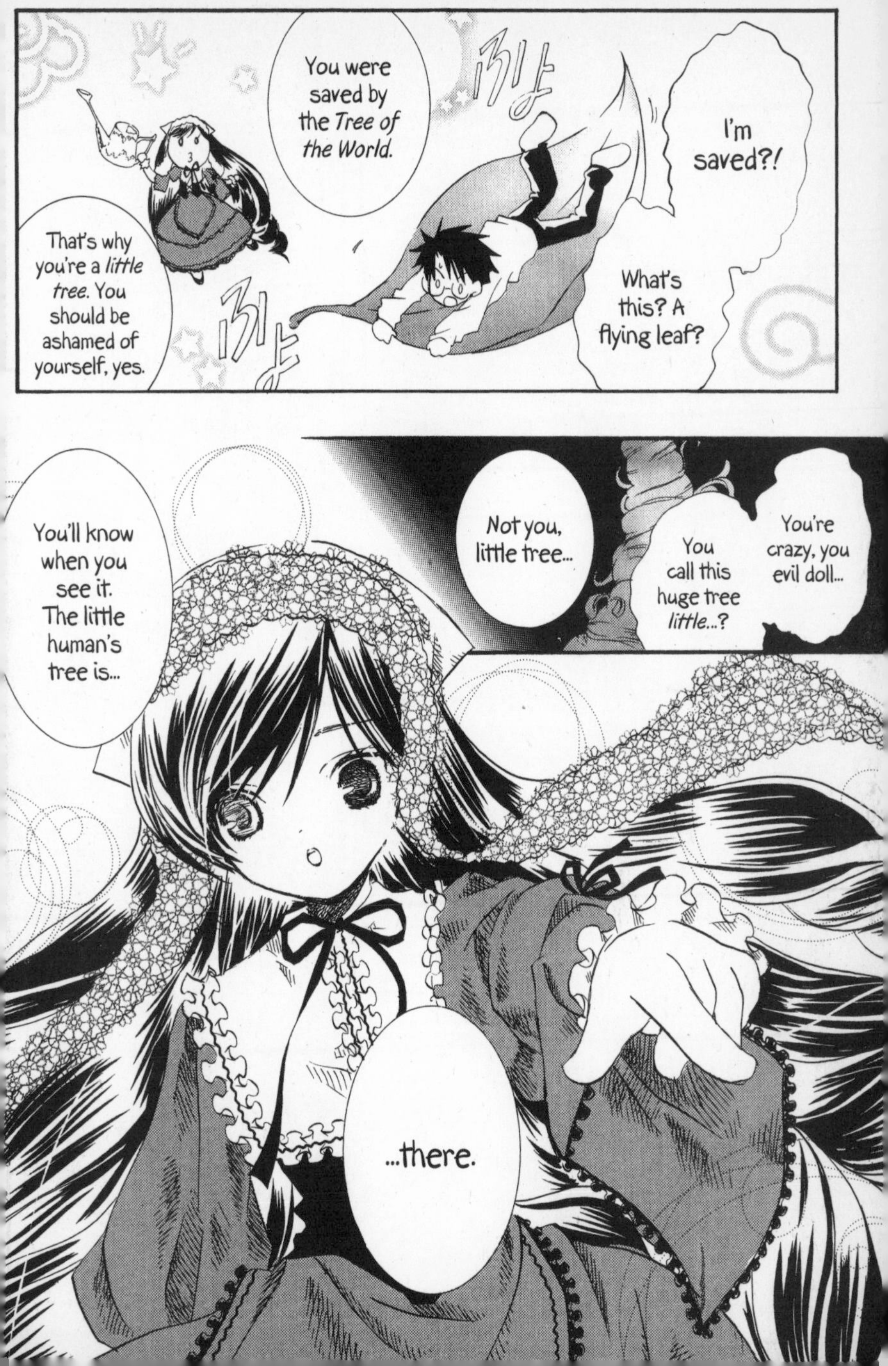
I'm saved?!
What's this? A flying leaf?
ふよ
You were saved by the *Tree of the World.*
ふよ
That's why you're a *little tree.* You should be ashamed of yourself, yes.
You're crazy, you evil doll...
You call this huge tree *little*...?
Not you, little tree...
You'll know when you see it. The little human's tree is...
...there.

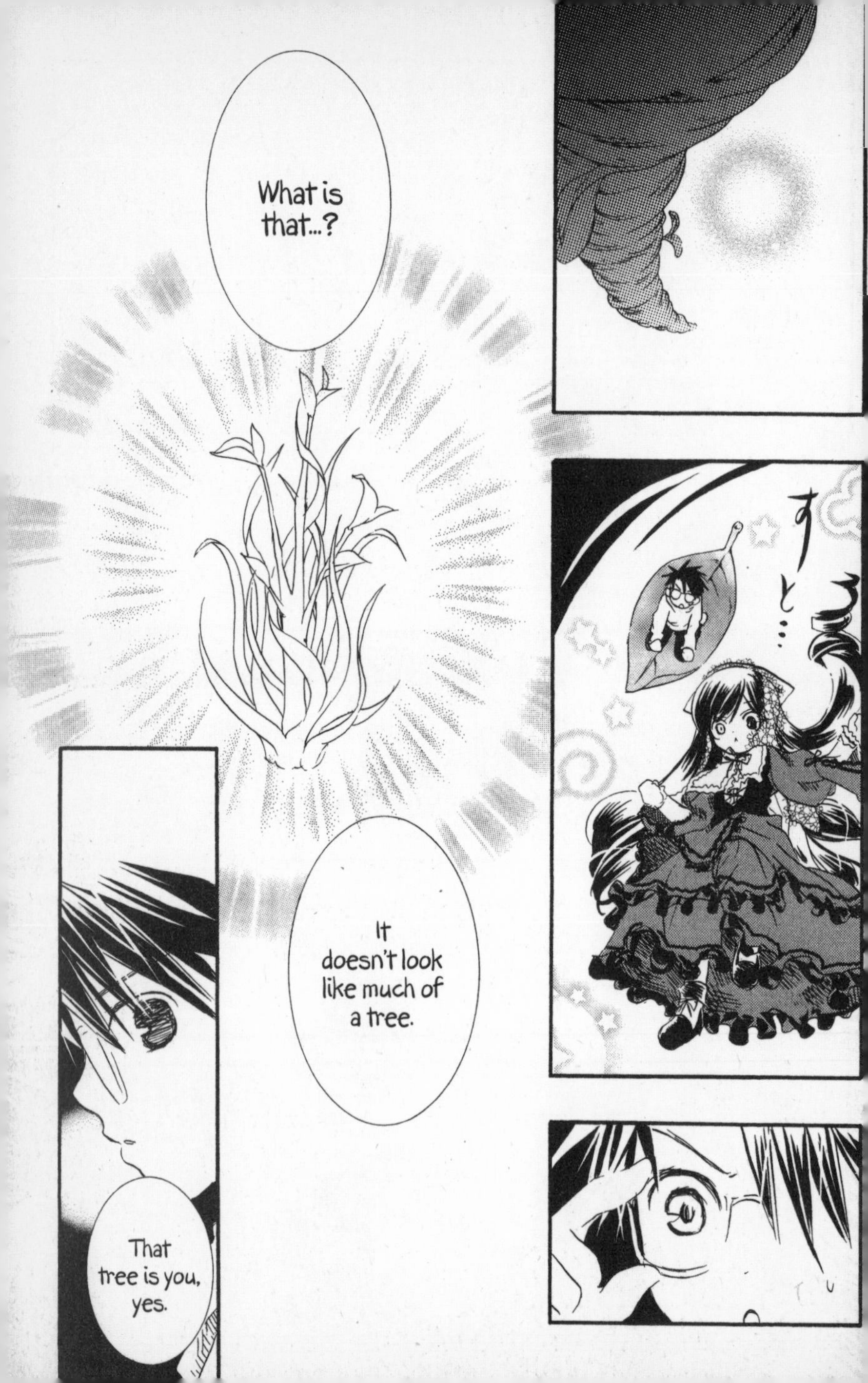
すと…
What is that...?
It doesn't look like much of a tree.
That tree is you, yes.

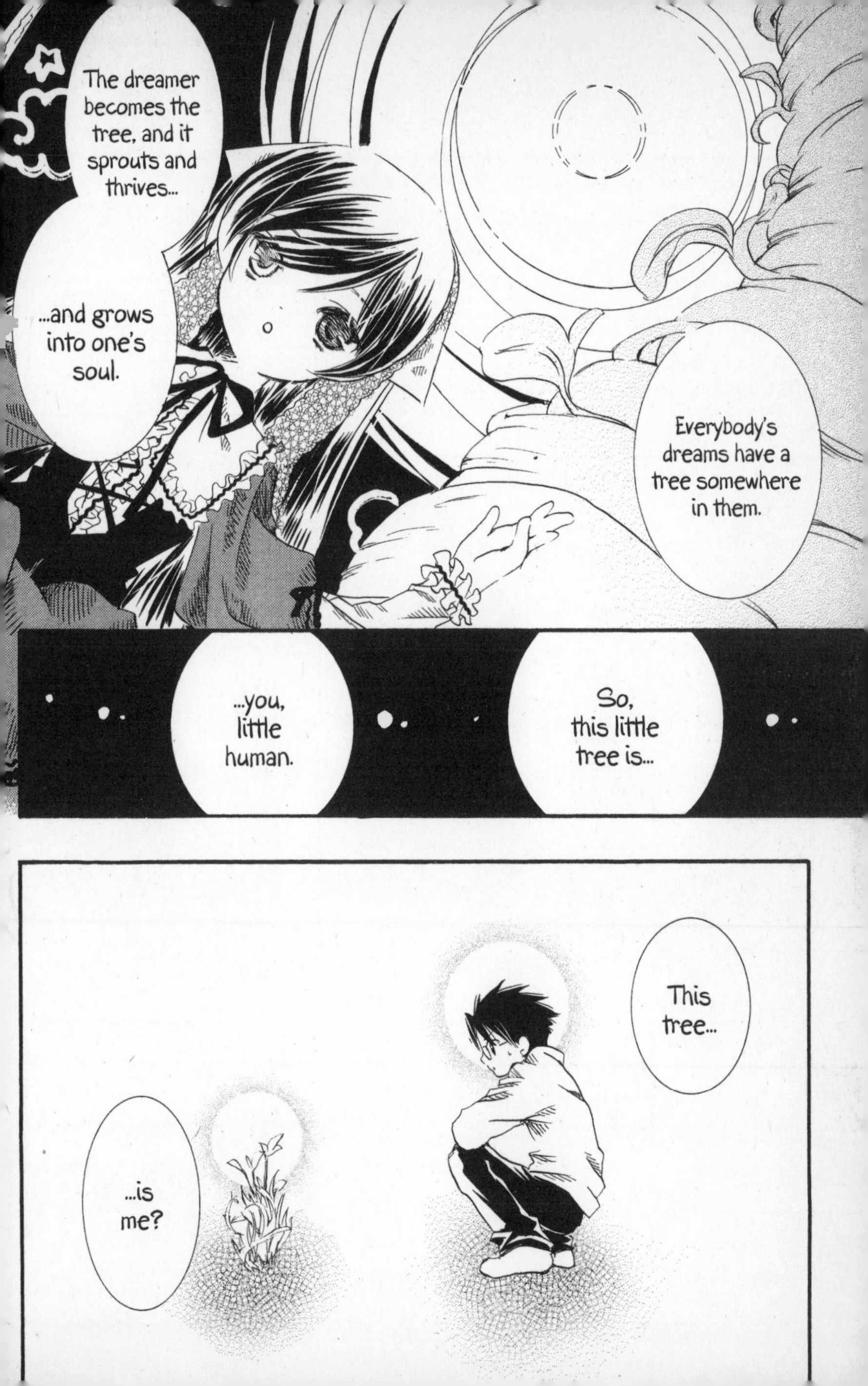
Everybody's dreams have a tree somewhere in them.
The dreamer becomes the tree, and it sprouts and thrives...
...and grows into one's soul.
So, this little tree is...
...you, little human.
This tree...
...is me?

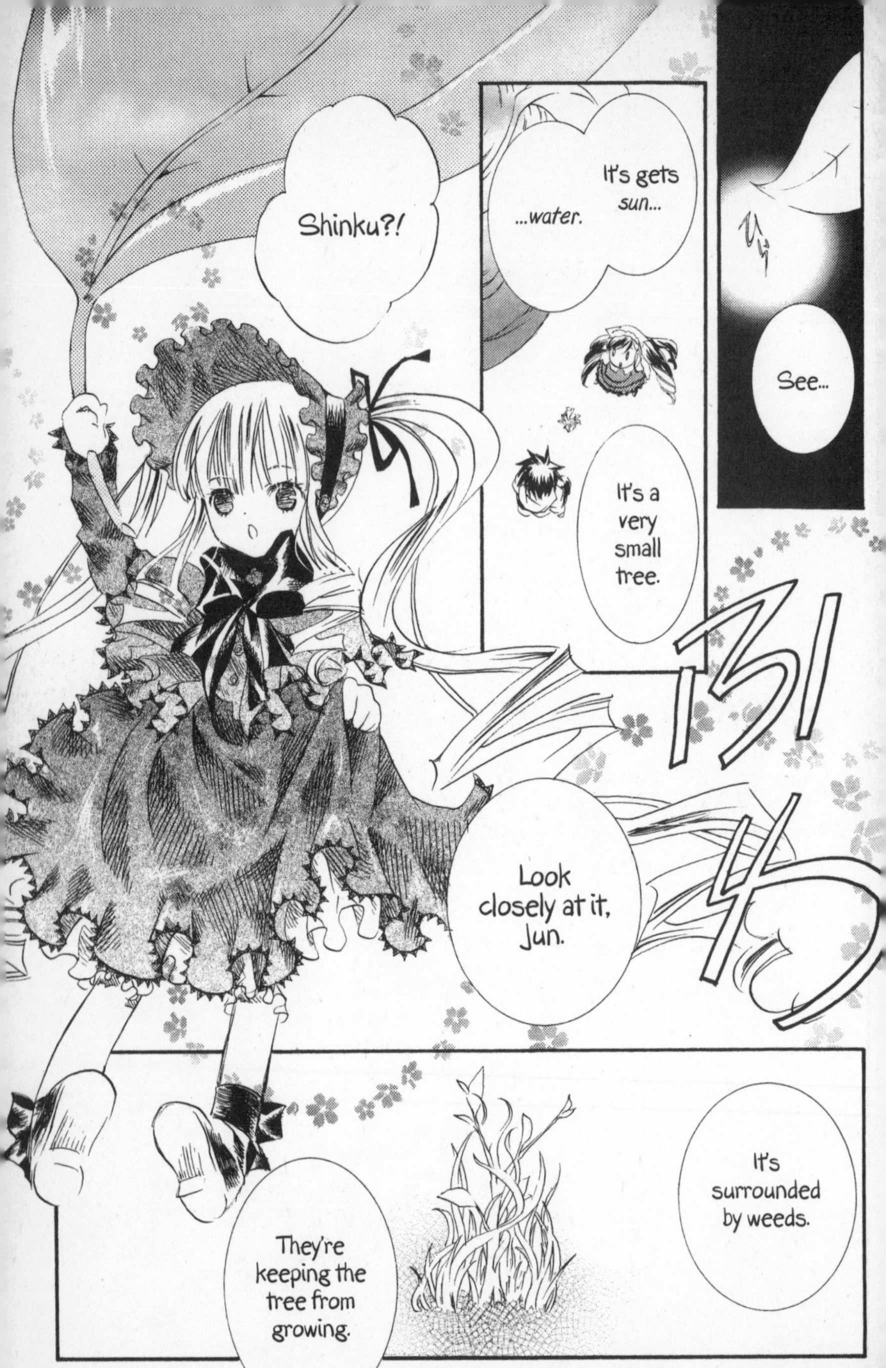
See...
It's gets sun...
...water.
It's a very small tree.
Shinku?!
Look closely at it, Jun.
It's surrounded by weeds.
They're keeping the tree from growing.

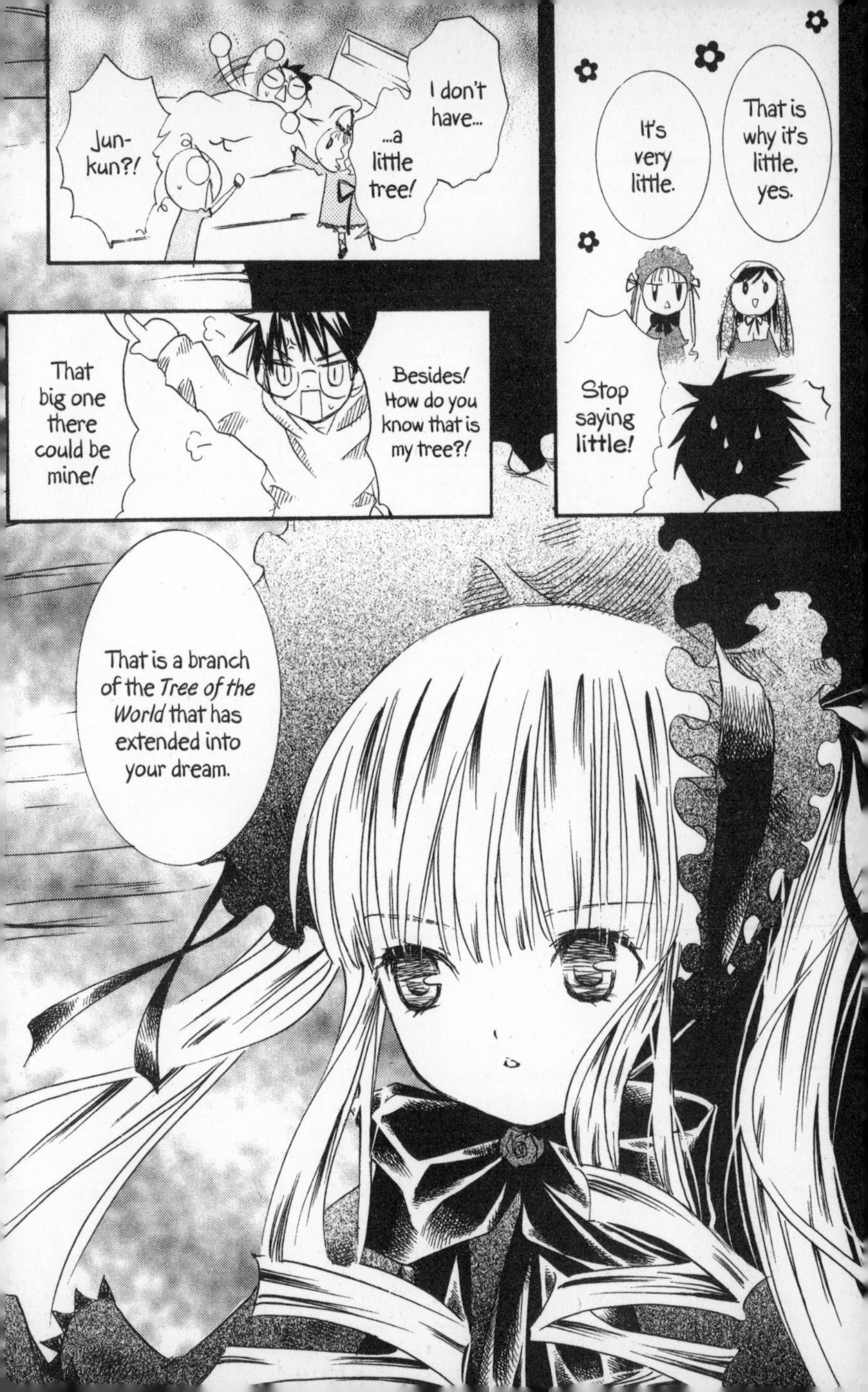
That is why it's little, yes.
It's very little.
Stop saying little!
I don't have... ...a little tree!
Jun-kun?!
Besides! How do you know that is my tree?!
That big one there could be mine!
That is a branch of the *Tree of the World* that has extended into your dream.

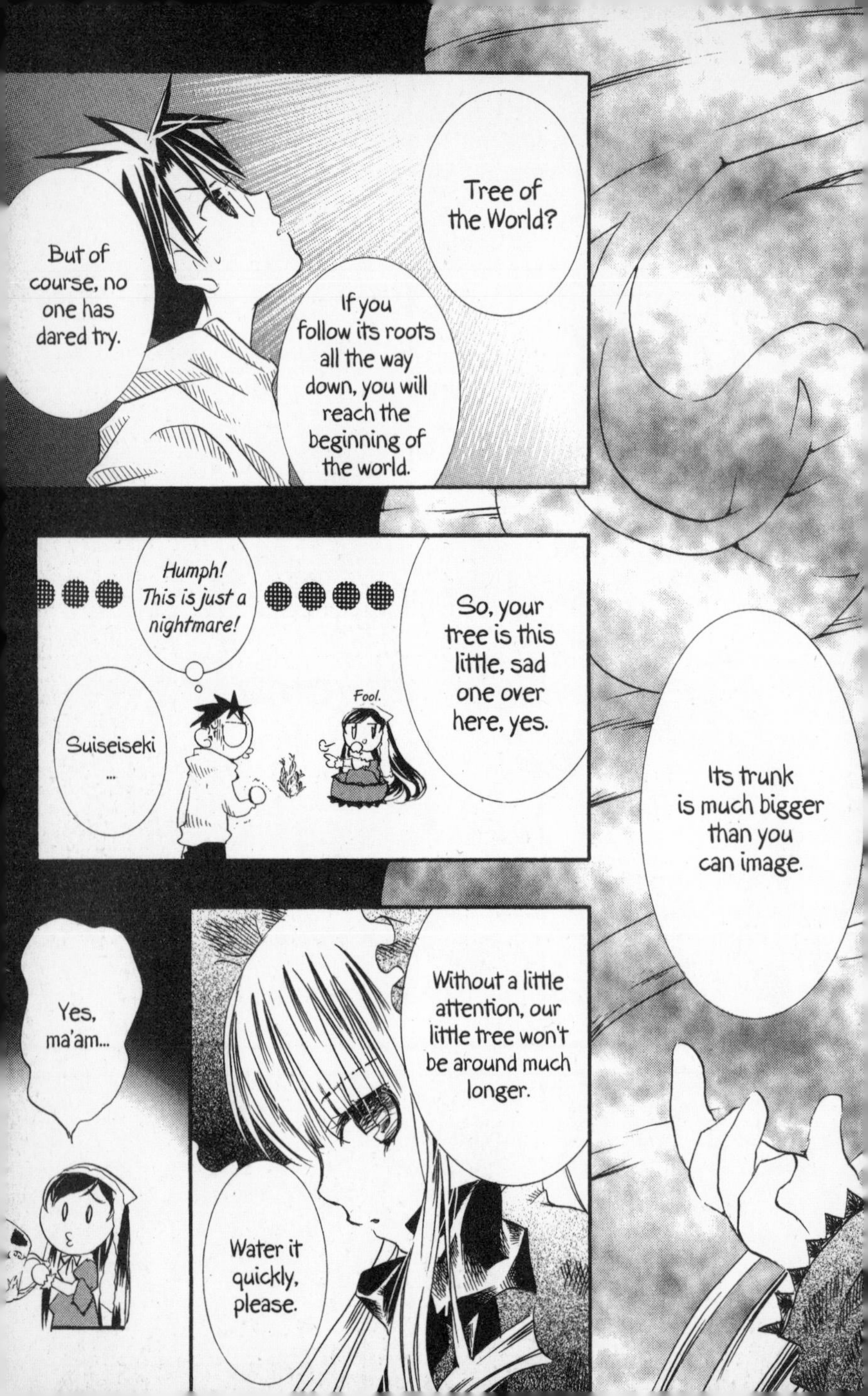
Tree of the World?
If you follow its roots all the way down, you will reach the beginning of the world.
But of course, no one has dared try.
Its trunk is much bigger than you can image.
So, your tree is this little, sad one over here, yes.
Fool.
Humph! This is just a nightmare!
Suiseiseki ...
Without a little attention, our little tree won't be around much longer.
Water it quickly, please.
Yes, ma'am...

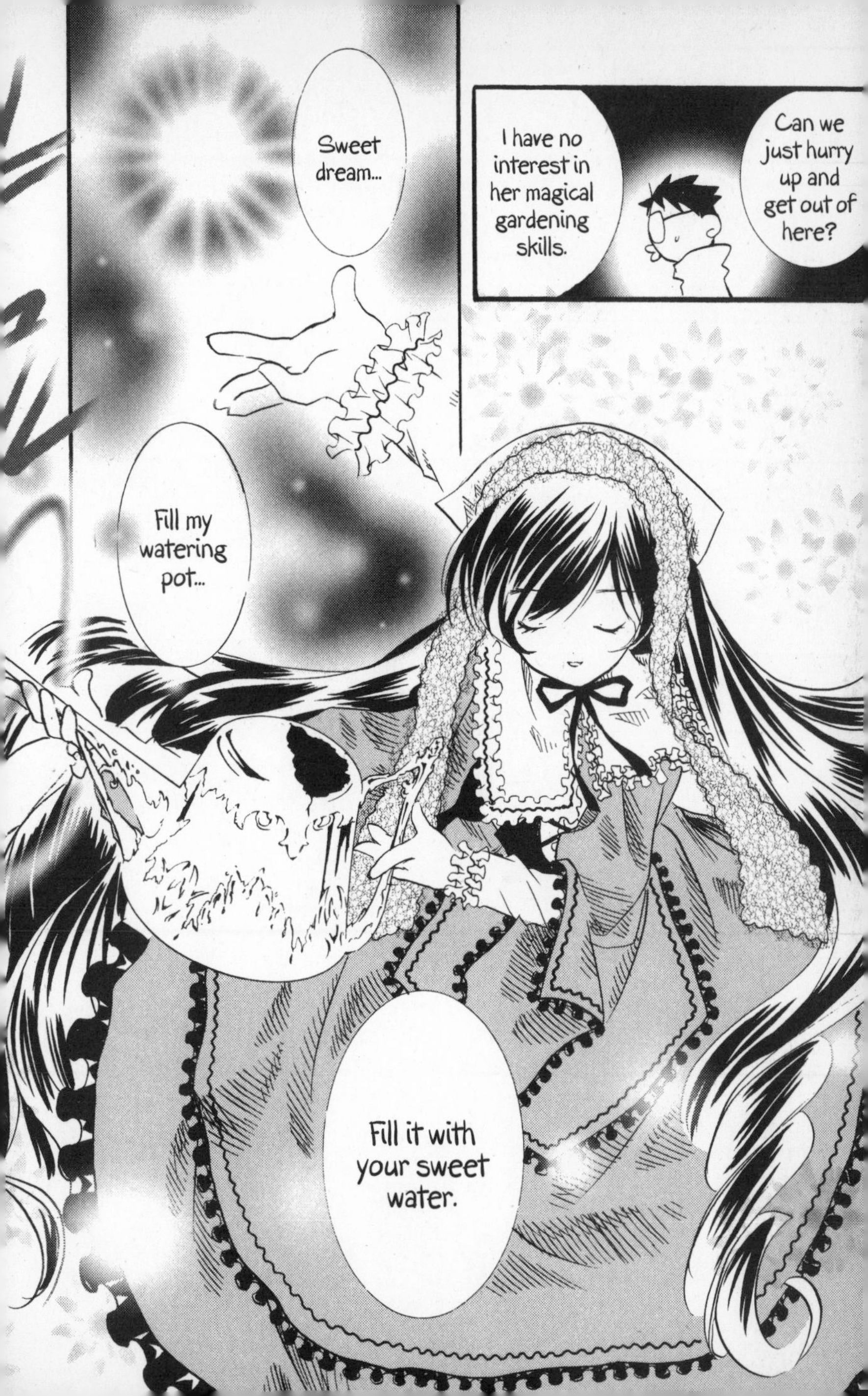
Can we just hurry up and get out of here?
I have no interest in her magical gardening skills.
Sweet dream...
Fill my watering pot...
Fill it with your sweet water.

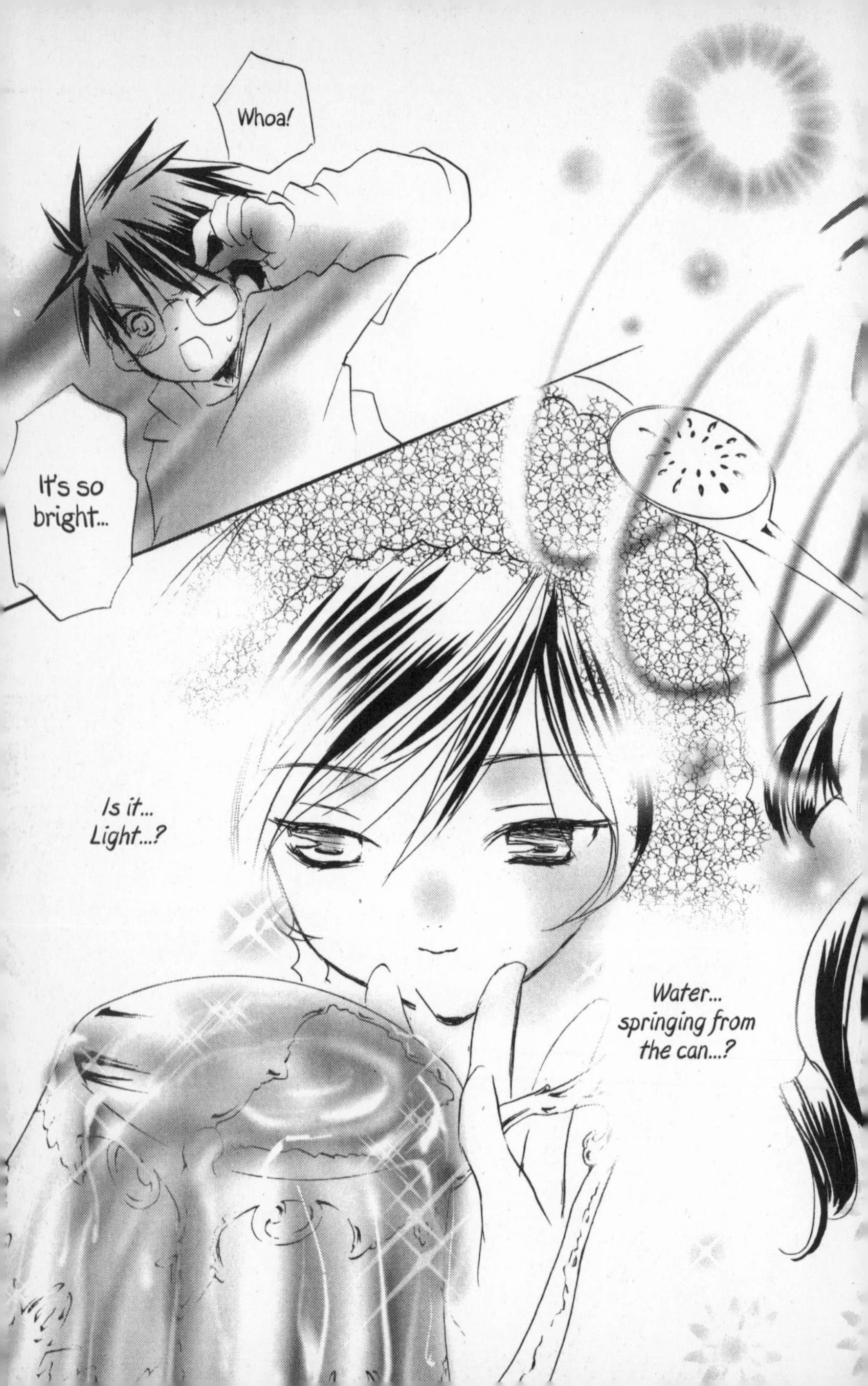
Whoa!
It's so bright...
Is it... Light...?
Water... springing from the can...?

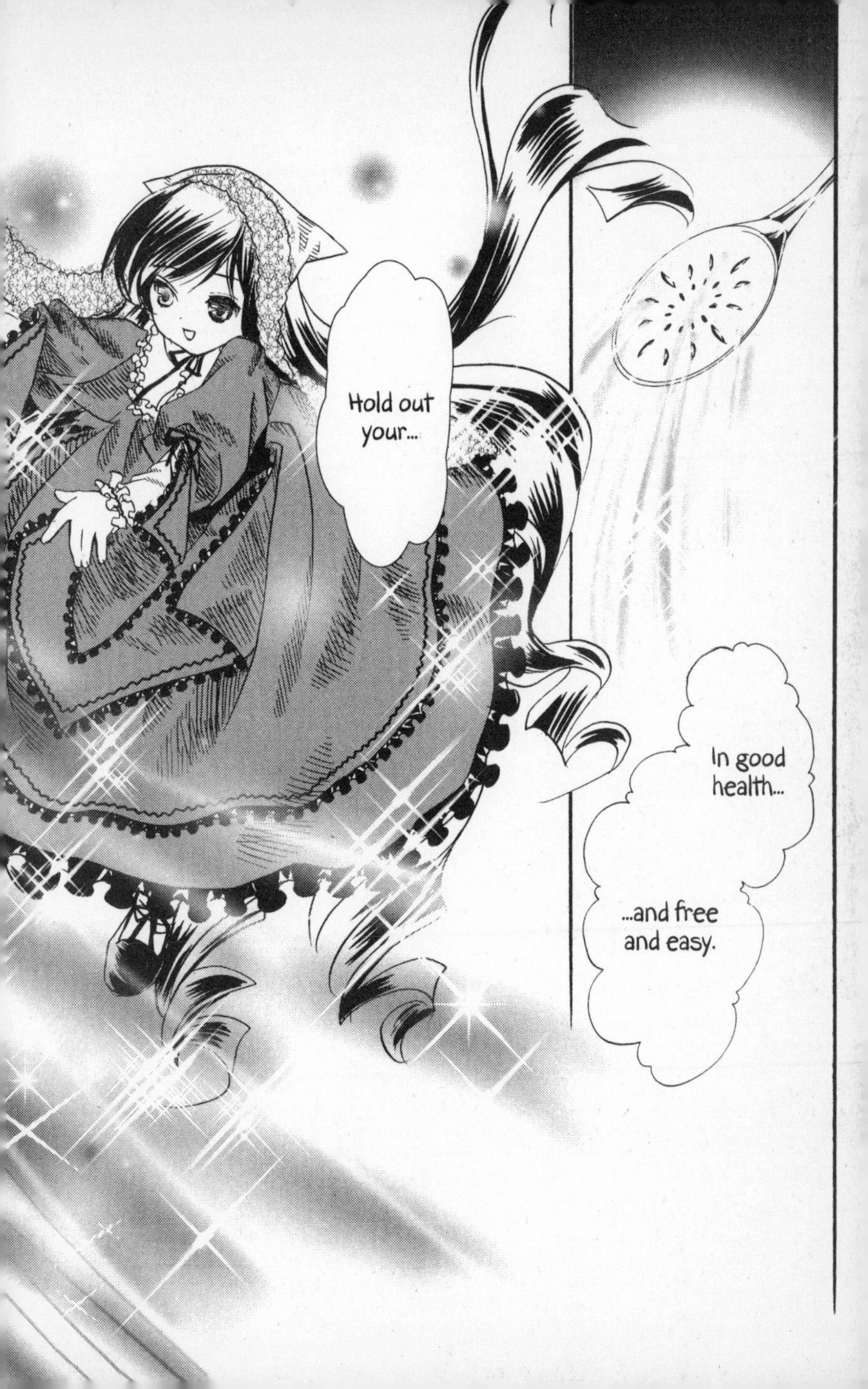
In good health...
...and free and easy.
Hold out your...

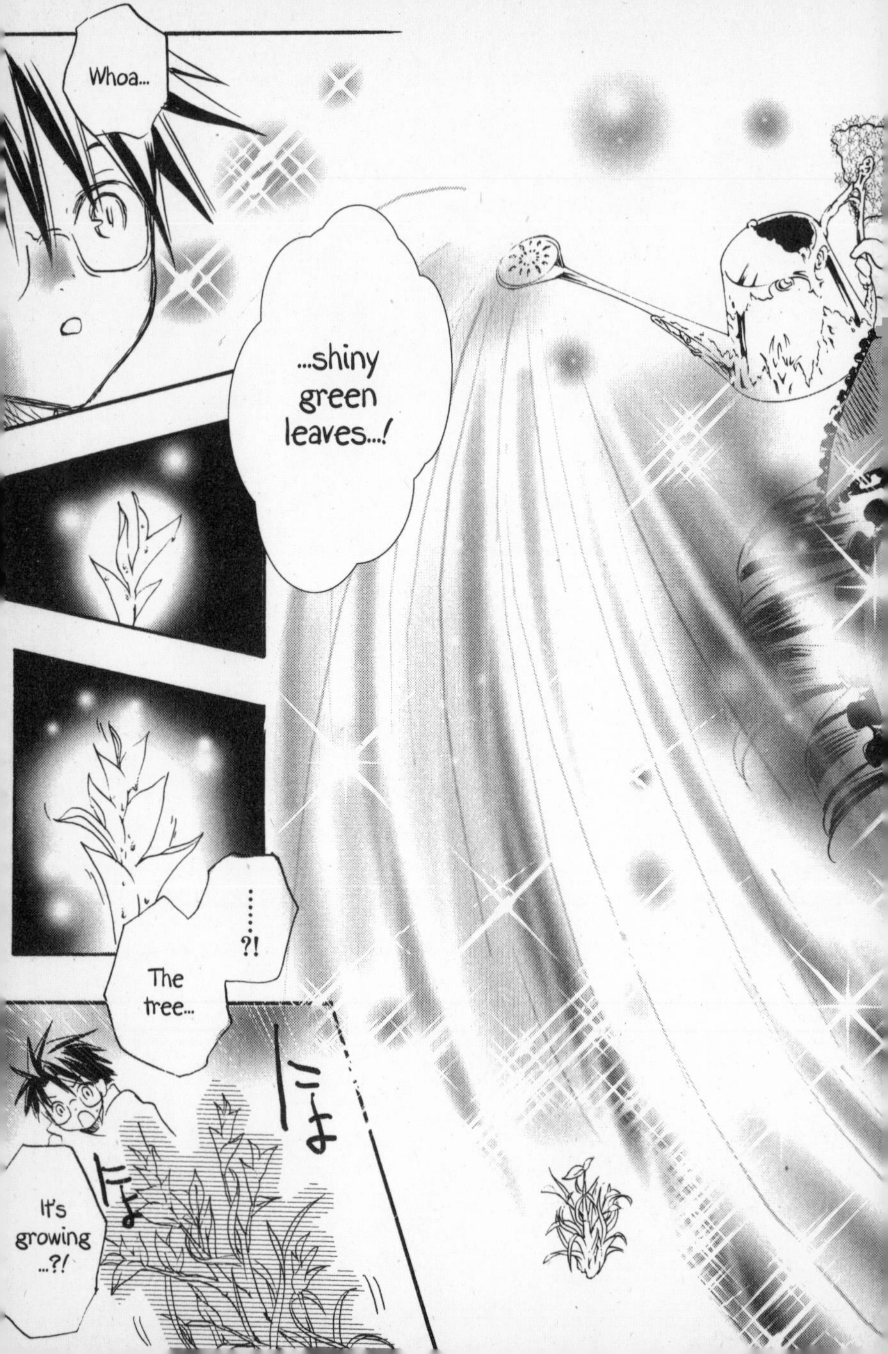
...shiny green leaves...!
Whoa...
......?!
The tree...
にょ
にょ
It's growing ...?!

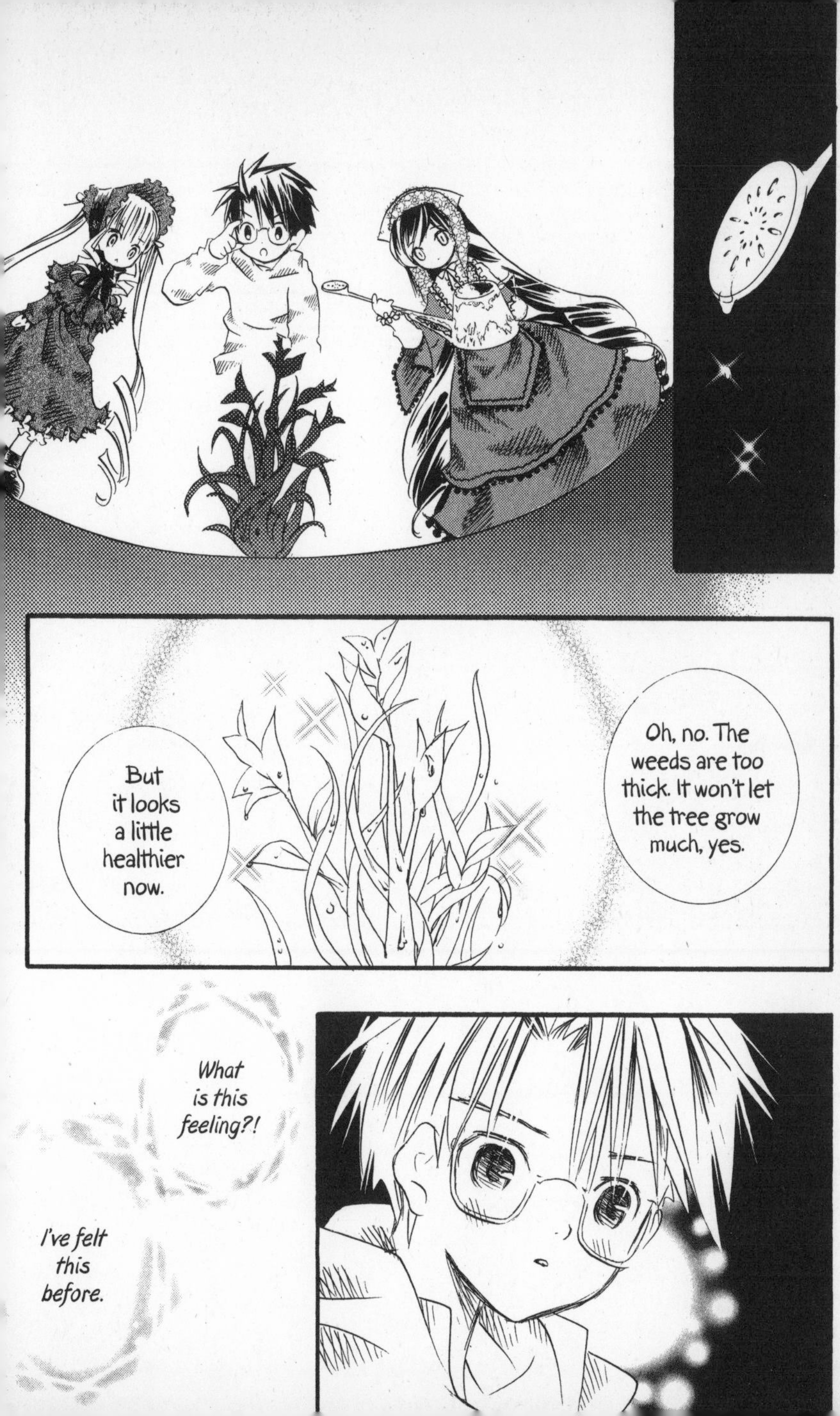
Oh, no. The weeds are too thick. It won't let the tree grow much, yes.
But it looks a little healthier now.
What is this feeling?!
I've felt this before.

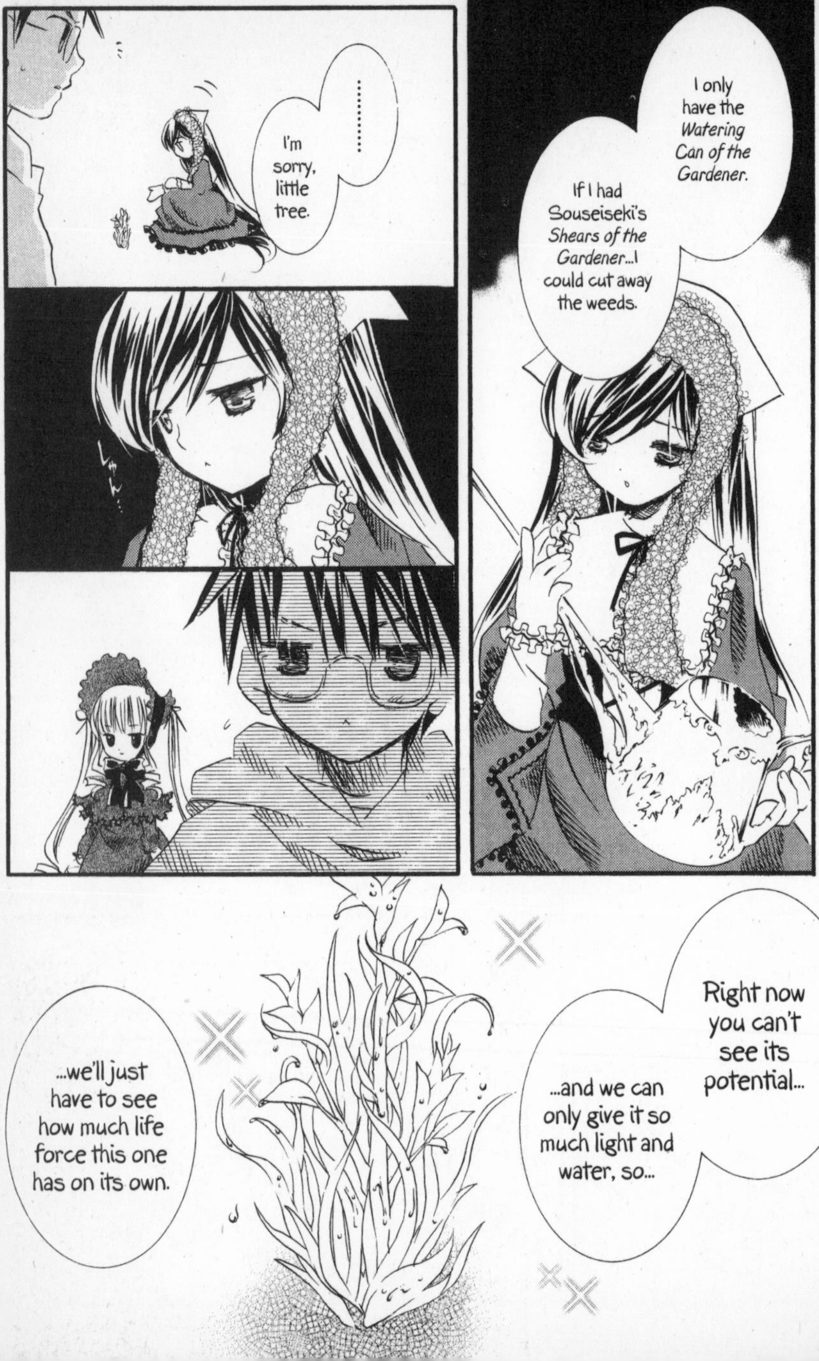
I only have the *Watering Can of the Gardener.*
If I had Souseiseki's *Shears of the Gardener*...I could cut away the weeds.
......
I'm sorry, little tree.
しゅん…
Right now you can't see its potential...
...and we can only give it so much light and water, so...
...we'll just have to see how much life force this one has on its own.

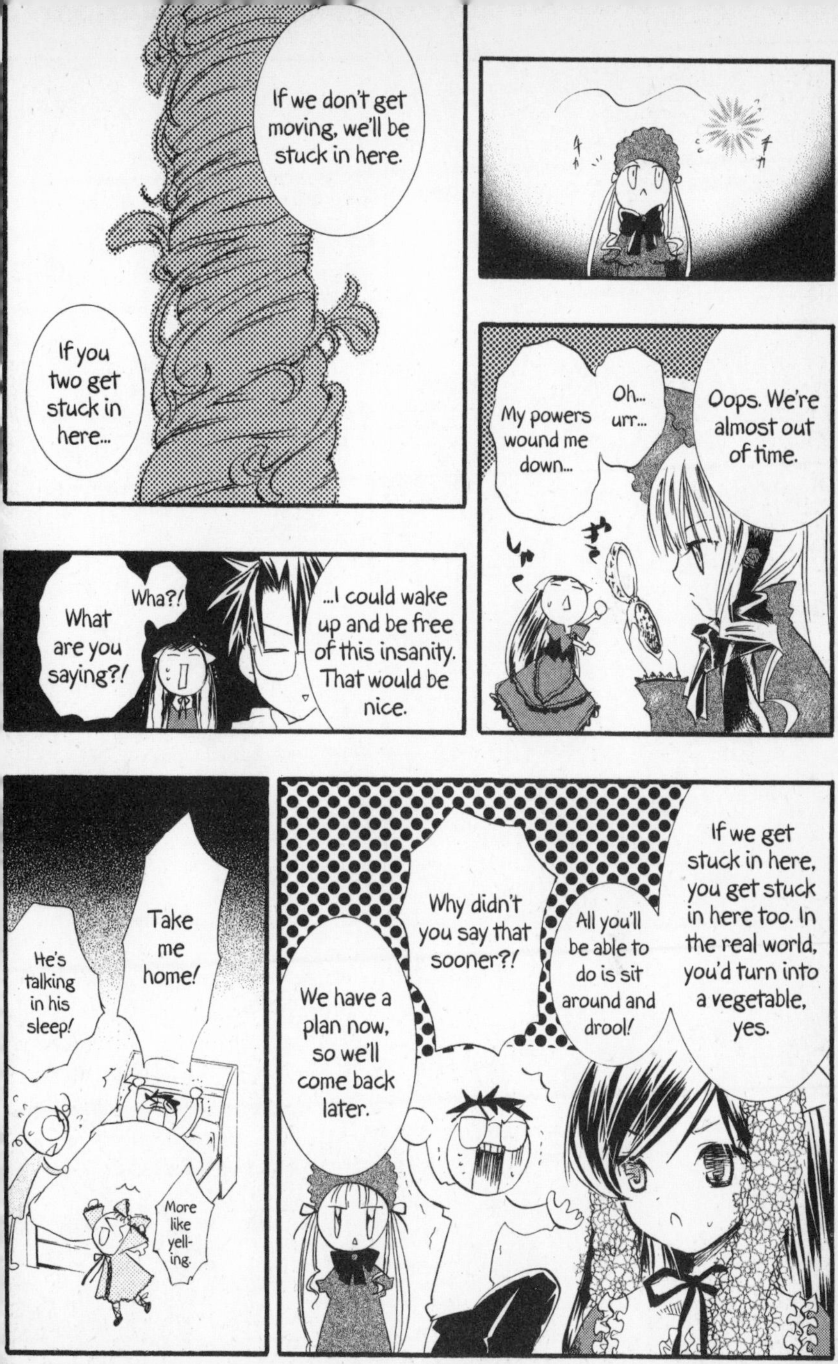
Oops. We're almost out of time.
Oh... urr...
My powers wound me down...
If we don't get moving, we'll be stuck in here.
If you two get stuck in here...
...I could wake up and be free of this insanity. That would be nice.
Wha?!
What are you saying?!
If we get stuck in here, you get stuck in here too. In the real world, you'd turn into a vegetable, yes.
All you'll be able to do is sit around and drool!
Why didn't you say that sooner?!
We have a plan now, so we'll come back later.
Take me home!
He's talking in his sleep!
More like yell-ing.

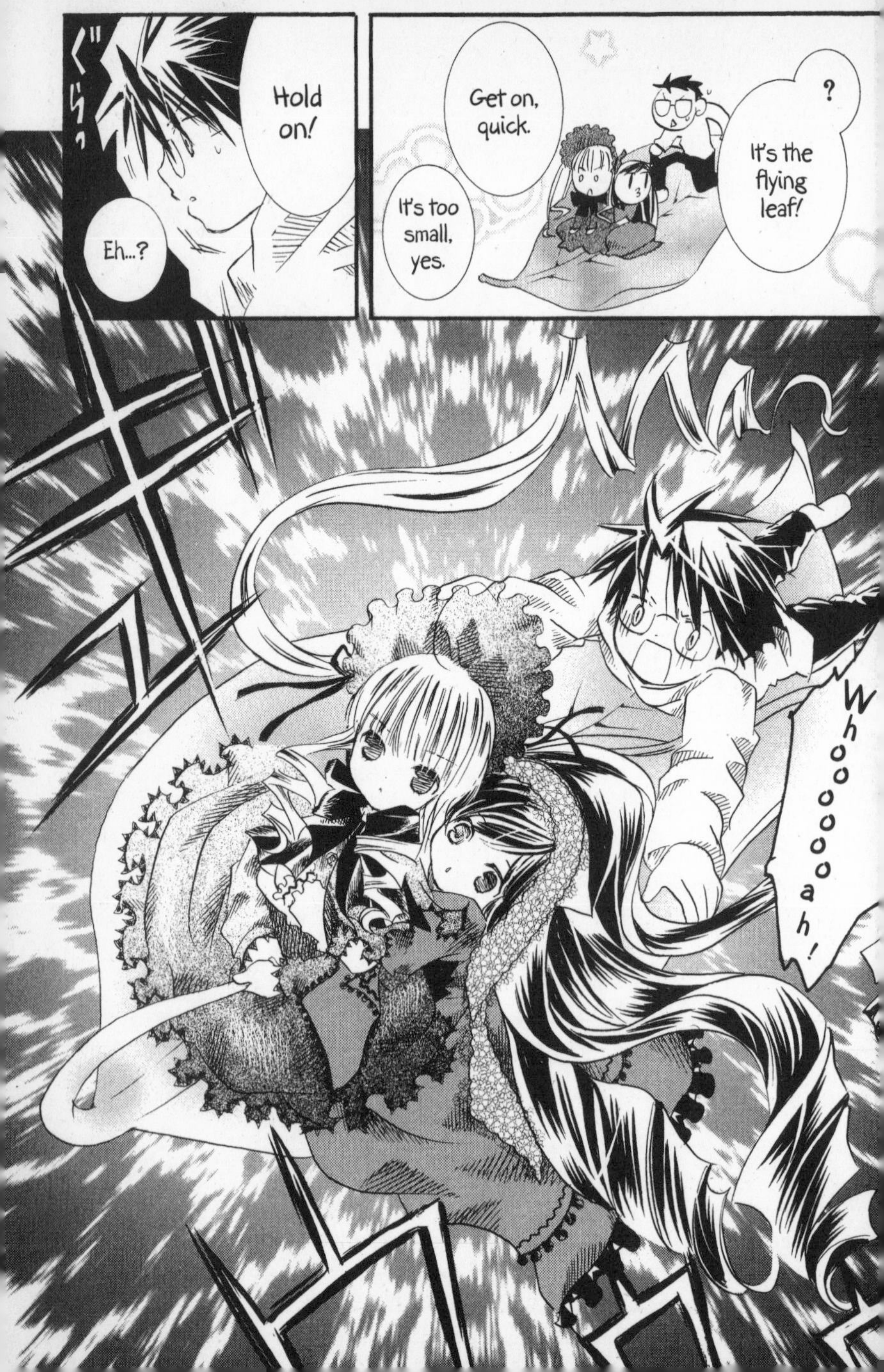
?
It's the flying leaf!
Get on, quick.
It's too small, yes.
ぐらっ
Hold on!
Eh...?
Whooooooah!

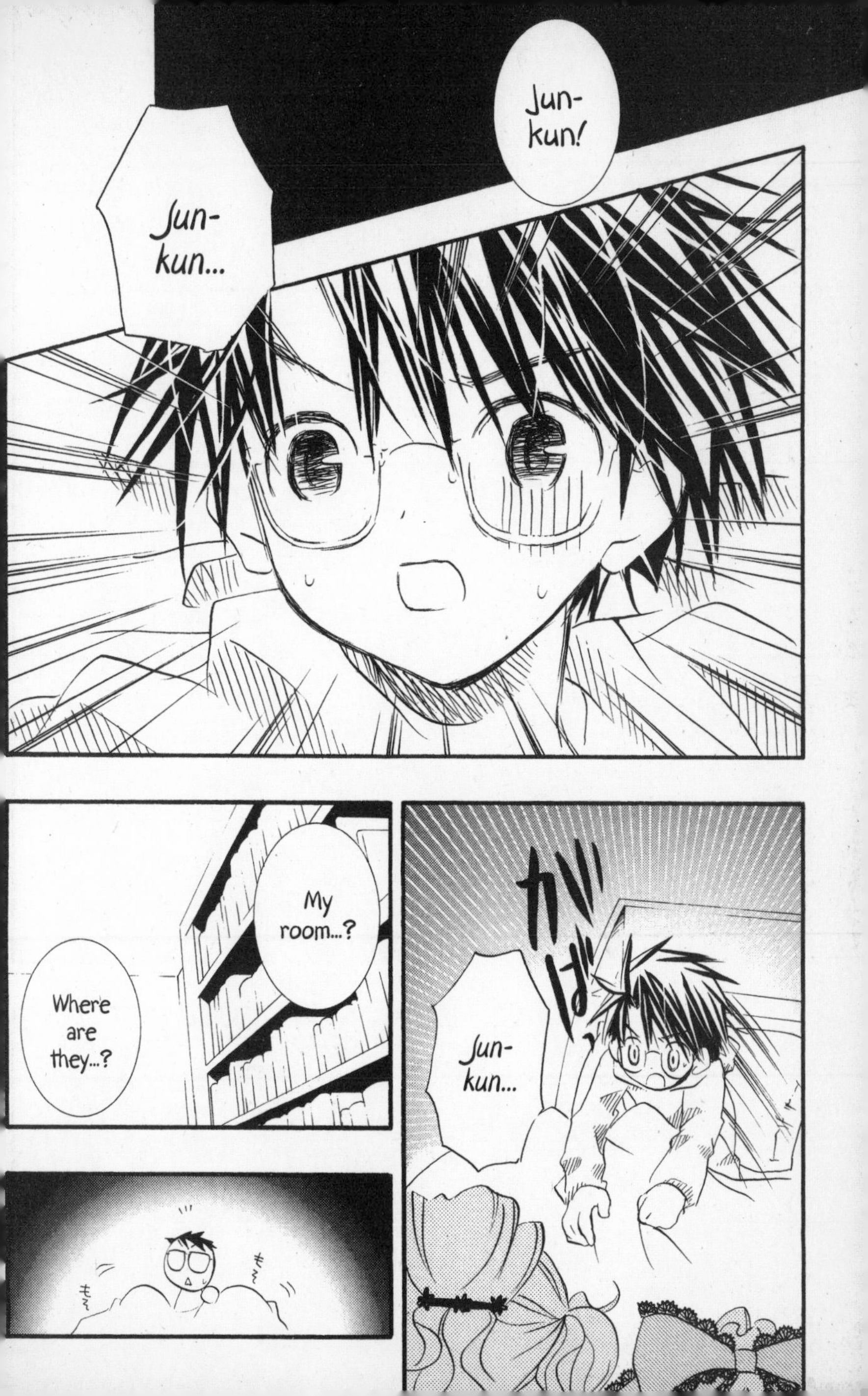
Jun-kun!
Jun-kun...
Jun-kun...
My room...?
Where are they...?

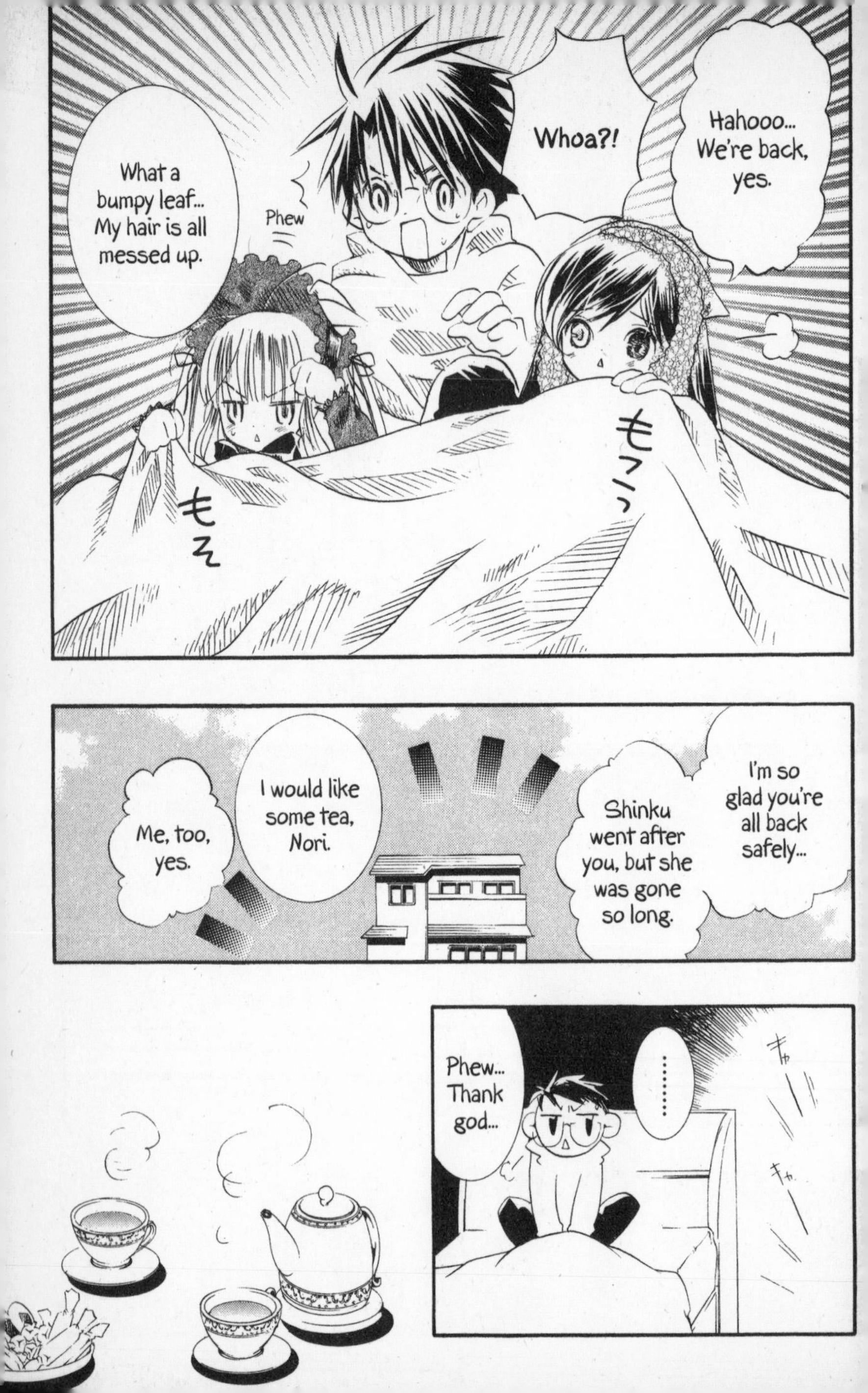
Hahooo... We're back, yes.
Whoa?!
Phew
What a bumpy leaf... My hair is all messed up.
I'm so glad you're all back safely...
Shinku went after you, but she was gone so long.
I would like some tea, Nori.
Me, too, yes.
......
Phew... Thank god...

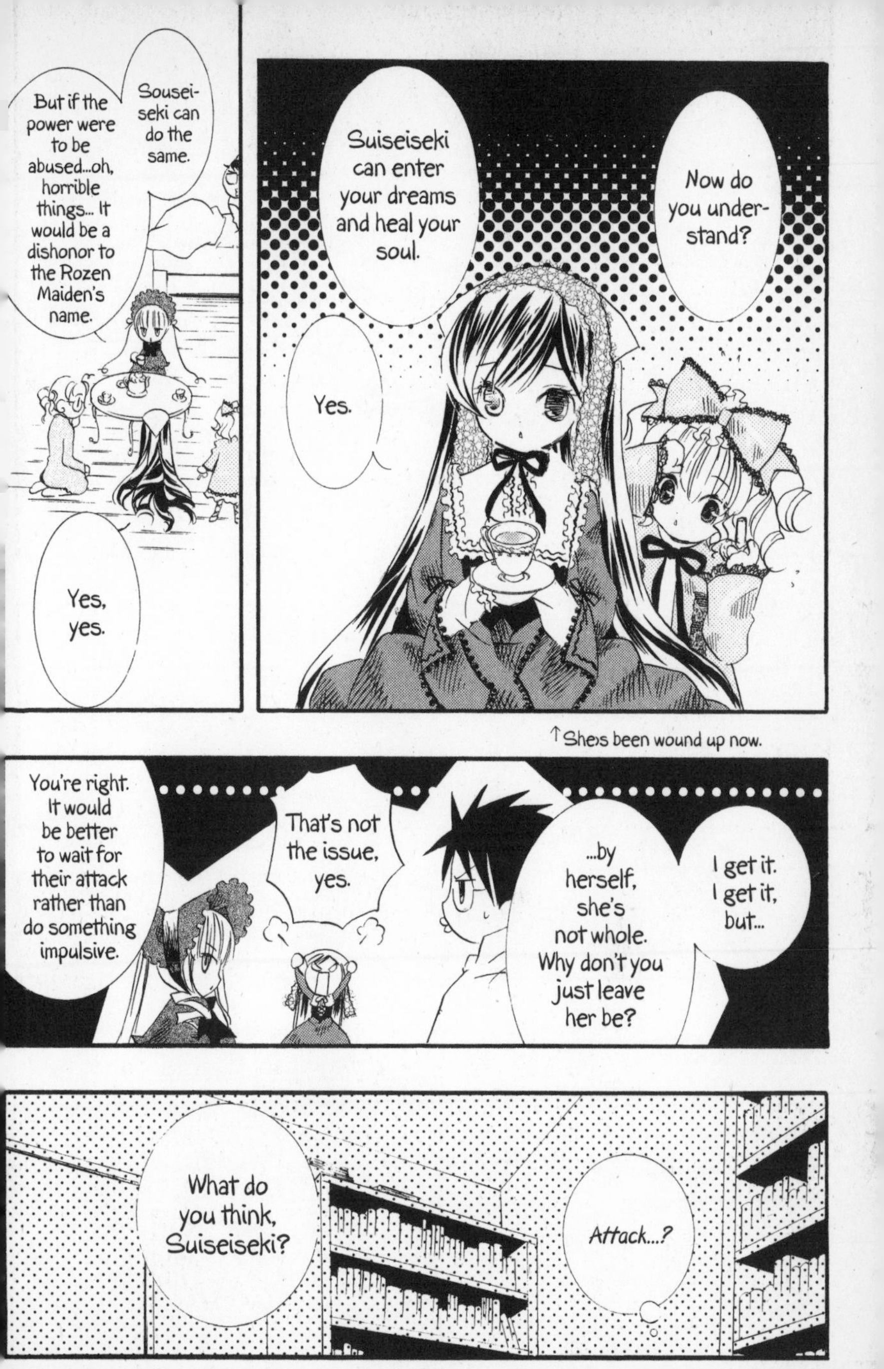
Now do you under-stand?
Suiseiseki can enter your dreams and heal your soul.
Yes.
Sousei-seki can do the same.
But if the power were to be abused...oh, horrible things... It would be a dishonor to the Rozen Maiden's name.
Yes, yes.
↑She's been wound up now.
I get it. I get it, but...
...by herself, she's not whole. Why don't you just leave her be?
That's not the issue, yes.
You're right. It would be better to wait for their attack rather than do something impulsive.
Attack...?
What do you think, Suiseiseki?

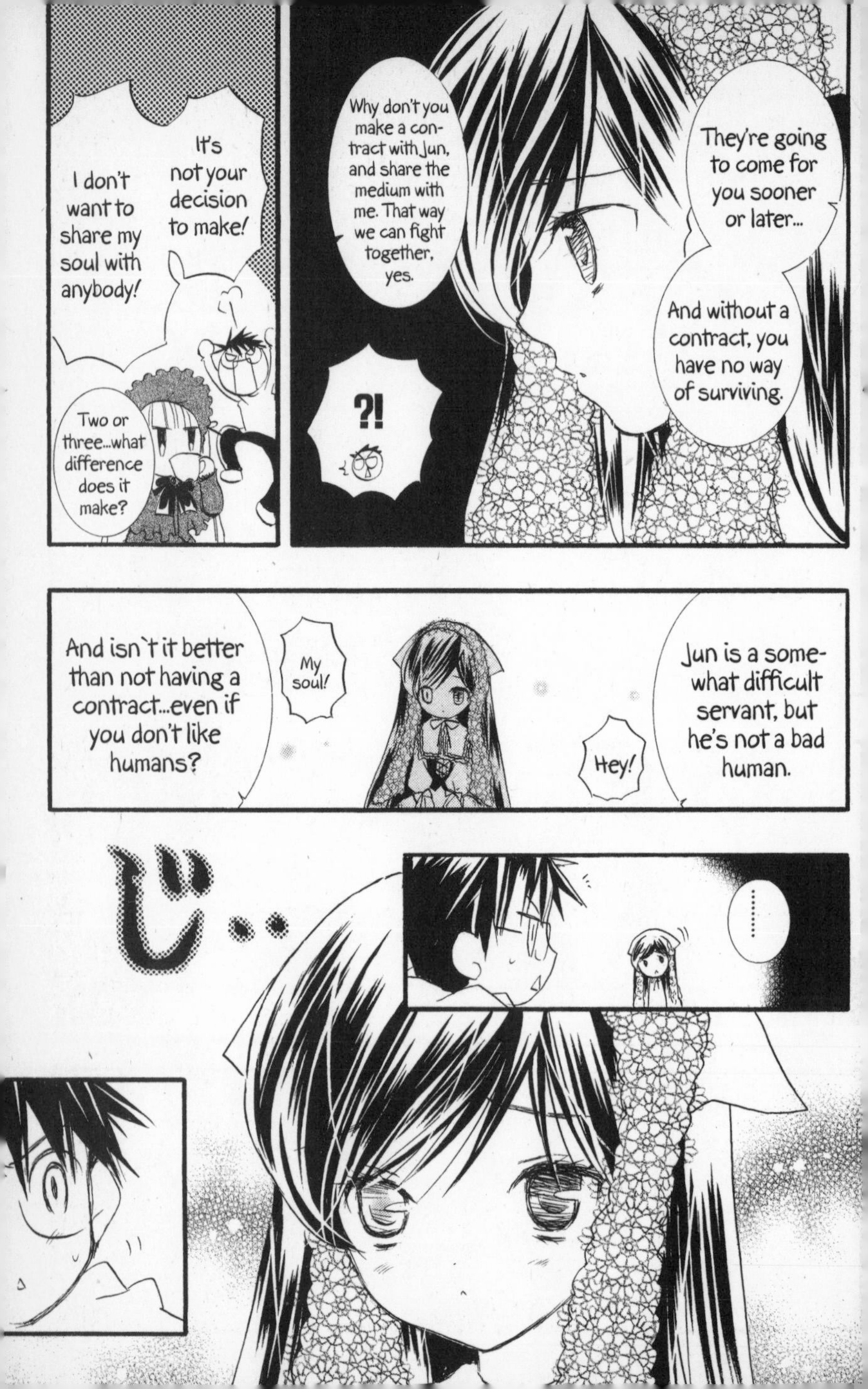
They're going to come for you sooner or later...
And without a contract, you have no way of surviving.
Why don't you make a contract with Jun, and share the medium with me. That way we can fight together, yes.
?!
It's not your decision to make!
I don't want to share my soul with anybody!
Two or three...what difference does it make?
Jun is a somewhat difficult servant, but he's not a bad human.
Hey!
My soul!
And isn`t it better than not having a contract...even if you don't like humans?
......
じ..

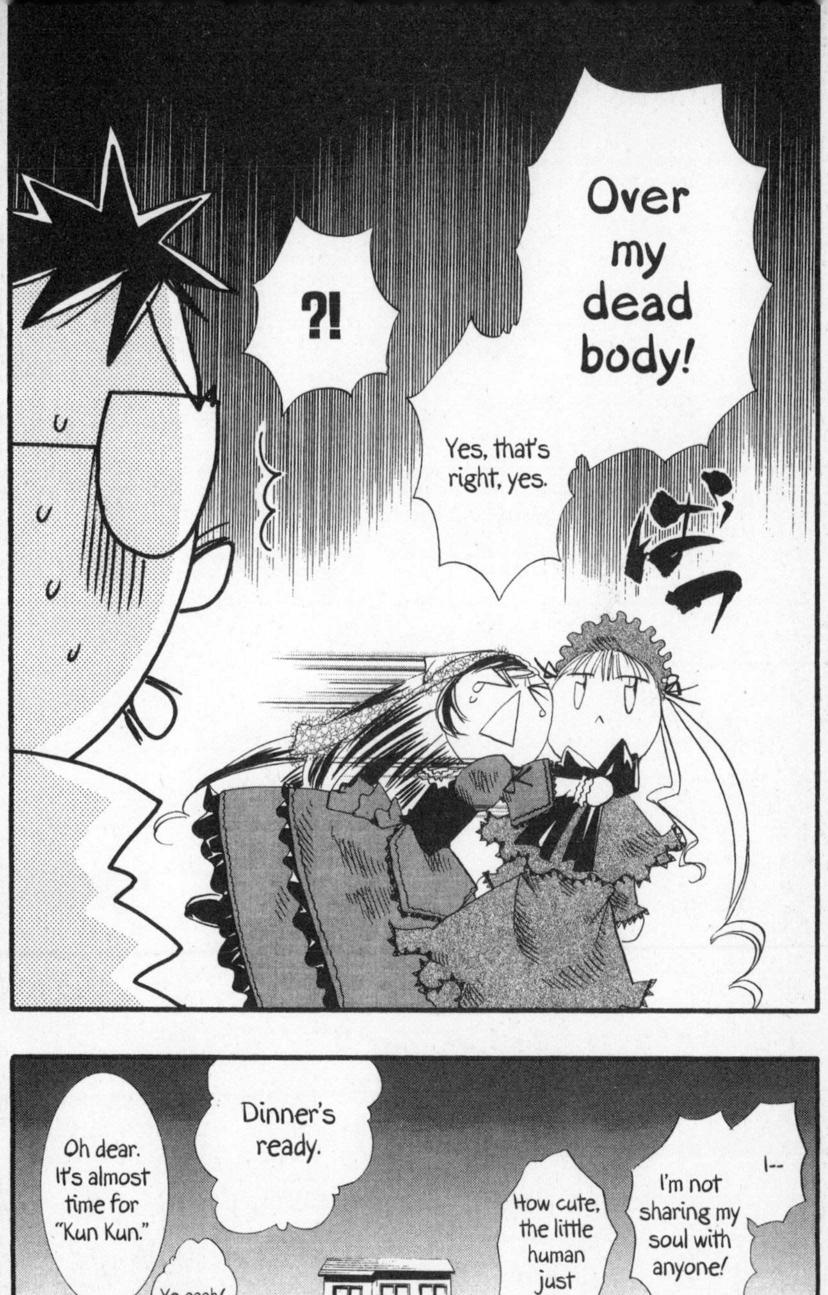
Over my dead body!
?!
Yes, that's right, yes.
I--
I'm not sharing my soul with anyone!
How cute, the little human just barked.
Dinner's ready.
Oh dear. It's almost time for "Kun Kun."
Ye-aaah!

Phase 13

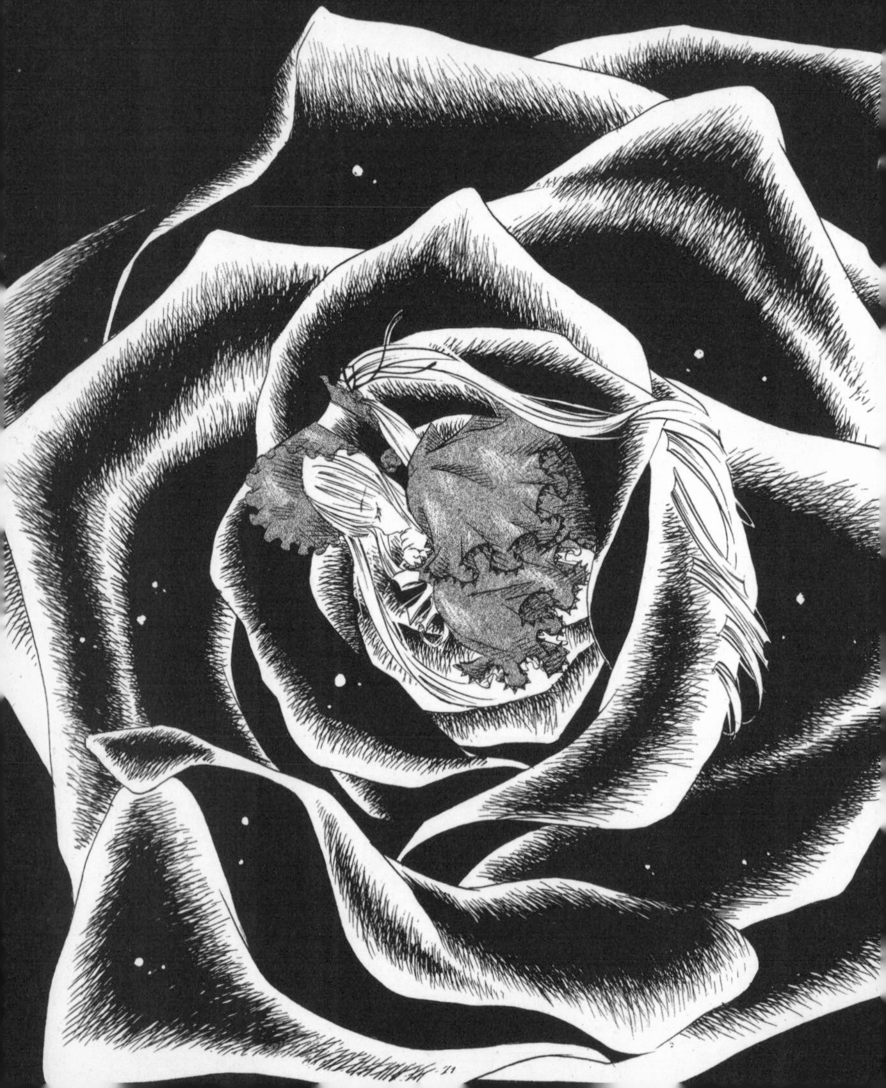

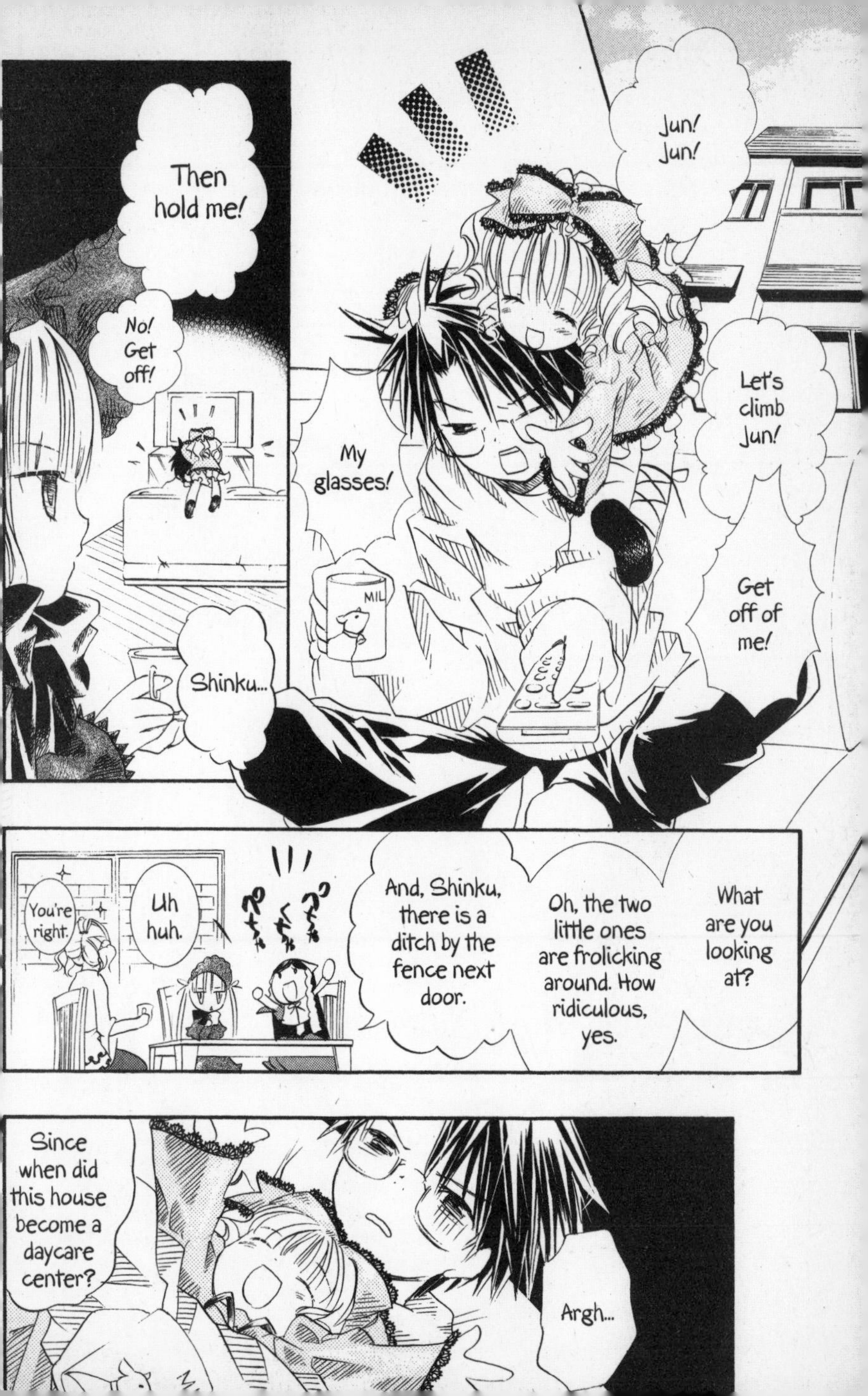
Jun! Jun!
Let's climb Jun!
Get off of me!
My glasses!
Then hold me!
No! Get off!
Shinku...
What are you looking at?
Oh, the two little ones are frolicking around. How ridiculous, yes.
And, Shinku, there is a ditch by the fence next door.
Uh huh.
You're right.
Argh...
Since when did this house become a daycare center?

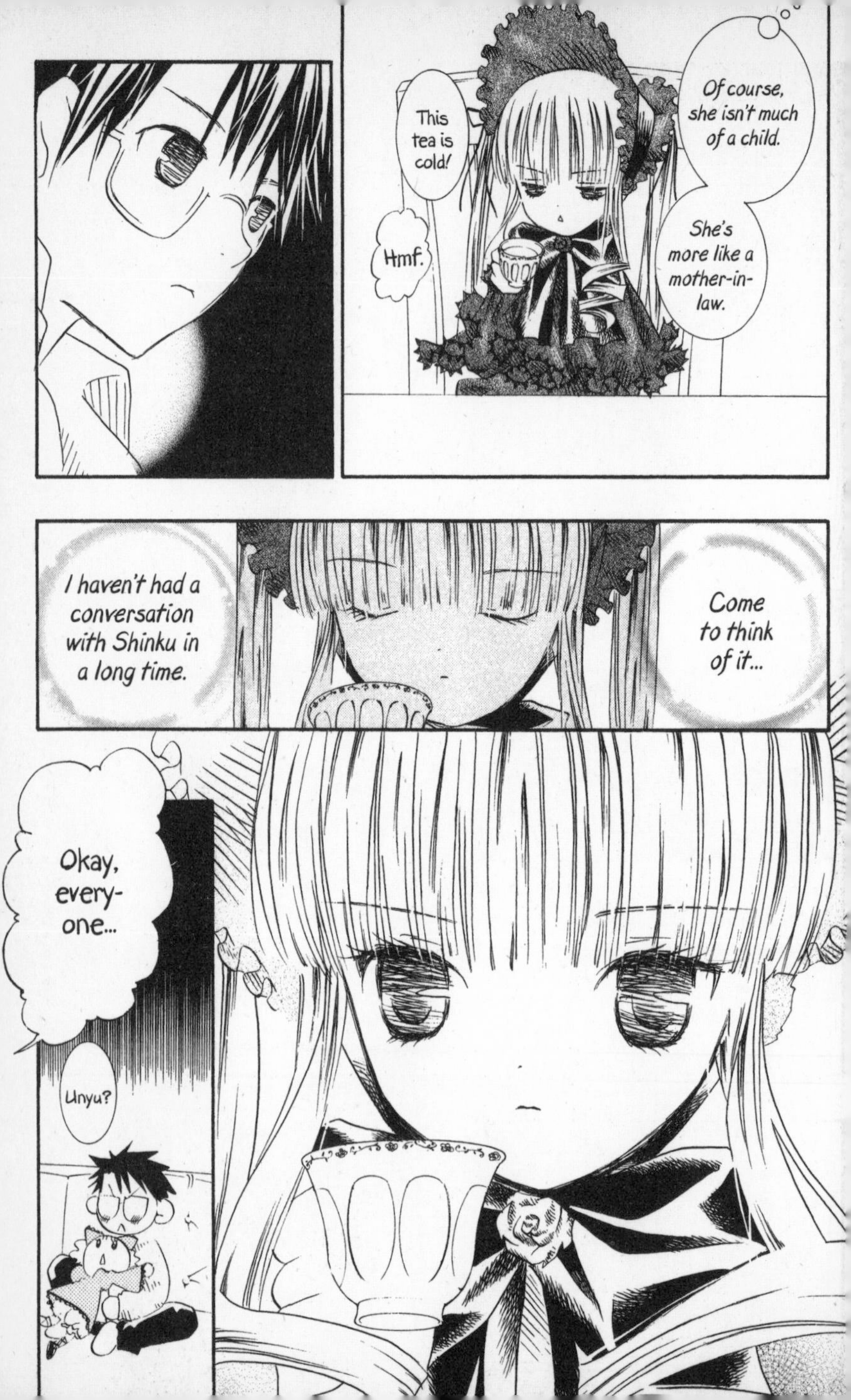
Of course, she isn't much of a child.
This tea is cold!
She's more like a mother-in-law.
Hmf.
Come to think of it...
I haven't had a conversation with Shinku in a long time.
Okay, everyone...
Unyu?

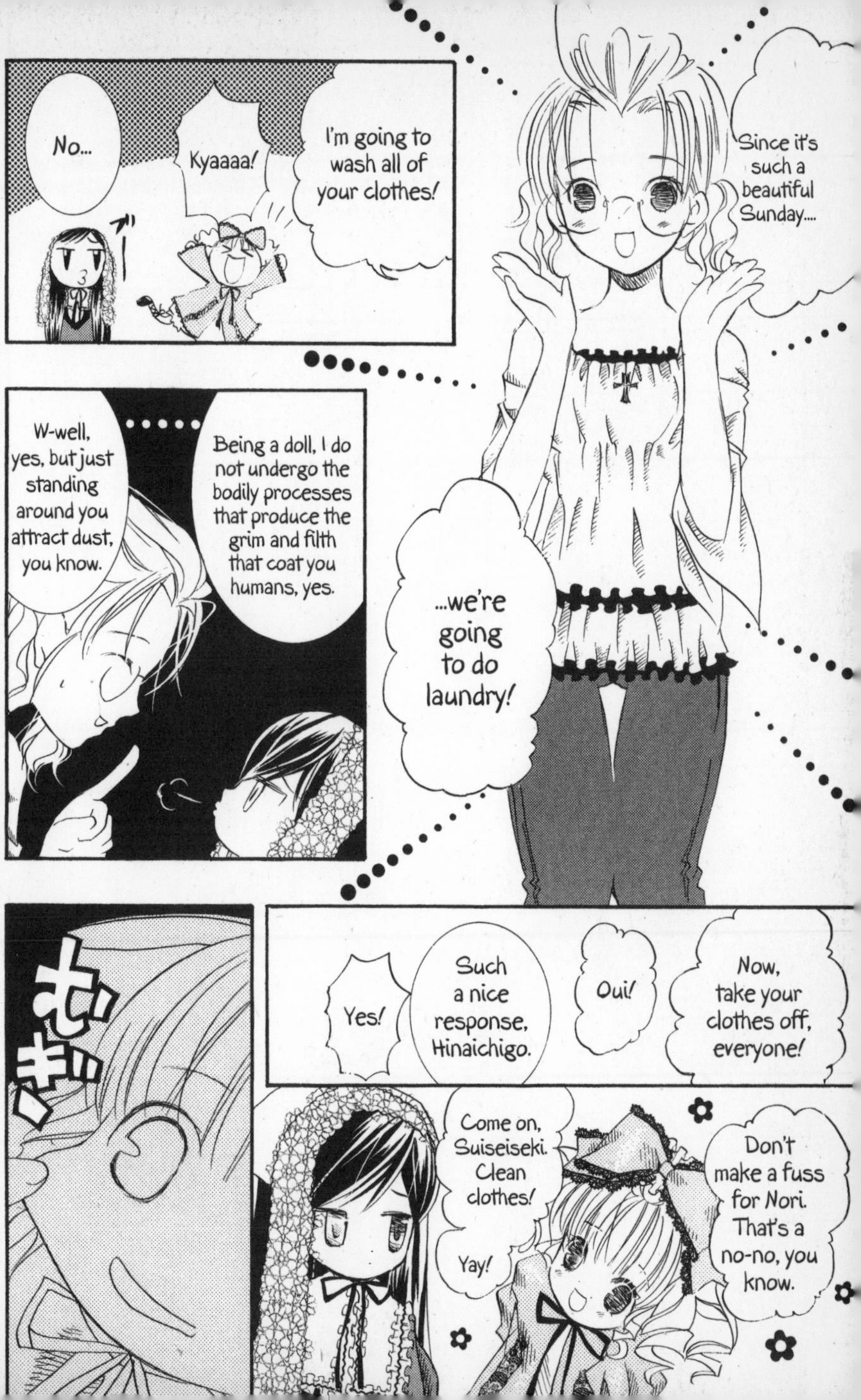
Since it's such a beautiful Sunday....
...we're going to do laundry!
I'm going to wash all of your clothes!
Kyaaaa!
No...
Being a doll, I do not undergo the bodily processes that produce the grim and filth that coat you humans, yes.
......
W-well, yes, but just standing around you attract dust, you know.
Now, take your clothes off, everyone!
Oui!
Such a nice response, Hinaichigo.
Yes!
Don't make a fuss for Nori. That's a no-no, you know.
Come on, Suiseiseki. Clean clothes!
Yay!

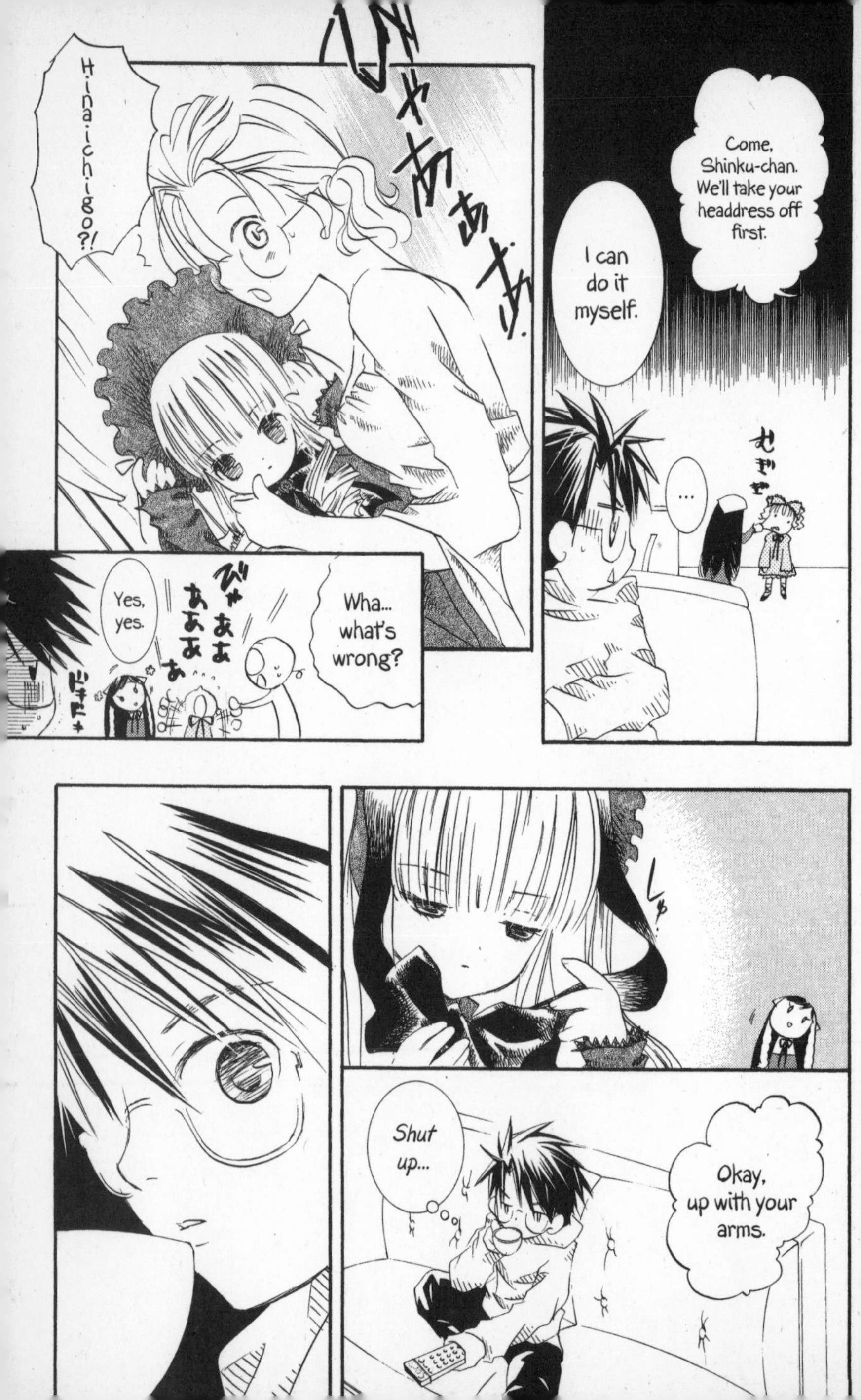

Come, Shinku-chan. We'll take your headdress off first.
I can do it myself.
...
Hi-na-ichi-goo?!
Wha... what's wrong?
Yes, yes.
Okay, up with your arms.
Shut up...

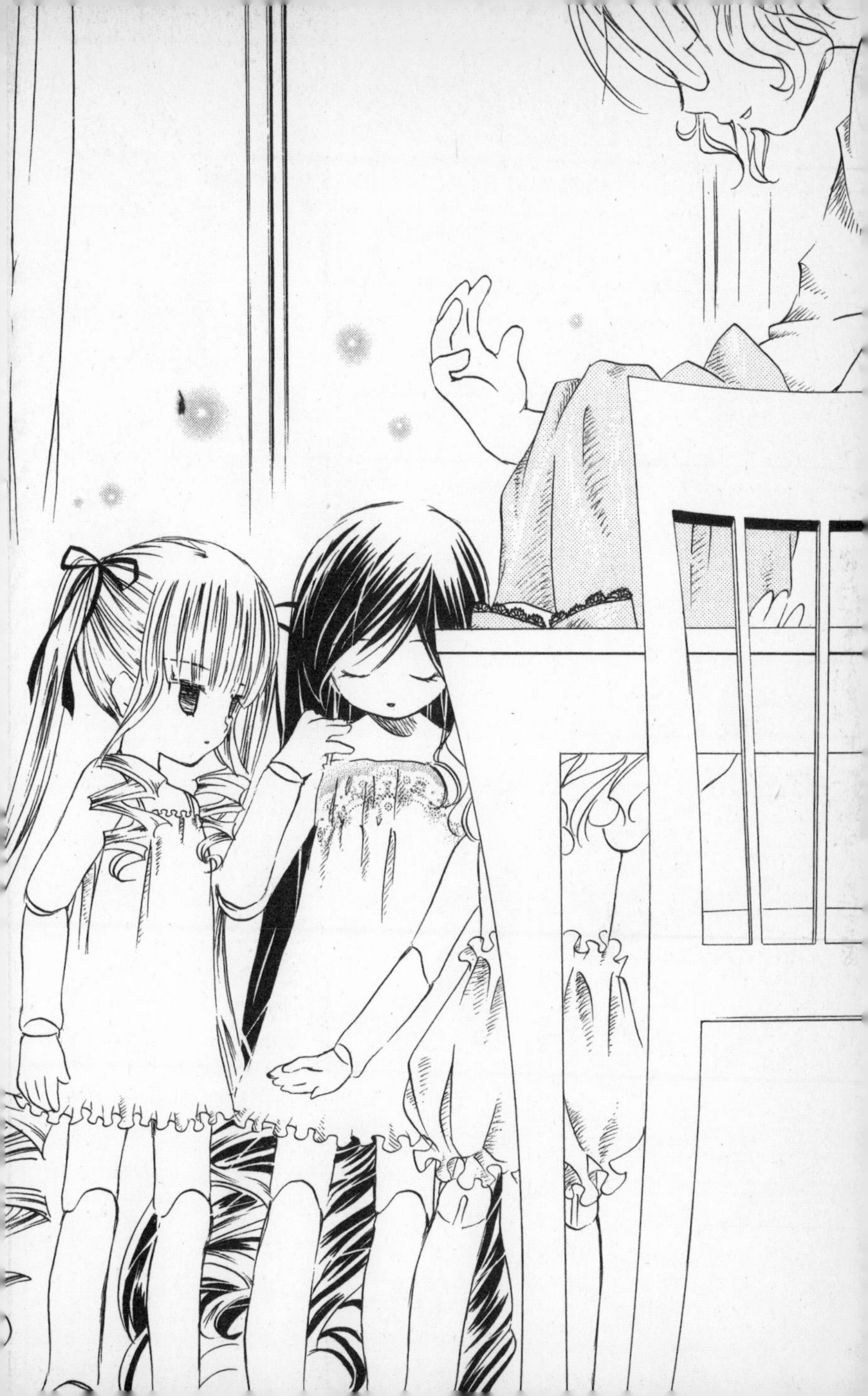

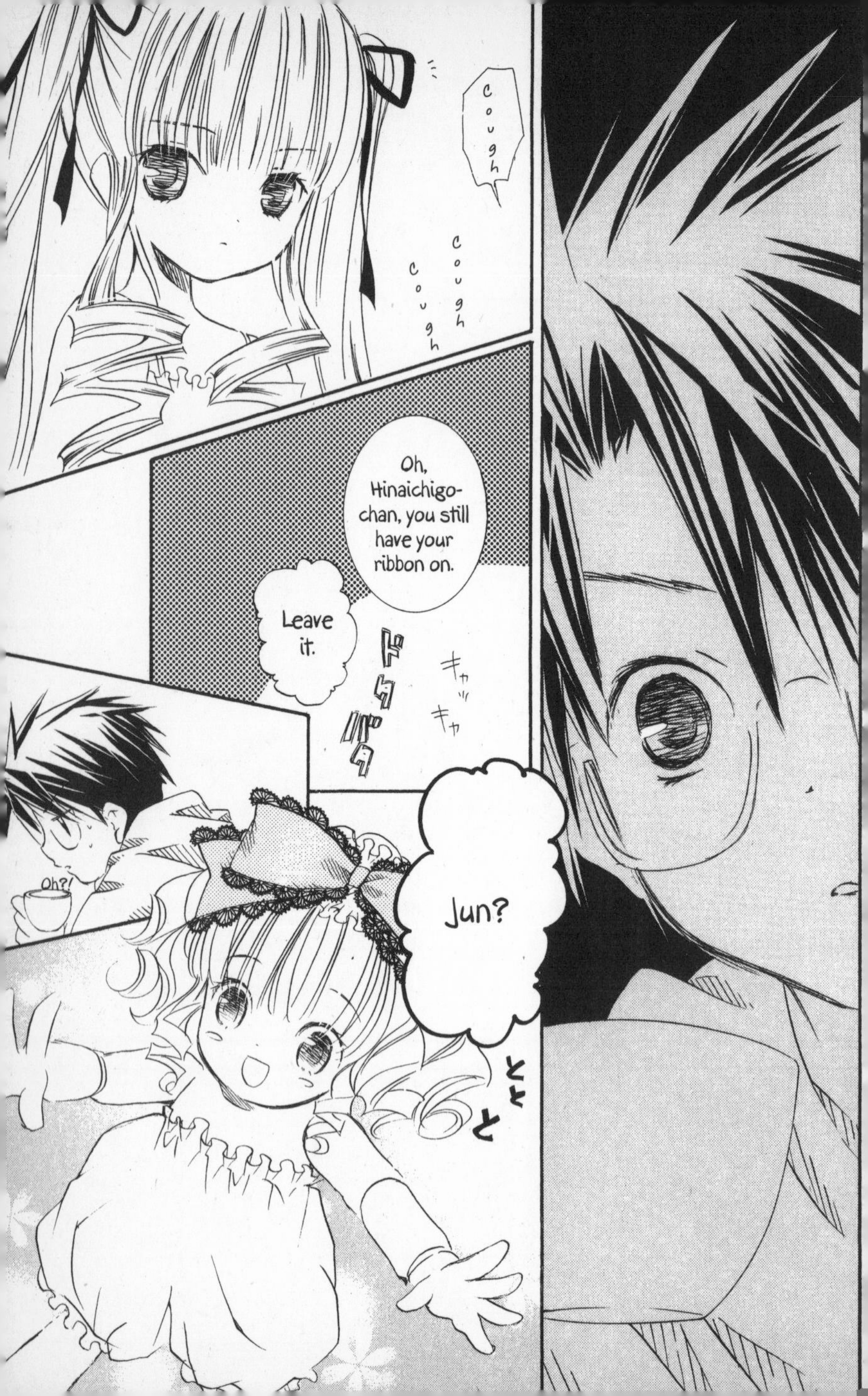
Cough
Cough
Cough
Oh, Hinaichigo-chan, you still have your ribbon on.
Leave it.
ドタバタ
キャッキャ
Oh?!
Jun?
ととと

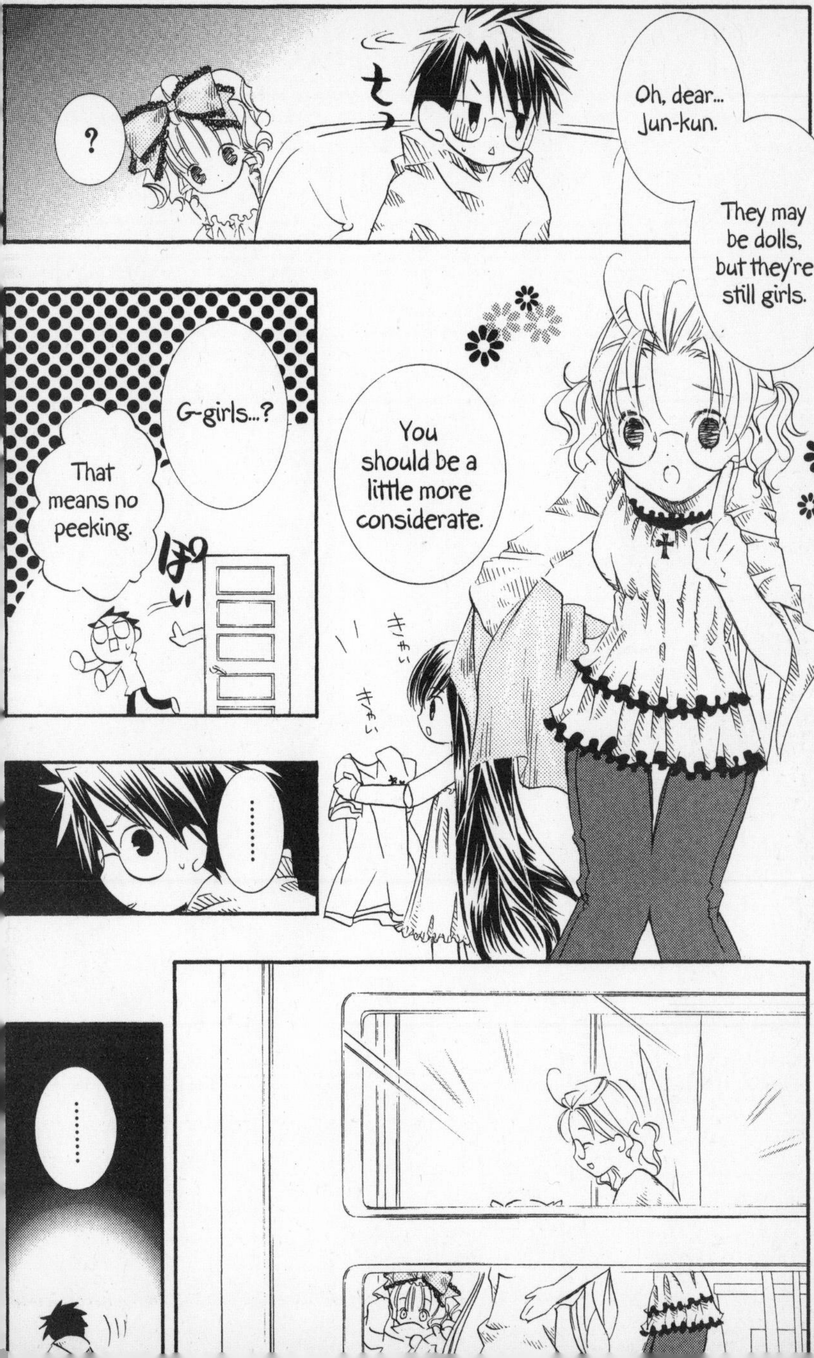

Oh, dear... Jun-kun.
?
They may be dolls, but they're still girls.
You should be a little more considerate.
きゃい
きゃい
G-girls...?
That means no peeking.
ぽい
....
....

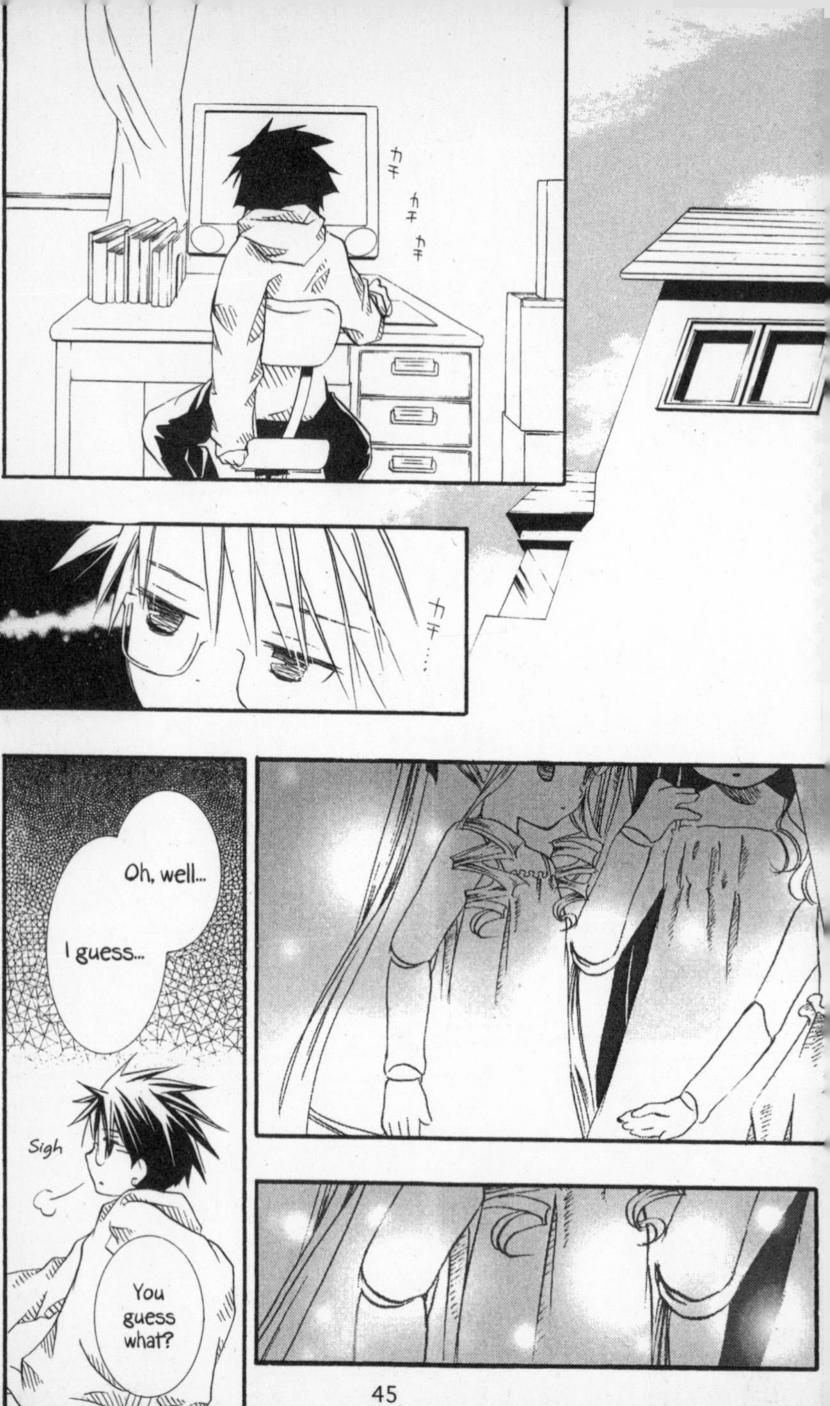
カチ
カチ
カチ
カチ…
Oh, well...
I guess...
Sigh
You guess what?

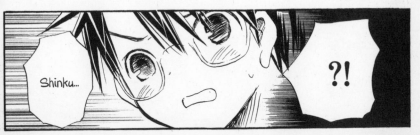

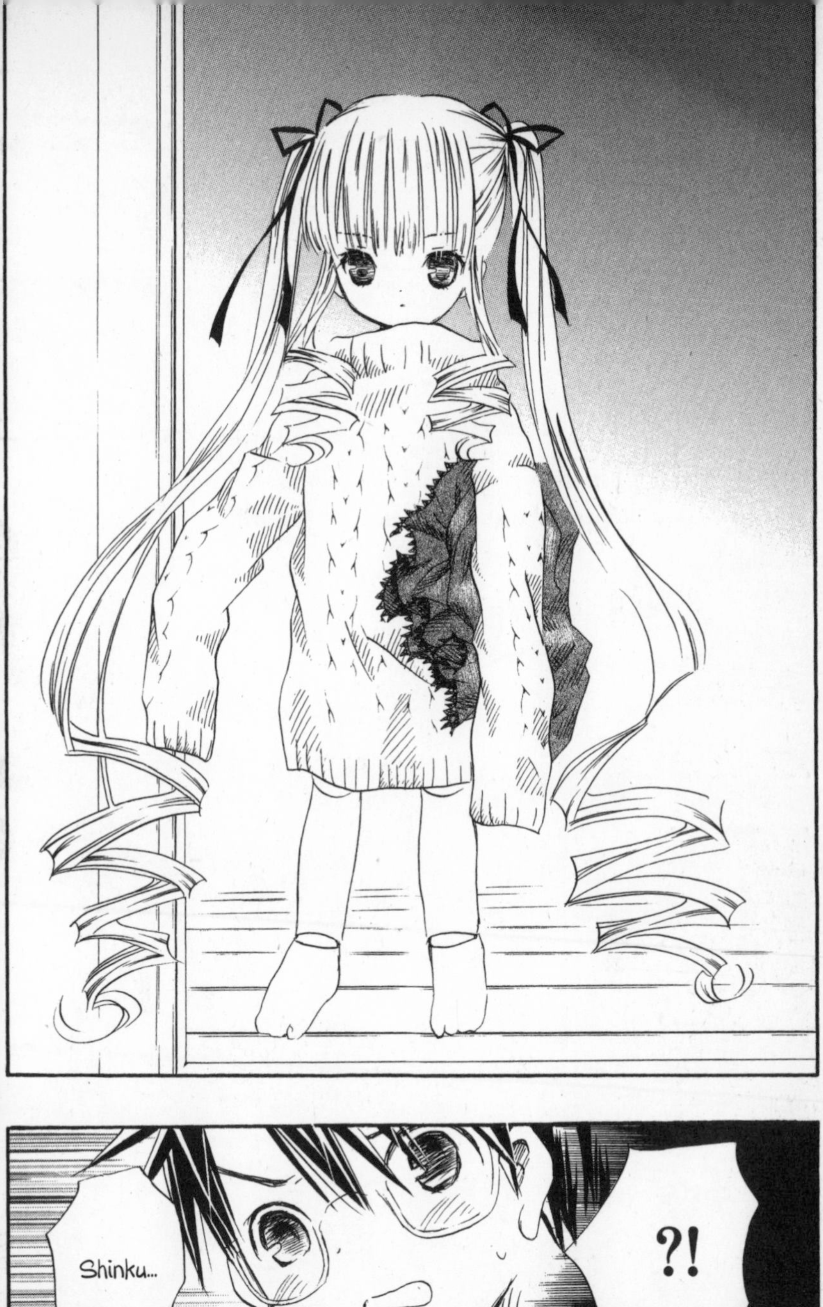
?!
Shinku...

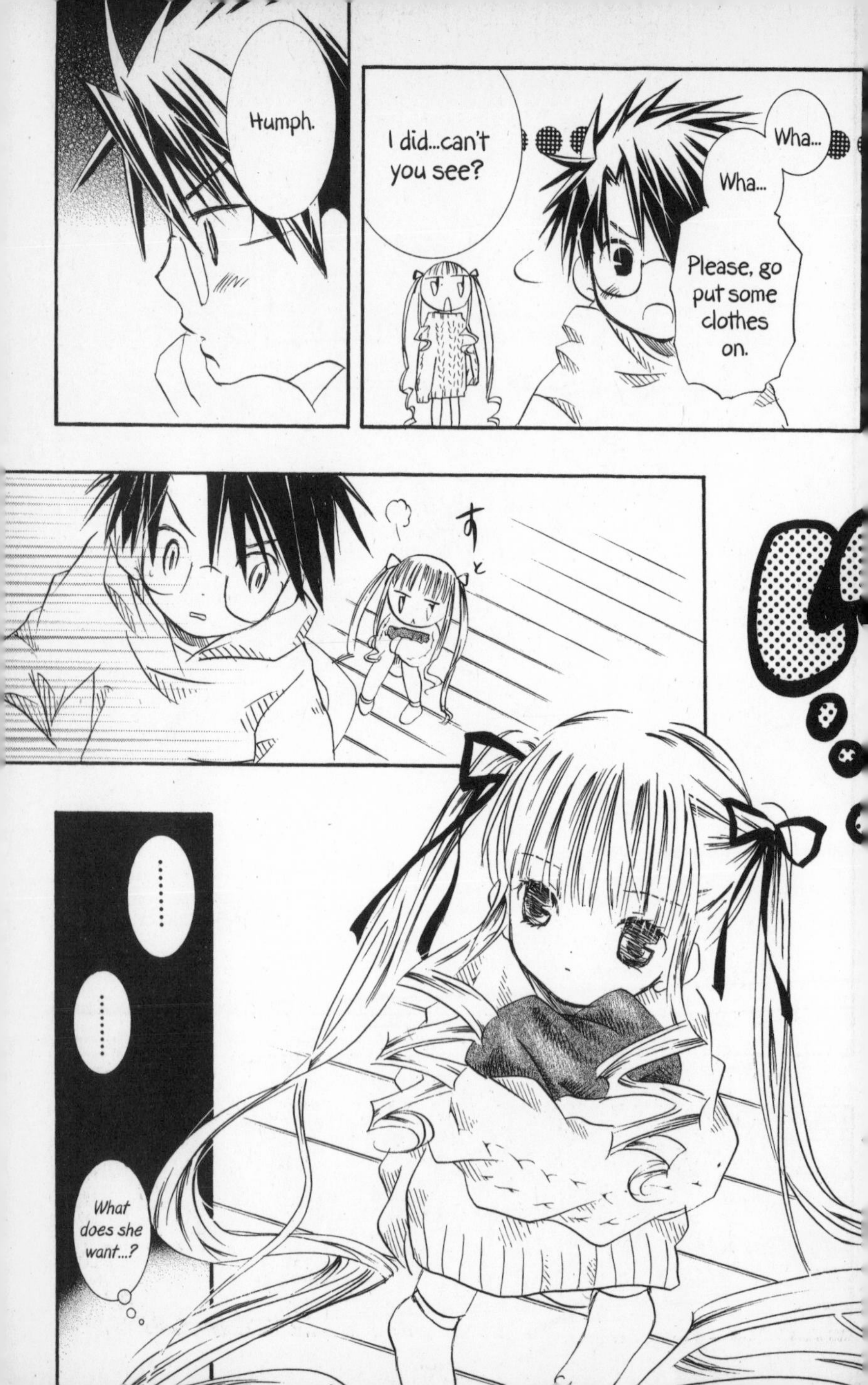
Wha...
Wha...
Please, go put some clothes on.
I did...can't you see?
Humph.
すと
....
....
What does she want...?

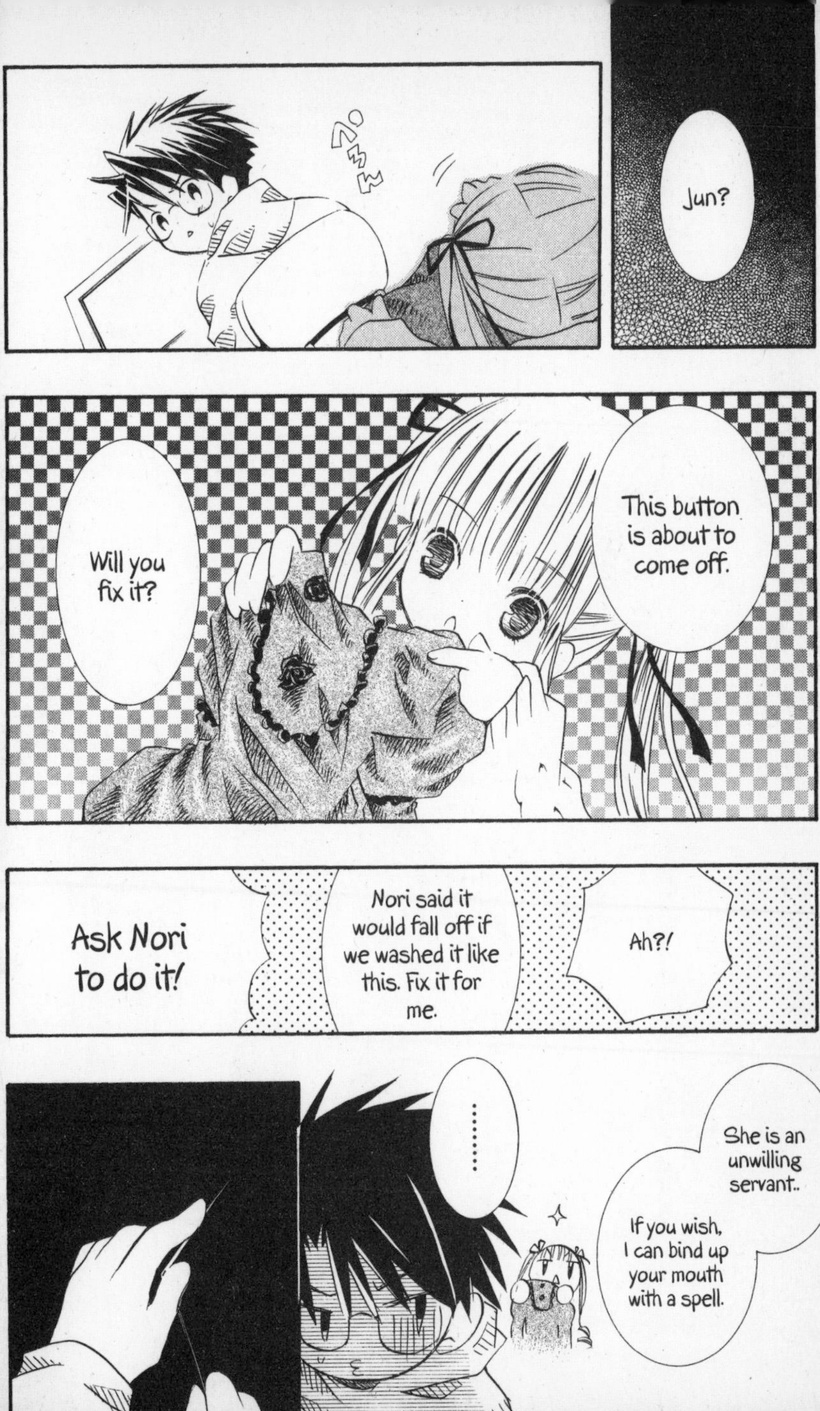
Jun?
This button is about to come off.
Will you fix it?
Ah?!
Nori said it would fall off if we washed it like this. Fix it for me.
Ask Nori to do it!
……
She is an unwilling servant..
If you wish, I can bind up your mouth with a spell.

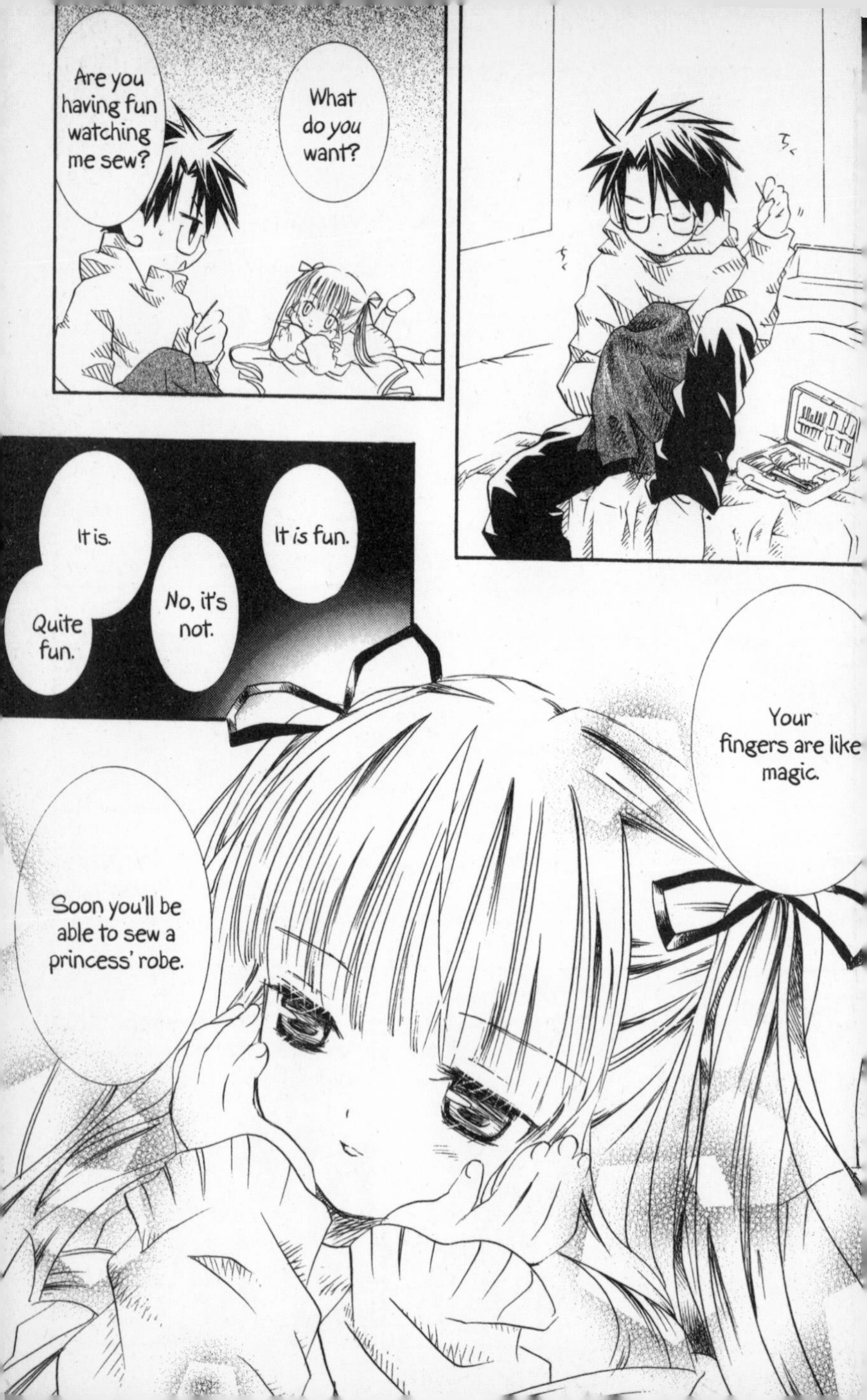
What do you want?
Are you having fun watching me sew?
It is fun.
No, it's not.
It is.
Quite fun.
Your fingers are like magic.
Soon you'll be able to sew a princess' robe.

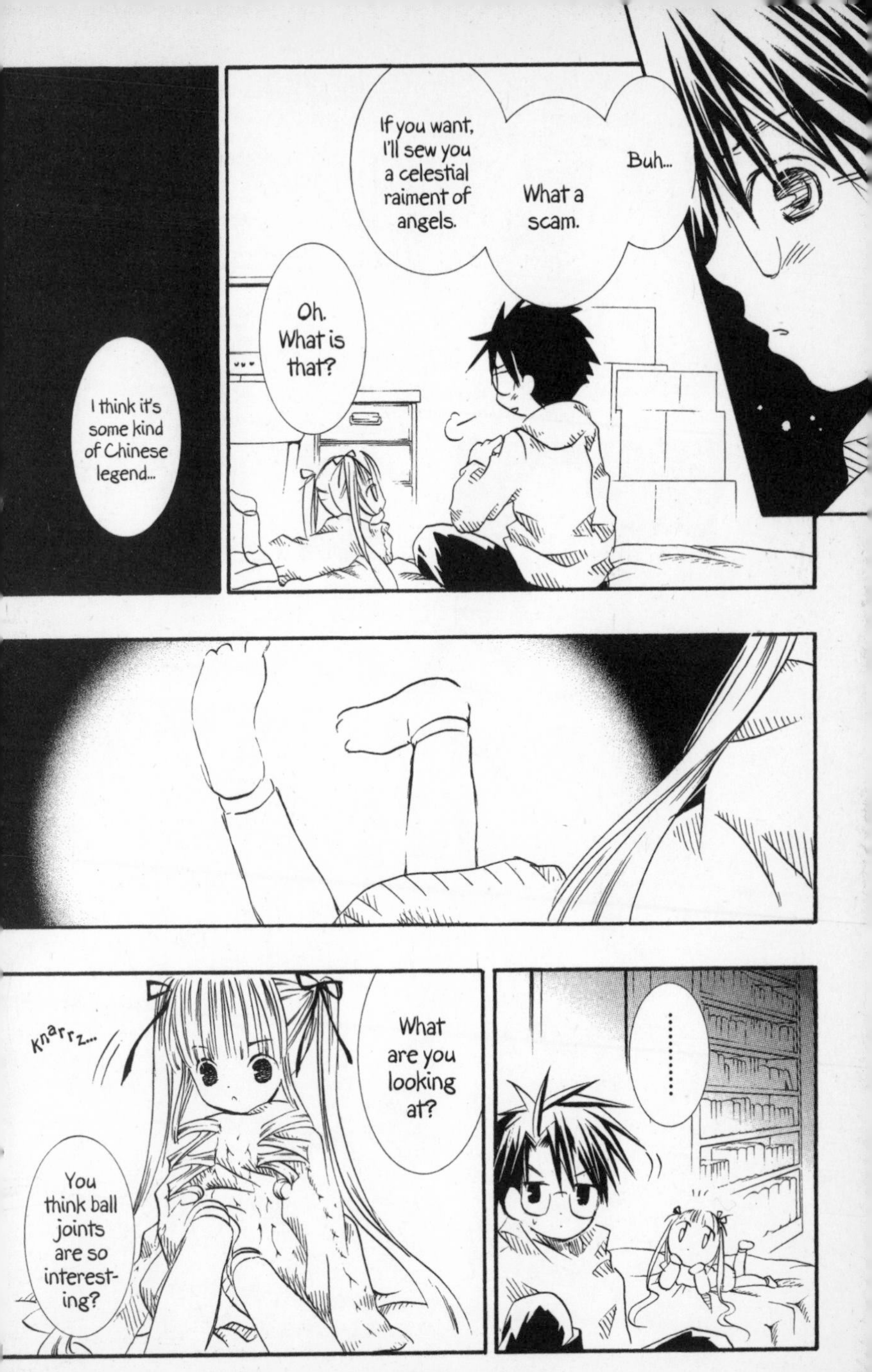

Buh...
What a scam.
If you want, I'll sew you a celestial raiment of angels.
Oh. What is that?
I think it's some kind of Chinese legend...
....
What are you looking at?
Knarrz...
You think ball joints are so interesting?

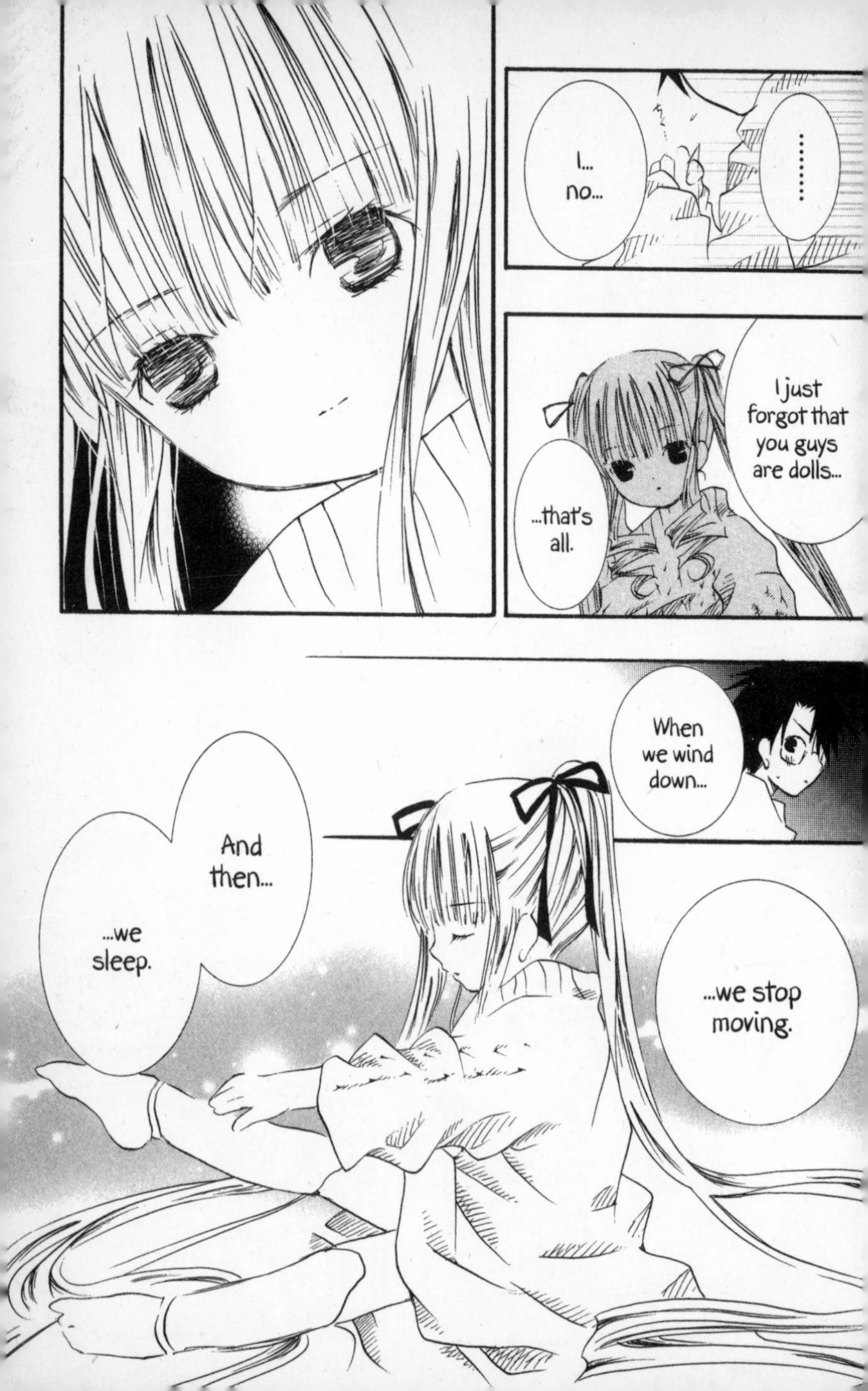
......
I... no...
I just forgot that you guys are dolls...
...that's all.
When we wind down...
...we stop moving.
And then...
...we sleep.

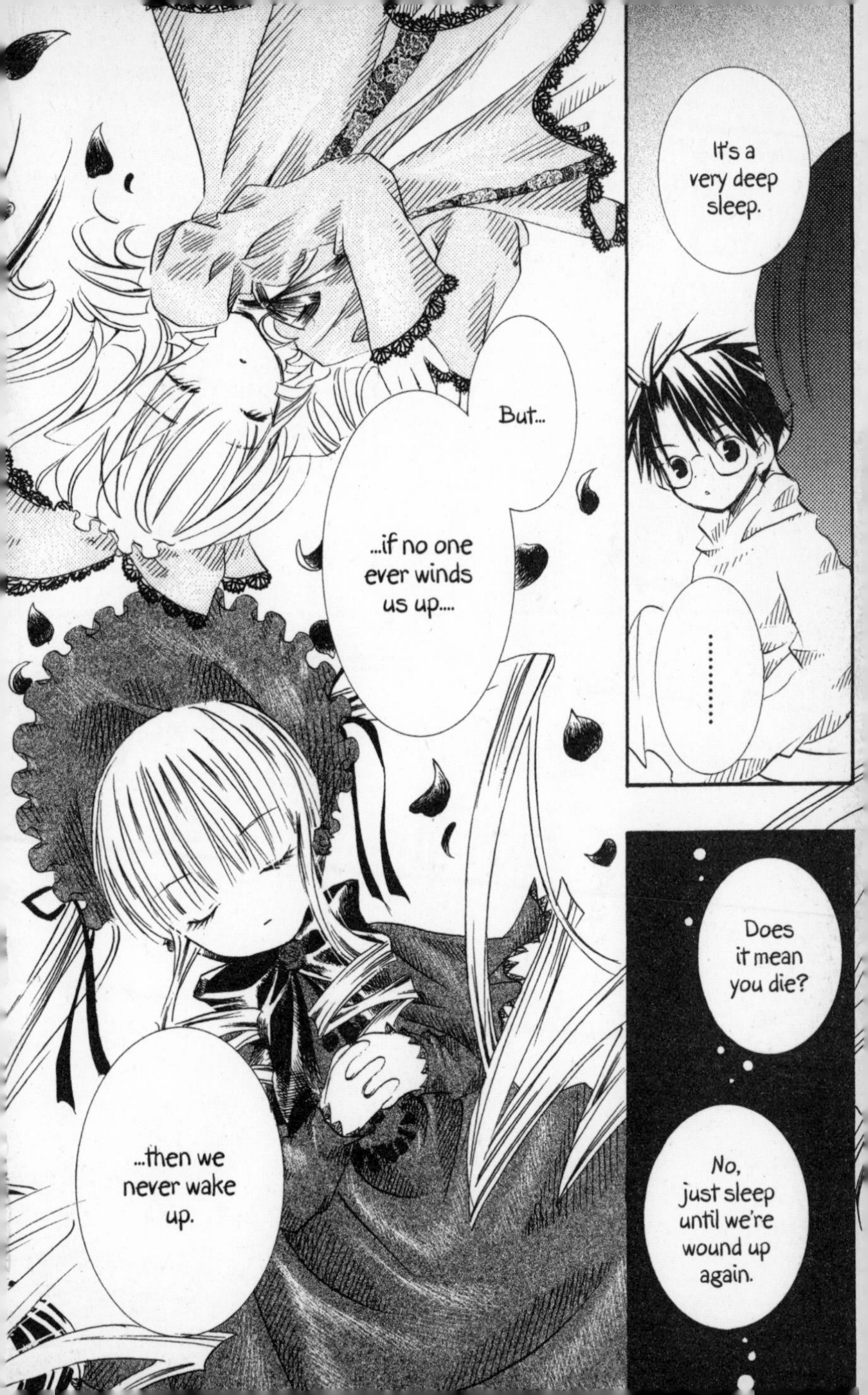
It's a very deep sleep.
....
Does it mean you die?
No, just sleep until we're wound up again.
But...
...if no one ever winds us up....
...then we never wake up.

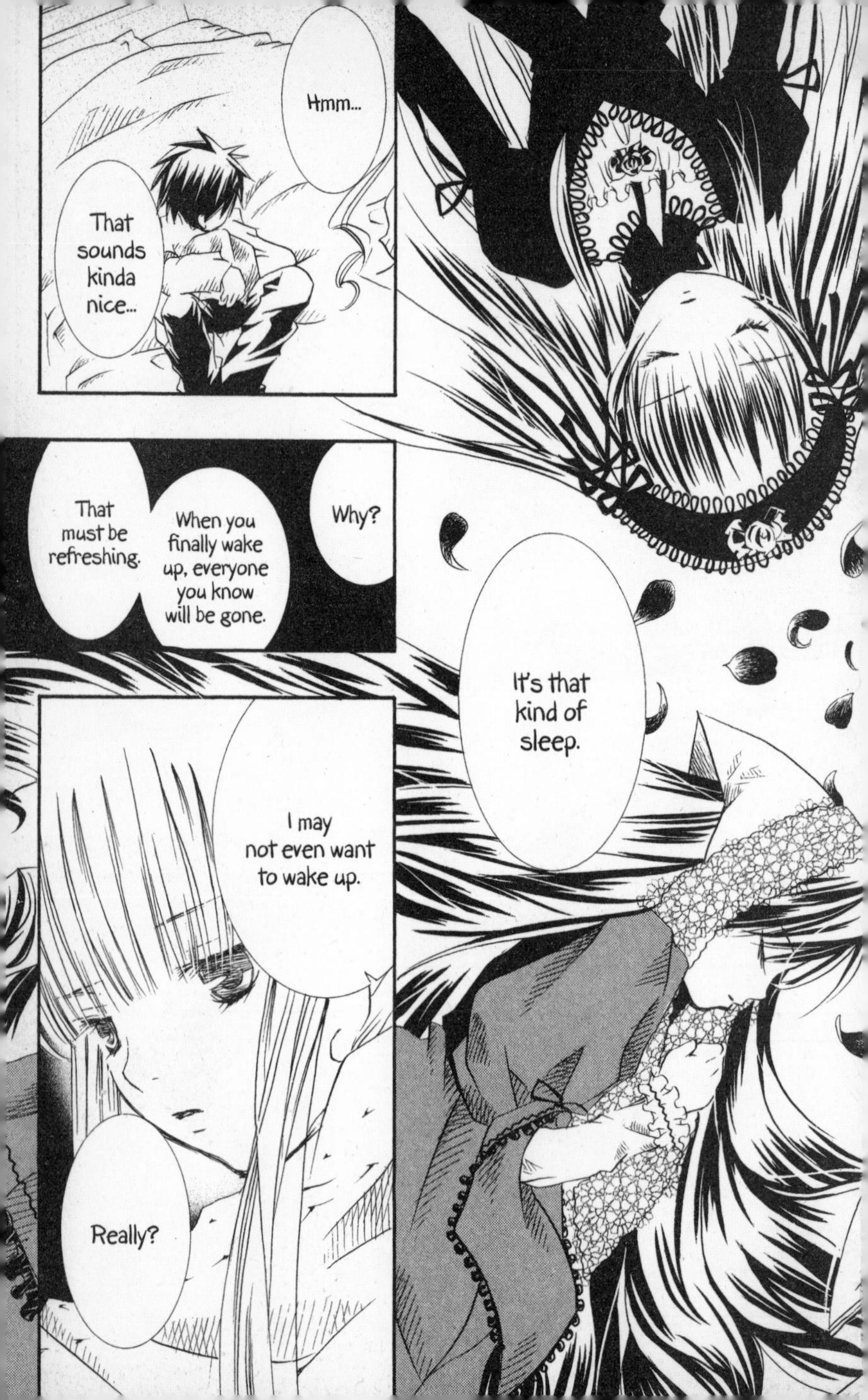
It's that kind of sleep.
Hmm...
That sounds kinda nice...
Why?
When you finally wake up, everyone you know will be gone.
That must be refreshing.
I may not even want to wake up.
Really?

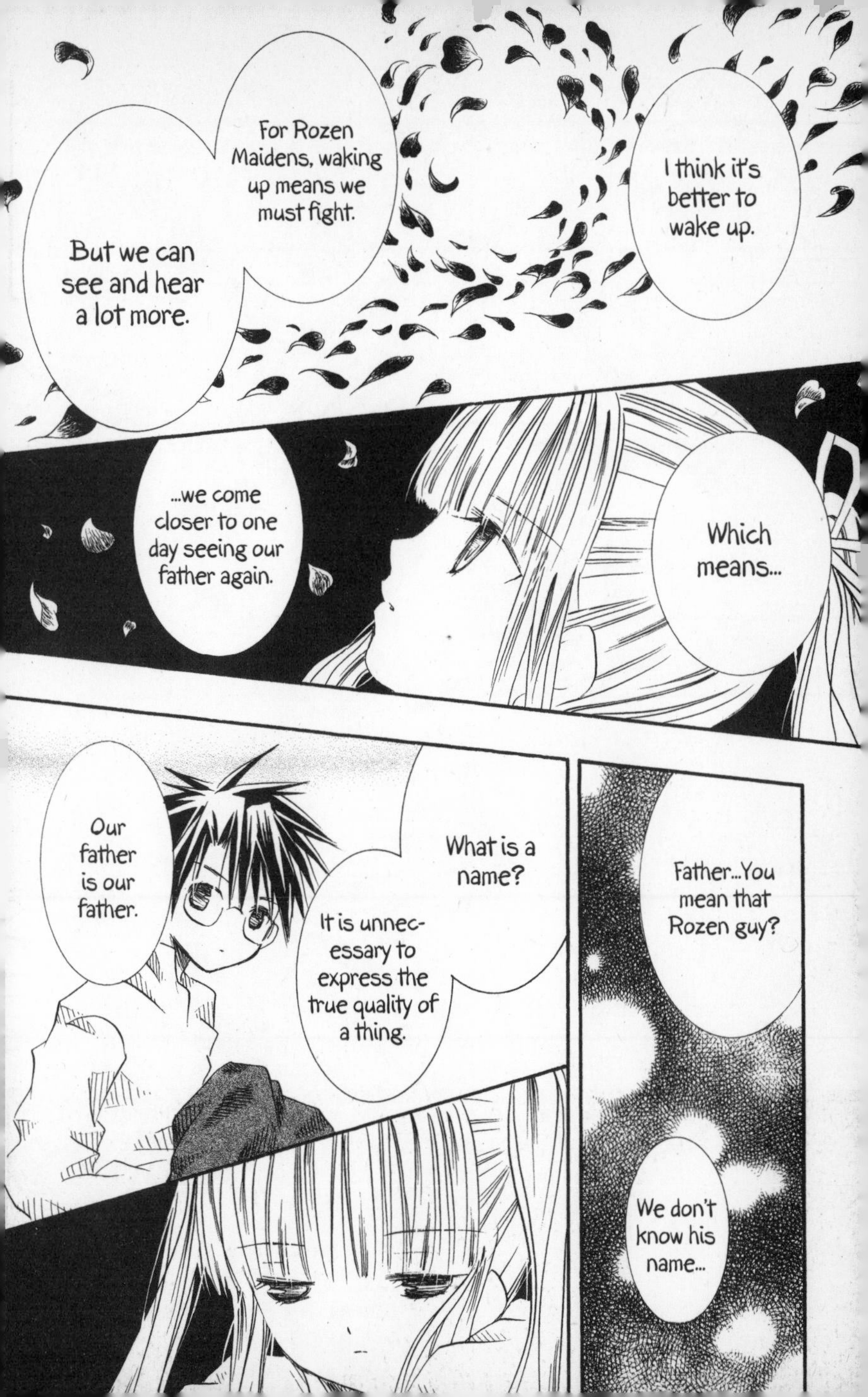

I think it's better to wake up.
For Rozen Maidens, waking up means we must fight.
But we can see and hear a lot more.
Which means...
...we come closer to one day seeing our father again.
Father...You mean that Rozen guy?
We don't know his name...
What is a name?
It is unnecessary to express the true quality of a thing.
Our father is our father.

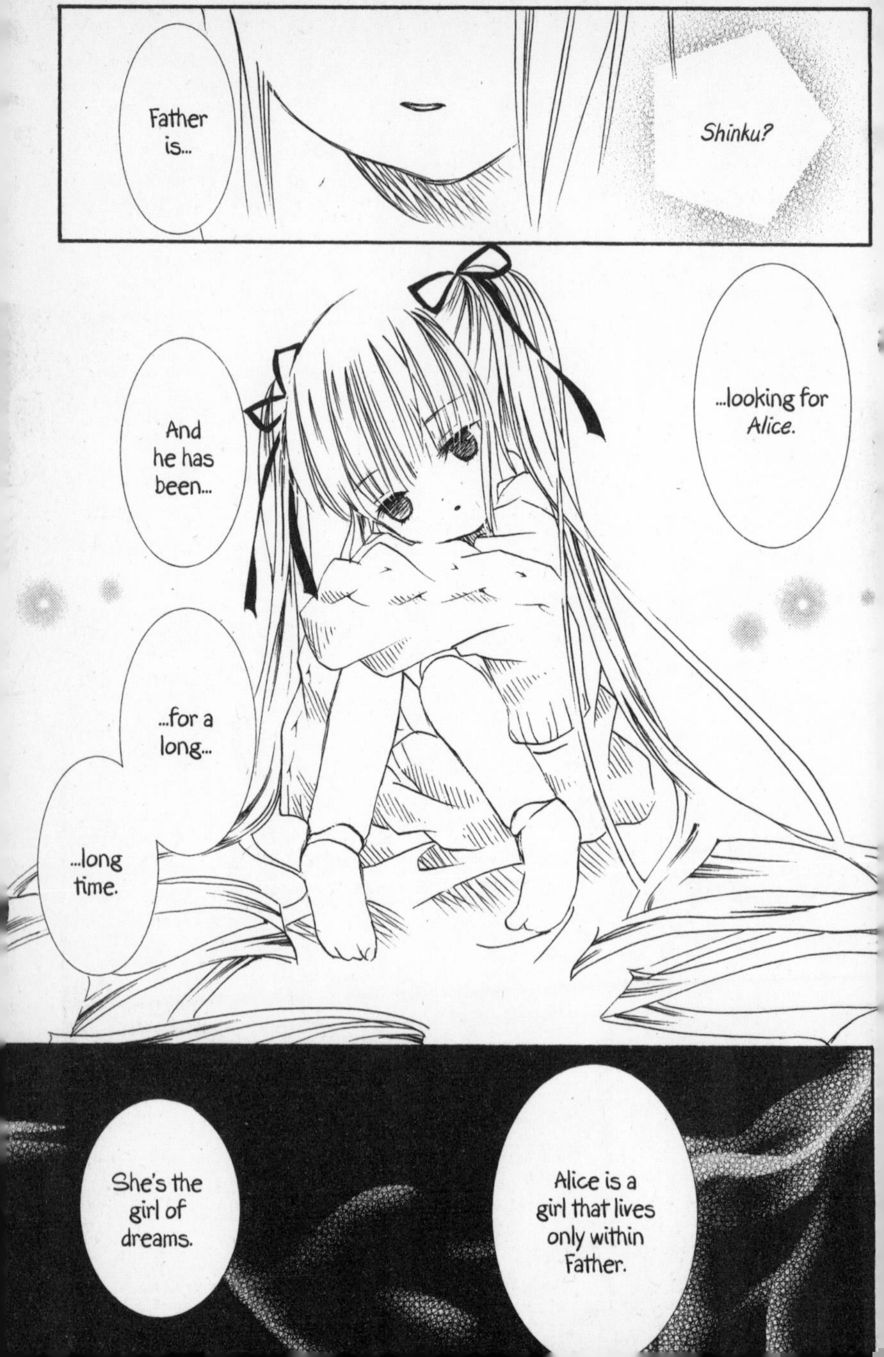
Shinku?
Father is...
...looking for Alice.
And he has been...
...for a long...
...long time.
Alice is a girl that lives only within Father.
She's the girl of dreams.

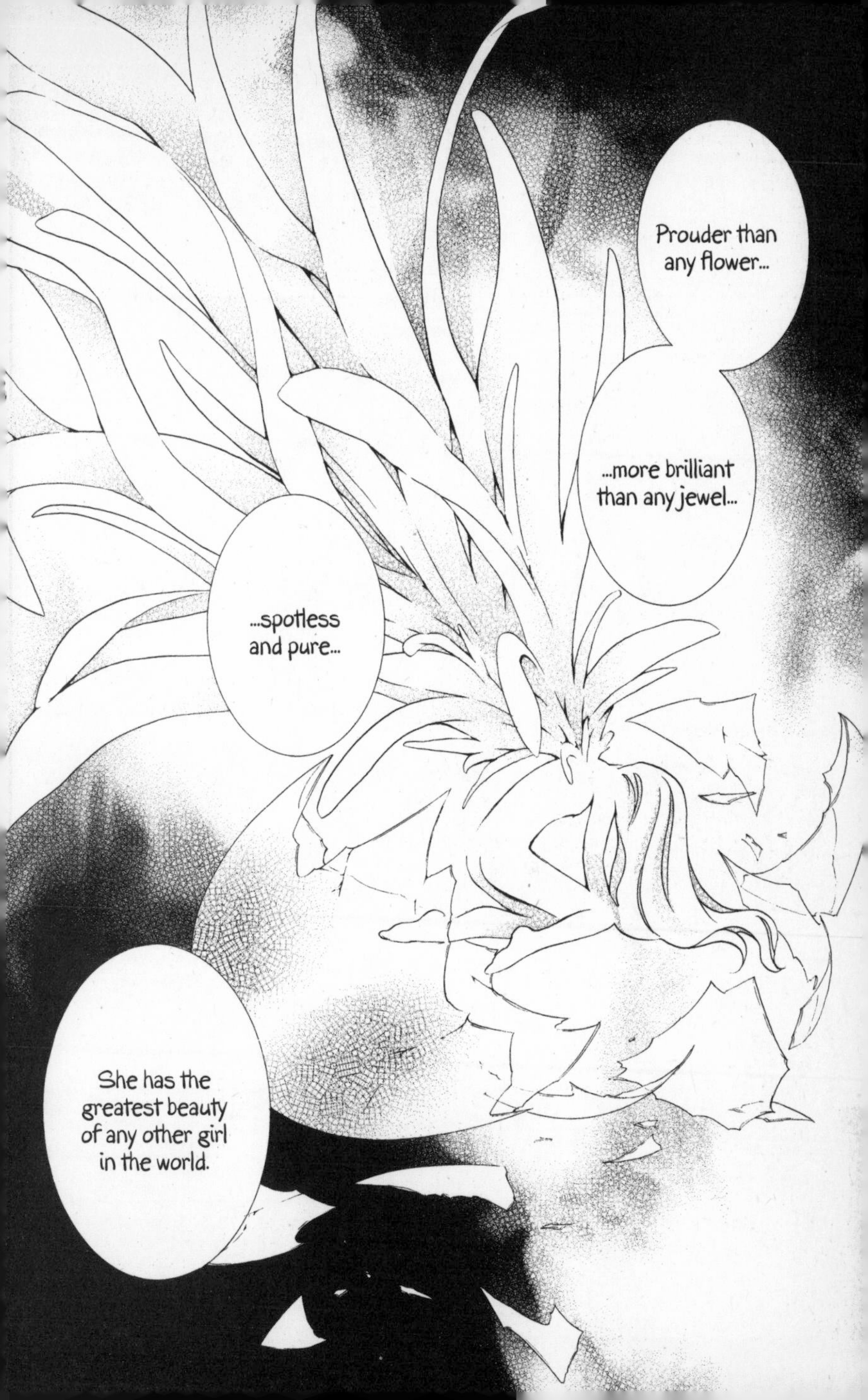
Prouder than any flower...
...more brilliant than any jewel...
...spotless and pure...
She has the greatest beauty of any other girl in the world.

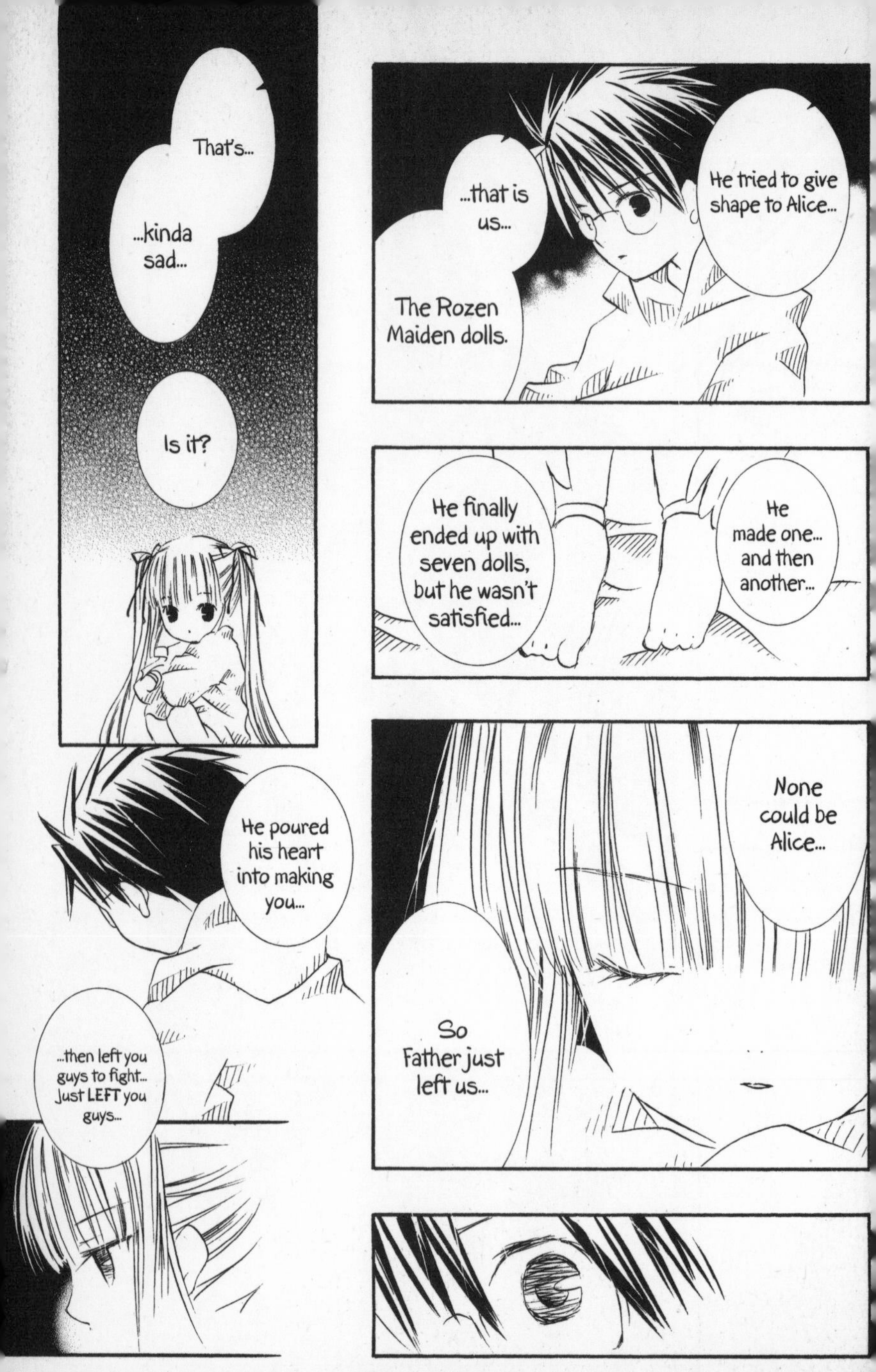
He tried to give shape to Alice...
...that is us...
The Rozen Maiden dolls.
He made one... and then another...
He finally ended up with seven dolls, but he wasn't satisfied...
That's...
...kinda sad...
Is it?
None could be Alice...
So Father just left us...
He poured his heart into making you...
...then left you guys to fight... Just LEFT you guys...

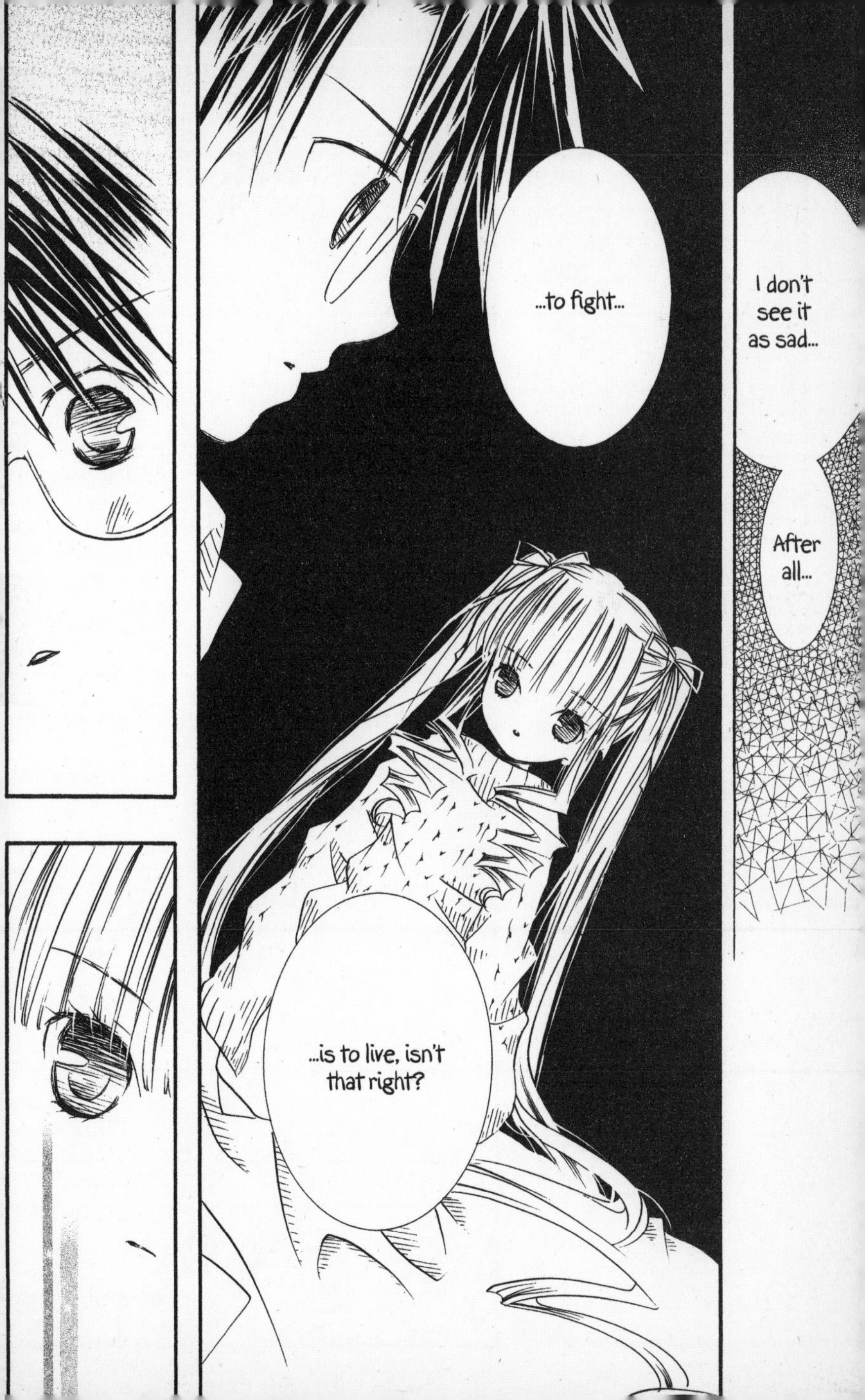
I don't see it as sad...
After all...
...to fight...
...is to live, isn't that right?

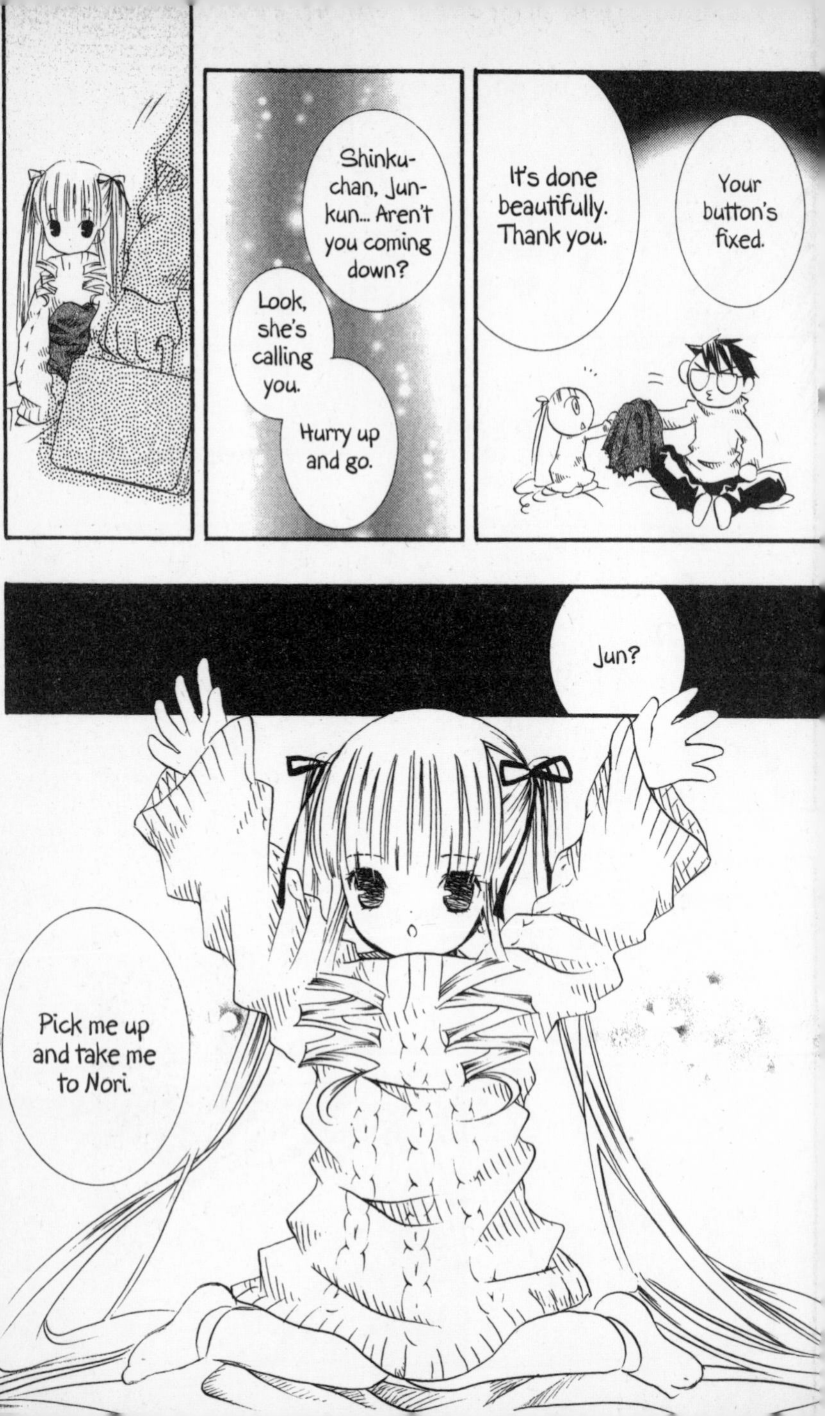
Your button's fixed.
It's done beautifully. Thank you.
Shinku-chan, Jun-kun... Aren't you coming down?
Look, she's calling you.
Hurry up and go.
Jun?
Pick me up and take me to Nori.

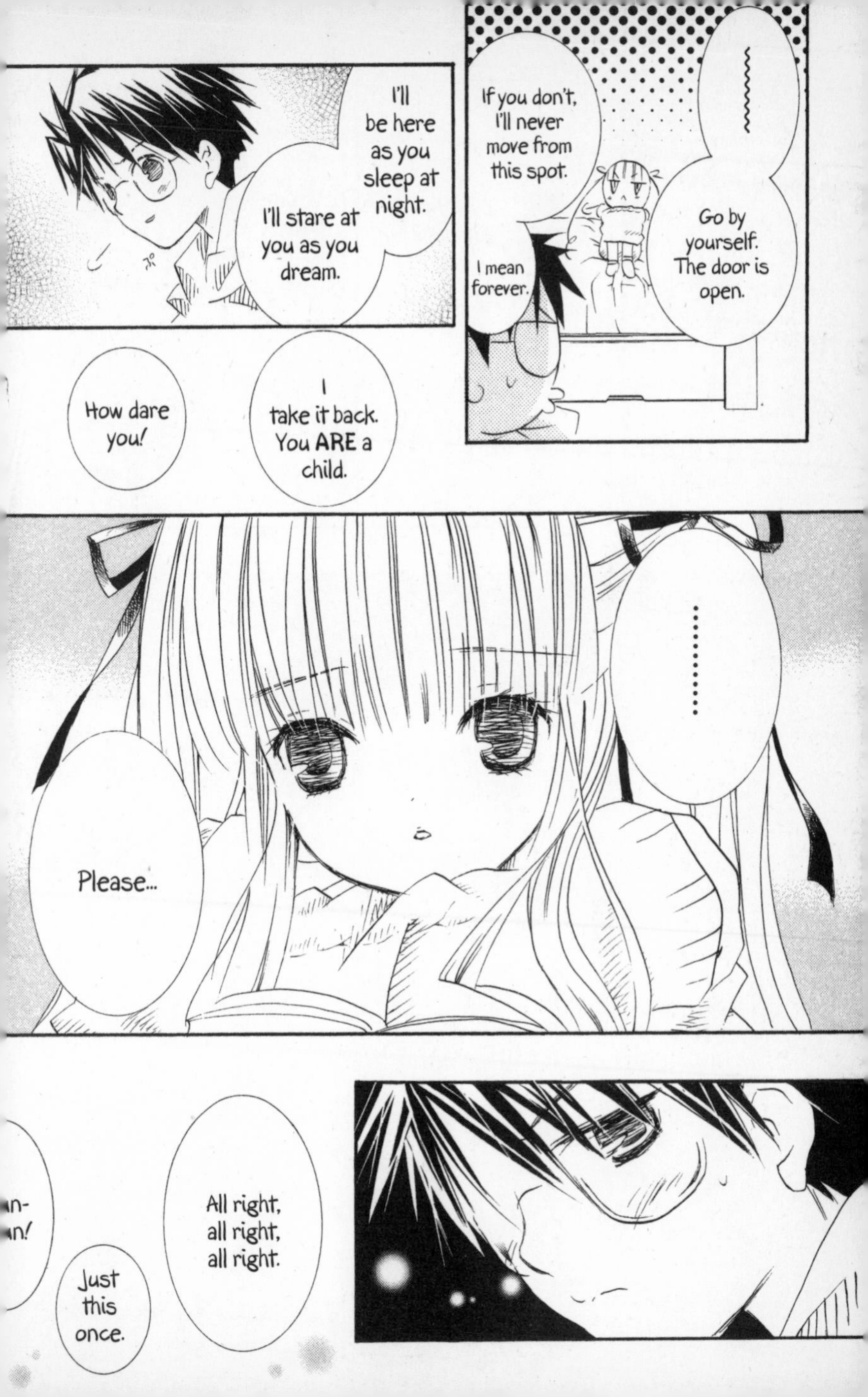
Go by yourself. The door is open.
If you don't, I'll never move from this spot.
I mean forever.
I'll be here as you sleep at night.
I'll stare at you as you dream.
I take it back. You ARE a child.
How dare you!
....
Please...
All right, all right, all right.
Just this once.

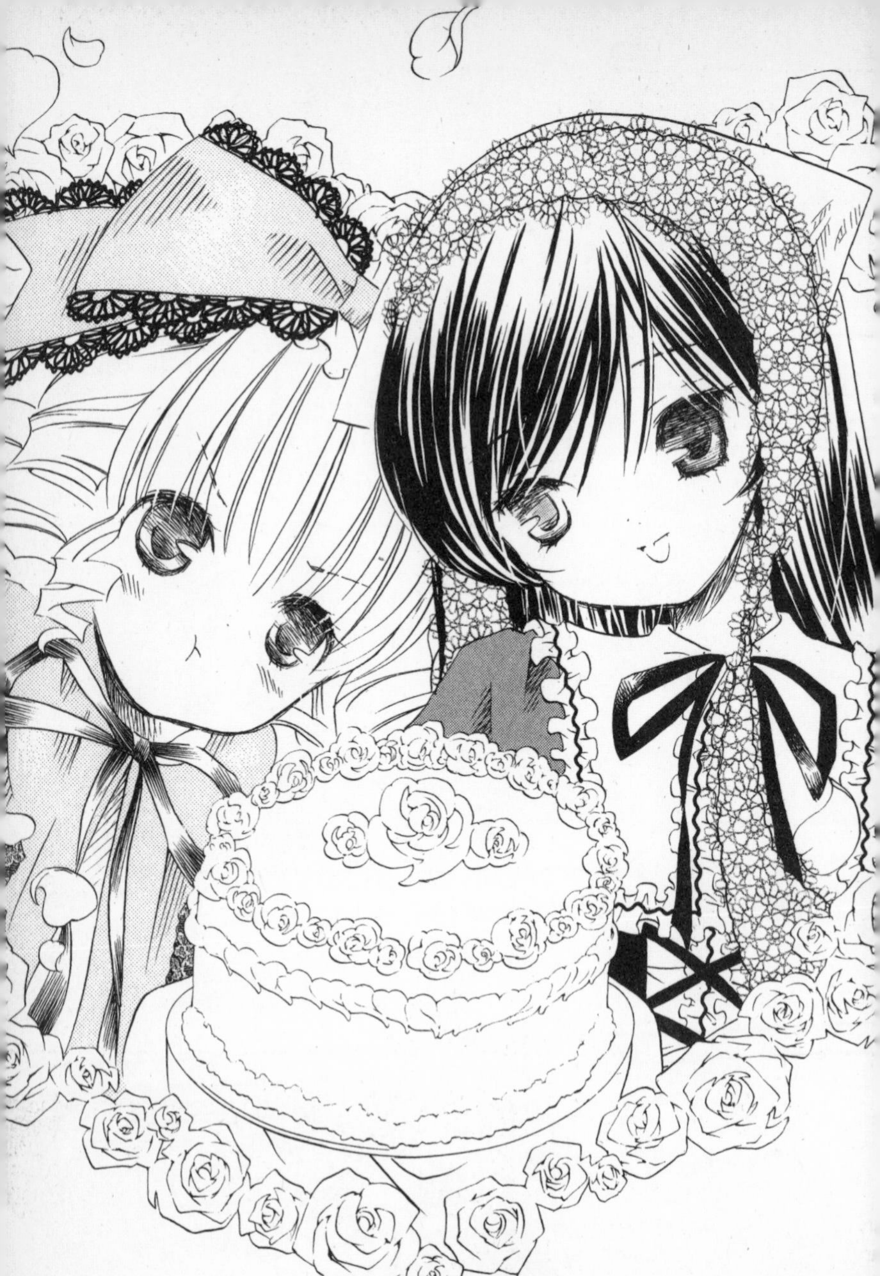

Phase 14

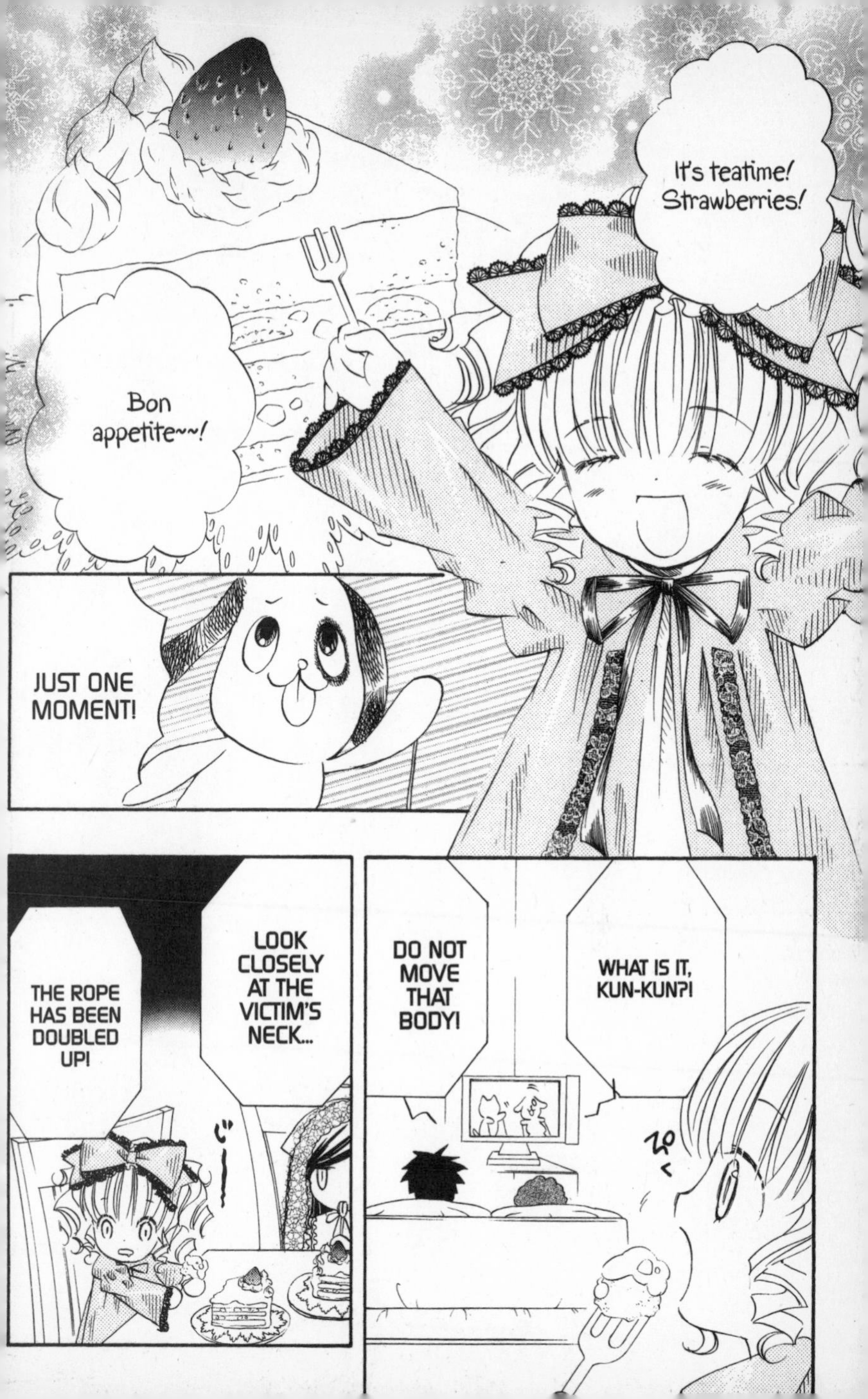
It's teatime! Strawberries!
Bon appetite~~!
JUST ONE MOMENT!
WHAT IS IT, KUN-KUN?!
DO NOT MOVE THAT BODY!
LOOK CLOSELY AT THE VICTIM'S NECK...
THE ROPE HAS BEEN DOUBLED UP!
じー

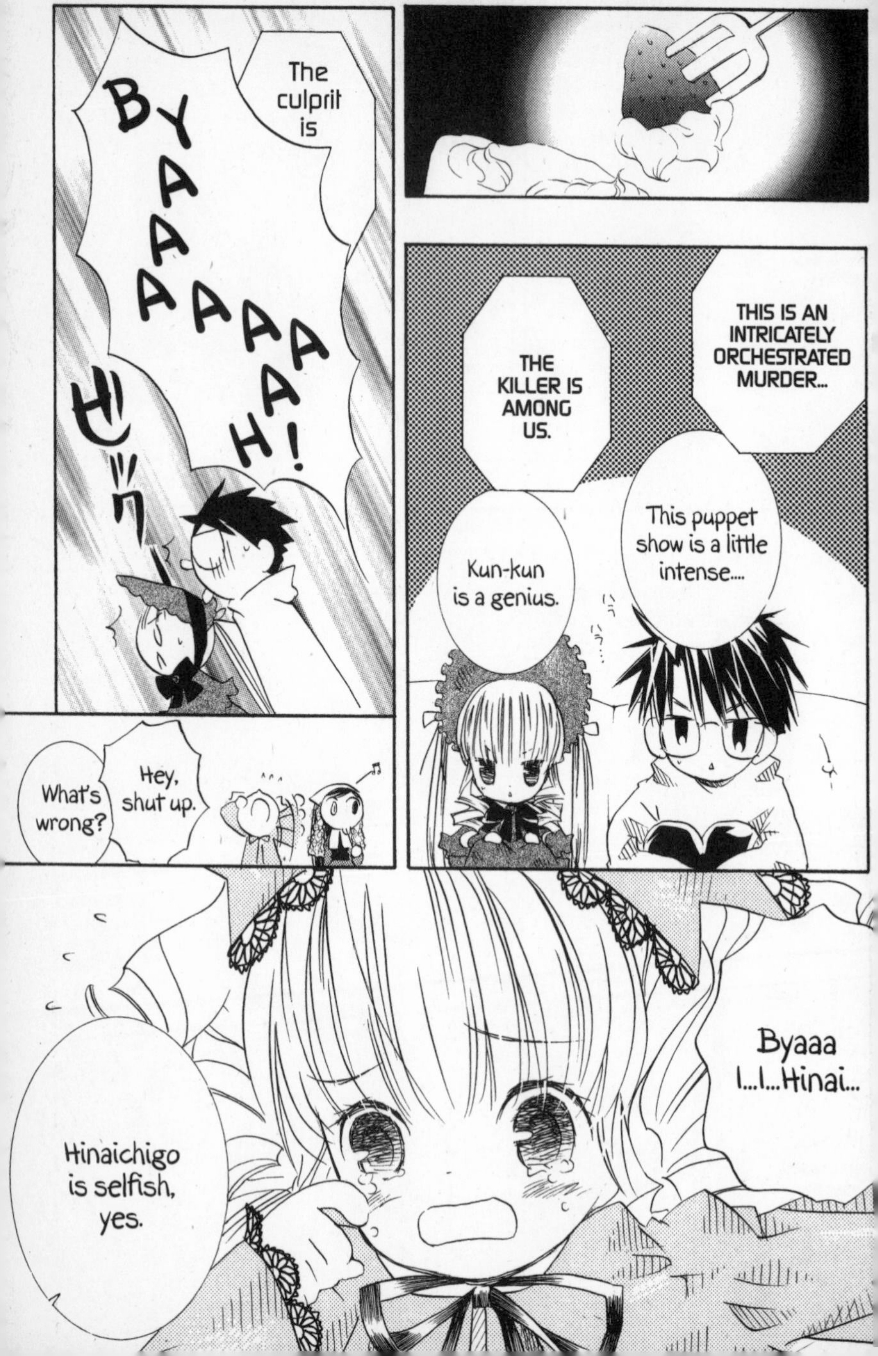
THIS IS AN INTRICATELY ORCHESTRATED MURDER...
THE KILLER IS AMONG US.
This puppet show is a little intense....
Kun-kun is a genius.
The culprit is
BYAAAAAAAAAH!
Hey, shut up.
What's wrong?
Byaaa I...I...Hinai...
Hinaichigo is selfish, yes.

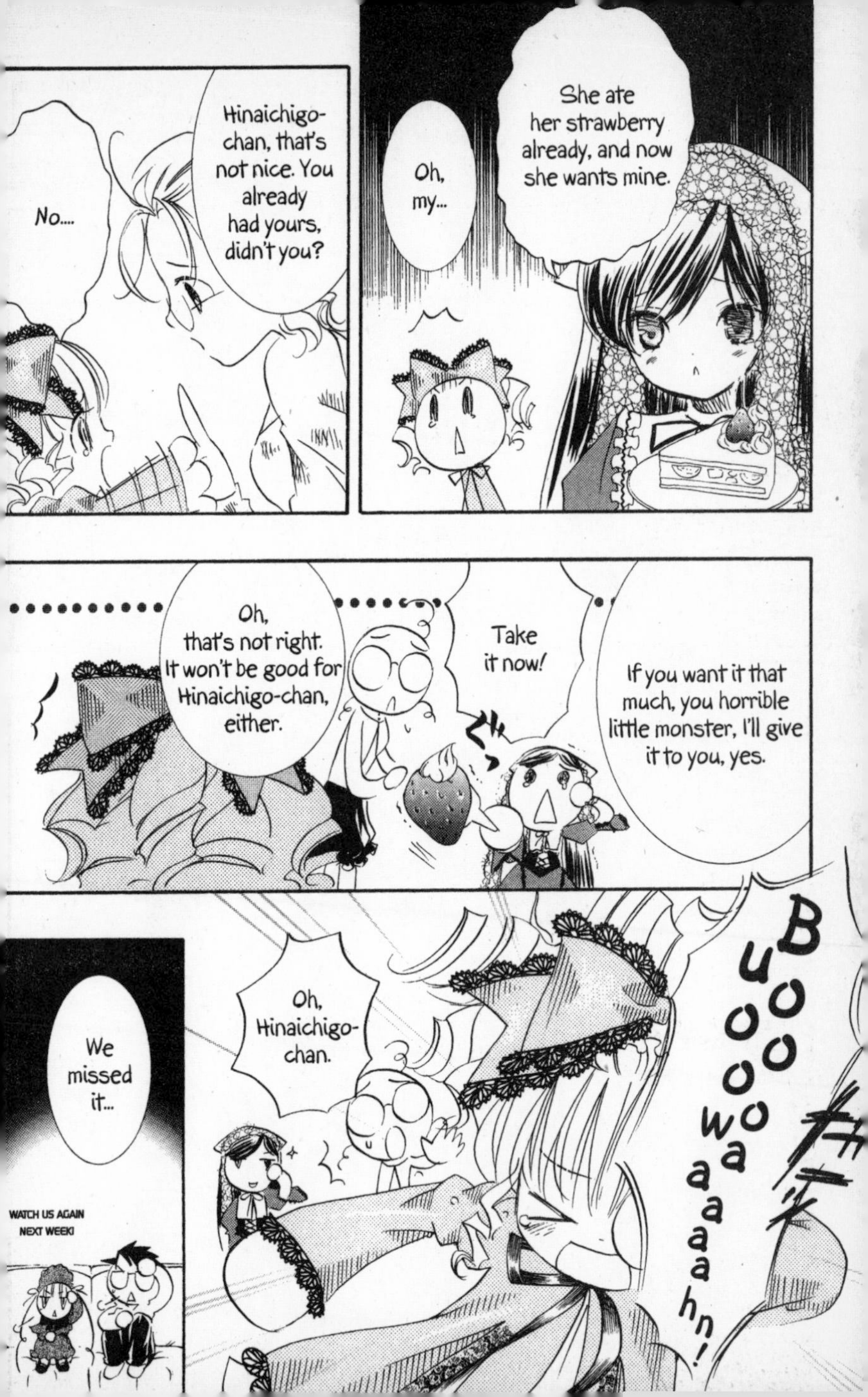
She ate her strawberry already, and now she wants mine.
Oh, my...
Hinaichigo-chan, that's not nice. You already had yours, didn't you?
No....
If you want it that much, you horrible little monster, I'll give it to you, yes.
Take it now!
Oh, that's not right. It won't be good for Hinaichigo-chan, either.
Buooooowaaaaaahn!
Oh, Hinaichigo-chan.
We missed it...
WATCH US AGAIN NEXT WEEK!

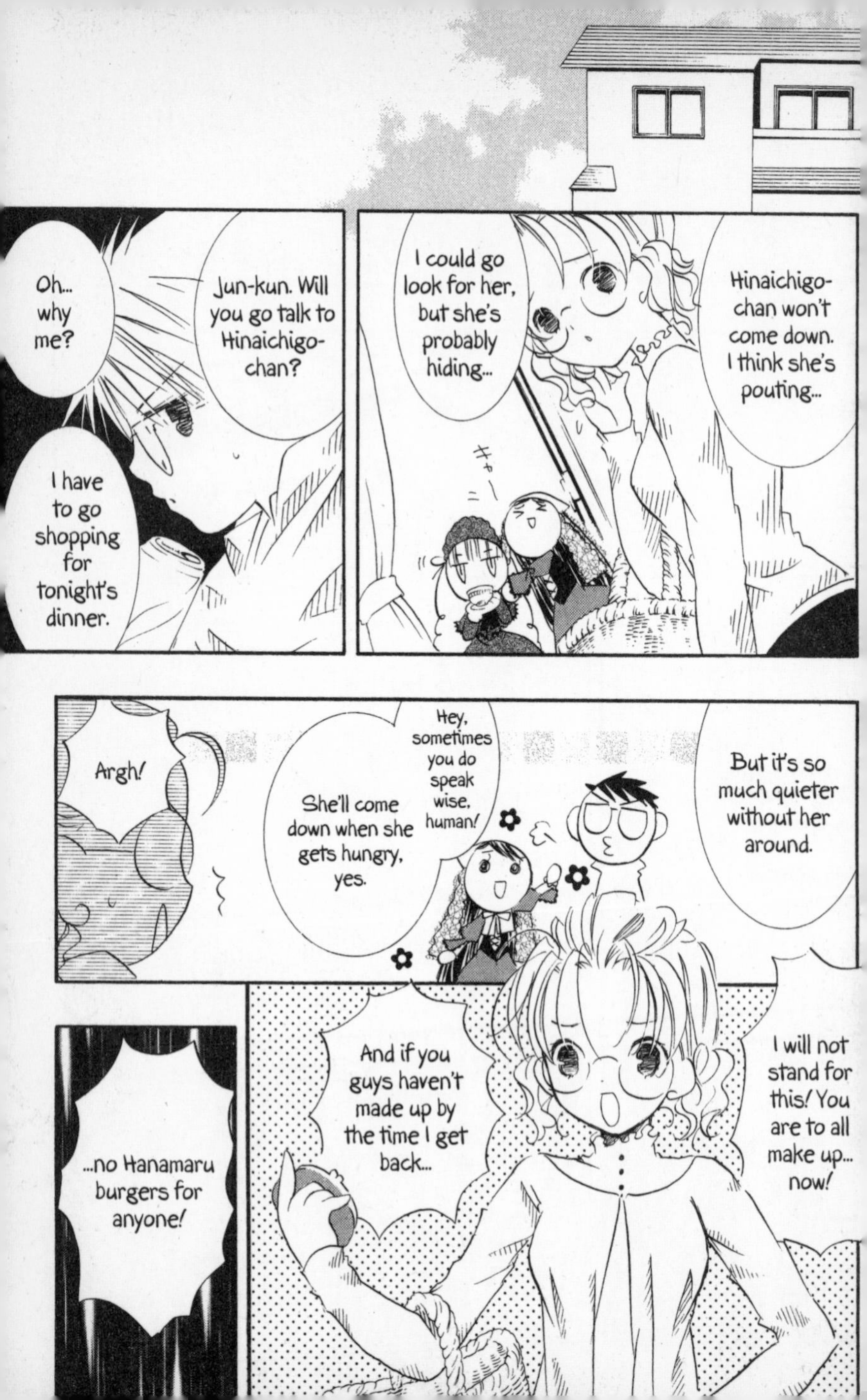
Hinaichigo-chan won't come down. I think she's pouting...
I could go look for her, but she's probably hiding...
キャ
Jun-kun. Will you go talk to Hinaichigo-chan?
Oh... why me?
I have to go shopping for tonight's dinner.
But it's so much quieter without her around.
Hey, sometimes you do speak wise, human!
She'll come down when she gets hungry, yes.
Argh!
I will not stand for this! You are to all make up... now!
And if you guys haven't made up by the time I get back...
...no Hanamaru burgers for anyone!

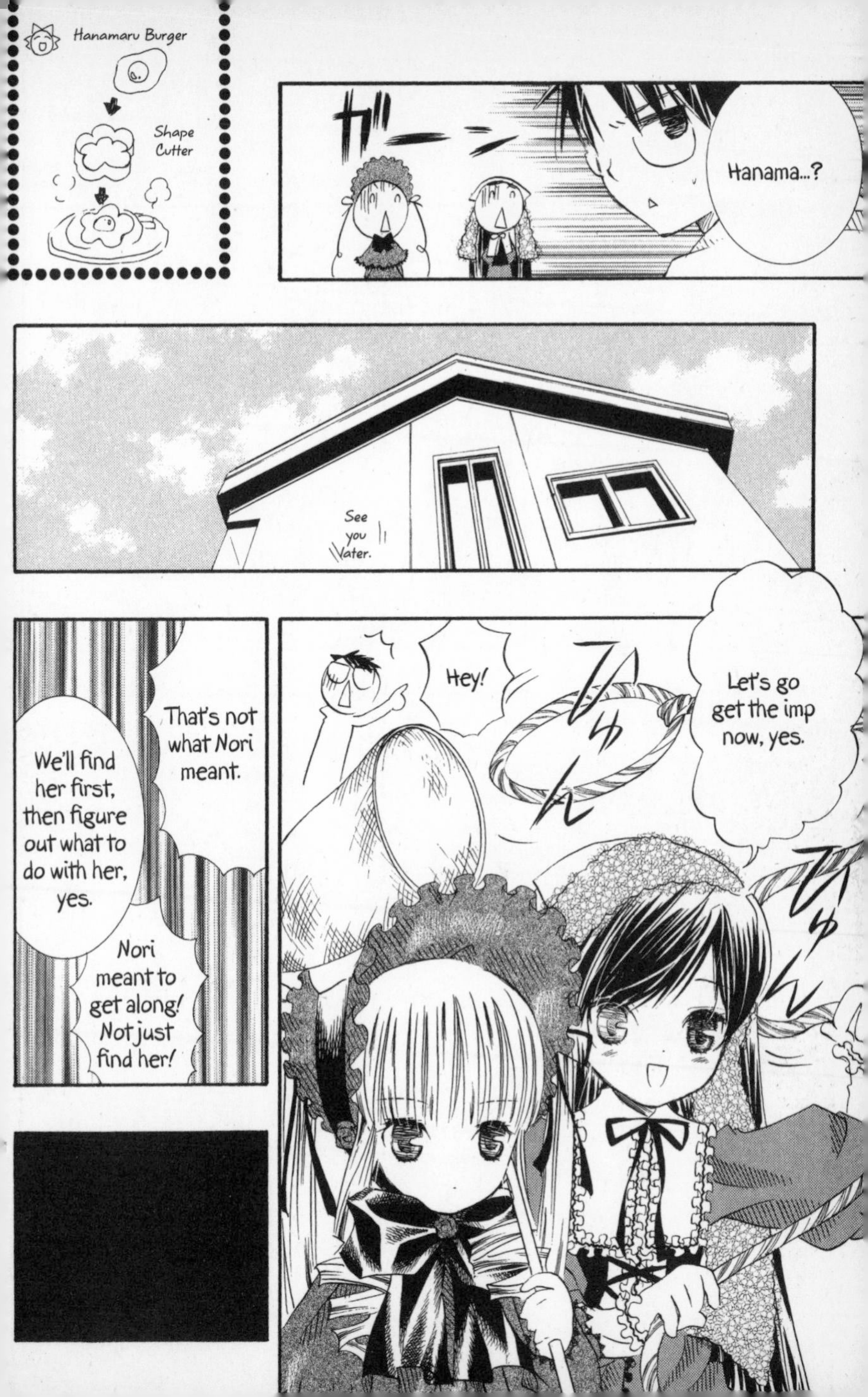
ガーー
Hanama...?
Hanamaru Burger
Shape Cutter
See you later.
Let's go get the imp now, yes.
Hey!
ひゅん
ひゅん
That's not what Nori meant.
We'll find her first, then figure out what to do with her, yes.
Nori meant to get along! Not just find her!

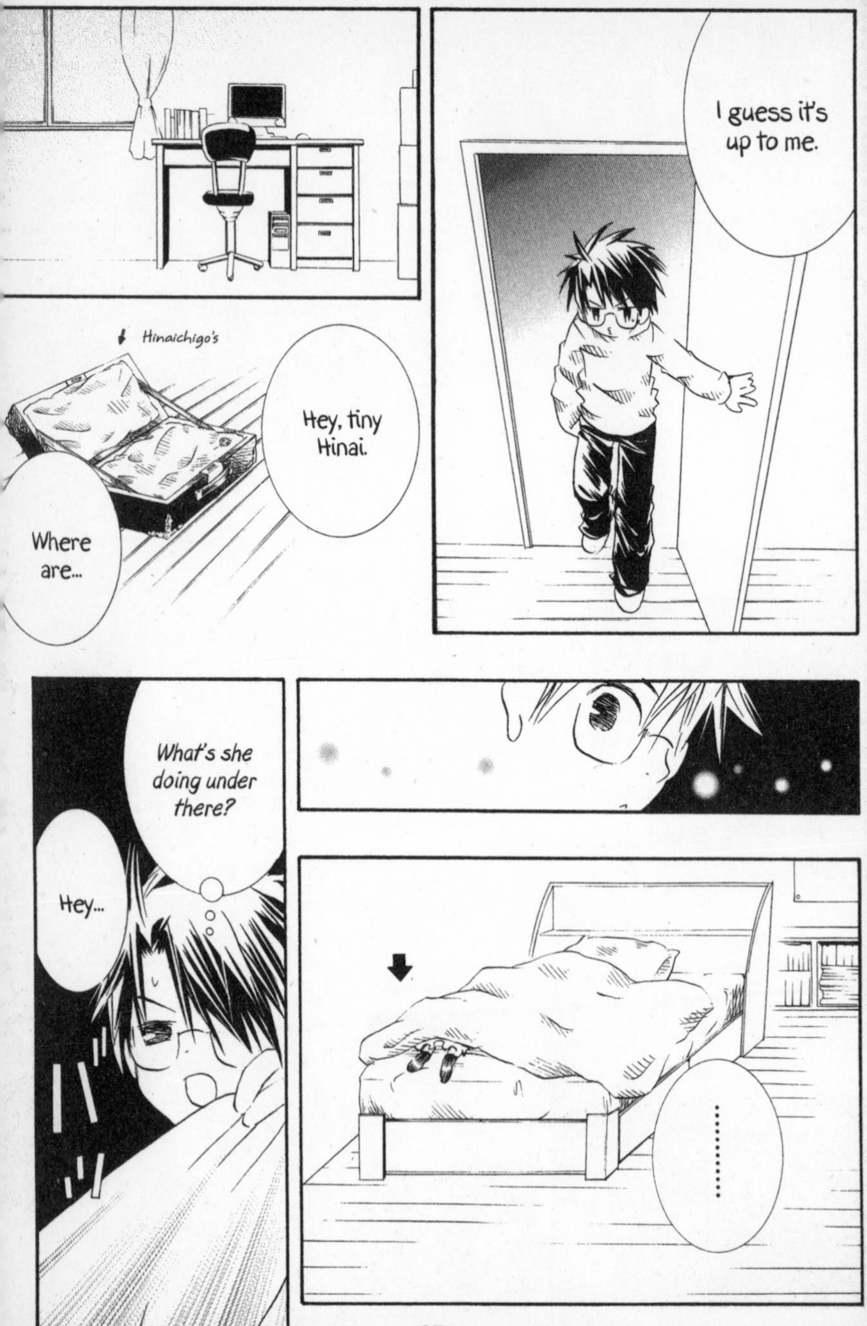
I guess it's up to me.
Hey, tiny Hinai.
Hinaichigo's
Where are...
......
What's she doing under there?
Hey...

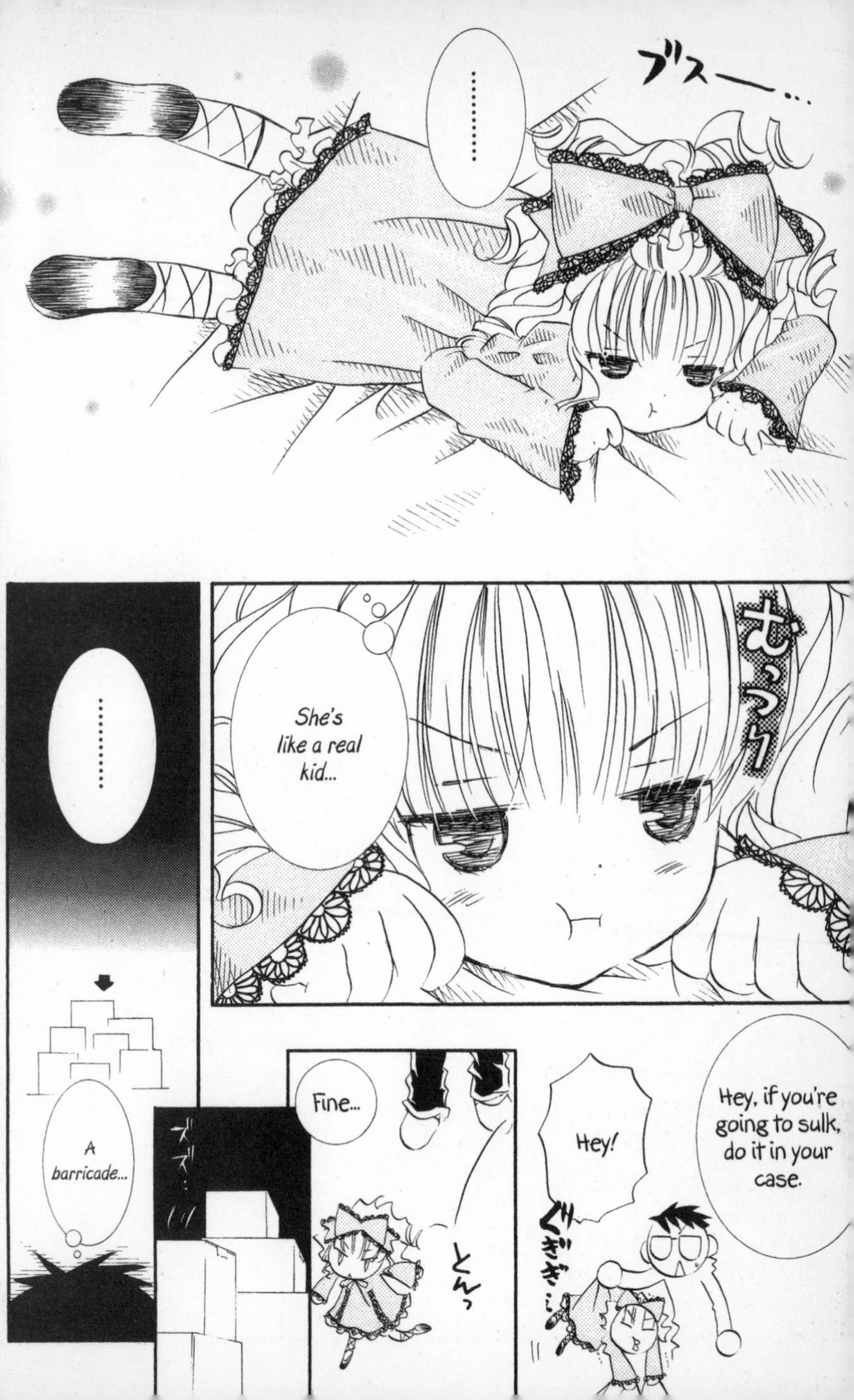
ブスー…
……
むぅっ
She's like a real kid...
Hey, if you're going to sulk, do it in your case.
Hey!
ぐぎぎ…
Fine...
とんっ
ズズ…
……
A barricade...

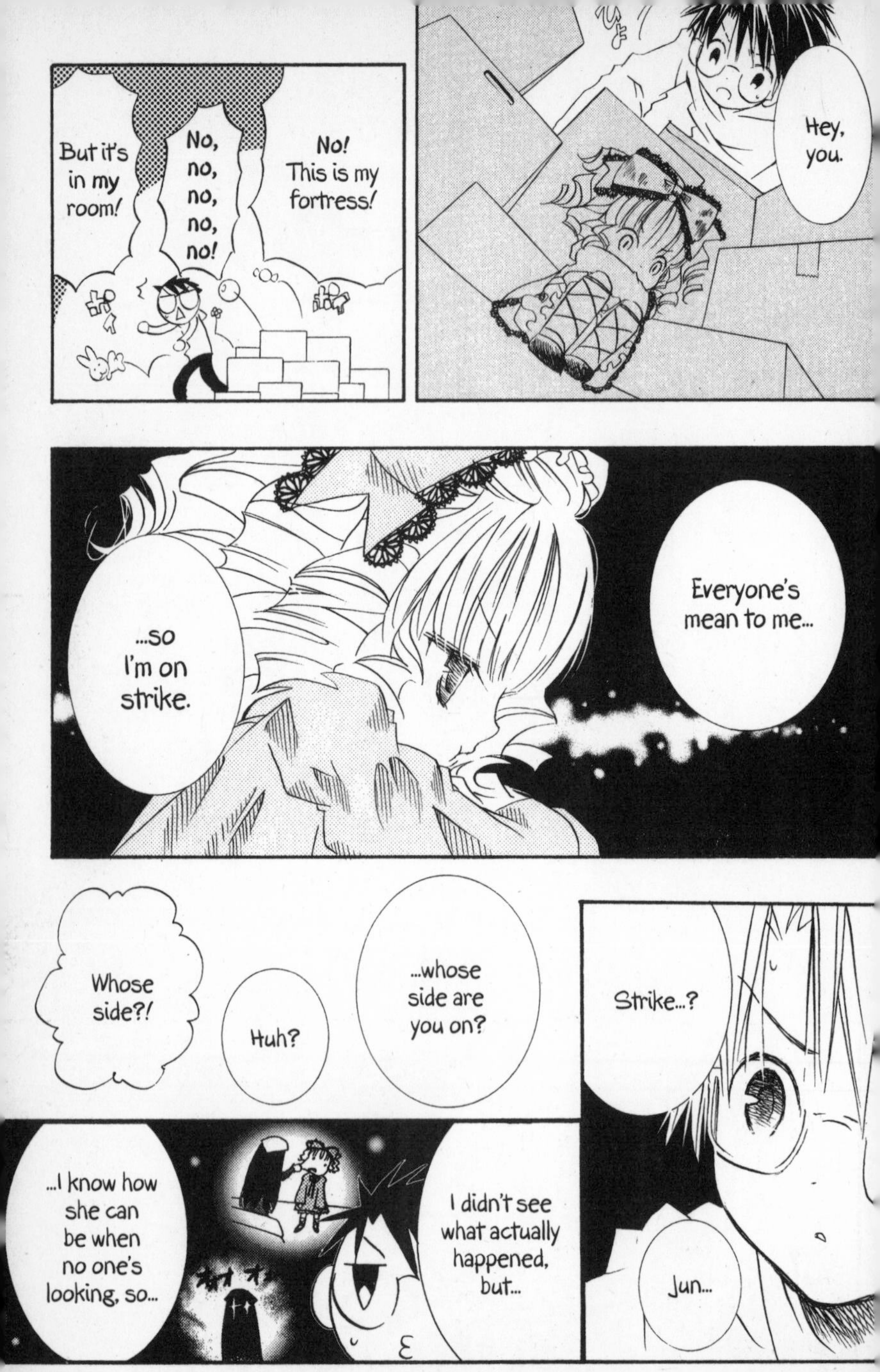
Hey, you.
No! This is my fortress!
No, no, no, no, no!
But it's in my room!
Everyone's mean to me...
...so I'm on strike.
Strike...?
Jun...
...whose side are you on?
Huh?
Whose side?!
I didn't see what actually happened, but...
...I know how she can be when no one's looking, so...

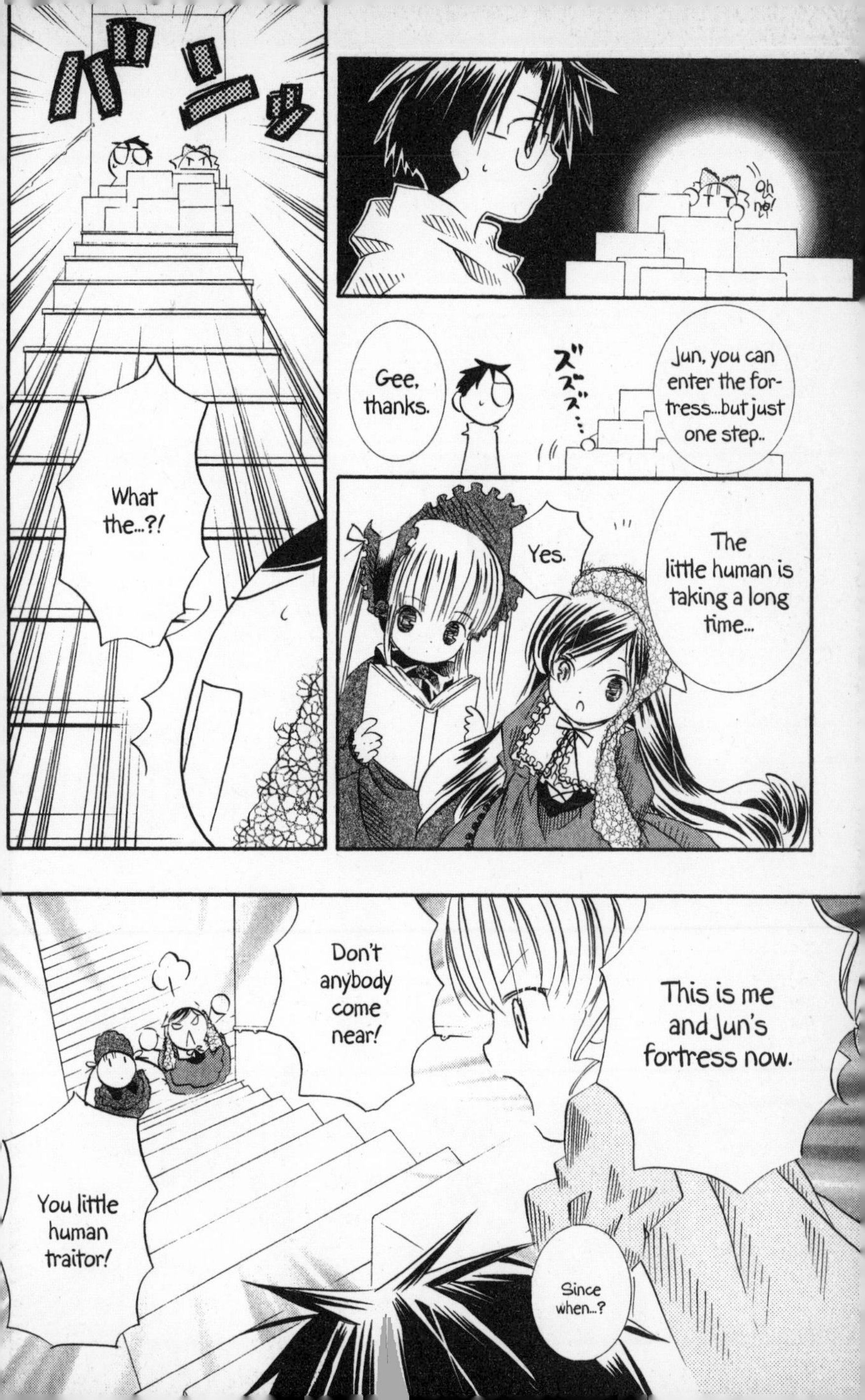

Oh no!
Jun, you can enter the fortress...but just one step..
ズズズ…
Gee, thanks.
The little human is taking a long time...
Yes.
バーンッ
What the...?!
This is me and Jun's fortress now.
Don't anybody come near!
Since when...?
You little human traitor!

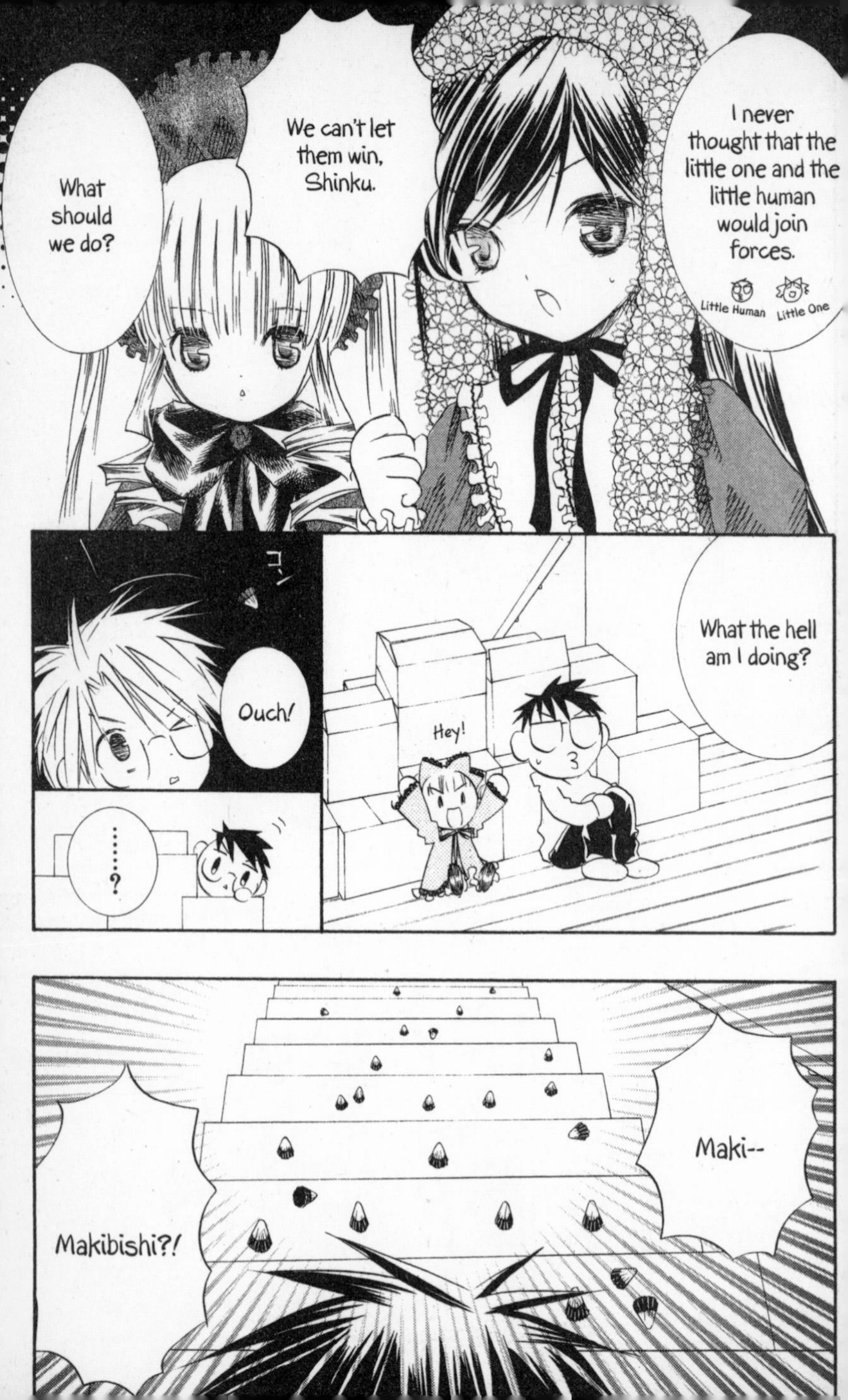
I never thought that the little one and the little human would join forces.
Little Human
Little One
We can't let them win, Shinku.
What should we do?
What the hell am I doing?
Hey!
Ouch!
......?
Maki--
Makibishi?!

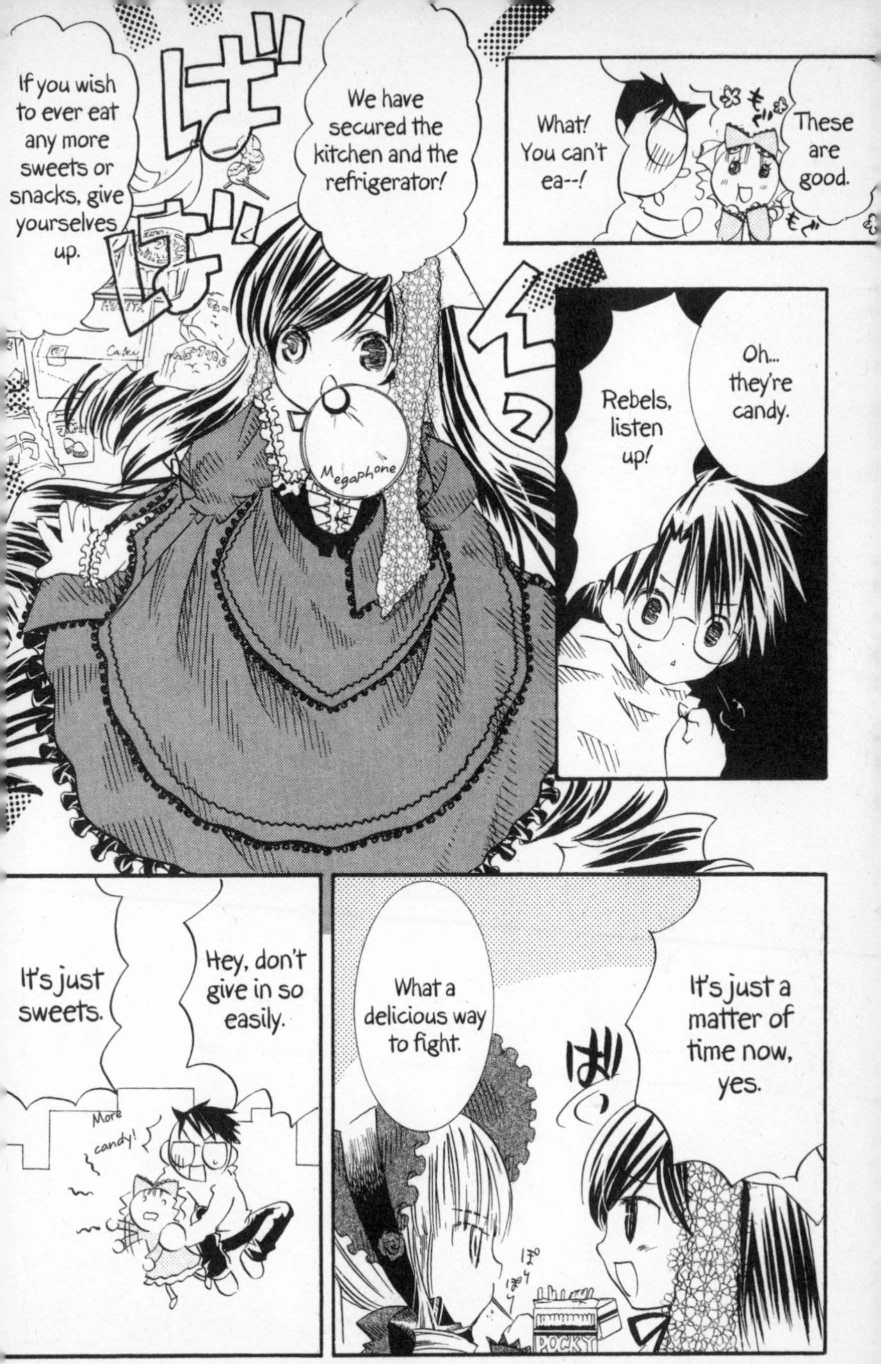
These are good.
What! You can't ea--!
Oh... they're candy.
Rebels, listen up!
We have secured the kitchen and the refrigerator!
If you wish to ever eat any more sweets or snacks, give yourselves up.
Megaphone
It's just a matter of time now, yes.
What a delicious way to fight.
POCKY
Hey, don't give in so easily.
It's just sweets.
More candy!

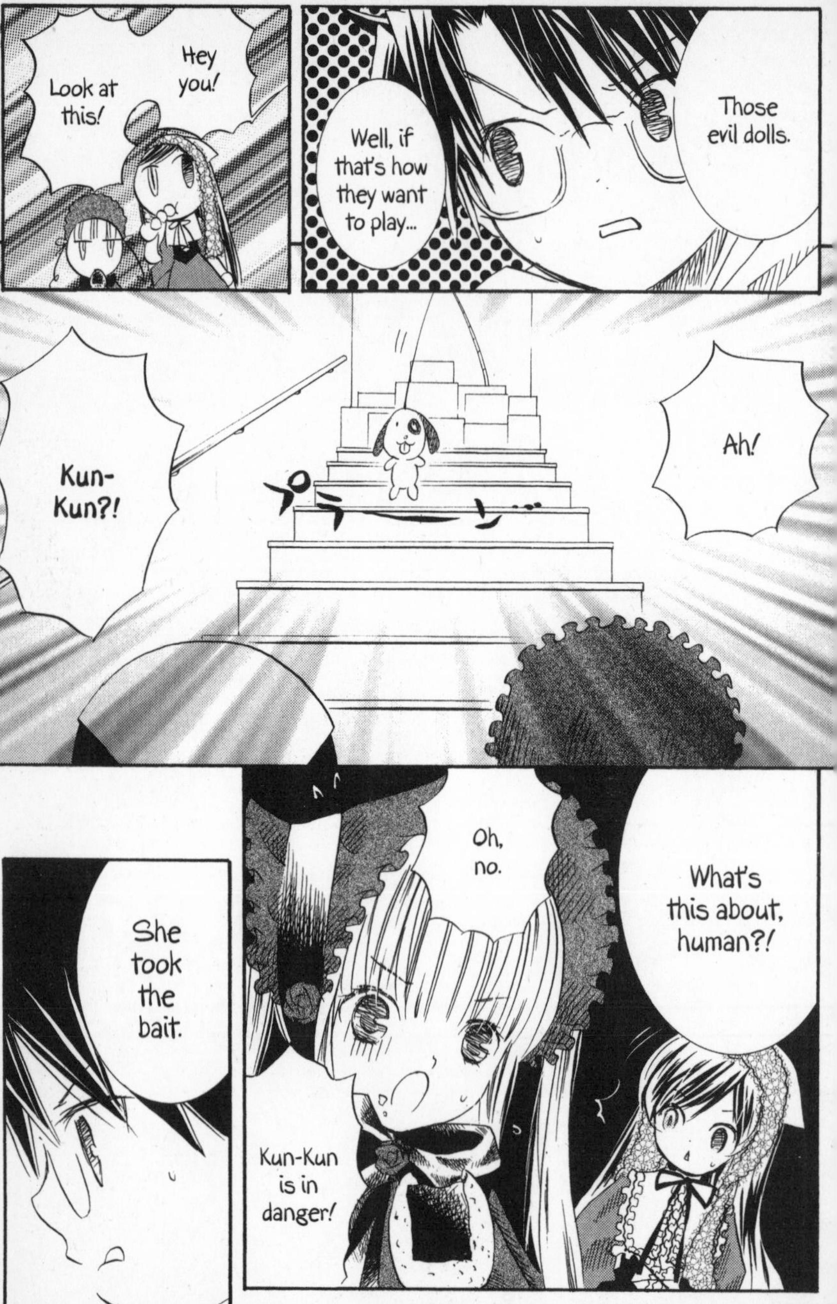
Those evil dolls.
Well, if that's how they want to play...
Hey you!
Look at this!
Ah!
Kun-Kun?!
What's this about, human?!
Oh, no.
Kun-Kun is in danger!
She took the bait.

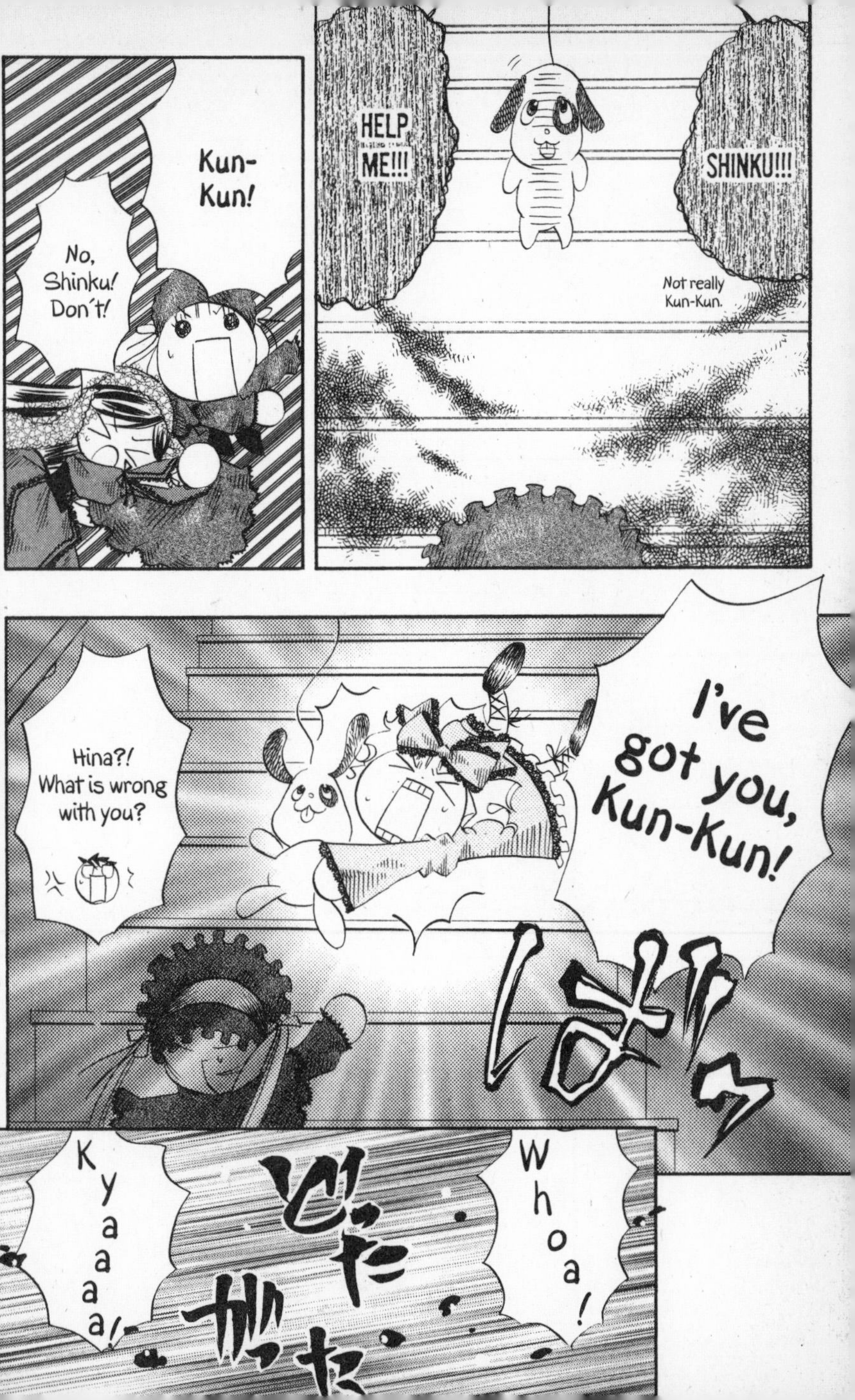
SHINKU!!!
HELP ME!!!
Not really Kun-Kun.
Kun-Kun!
No, Shinku! Don´t!
I've got you, Kun-kun!
Hina?! What is wrong with you?
Whoa!
Kyaaaaa!

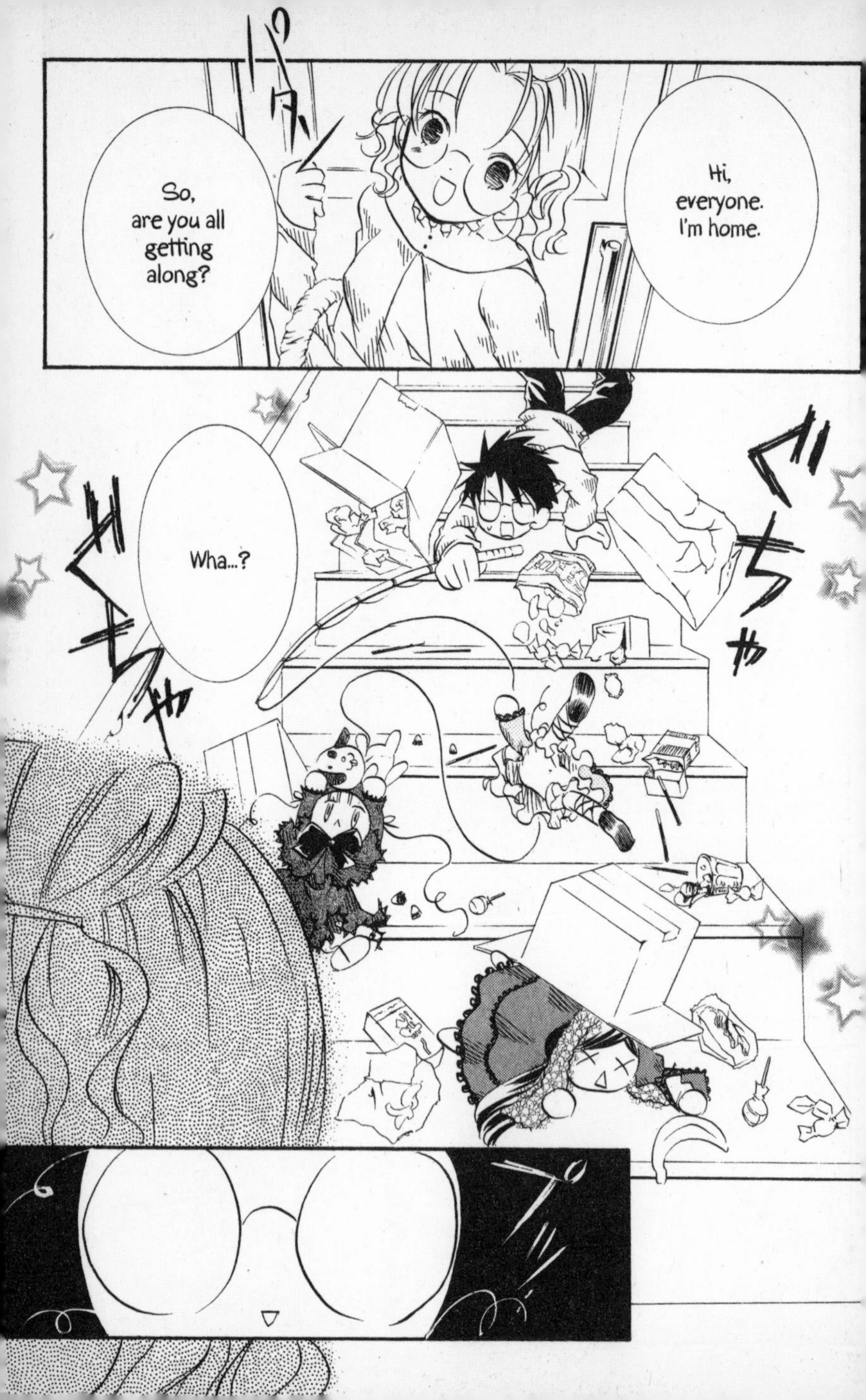
Hi, everyone. I'm home.
So, are you all getting along?
Wha...?

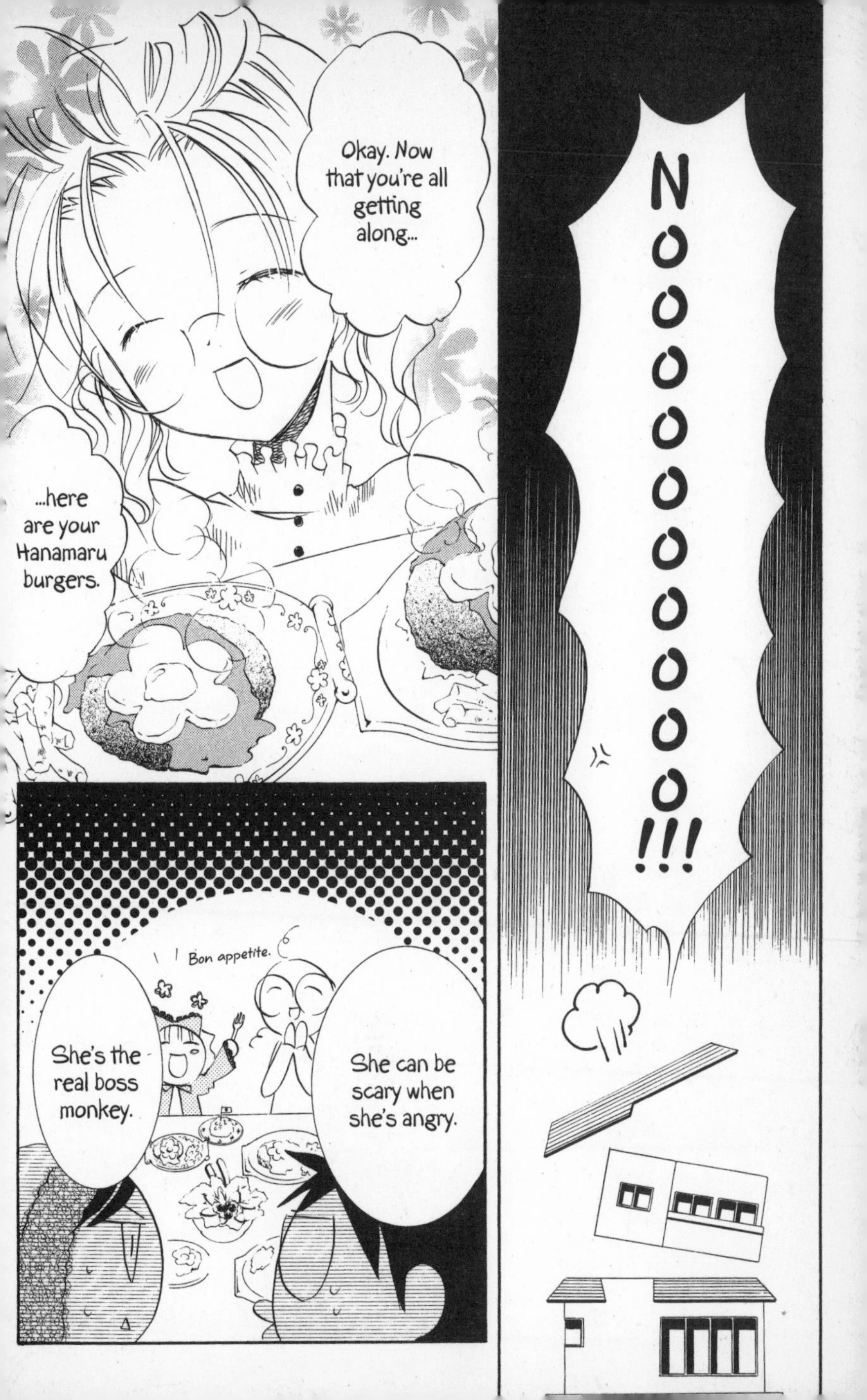
NOOOOOOOOOOO!!!
Okay. Now that you're all getting along...
...here are your Hanamaru burgers.
Bon appetite.
She can be scary when she's angry.
She's the real boss monkey.

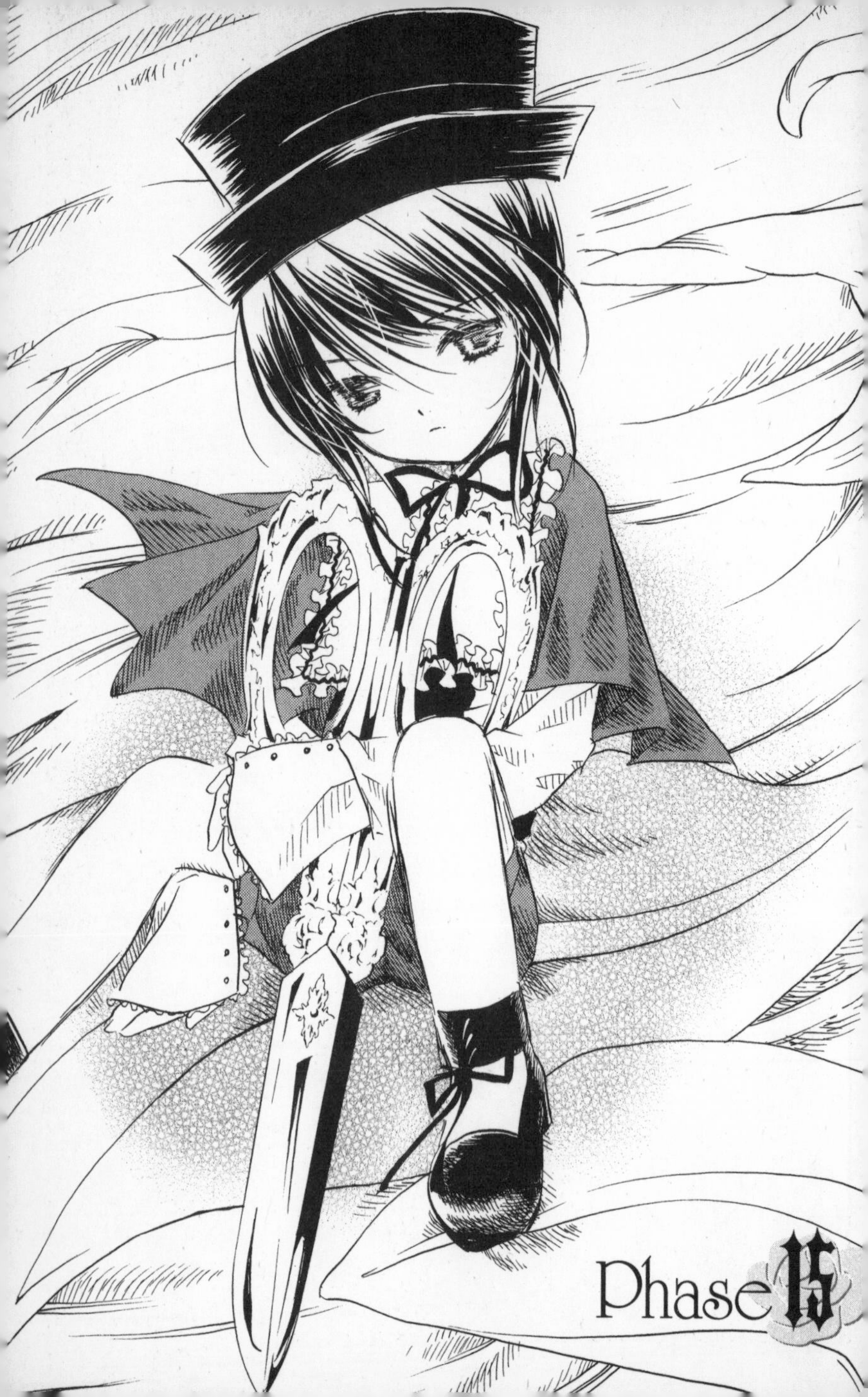
Phase 15

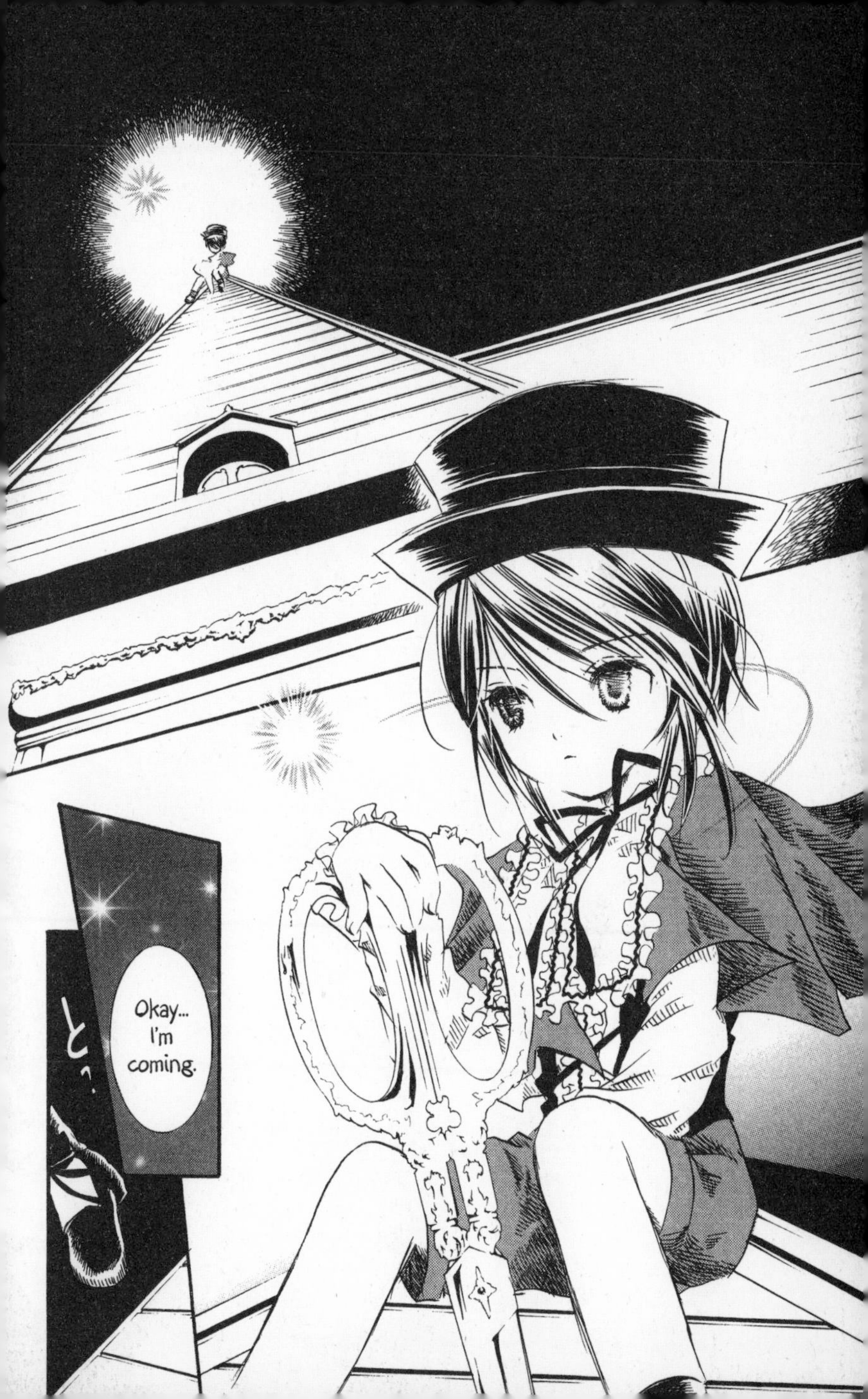
Okay... I'm coming.

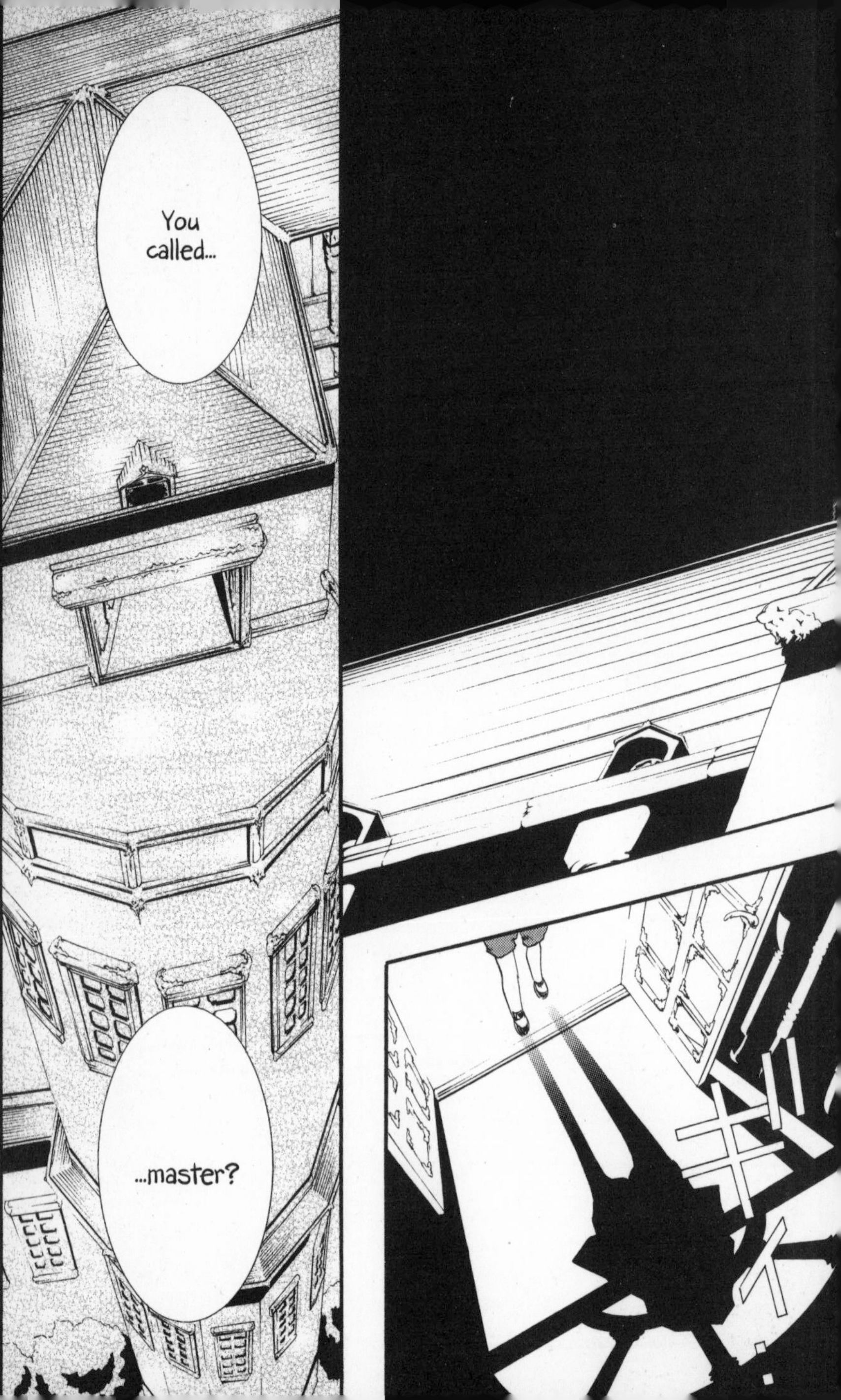

ギィ…
You called...
...master?

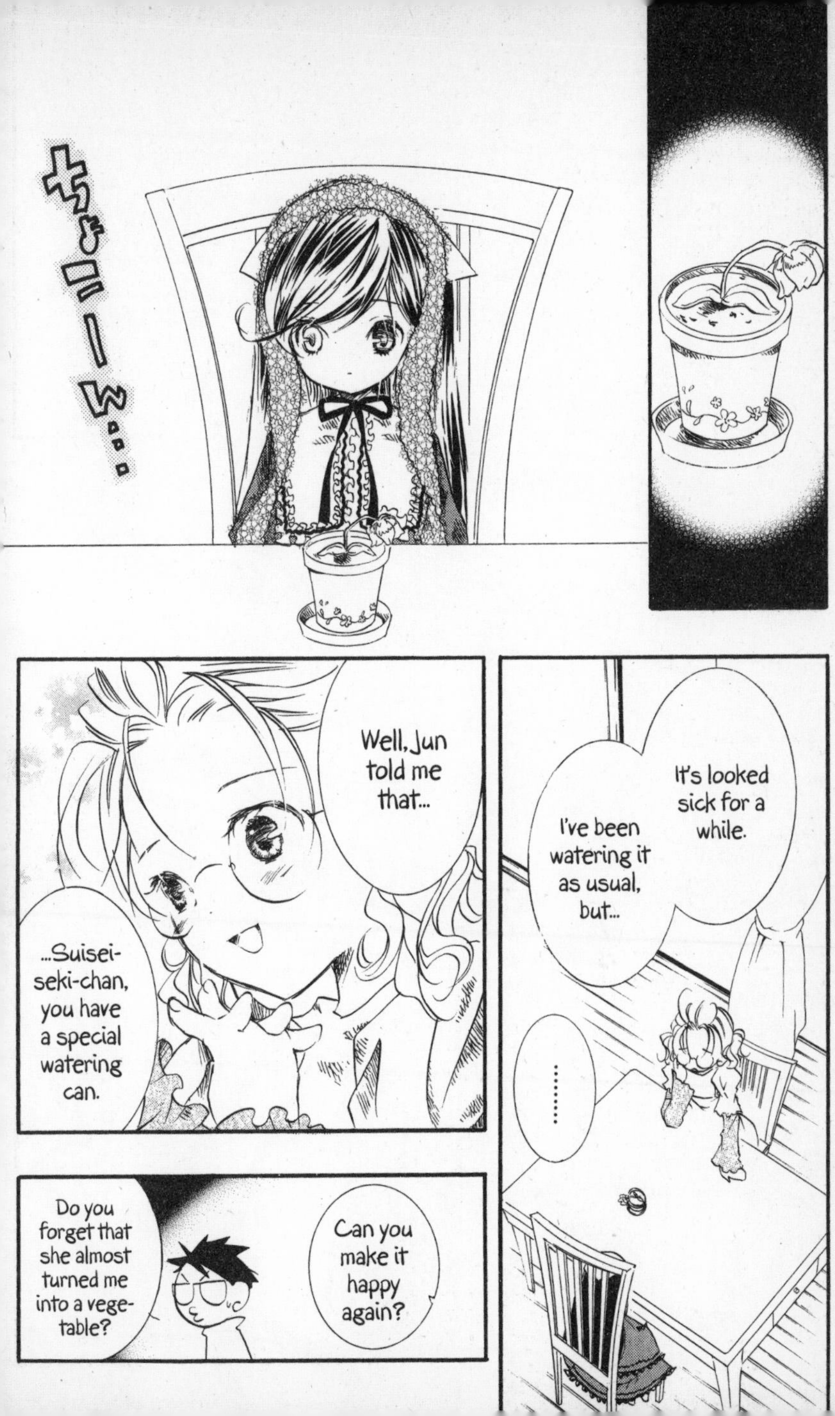
ちょこーん…
It's looked sick for a while.
I've been watering it as usual, but...
......
Well, Jun told me that...
...Suisei-seki-chan, you have a special watering can.
Can you make it happy again?
Do you forget that she almost turned me into a vege-table?

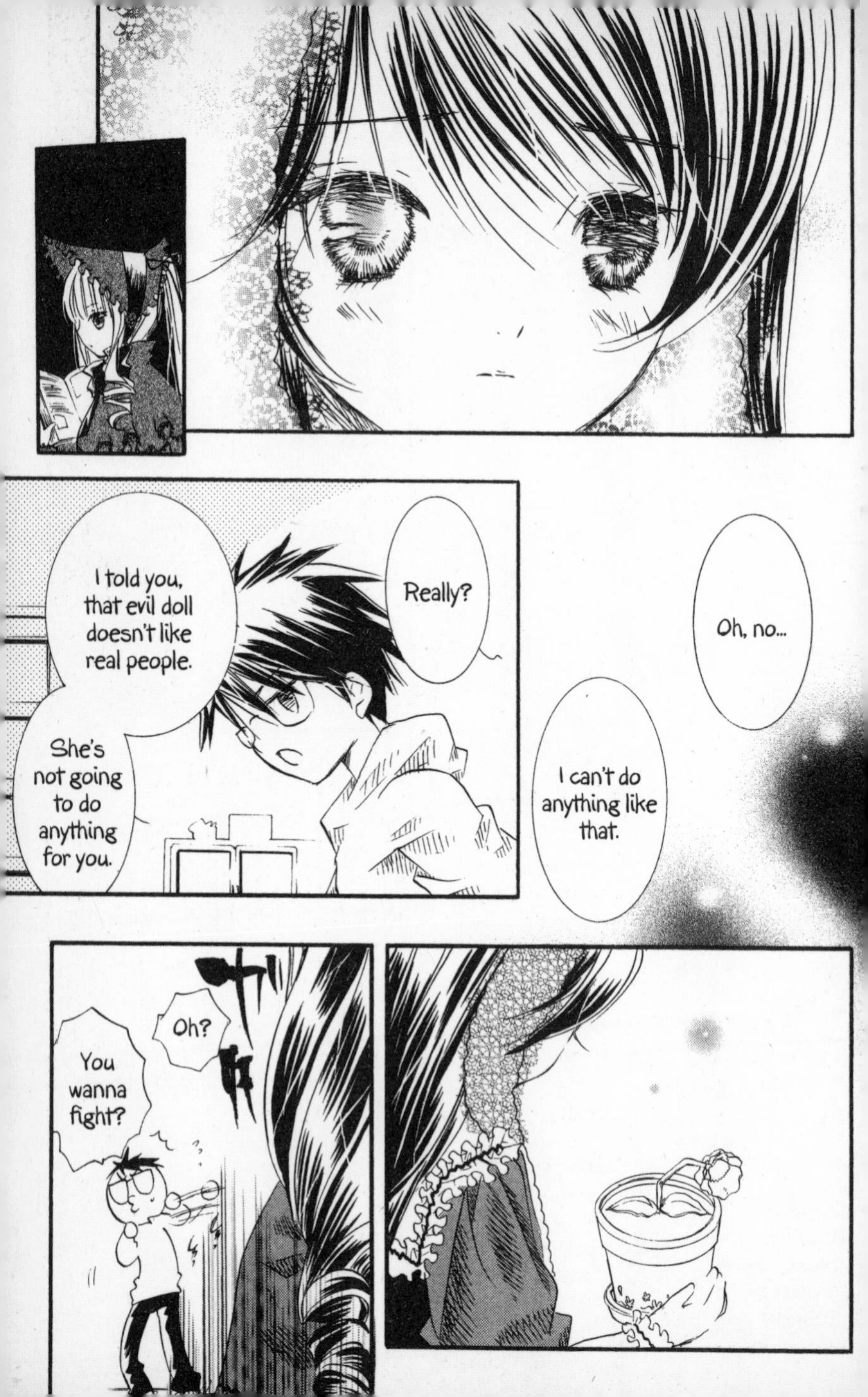
Oh, no...
I can't do anything like that.
Really?
I told you, that evil doll doesn't like real people.
She's not going to do anything for you.
Oh?
You wanna fight?

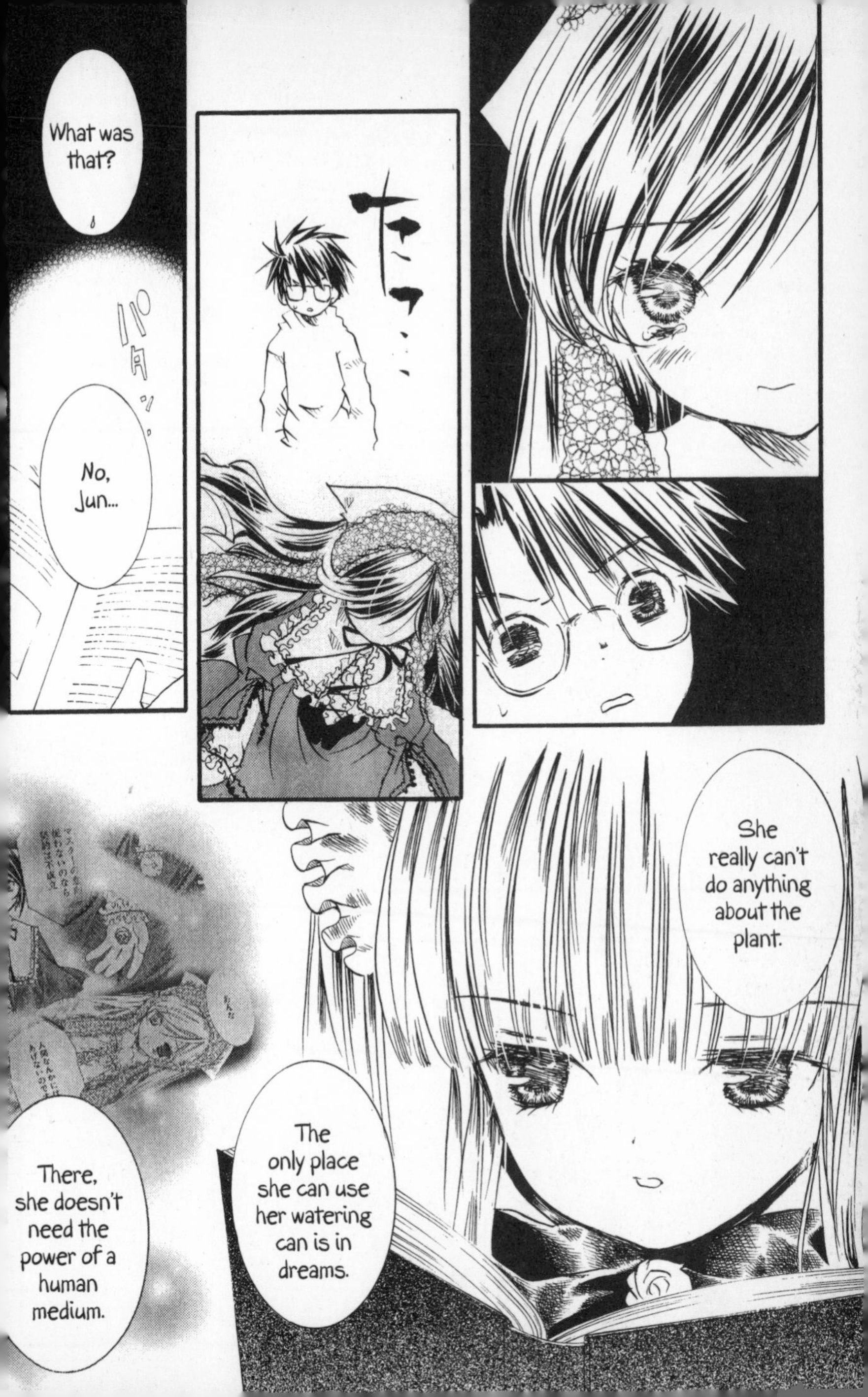
What was that?
No, Jun...
She really can't do anything about the plant.
The only place she can use her watering can is in dreams.
There, she doesn't need the power of a human medium.

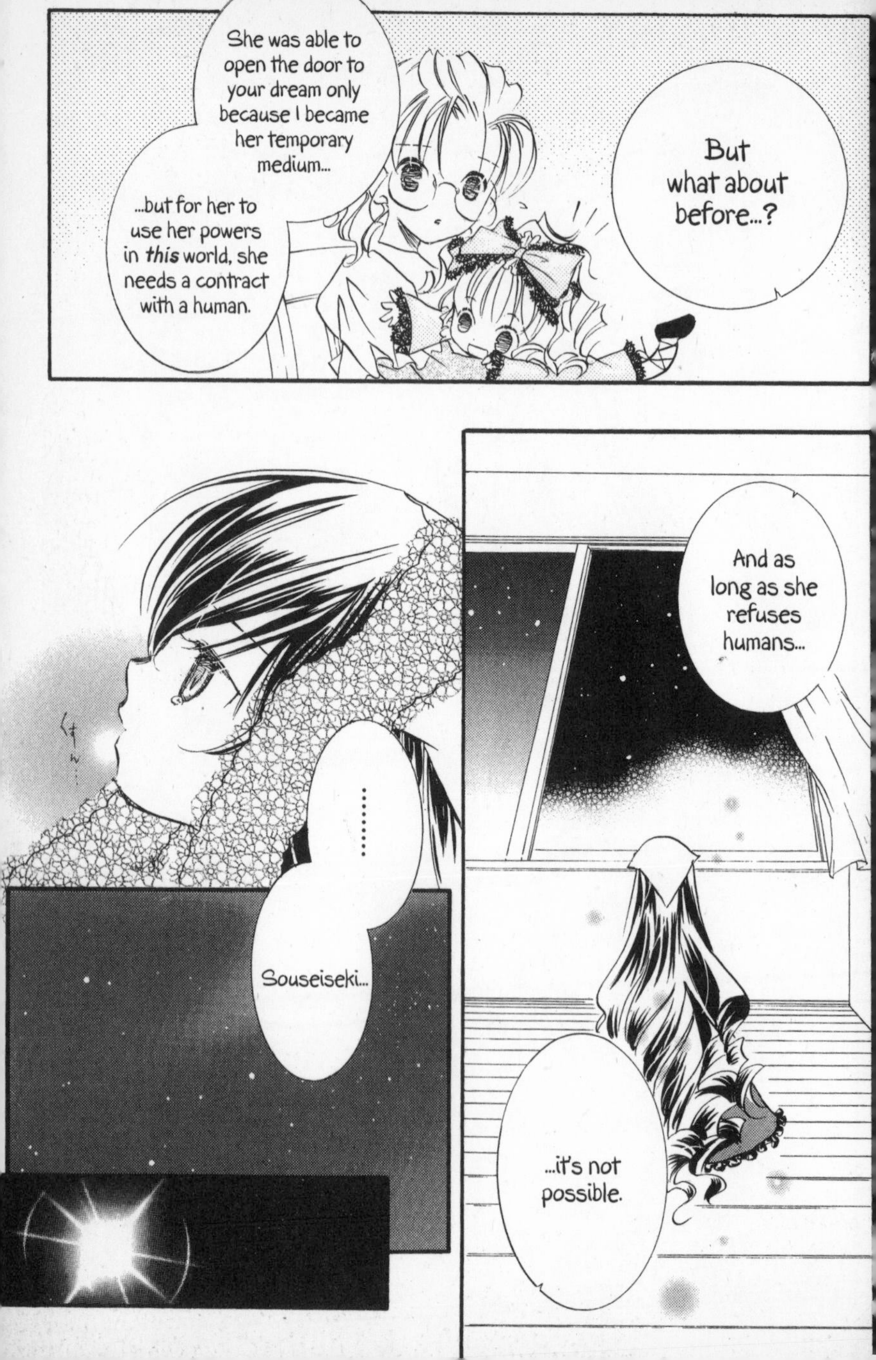

She was able to open the door to your dream only because I became her temporary medium...
...but for her to use her powers in *this* world, she needs a contract with a human.
But what about before...?
And as long as she refuses humans...
...it's not possible.
......
Souseiseki...

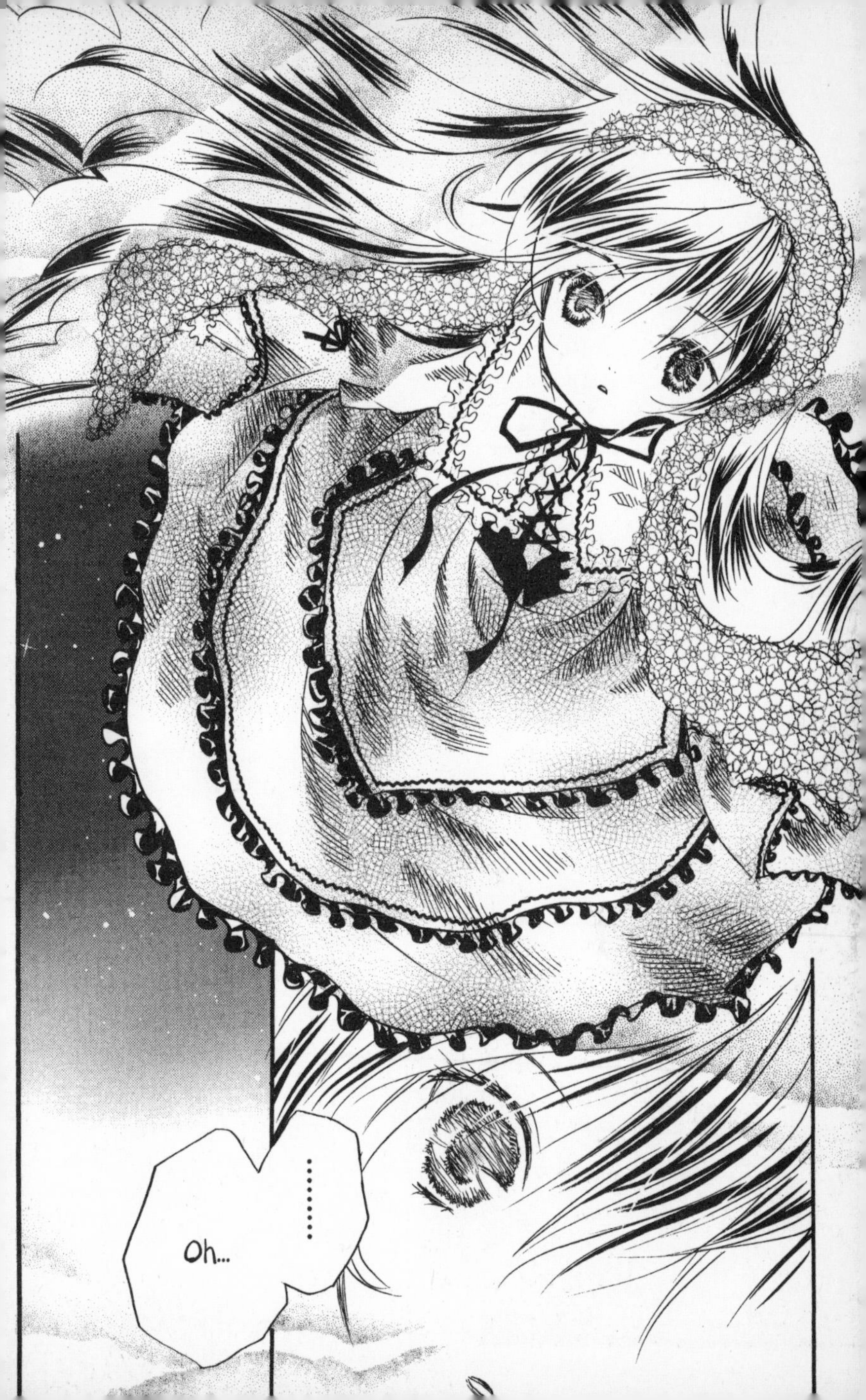

......
Oh...

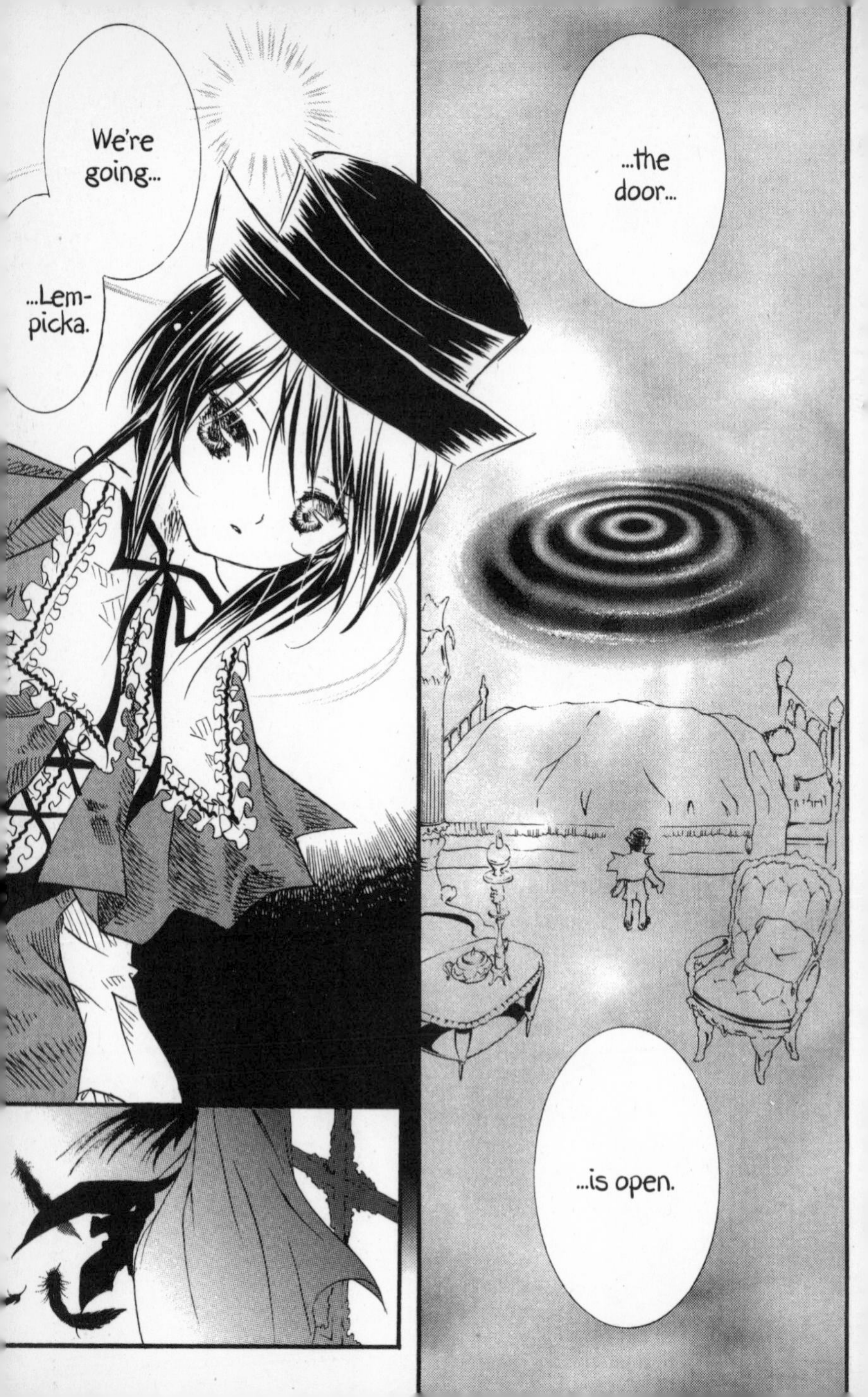
...the door...
...is open.
We're going...
...Lem-picka.

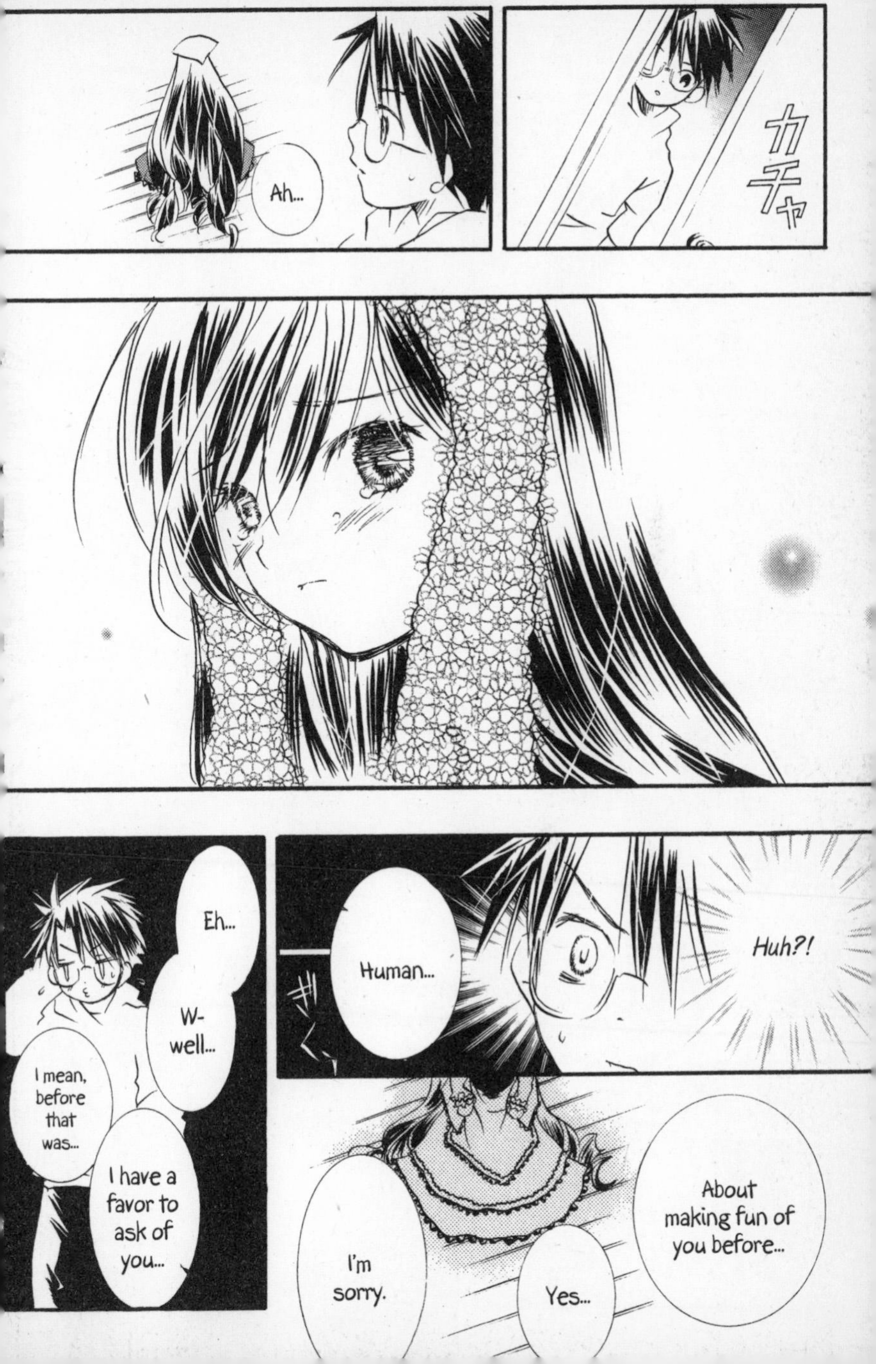
カチャ
Ah...
Human...
Huh?!
About making fun of you before...
Yes...
I'm sorry.
Eh...
W-well...
I mean, before that was...
I have a favor to ask of you...

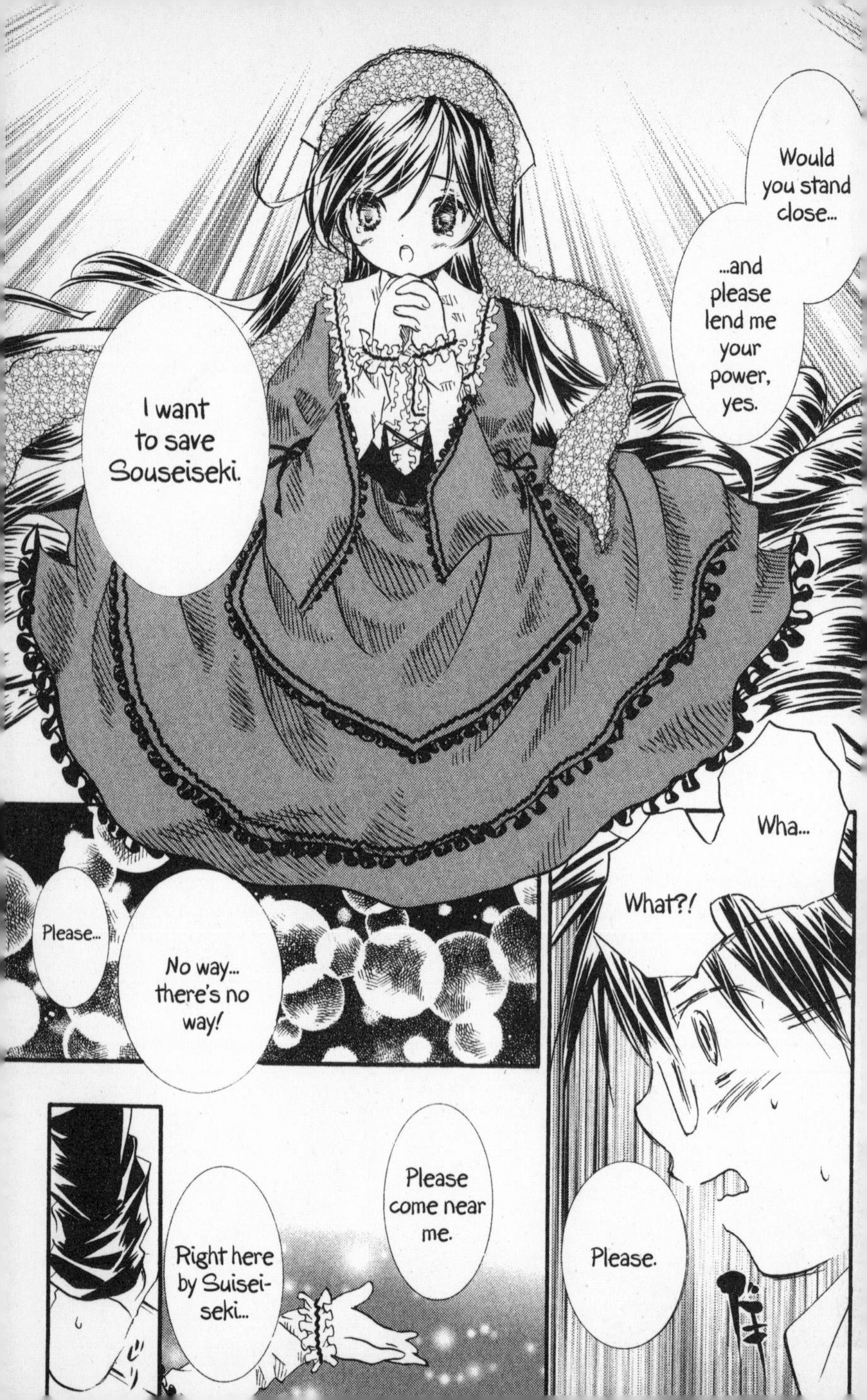

Would you stand close...
...and please lend me your power, yes.
I want to save Souseiseki.
Wha...
What?!
Please.
No way... there's no way!
Please...
Please come near me.
Right here by Suisei-seki...

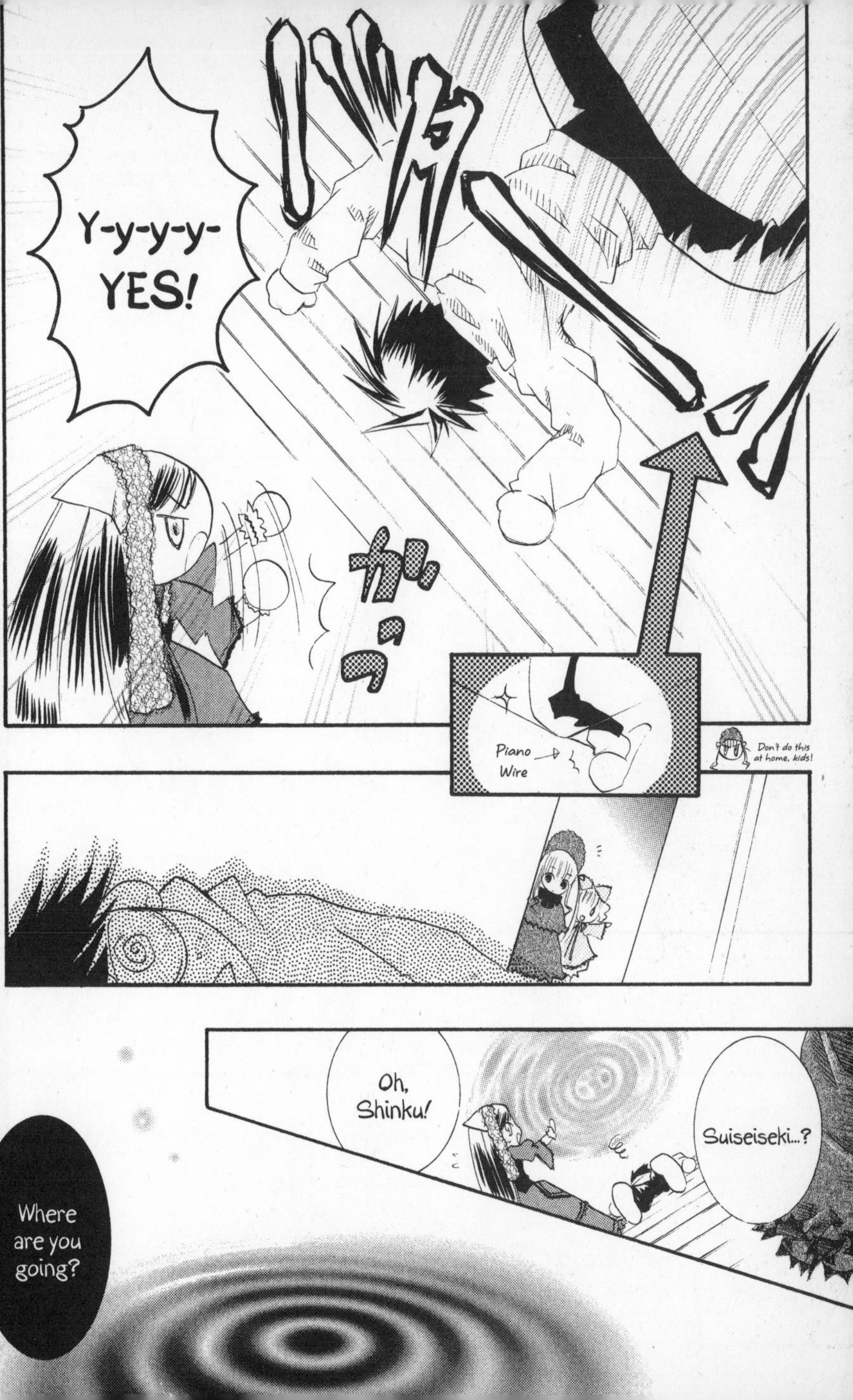
Y-y-y-y-YES!
がっっ
Piano Wire
Don't do this at home, kids!
Suiseiseki...?
Oh, Shinku!
Where are you going?

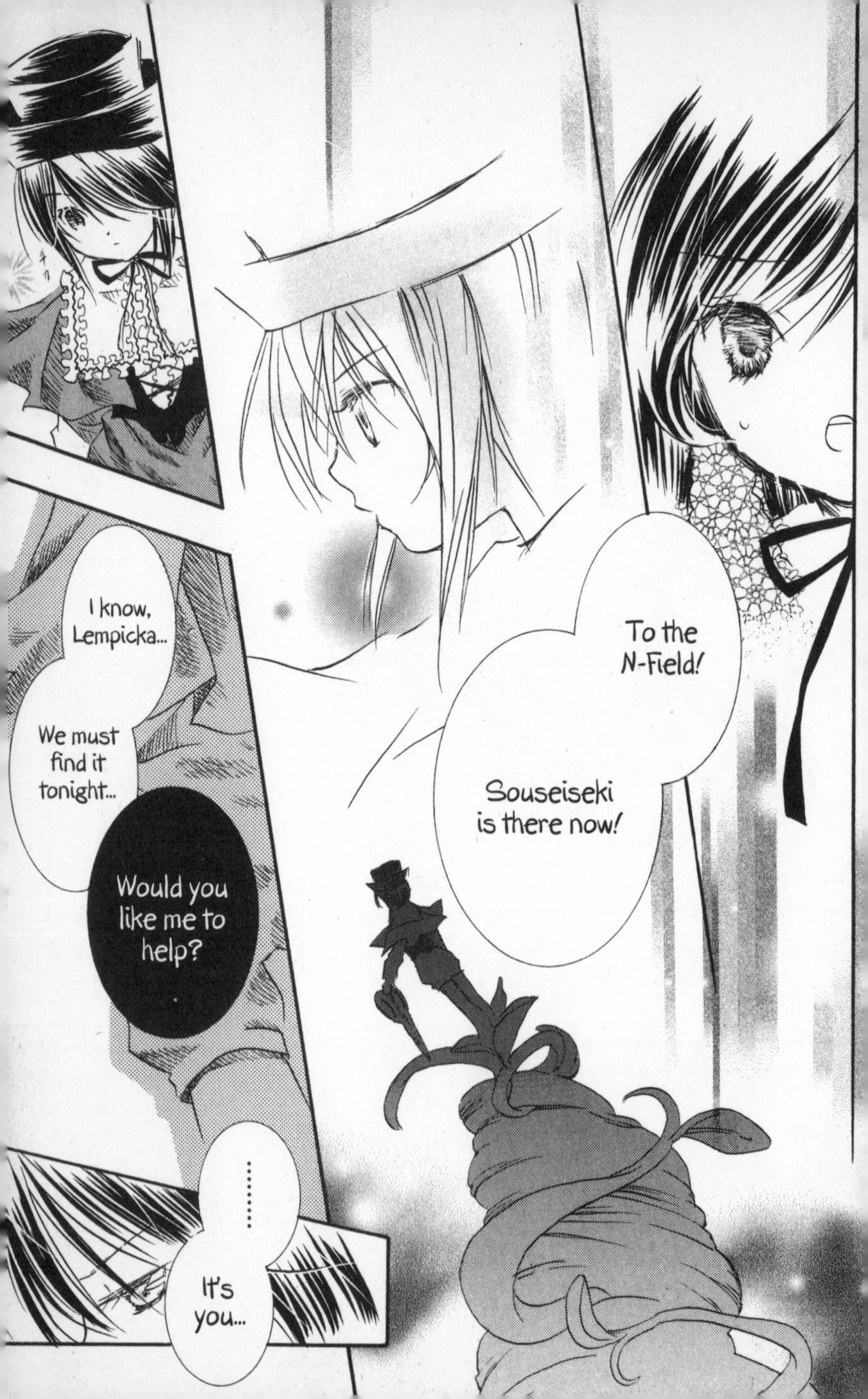
To the N-Field!
Souseiseki is there now!
I know, Lempicka...
We must find it tonight...
Would you like me to help?
......
It's you...

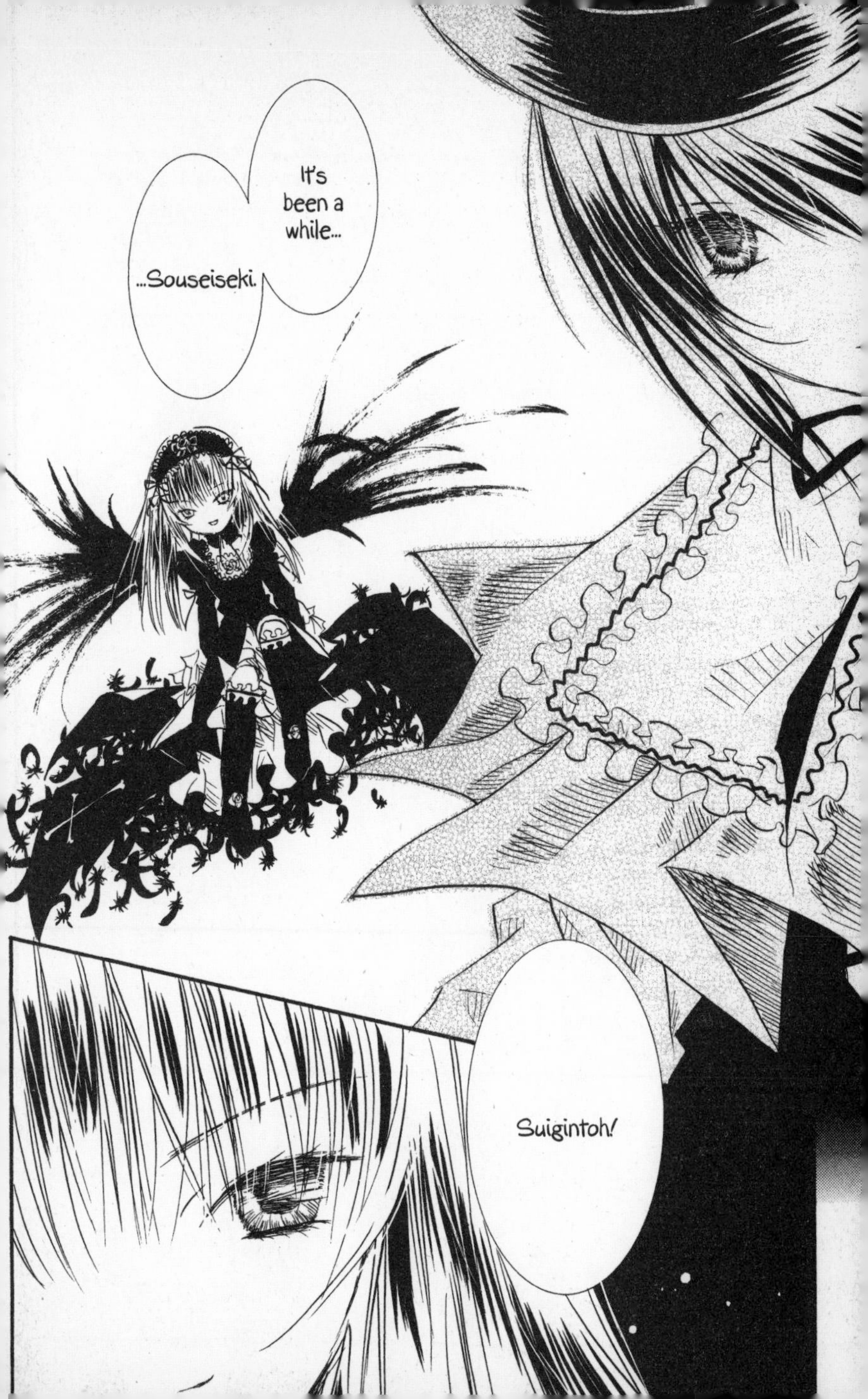
It's been a while...
...Souseiseki.
Suigintoh!

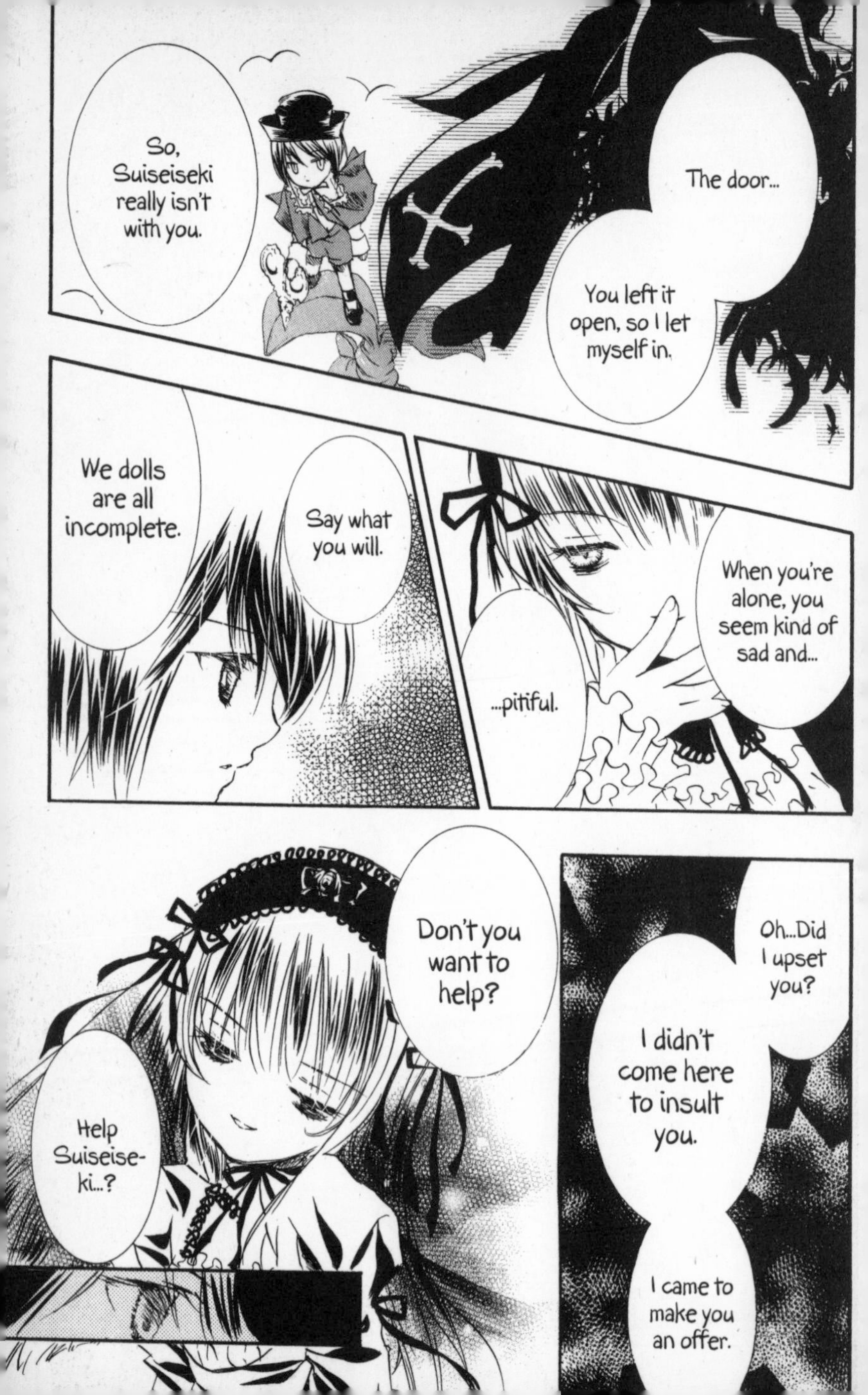
The door...
You left it open, so I let myself in.
So, Suiseiseki really isn't with you.
When you're alone, you seem kind of sad and...
...pitiful.
Say what you will.
We dolls are all incomplete.
Oh...Did I upset you?
I didn't come here to insult you.
I came to make you an offer.
Don't you want to help?
Help Suiseiseki...?

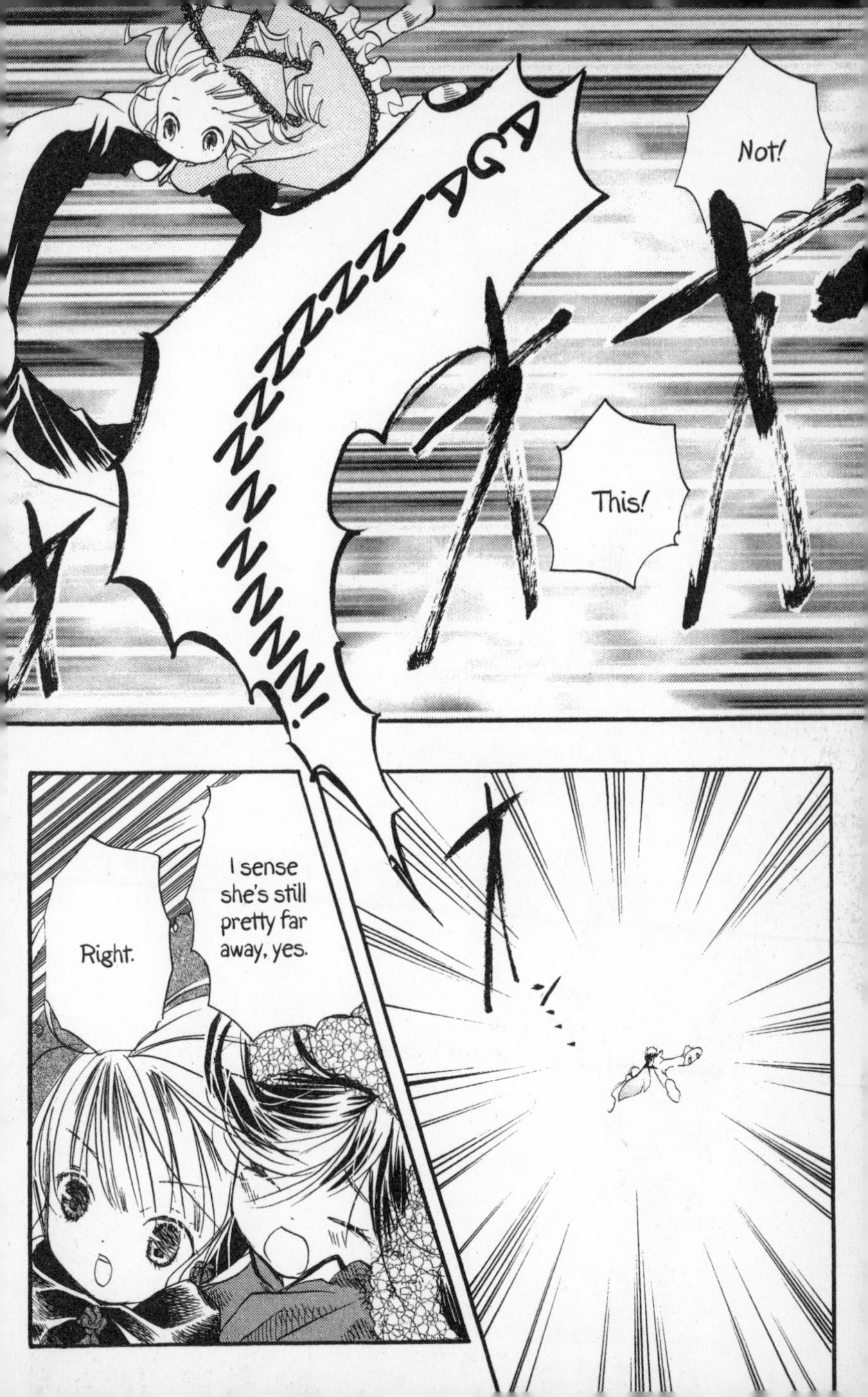

Not!
This!
DGA-ZZZZZZNNNNNNN!
I sense she's still pretty far away, yes.
Right.

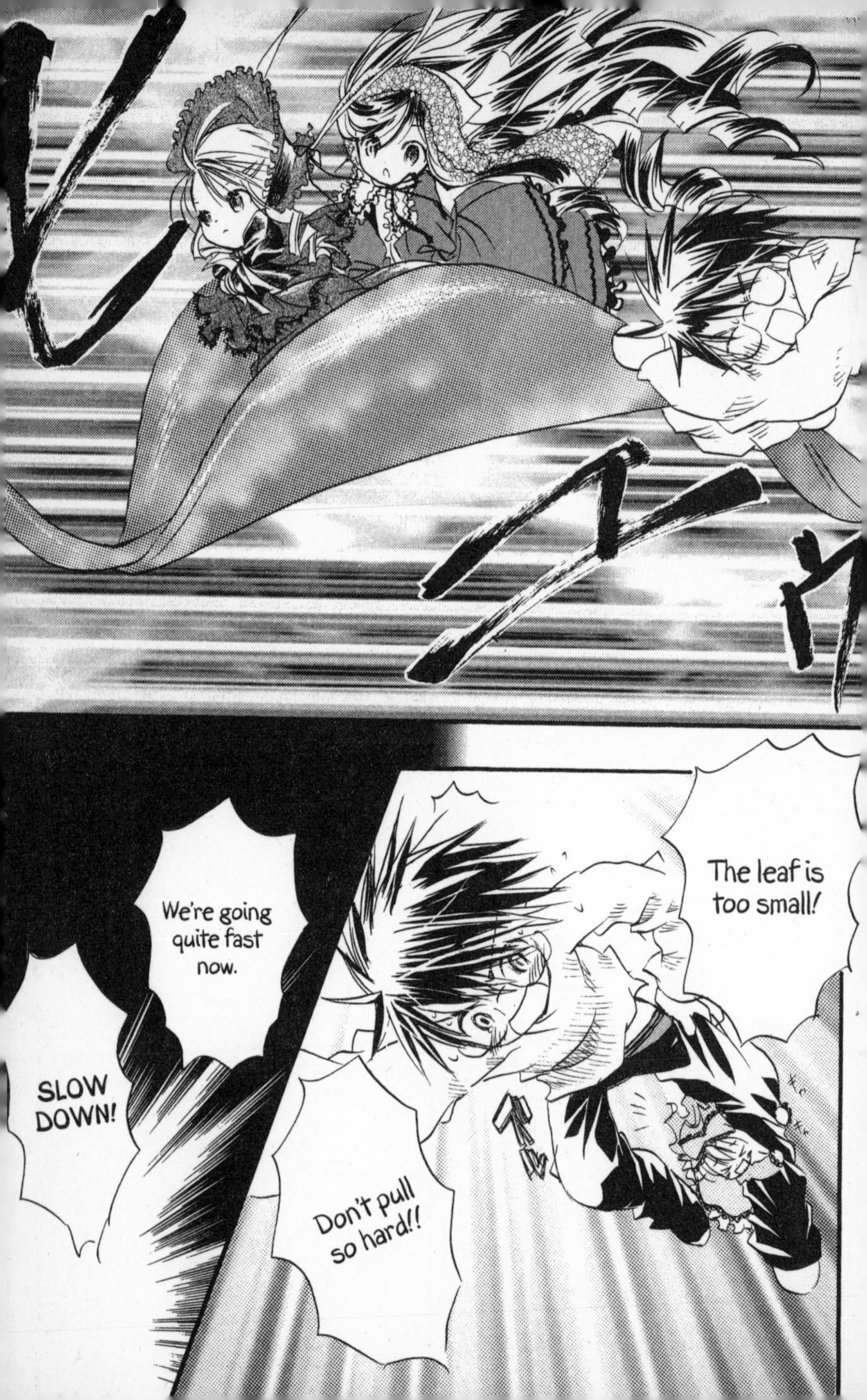
The leaf is too small!
Don't pull so hard!!
We're going quite fast now.
SLOW DOWN!

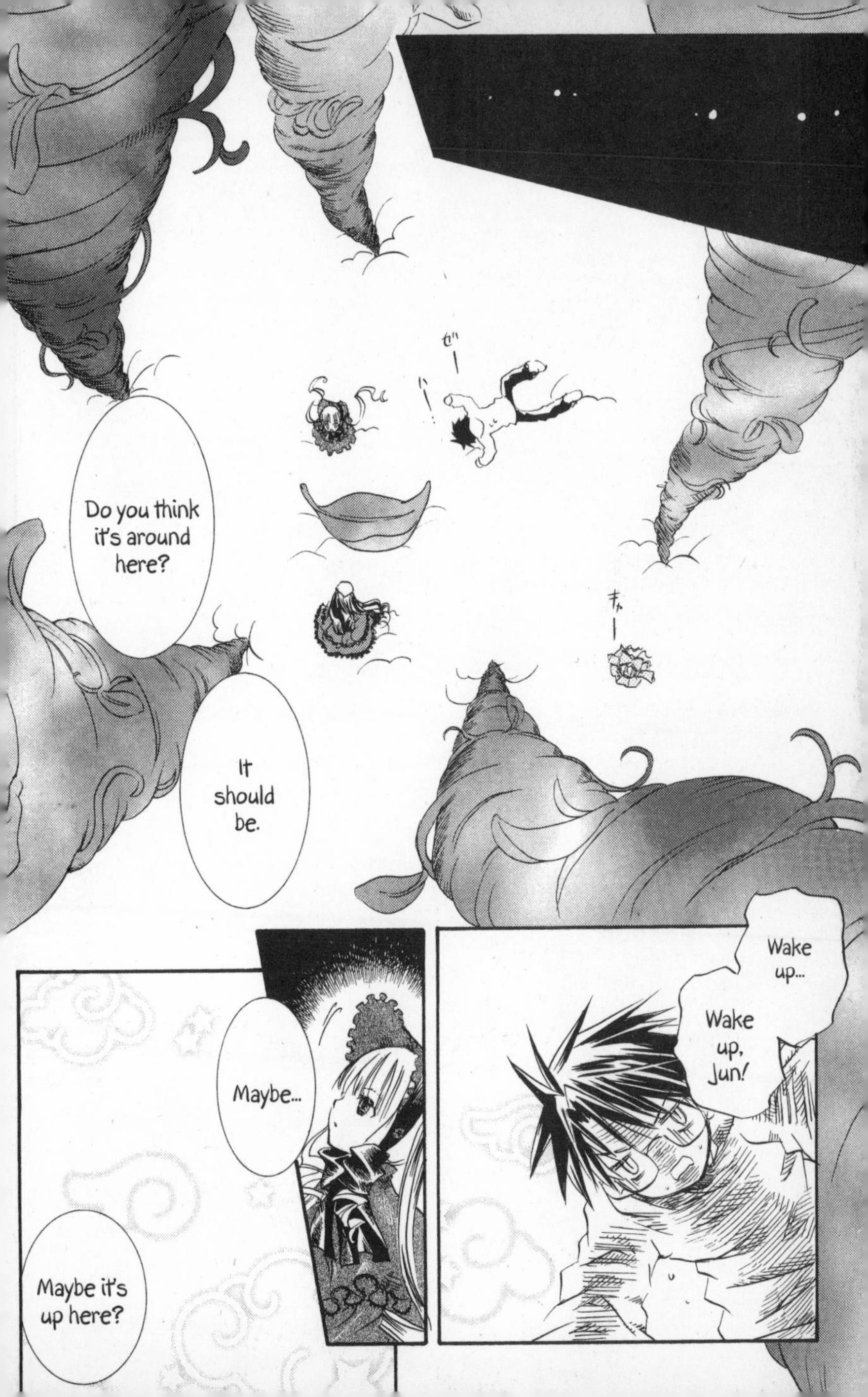
Do you think it's around here?
It should be.
Wake up...
Wake up, Jun!
Maybe...
Maybe it's up here?

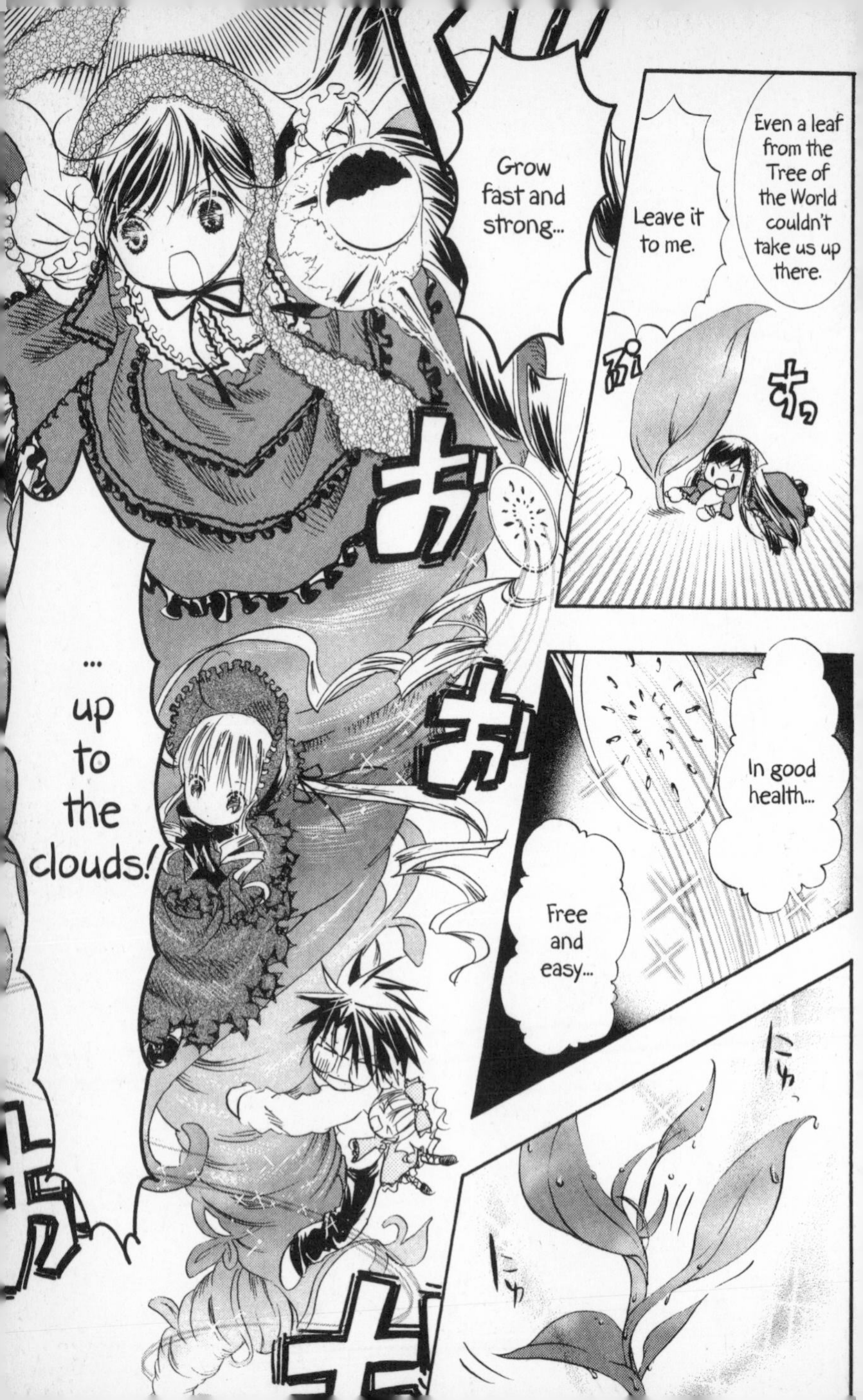
Even a leaf from the Tree of the World couldn't take us up there.
Leave it to me.
In good health...
Free and easy...
Grow fast and strong...
... up to the clouds!

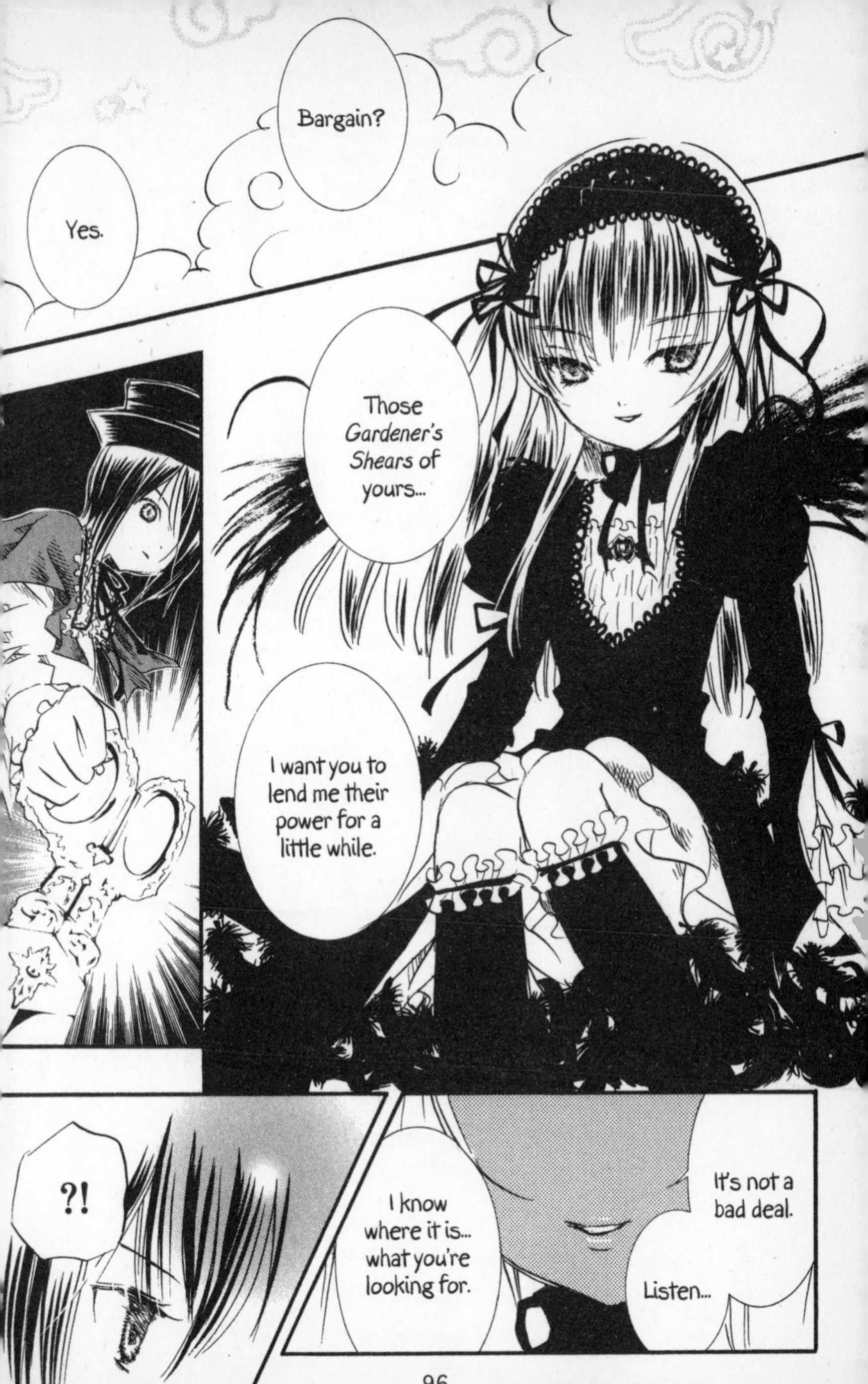
Bargain?
Yes.
Those Gardener's Shears of yours...
I want you to lend me their power for a little while.
It's not a bad deal.
Listen...
I know where it is... what you're looking for.
?!

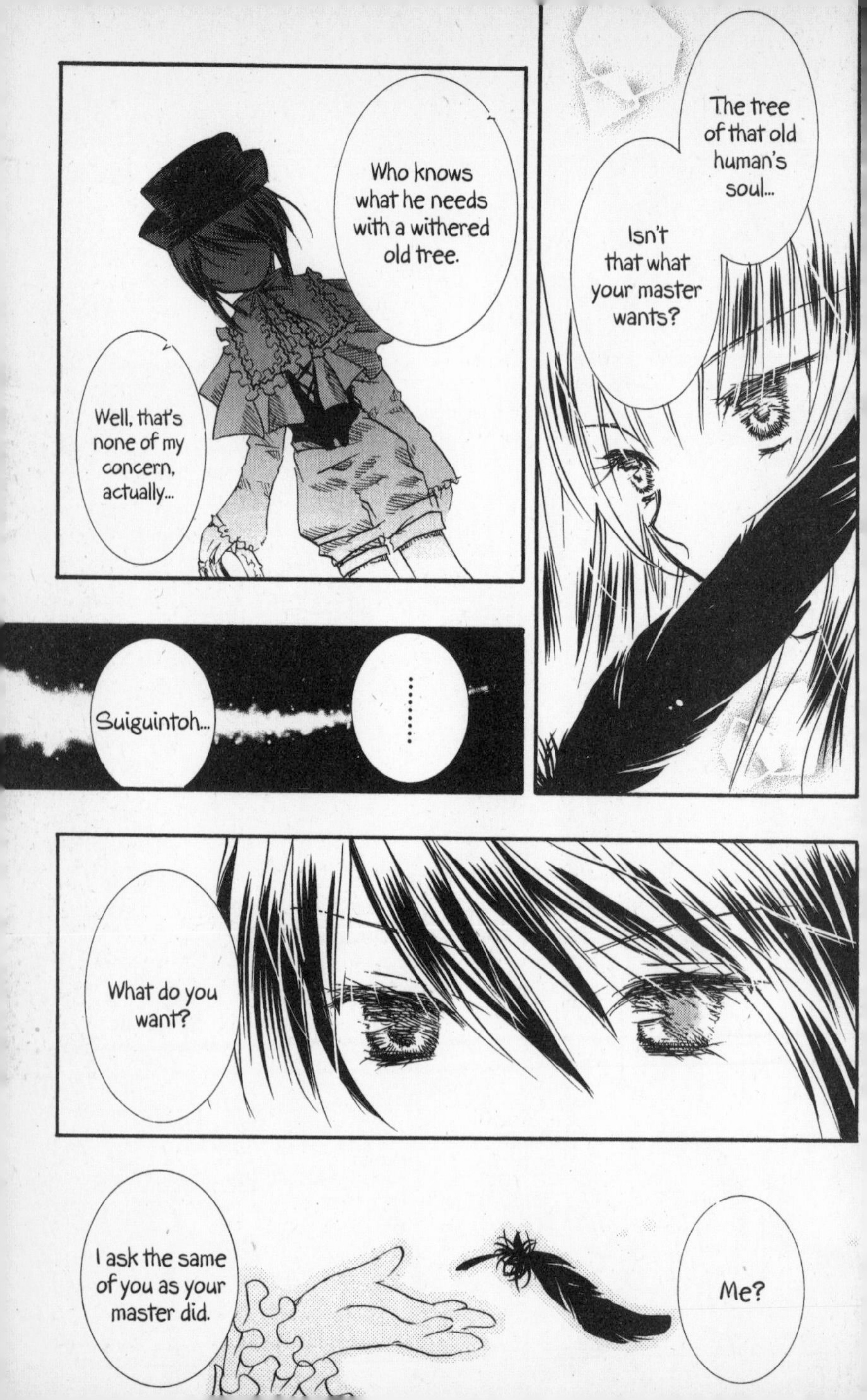
The tree of that old human's soul...
Isn't that what your master wants?
Who knows what he needs with a withered old tree.
Well, that's none of my concern, actually...
....
Suiguintoh...
What do you want?
Me?
I ask the same of you as your master did.

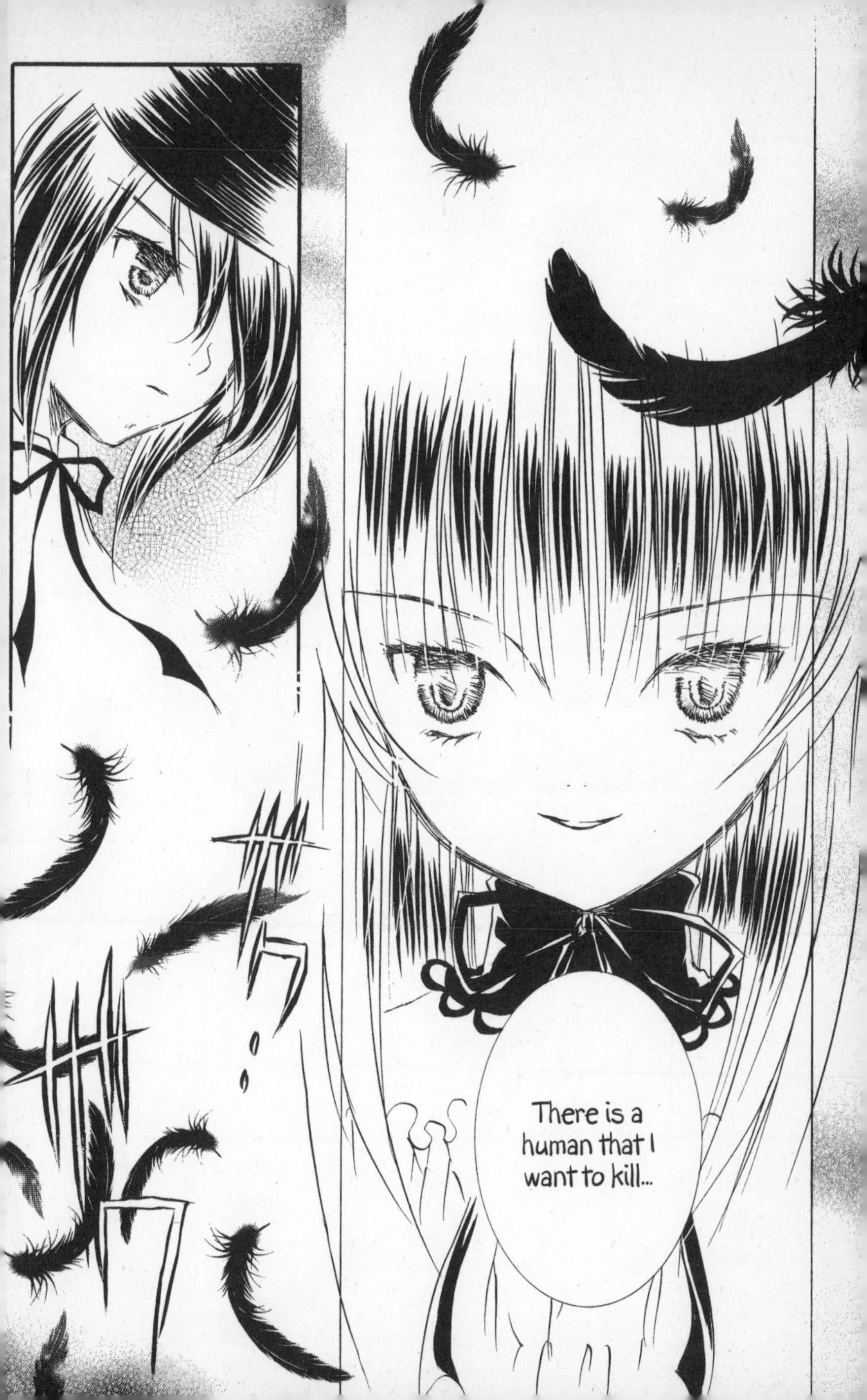
There is a human that I want to kill...

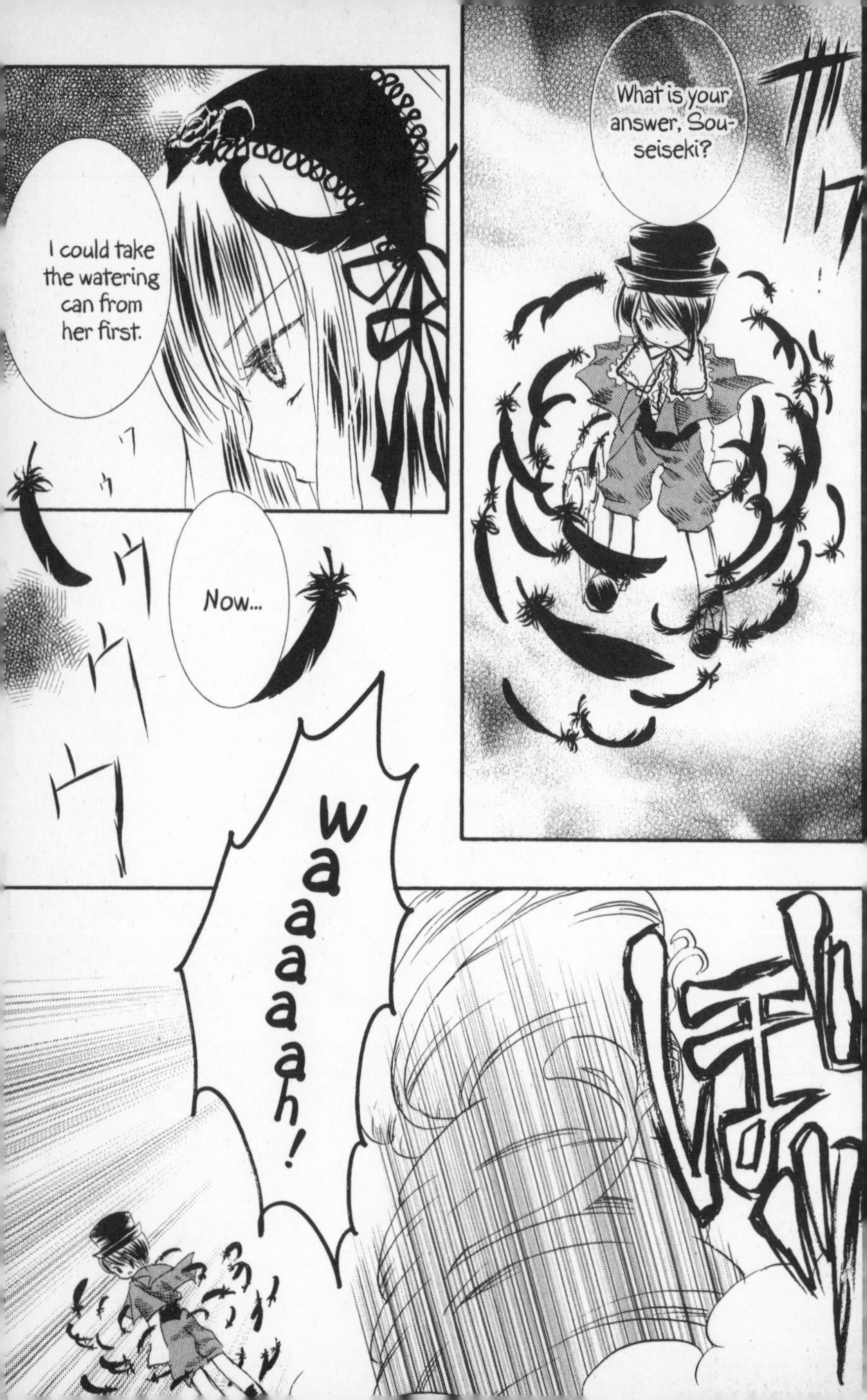
What is your answer, Sou-seiseki?
I could take the watering can from her first.
Now...
Waaaaaah!

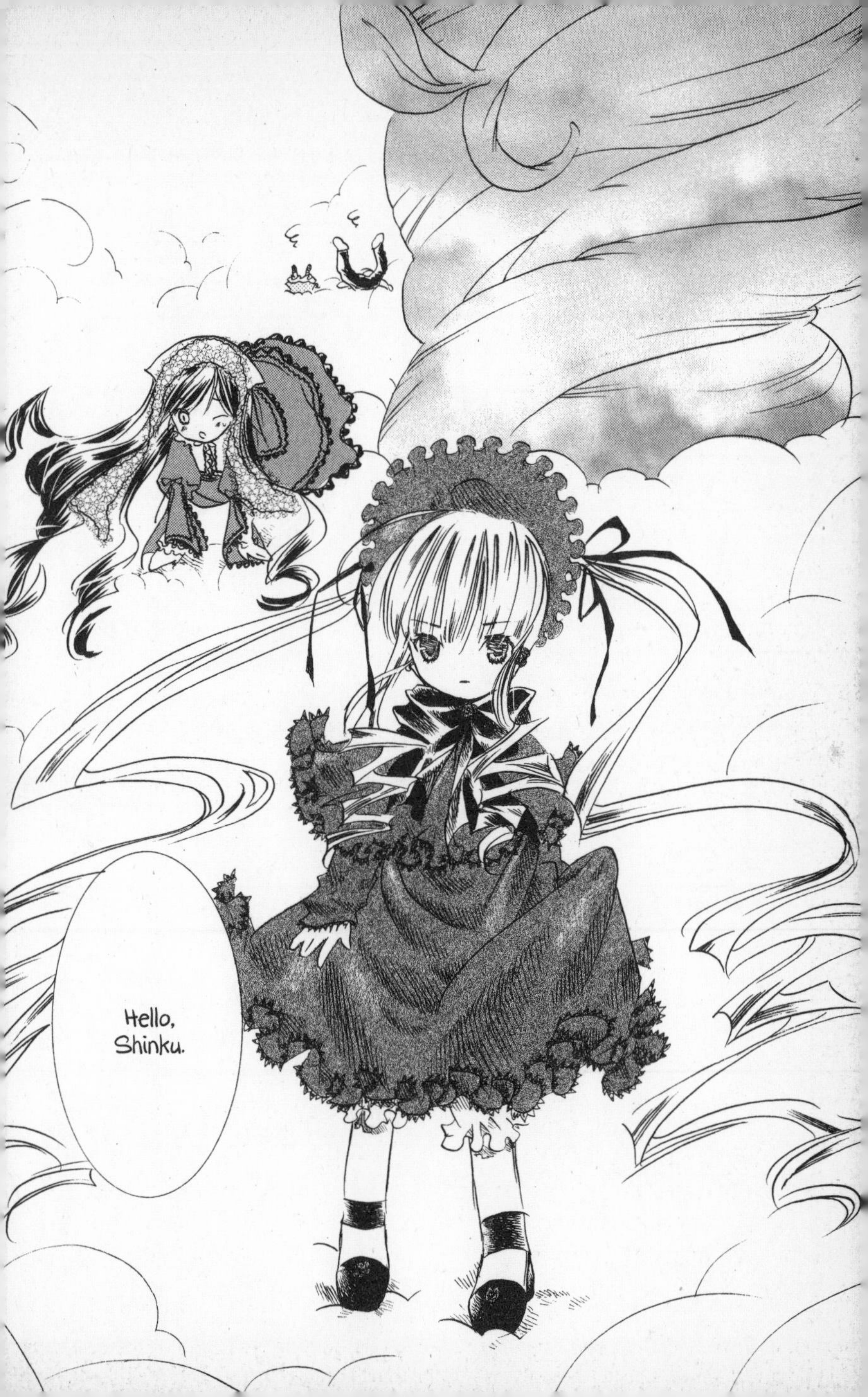
Hello, Shinku.

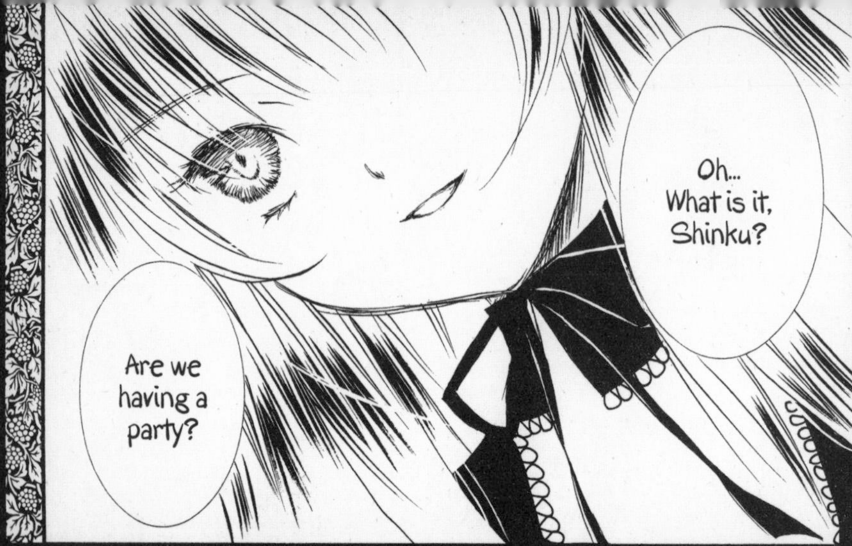
Oh... What is it, Shinku?
Are we having a party?

Phase 16

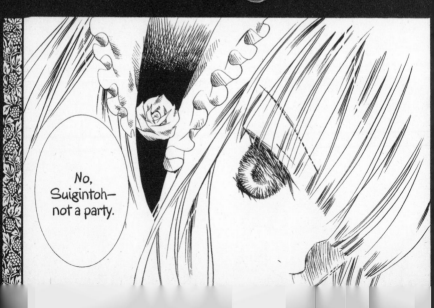

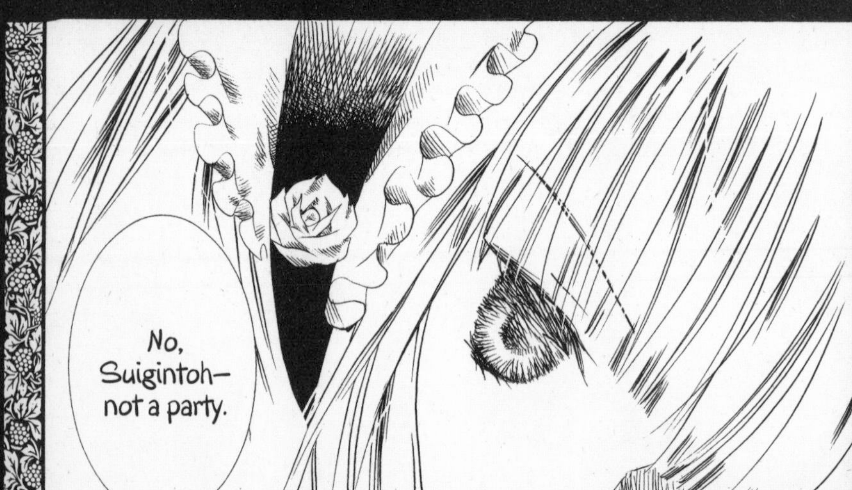
No, Suigintoh— not a party.

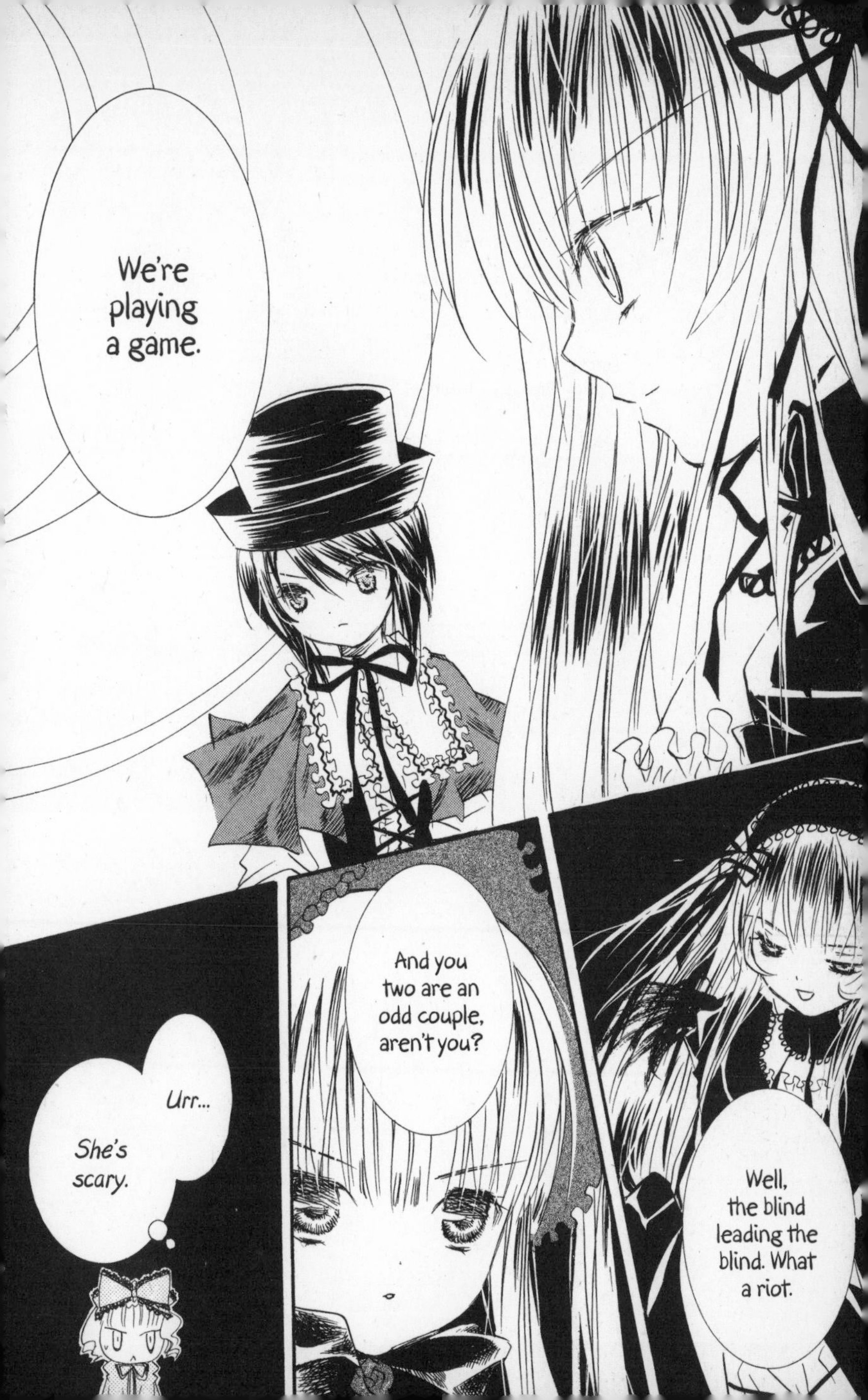
We're playing a game.
Well, the blind leading the blind. What a riot.
And you two are an odd couple, aren't you?
Urr...
She's scary.

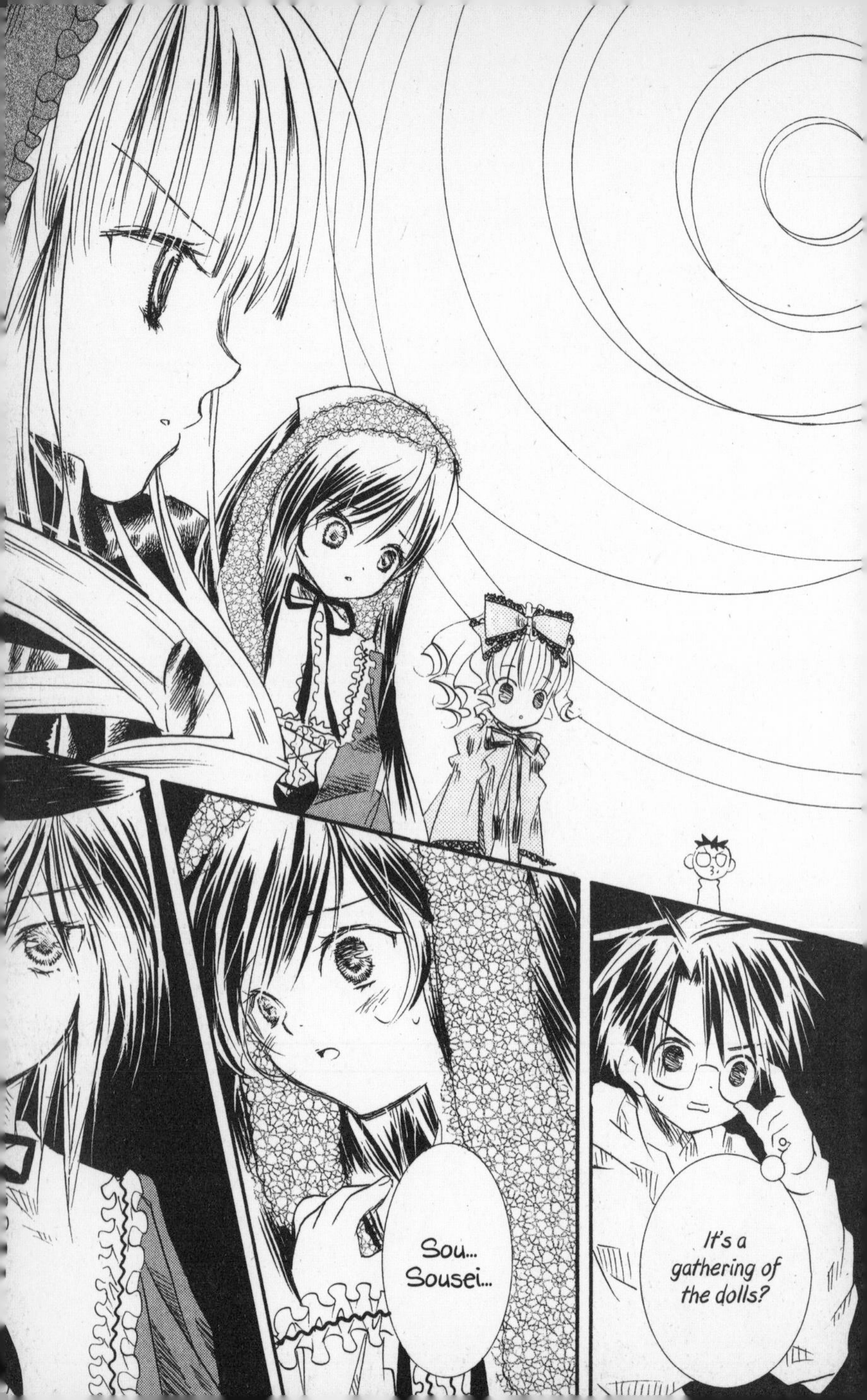
It's a gathering of the dolls?
Sou... Sousei...

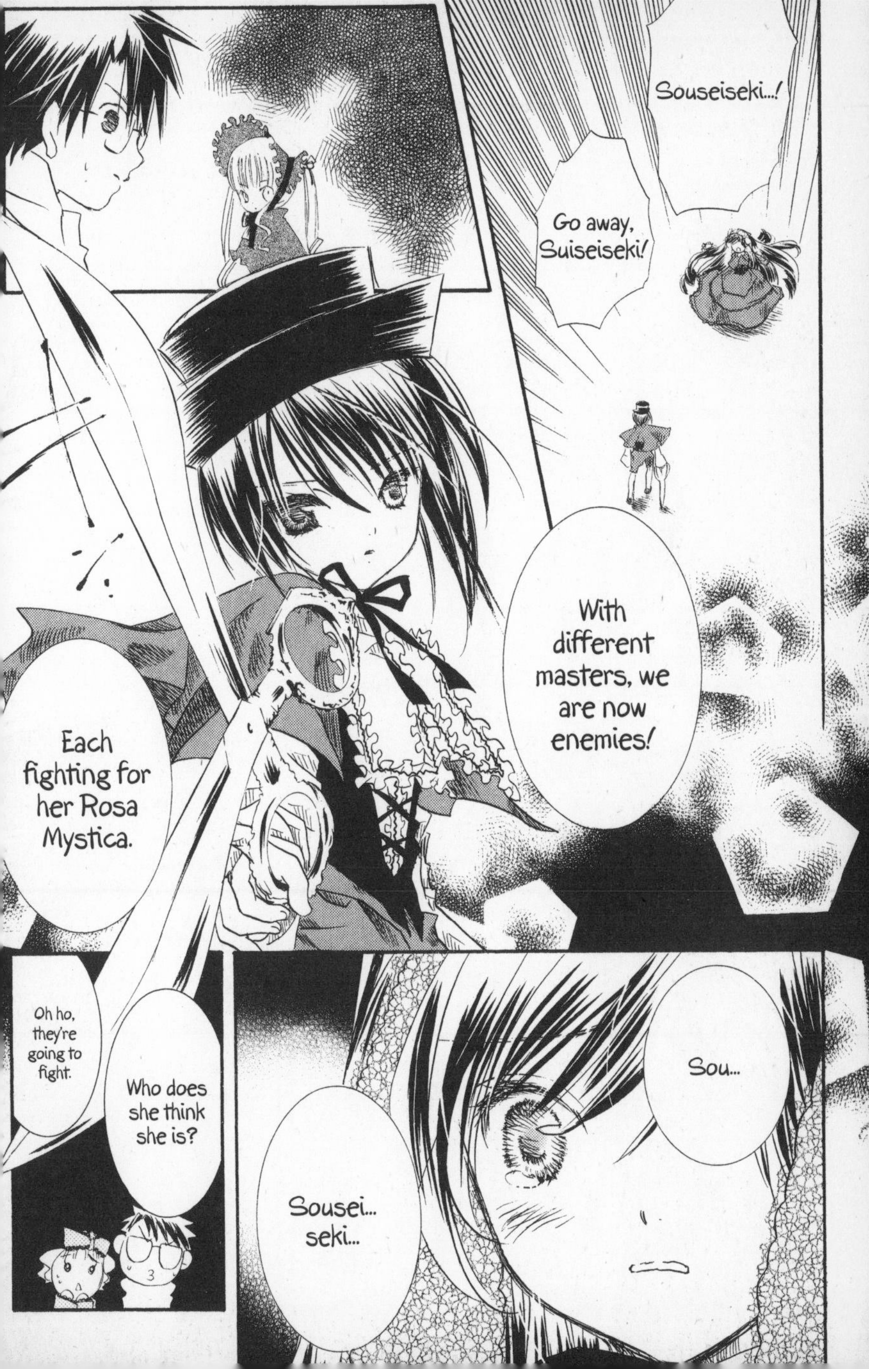
Souseiseki...!
Go away, Suiseiseki!
With different masters, we are now enemies!
Each fighting for her Rosa Mystica.
Sou...
Sousei... seki...
Who does she think she is?
Oh ho, they're going to fight.

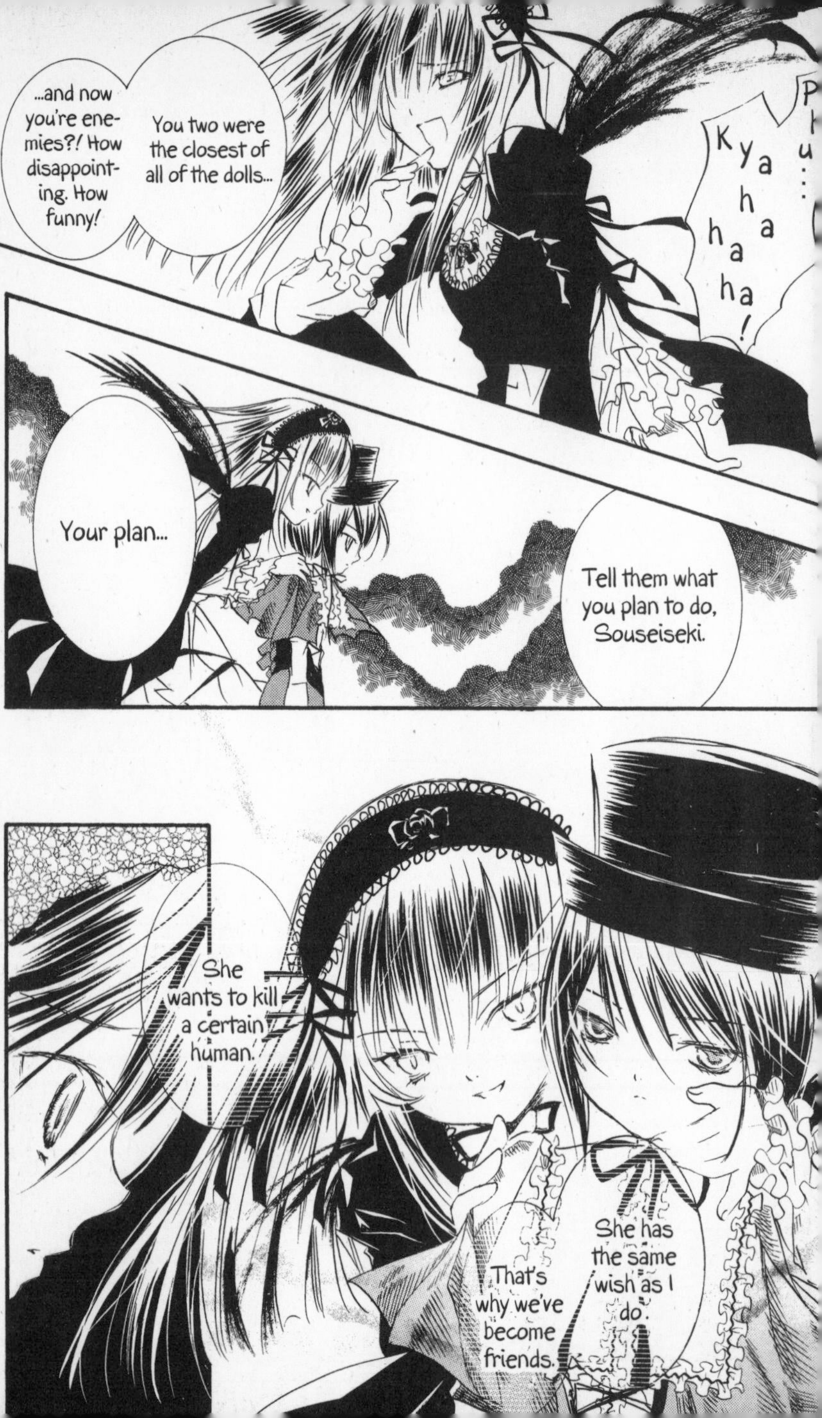
Pfu...
Kyahahahaha!
You two were the closest of all of the dolls...
...and now you're enemies?! How disappointing. How funny!
Tell them what you plan to do, Souseiseki.
Your plan...
She wants to kill a certain human.
She has the same wish as I do.
That's why we've become friends.

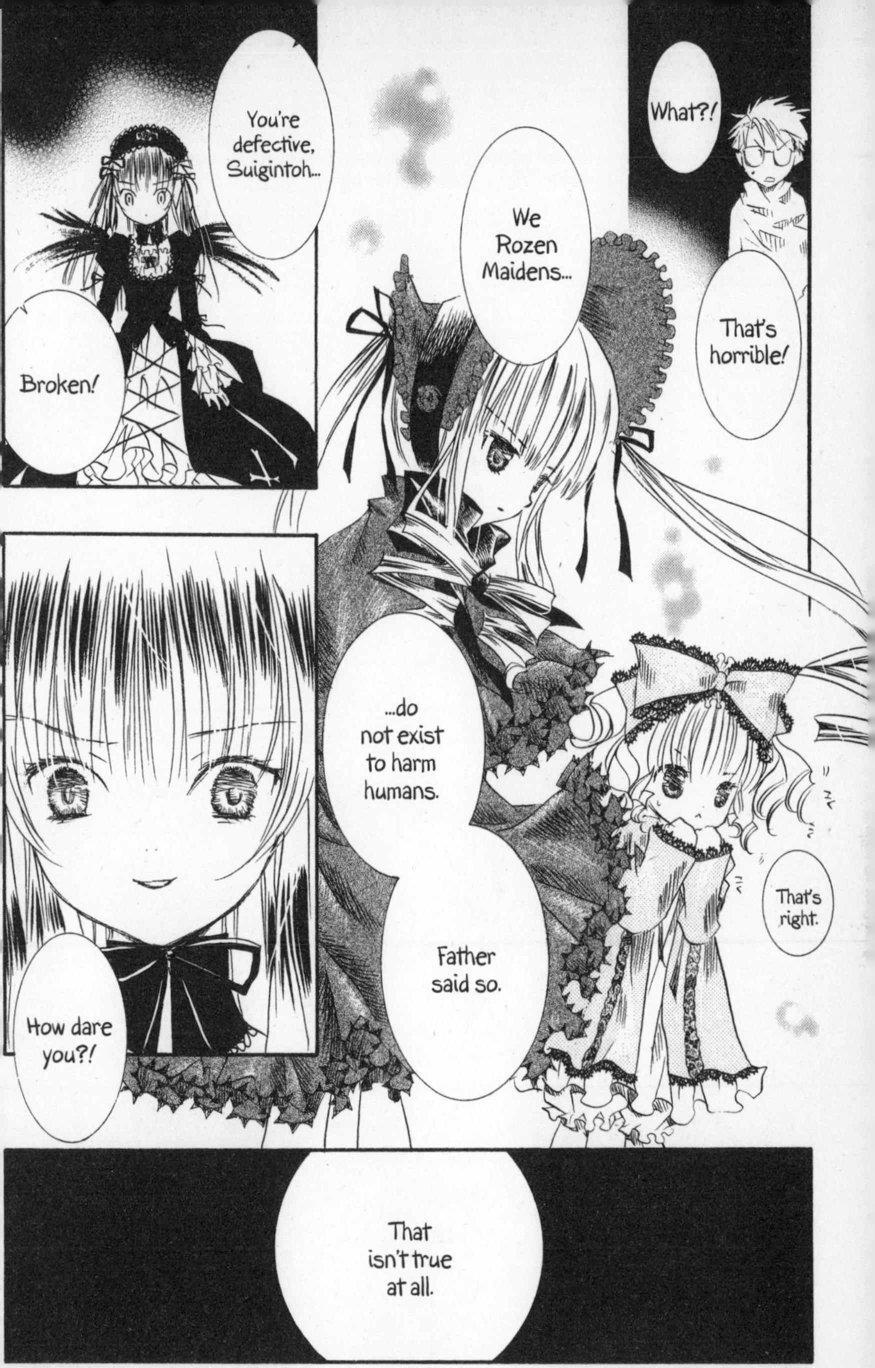

What?!
That's horrible!
We Rozen Maidens...
...do not exist to harm humans.
Father said so.
That's right.
You're defective, Suigintoh...
Broken!
How dare you?!
That isn't true at all.

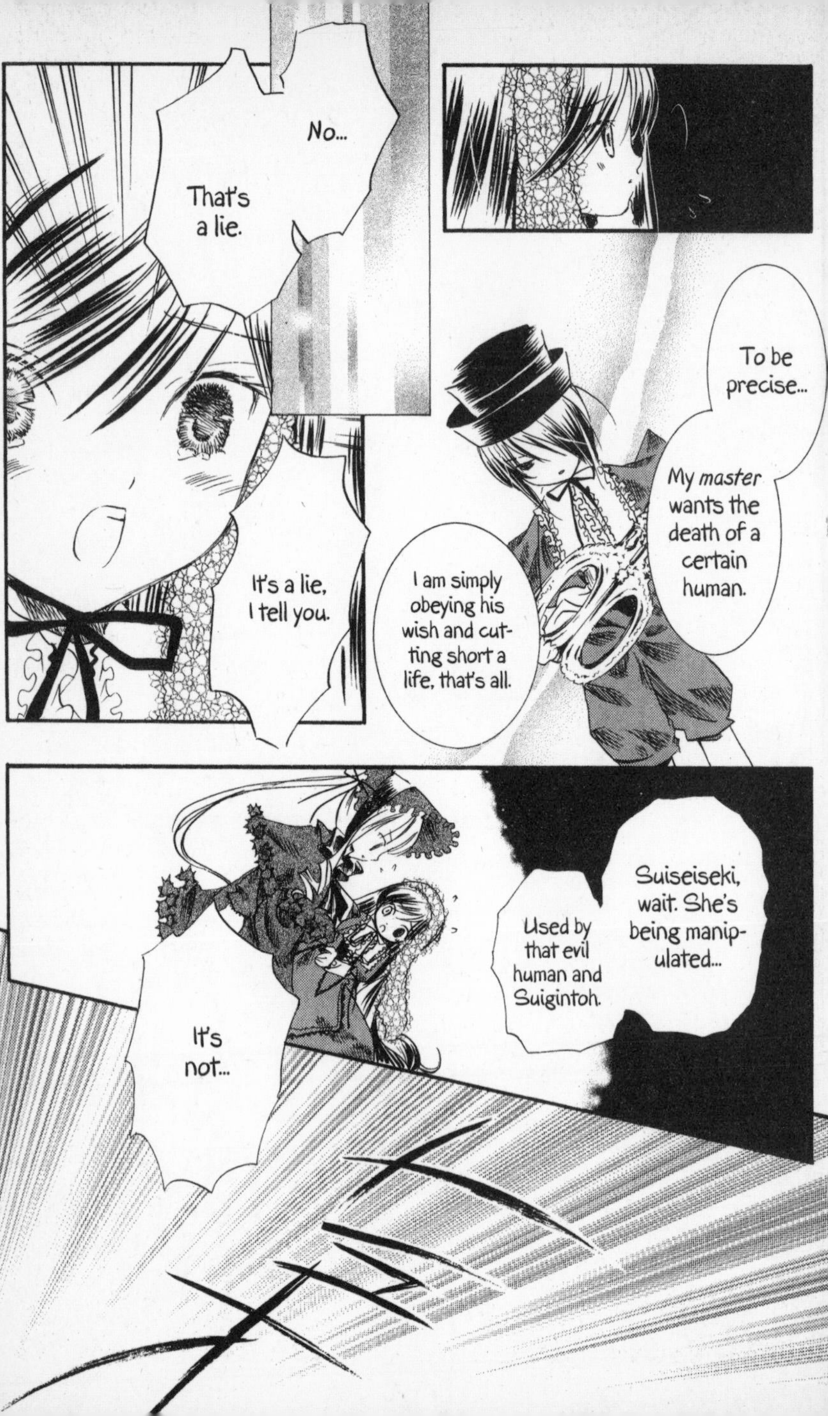
To be precise...
My *master* wants the death of a certain human.
I am simply obeying his wish and cutting short a life, that's all.
No...
That's a lie.
It's a lie, I tell you.
Suiseiseki, wait. She's being manipulated...
Used by that evil human and Suigintoh.
It's not...

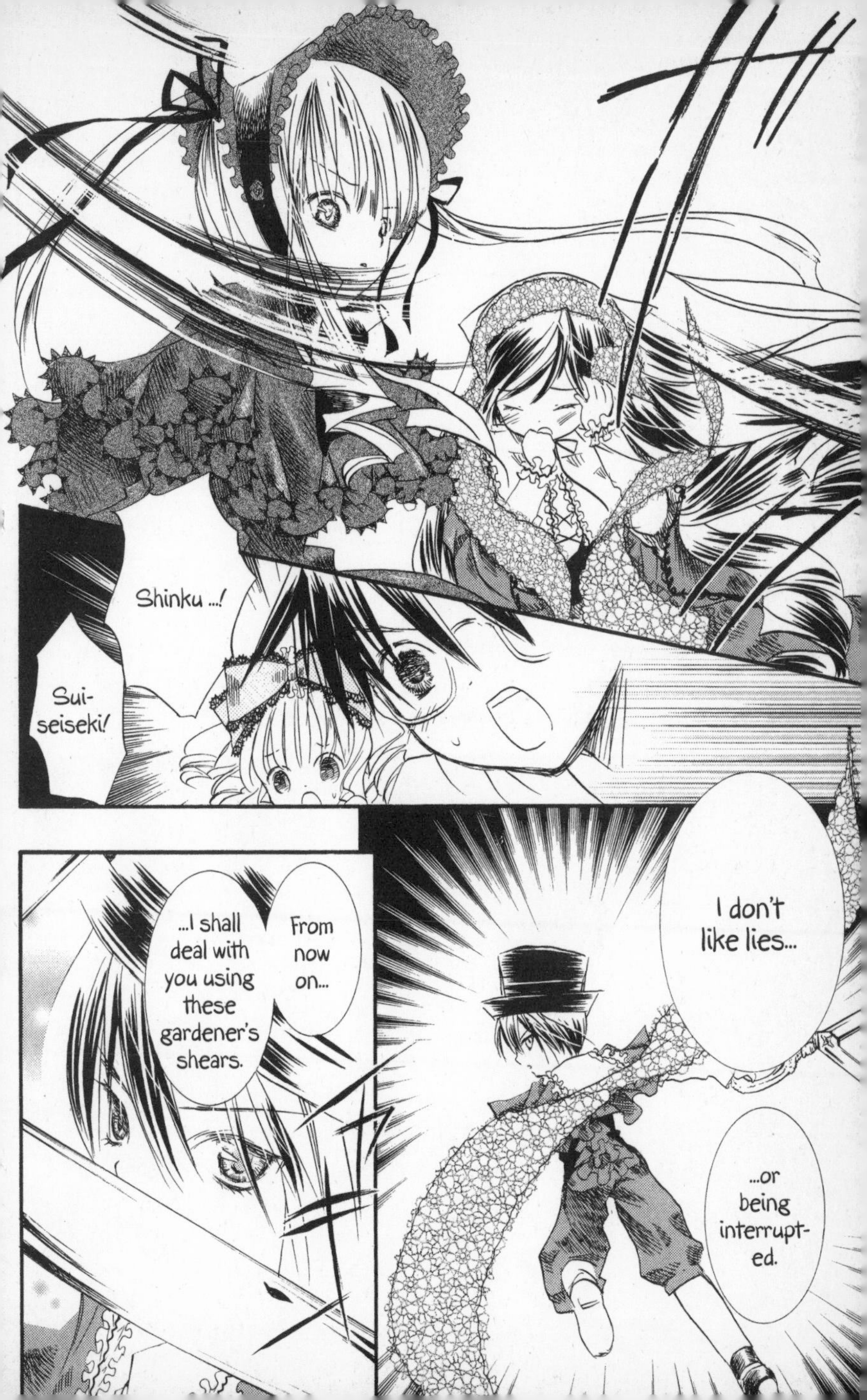
Shinku ...!
Sui-seiseki!
I don't like lies...
...or being interrupt-ed.
From now on...
...I shall deal with you using these gardener's shears.

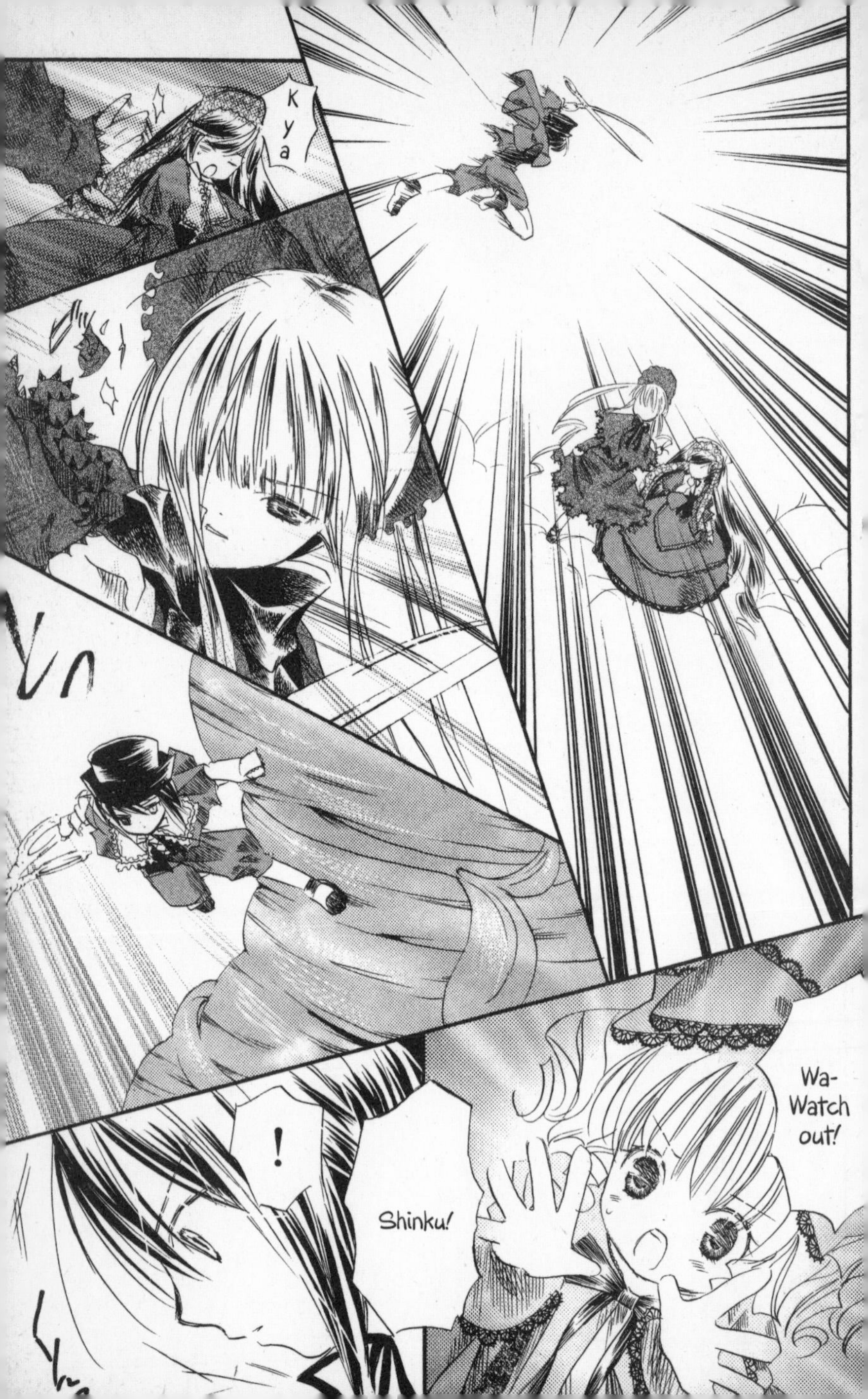
Kya
Wa-Watch out!
!
Shinku!

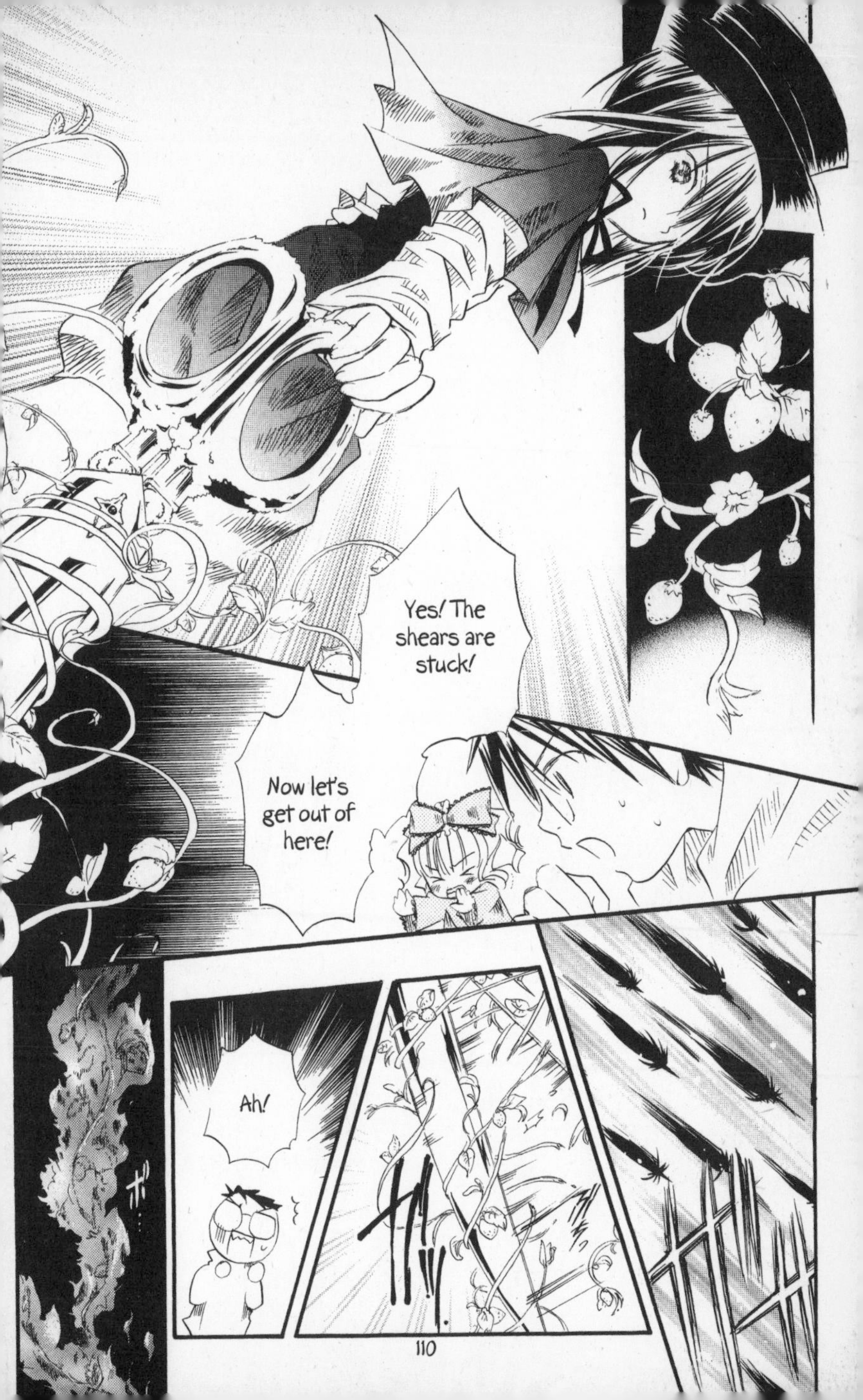
Yes! The shears are stuck!
Now let's get out of here!
Ah!

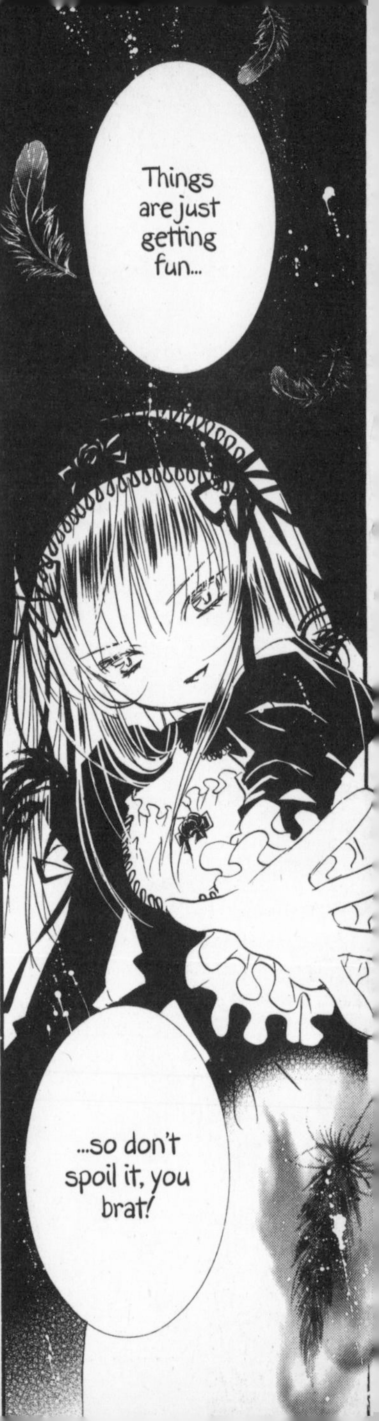
Things are just getting fun...
...so don't spoil it, you brat!
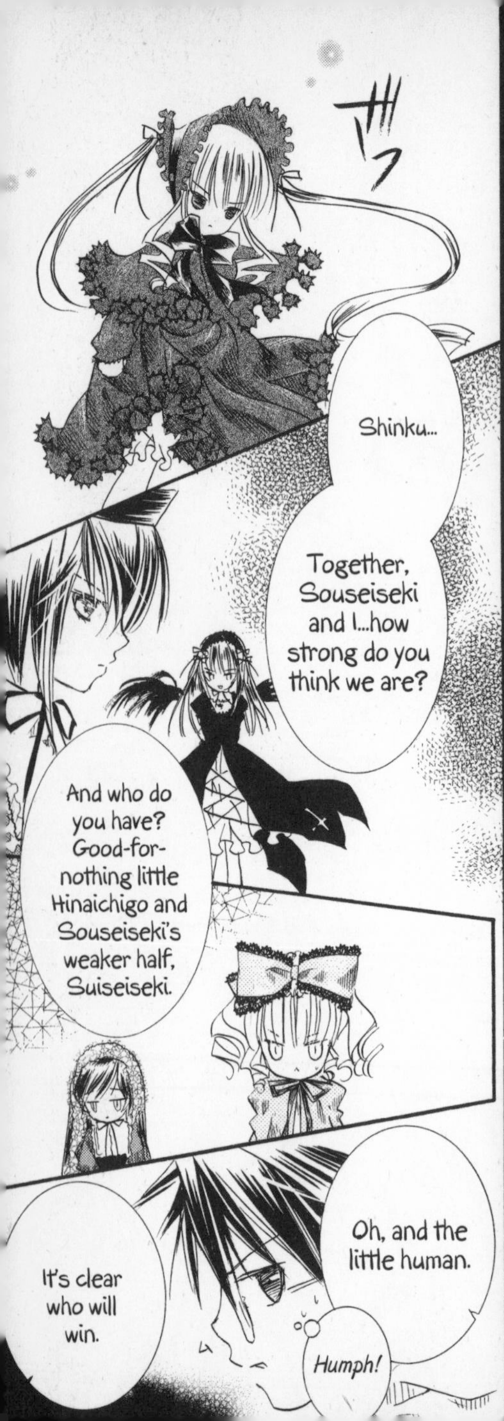
ザッ
Shinku...
Together, Souseiseki and I...how strong do you think we are?
And who do you have? Good-for-nothing little Hinaichigo and Souseiseki's weaker half, Suiseiseki.
Oh, and the little human.
Humph!
It's clear who will win.

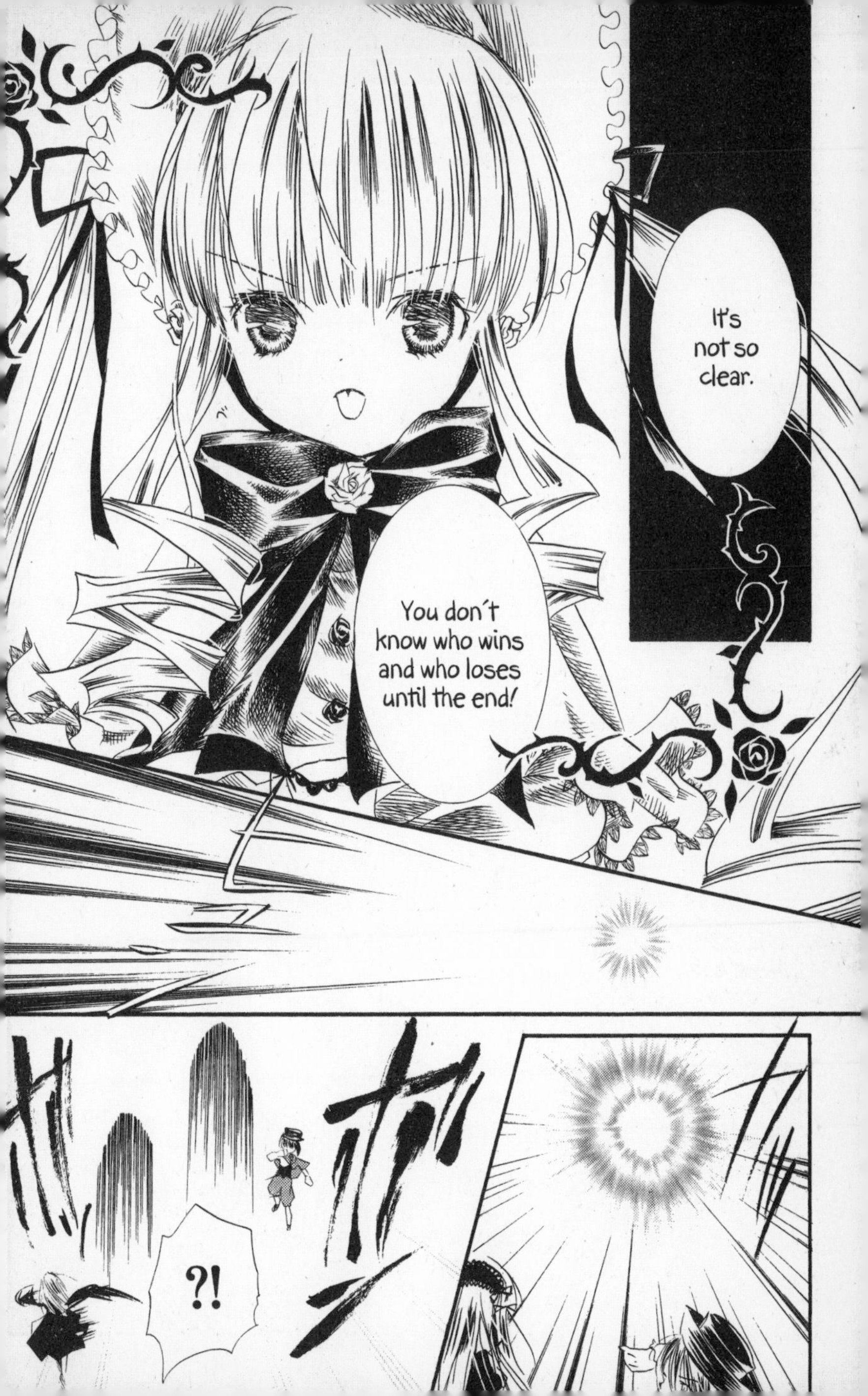
It's not so clear.
You don´t know who wins and who loses until the end!
?!

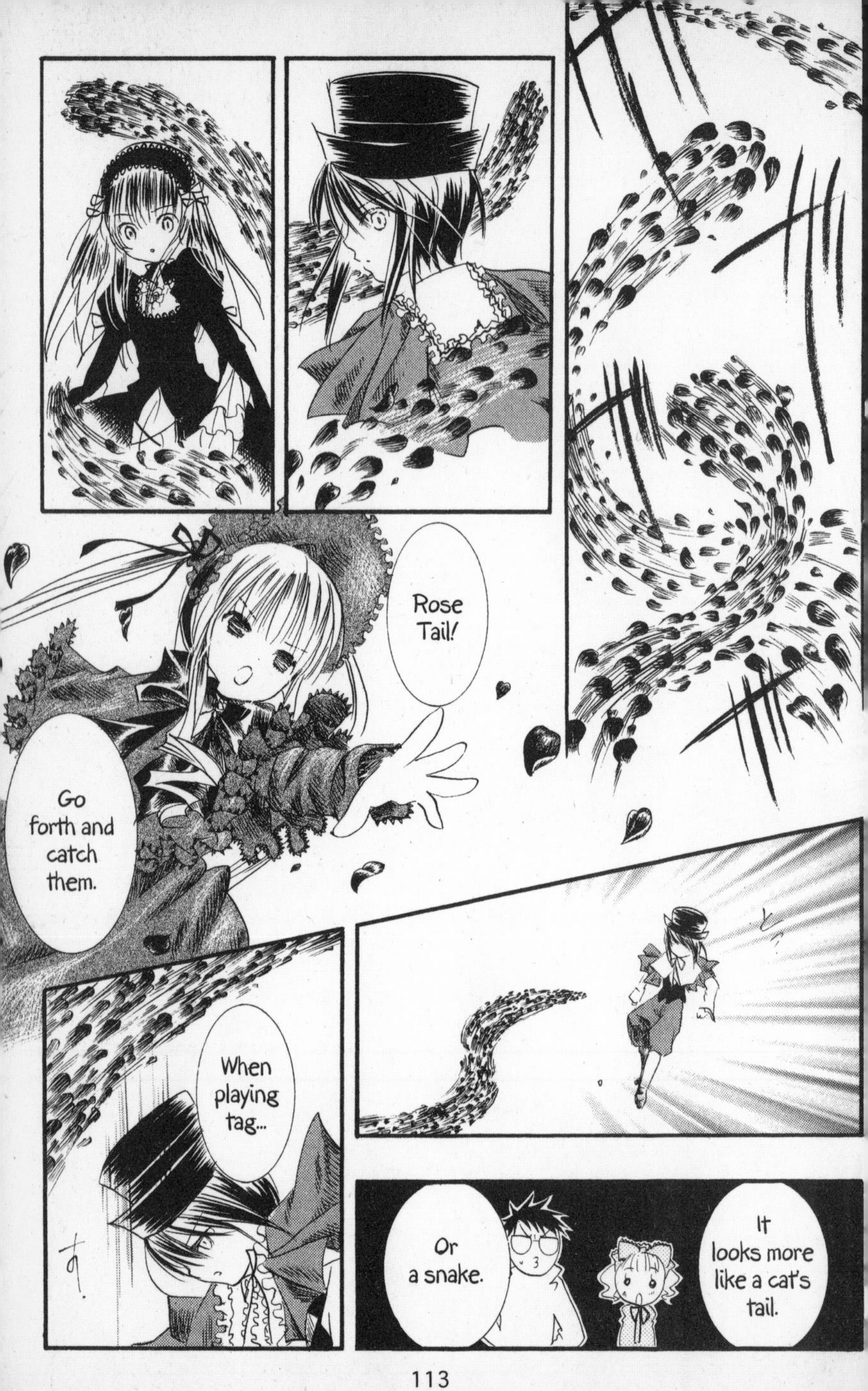
Rose Tail!
Go forth and catch them.
It looks more like a cat's tail.
Or a snake.
When playing tag...

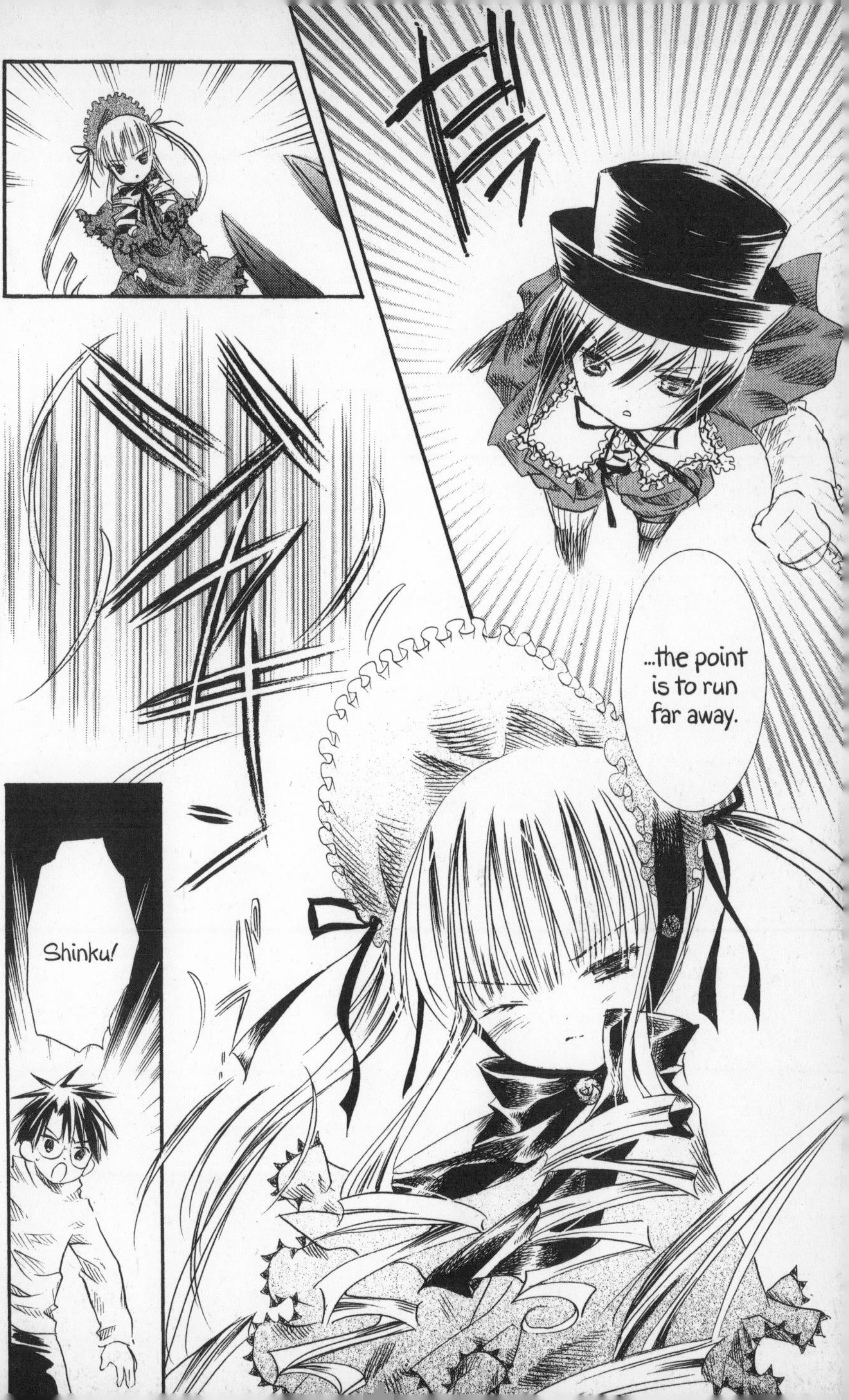
...the point is to run far away.
Shinku!

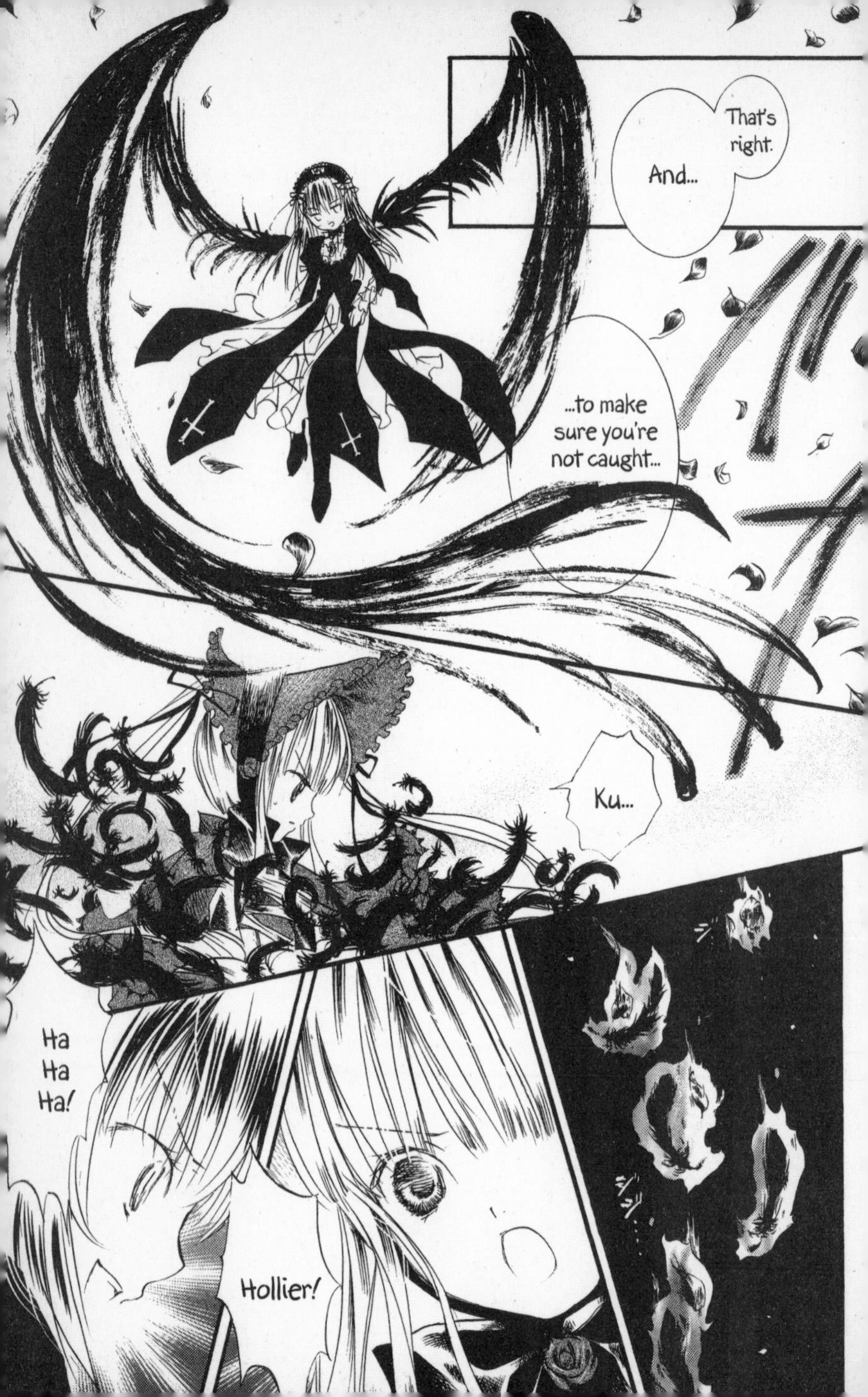

That's right.
And...
...to make sure you're not caught...
Ku...
Ha Ha Ha!
Hollier!

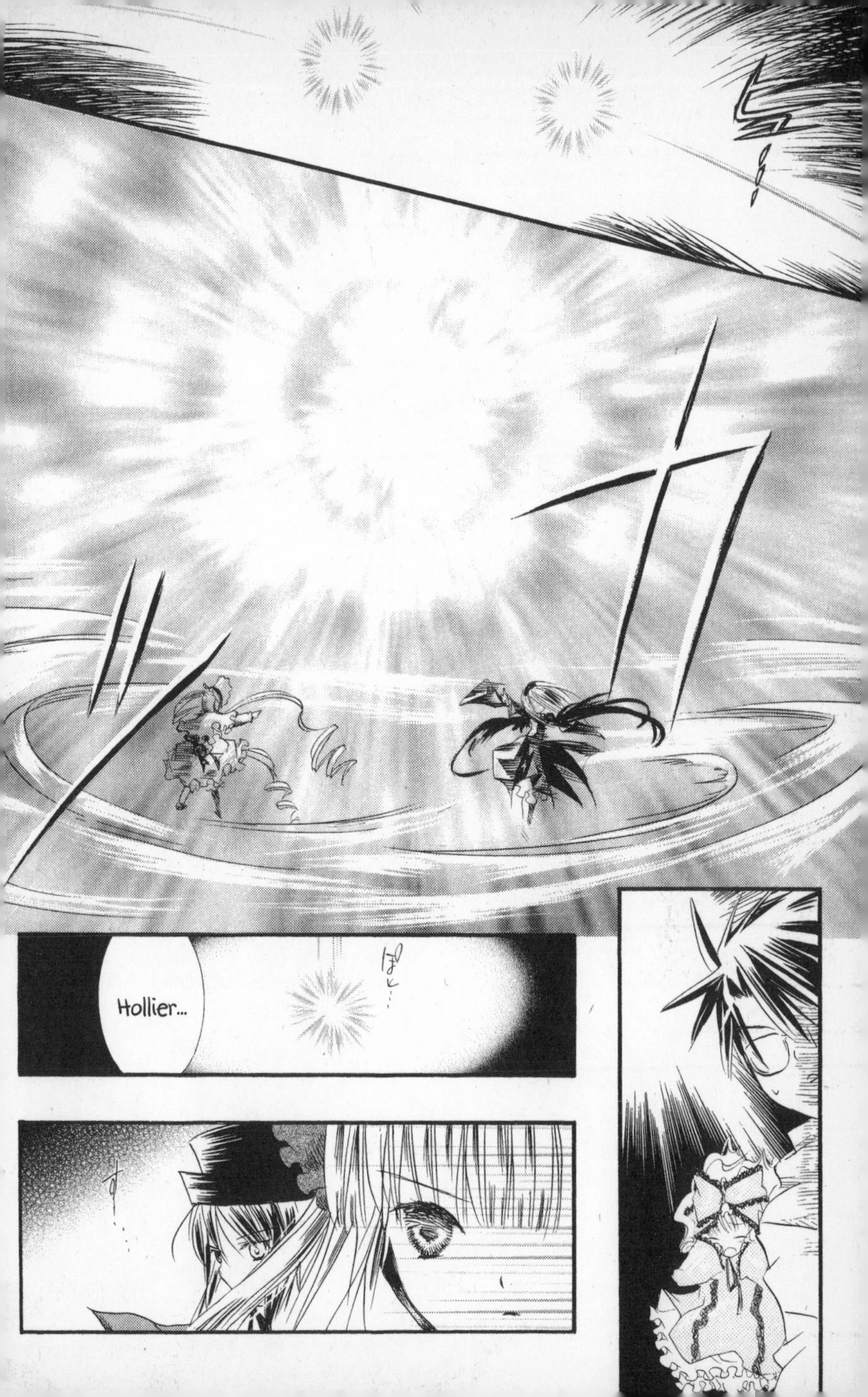
Hollier...

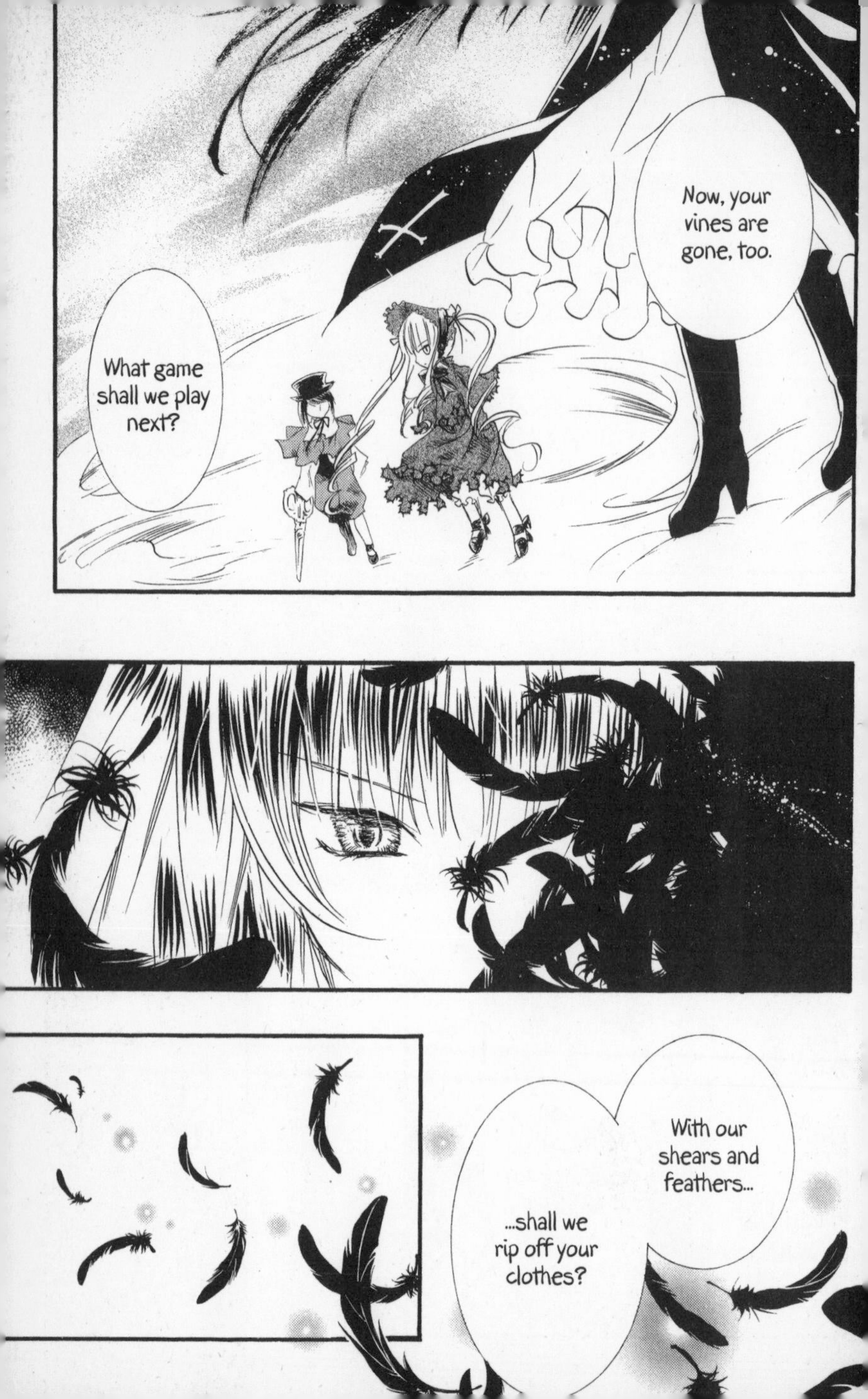
Now, your vines are gone, too.
What game shall we play next?
With our shears and feathers...
...shall we rip off your clothes?

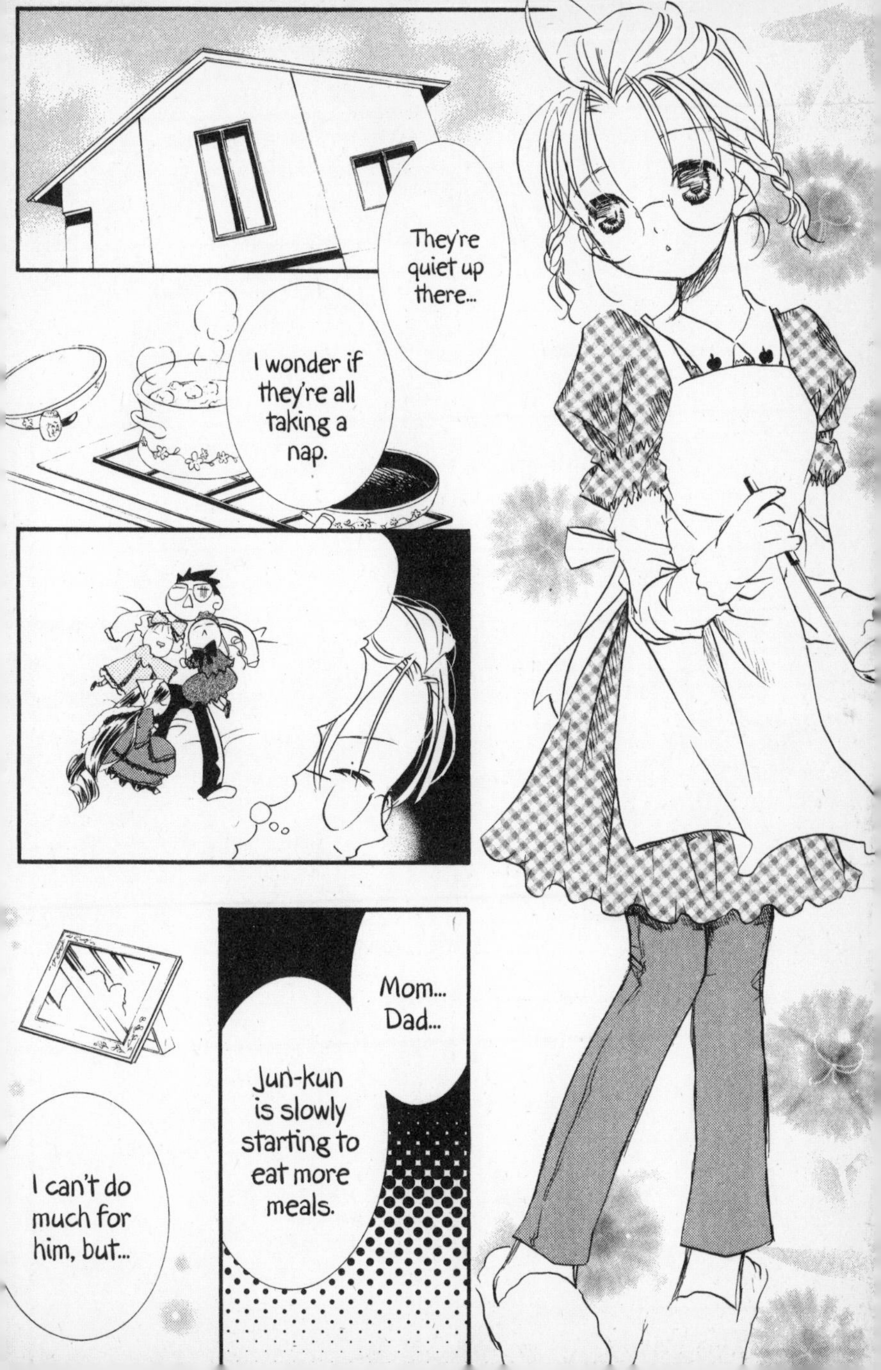
They're quiet up there...
I wonder if they're all taking a nap.
Mom... Dad...
Jun-kun is slowly starting to eat more meals.
I can't do much for him, but...

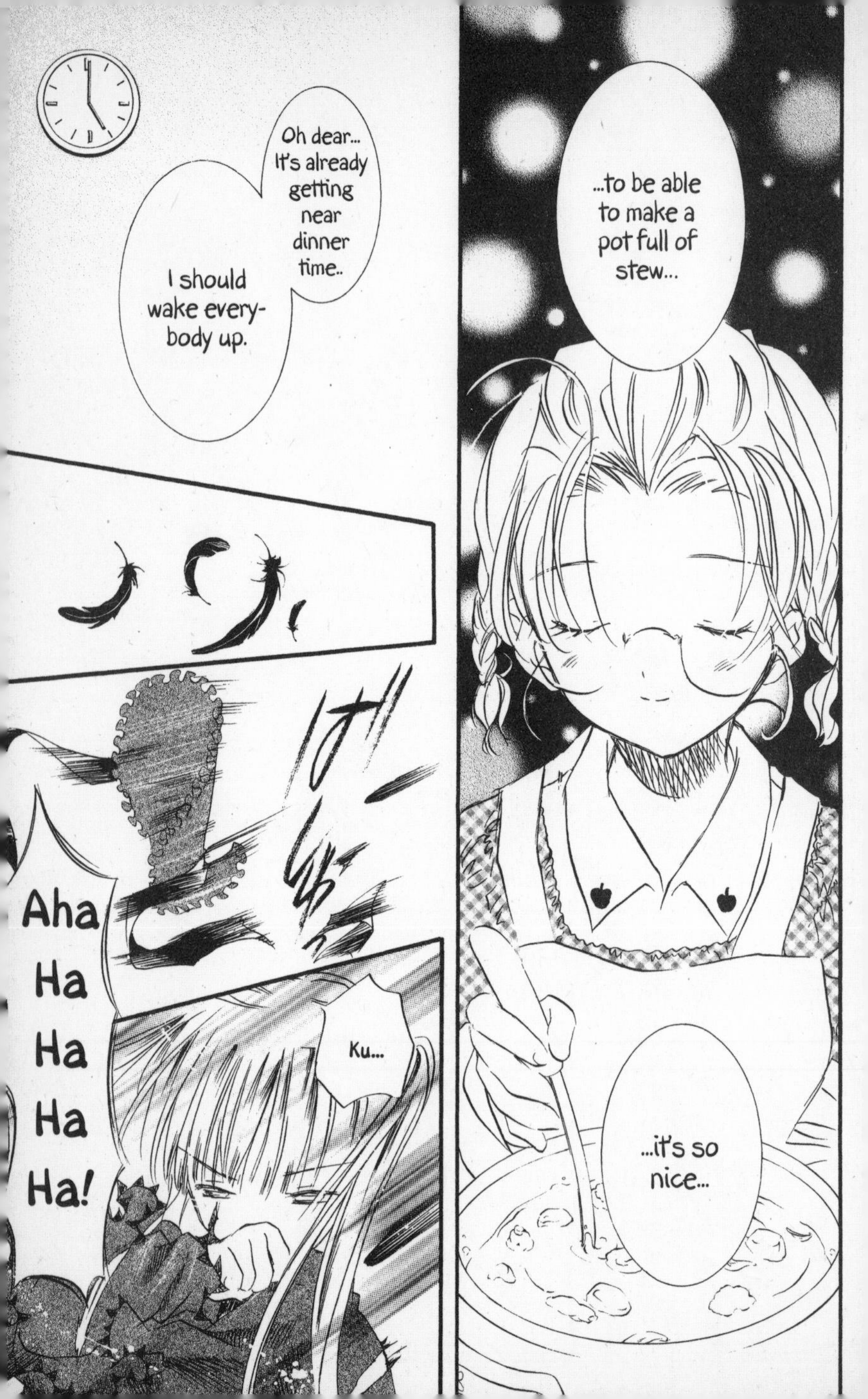

...to be able to make a pot full of stew...
...it's so nice...
Oh dear... It's already getting near dinner time..
I should wake every-body up.
Ku...
Aha Ha Ha Ha Ha!

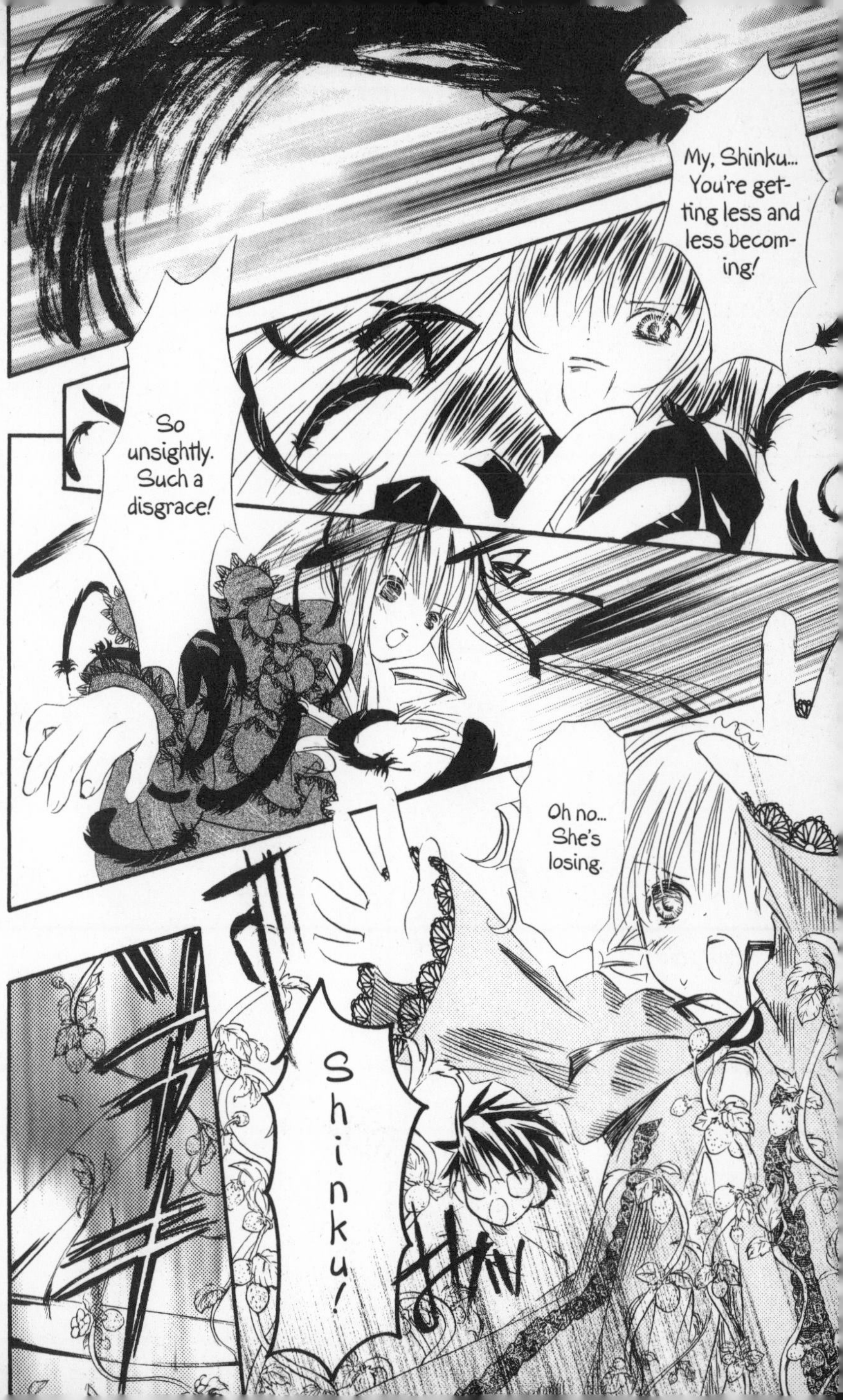
My, Shinku... You're getting less and less becoming!
So unsightly. Such a disgrace!
Oh no... She's losing.
Shinku!

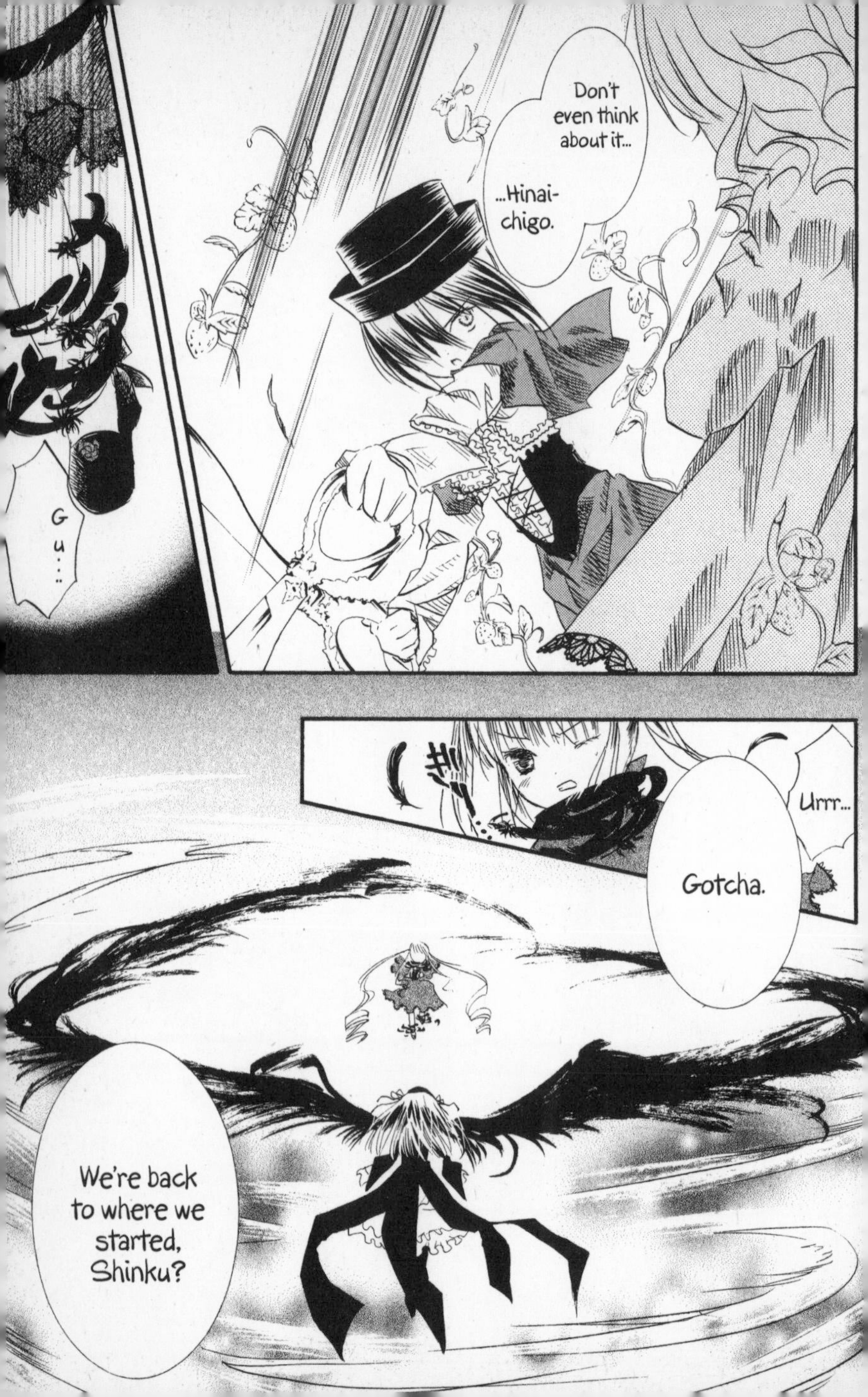
Don't even think about it...
...Hinai-chigo.
Gu...
Urrr...
Gotcha.
We're back to where we started, Shinku?

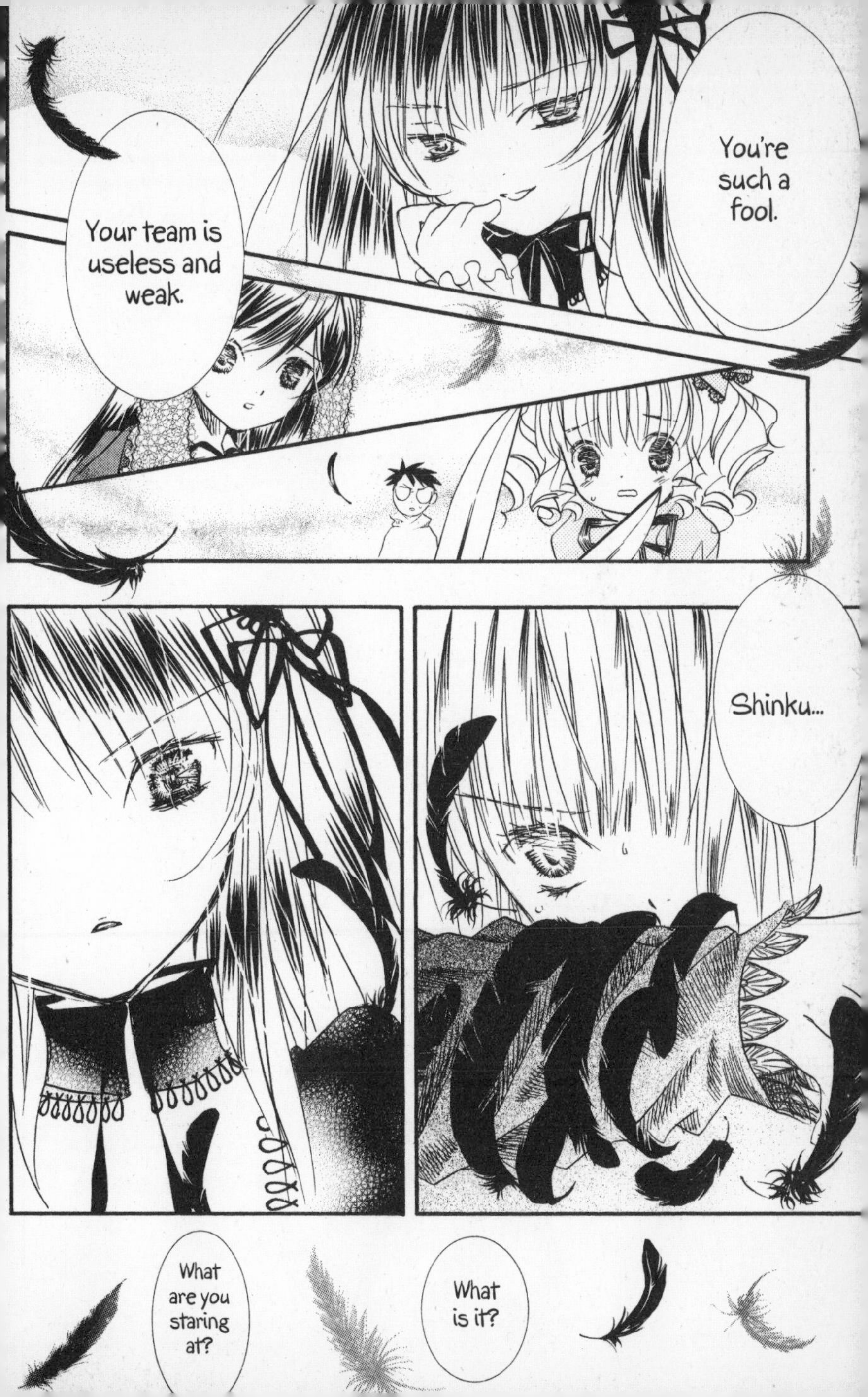
You're such a fool.
Your team is useless and weak.
Shinku...
What is it?
What are you staring at?

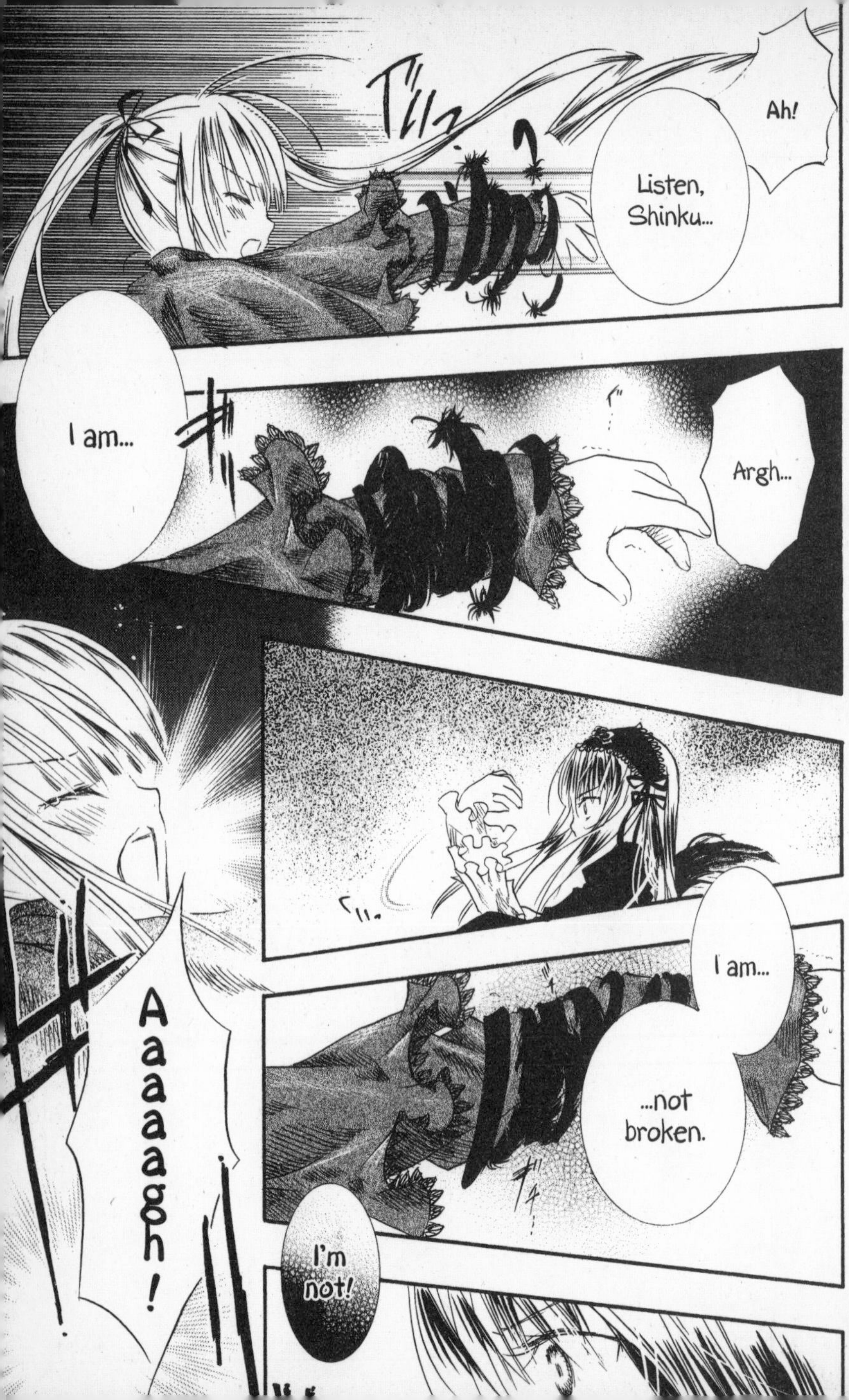

Ah!
Listen, Shinku...
I am...
Argh...
I am...
...not broken.
I'm not!
Aaaaaagh!

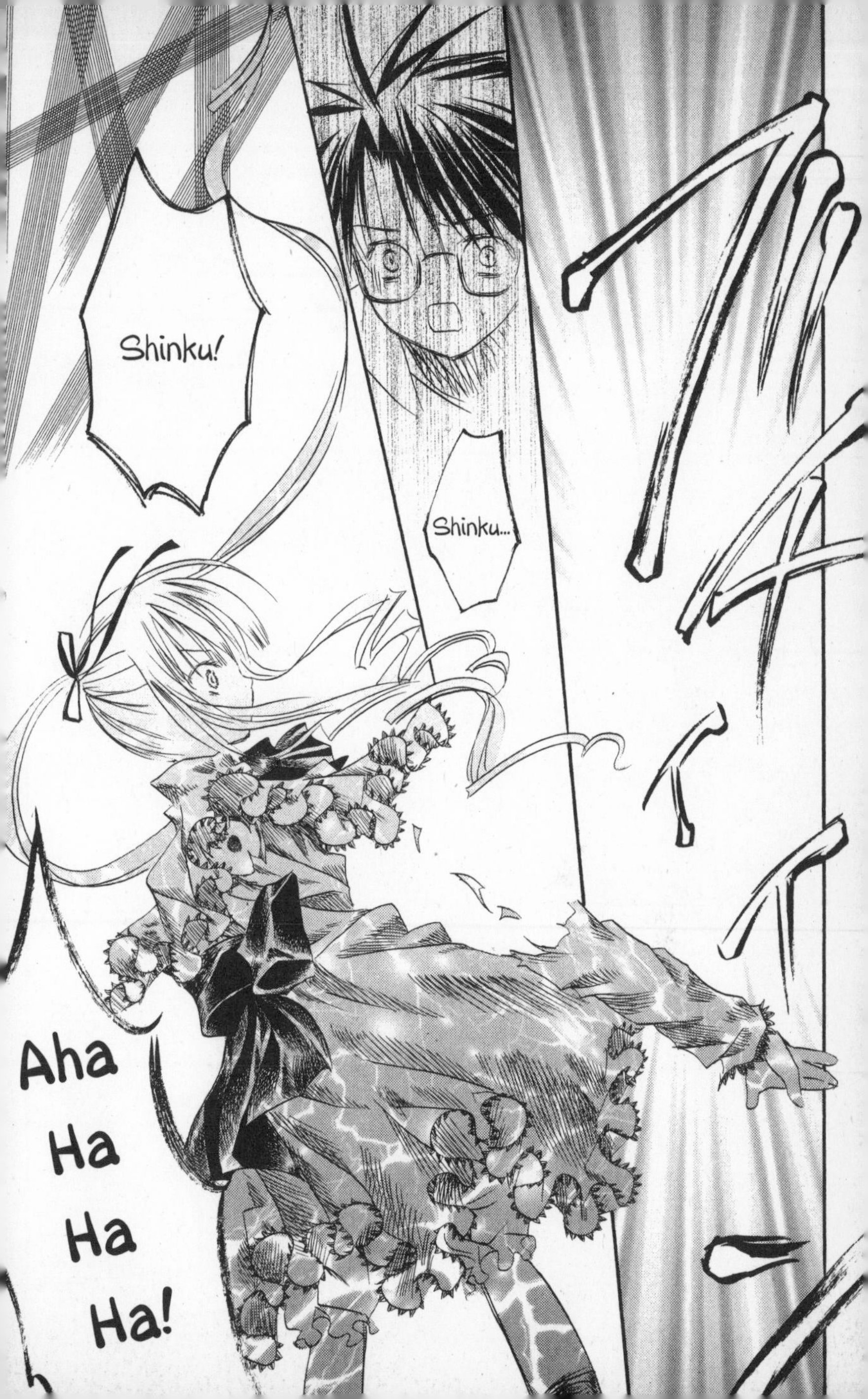
Shinku...
Shinku!
Aha Ha Ha Ha!

Phase 17

What don't you need?
"A broken toy."
What don't you like?
"Something imperfect."
What do you fear?
"Lacking something."

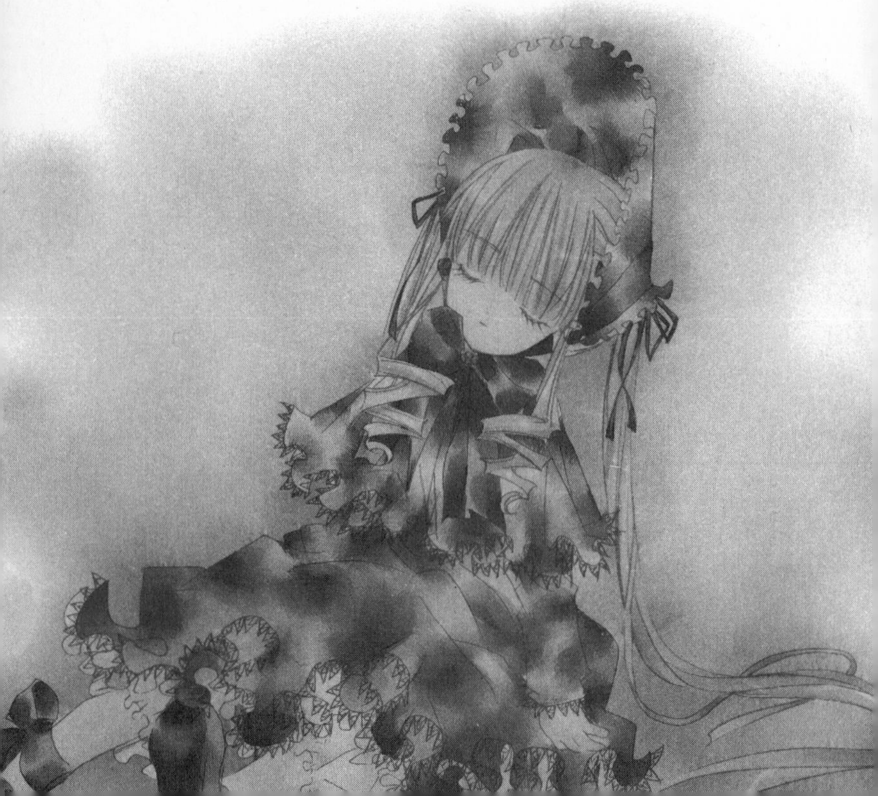

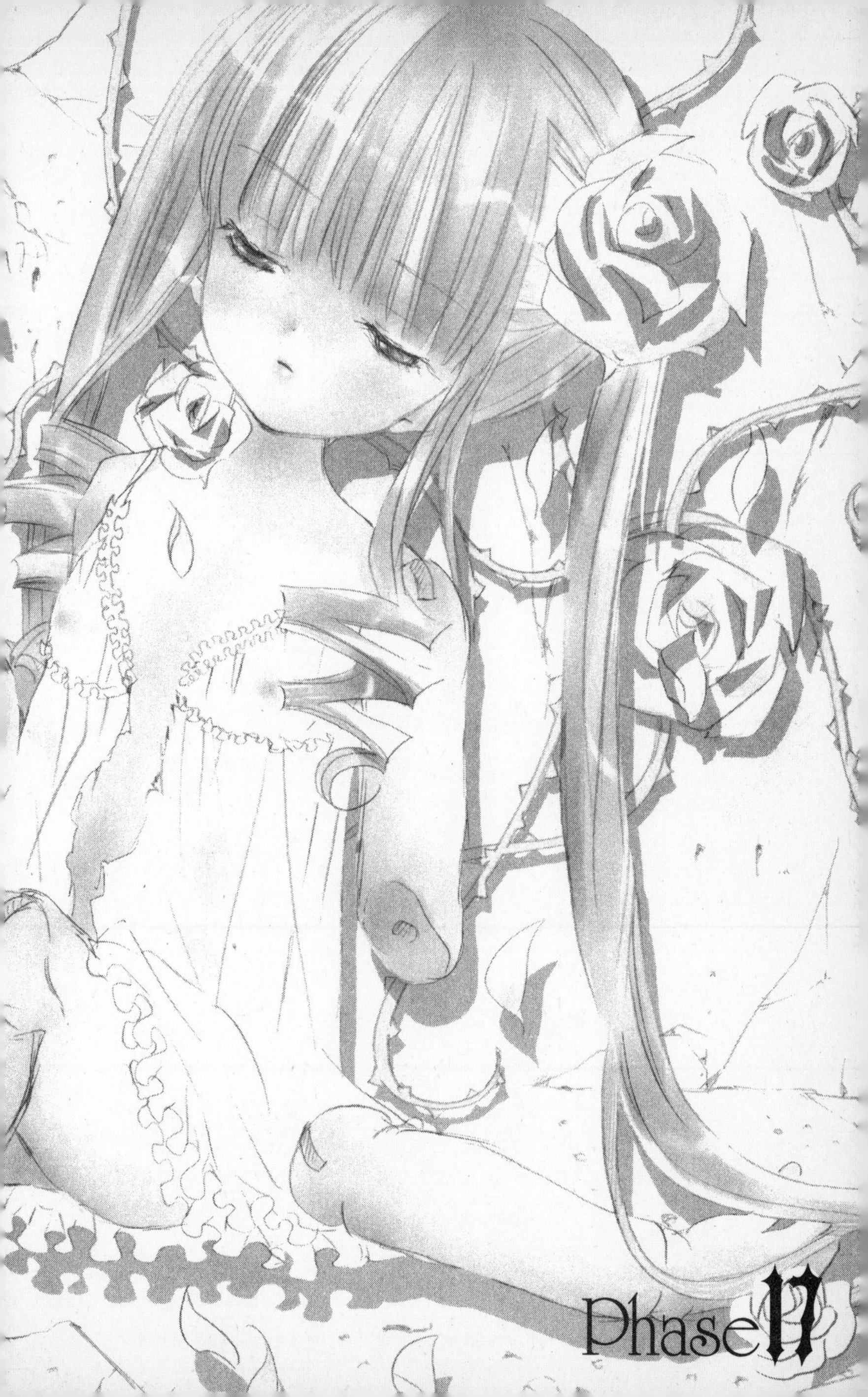
Phase 17

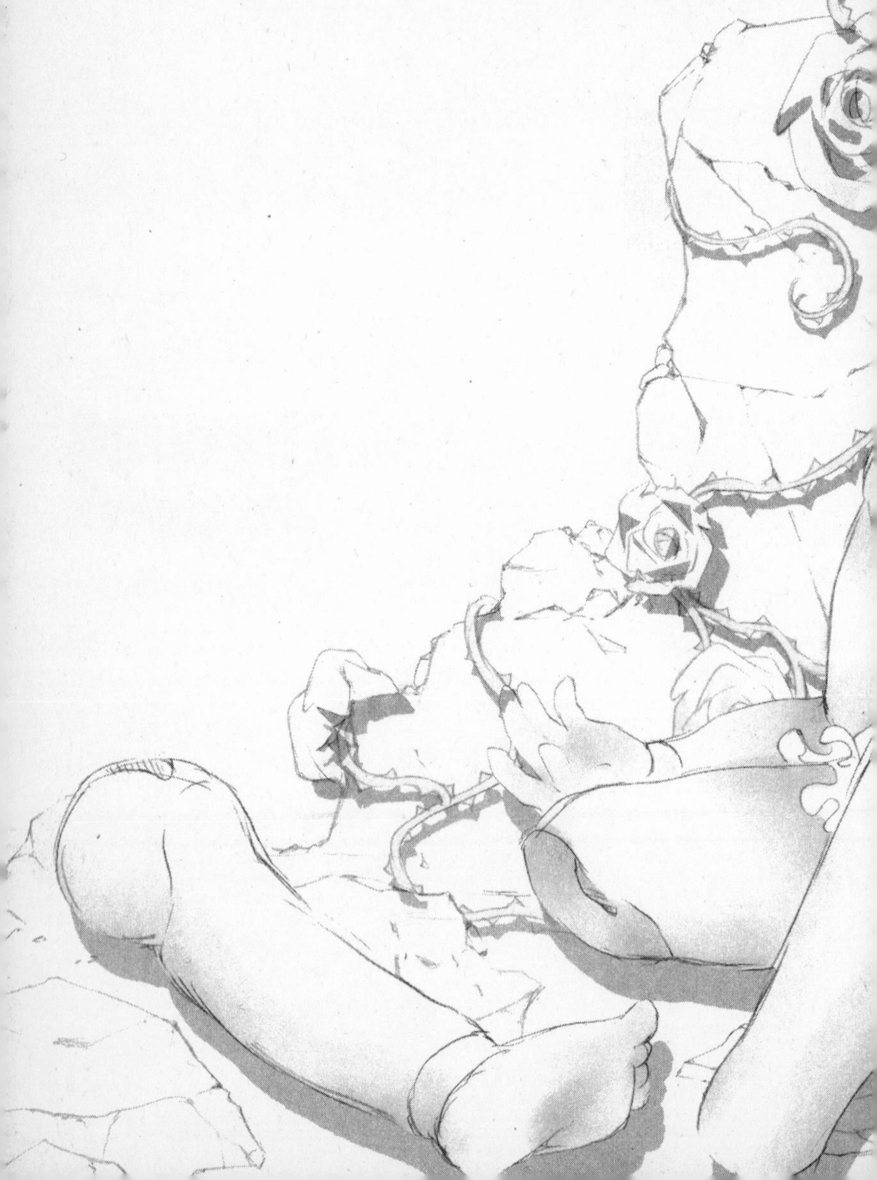

ローゼン メイデン

Rozen Maiden

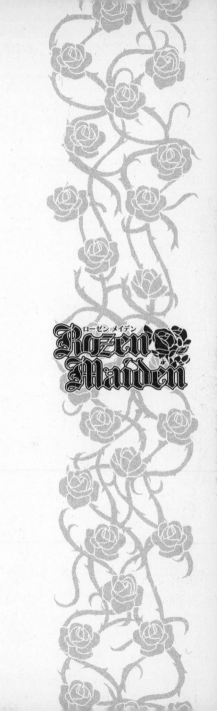

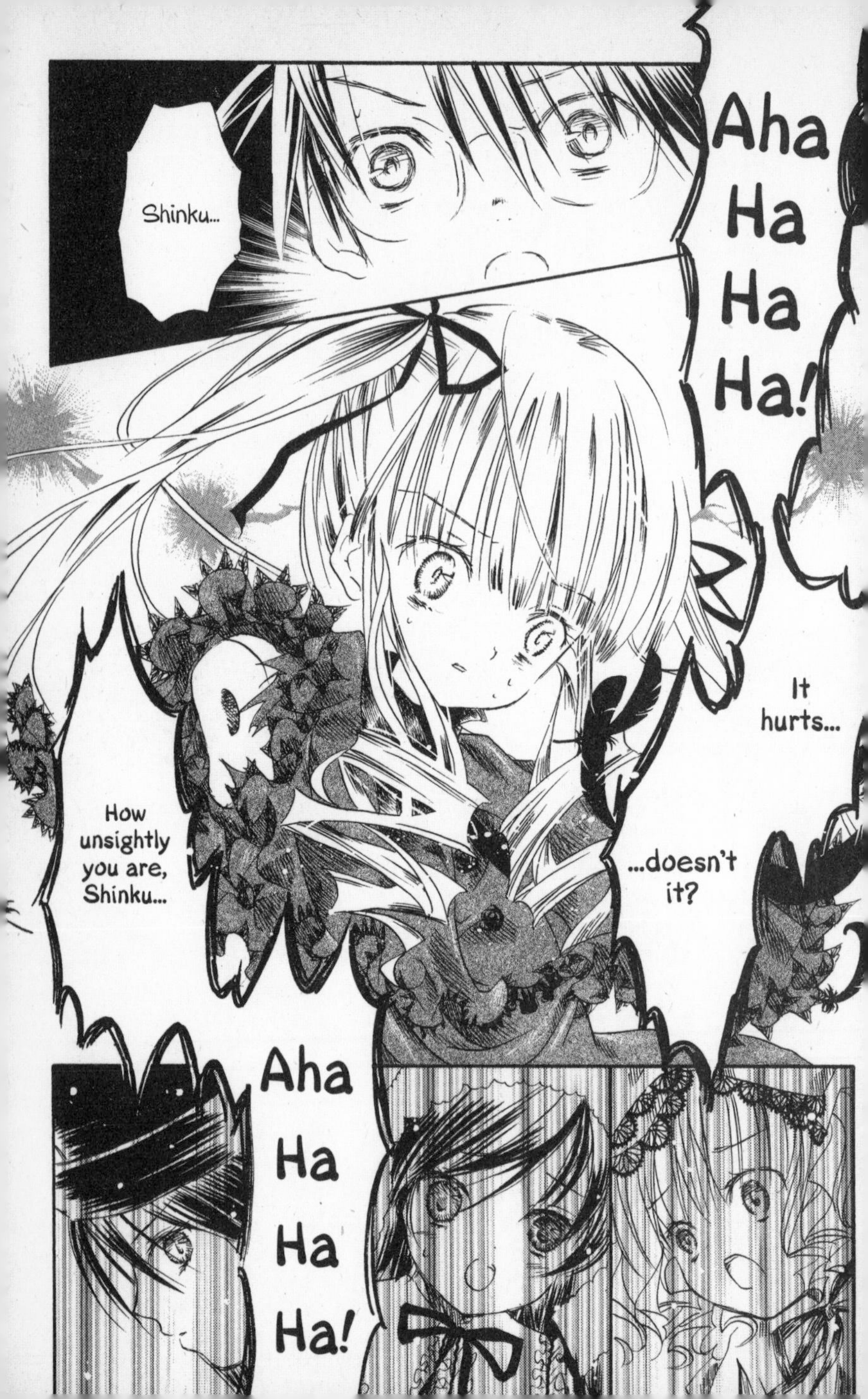
Aha Ha Ha Ha!
Shinku...
It hurts...
...doesn't it?
How unsightly you are, Shinku...
Aha Ha Ha Ha!

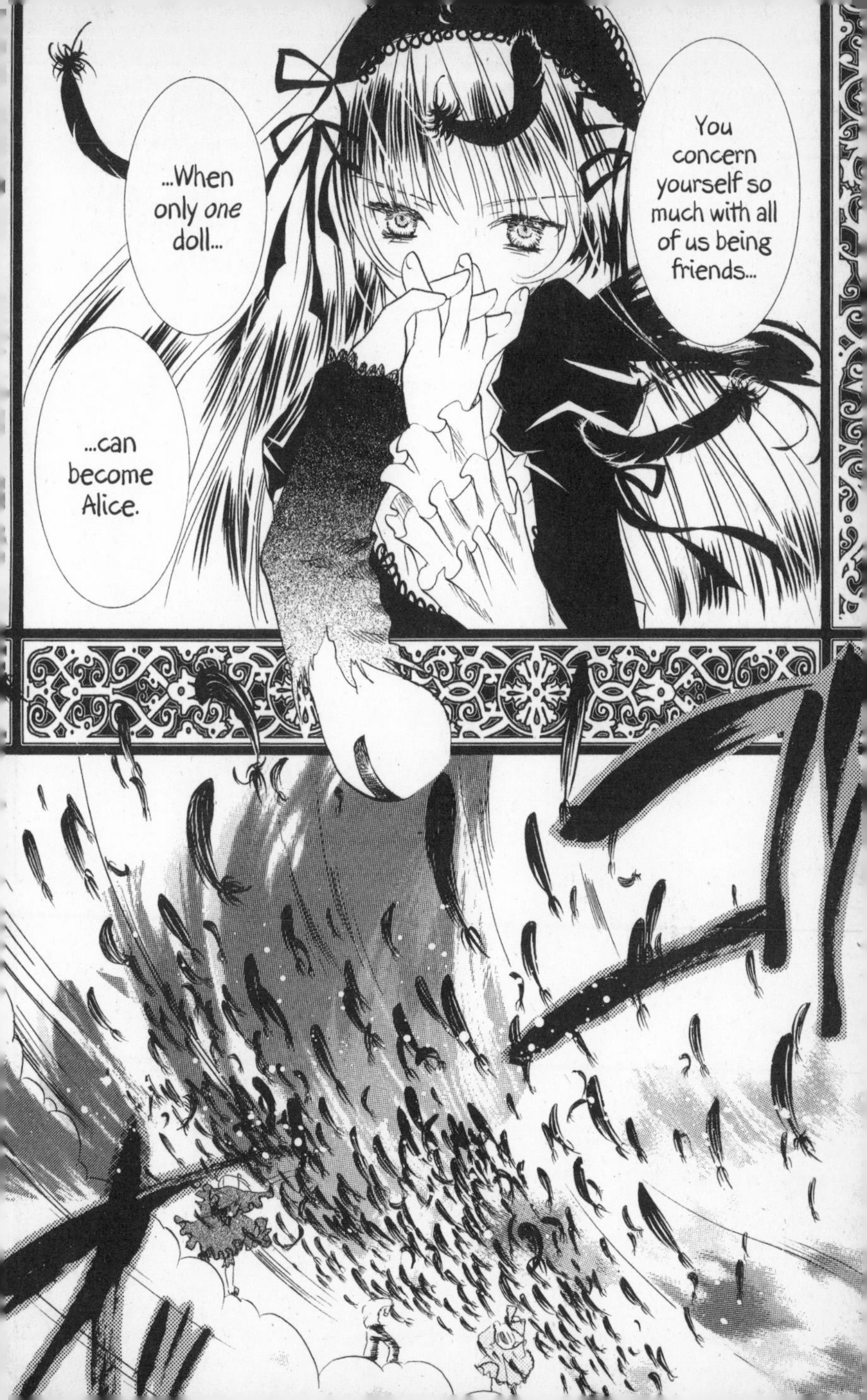
You concern yourself so much with all of us being friends...
...When only *one* doll...
...can become Alice.

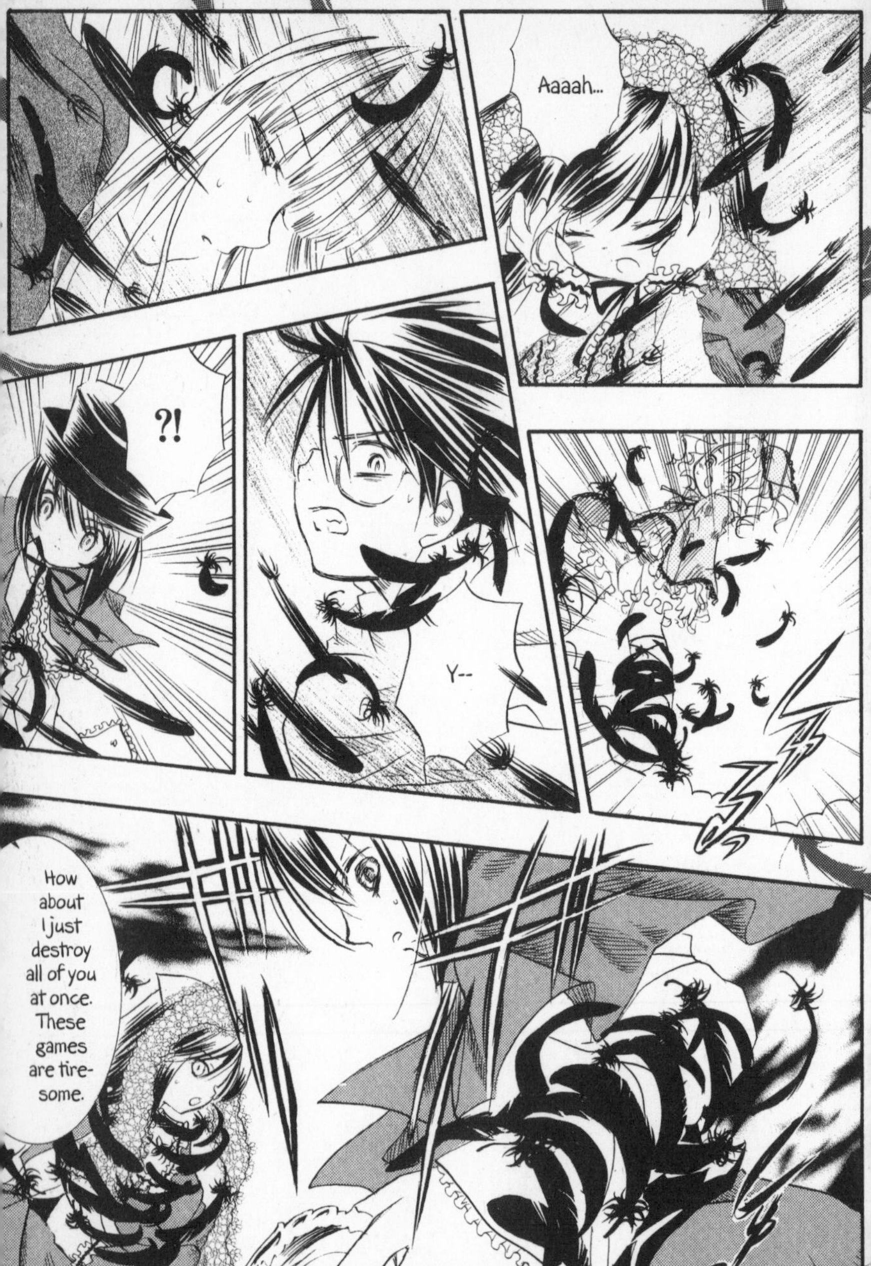
Aaaah...
Y--
?!
How about I just destroy all of you at once. These games are tire-some.

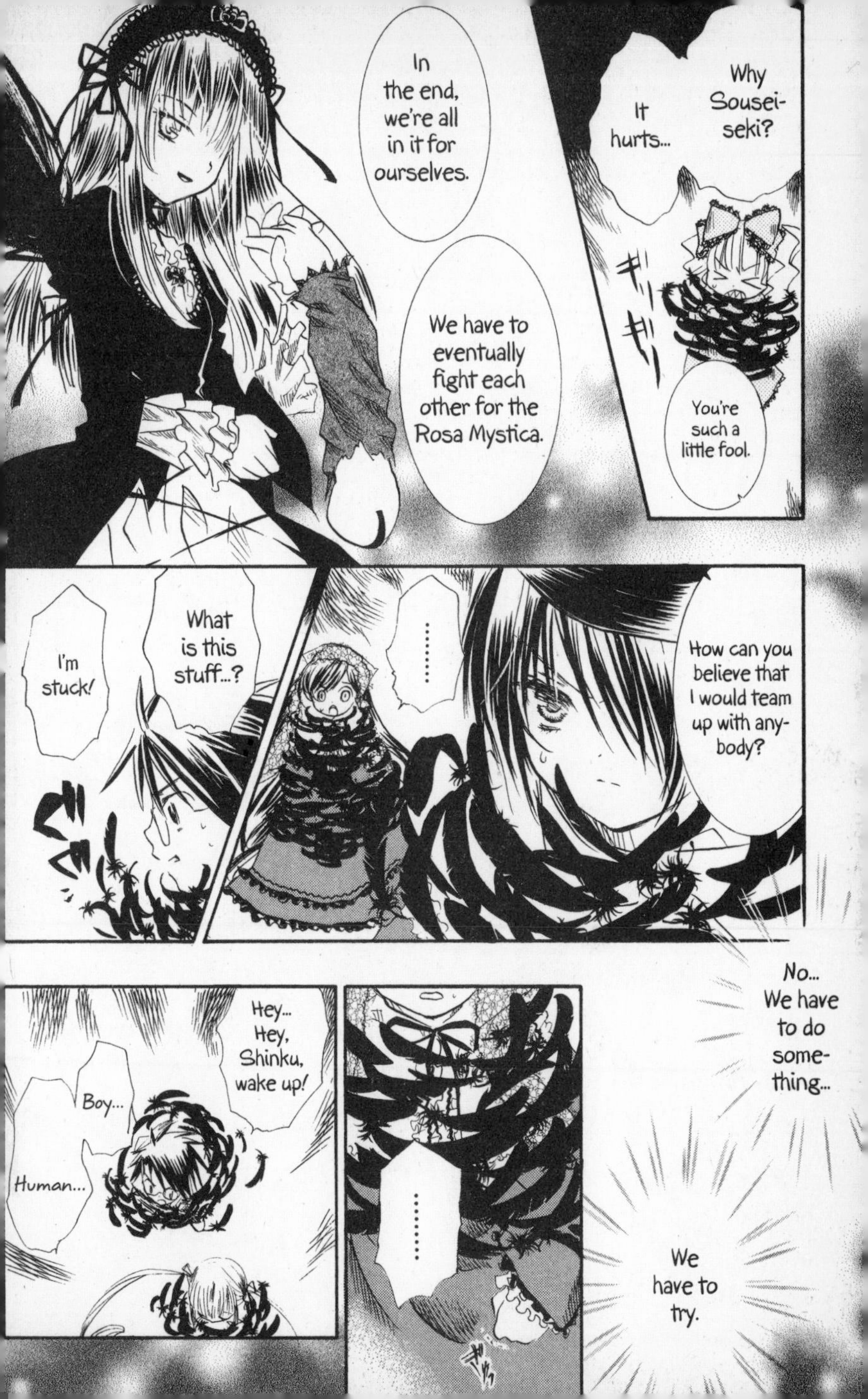
Why Sousei-seki?
It hurts...
You're such a little fool.
In the end, we're all in it for ourselves.
We have to eventually fight each other for the Rosa Mystica.
How can you believe that I would team up with any-body?
......
What is this stuff...?
I'm stuck!
No... We have to do some-thing...
We have to try.
......
Hey... Hey, Shinku, wake up!
Boy...
Human...

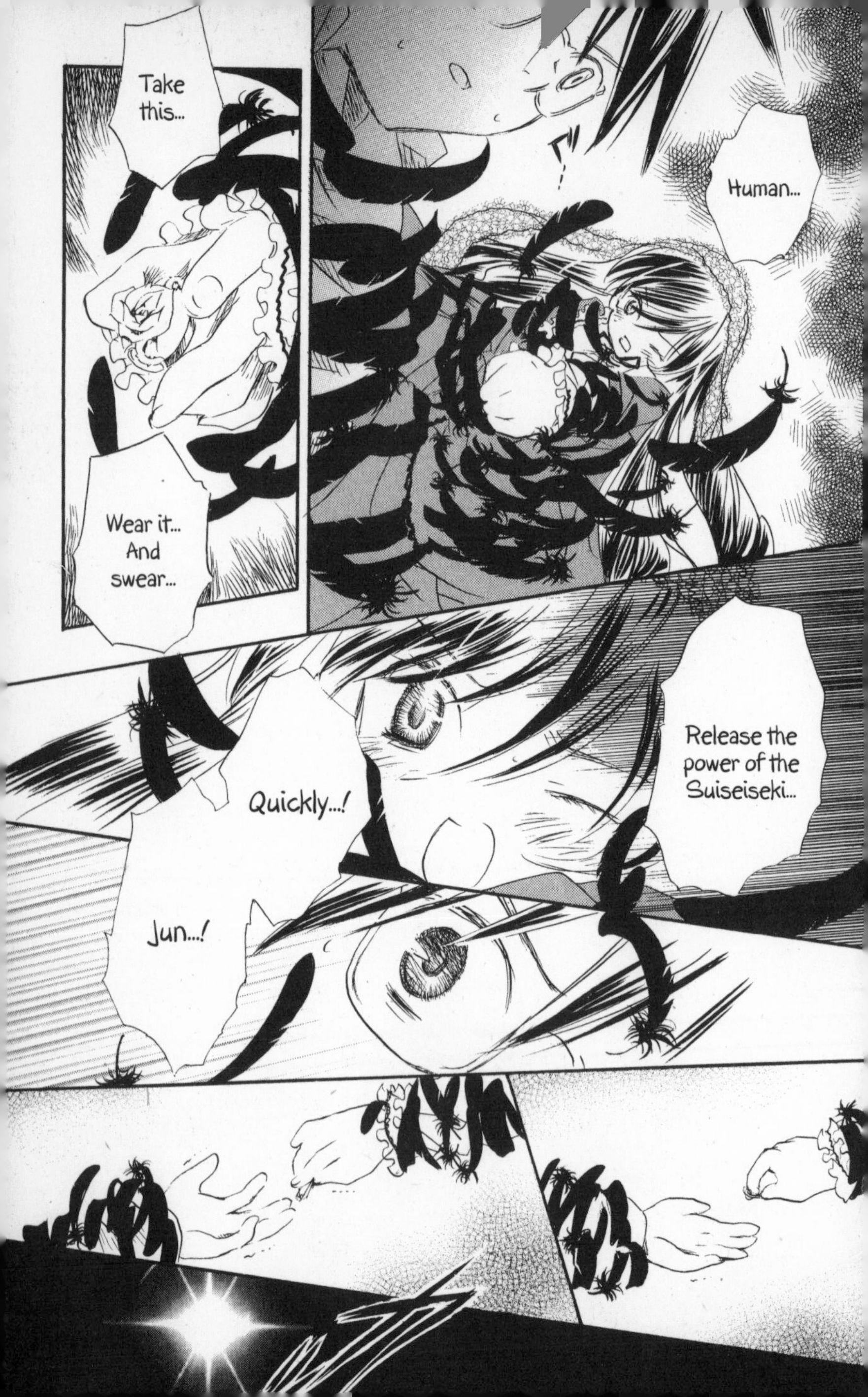
Human...
Take this...
Wear it... And swear...
Release the power of the Suiseiseki...
Quickly...!
Jun...!

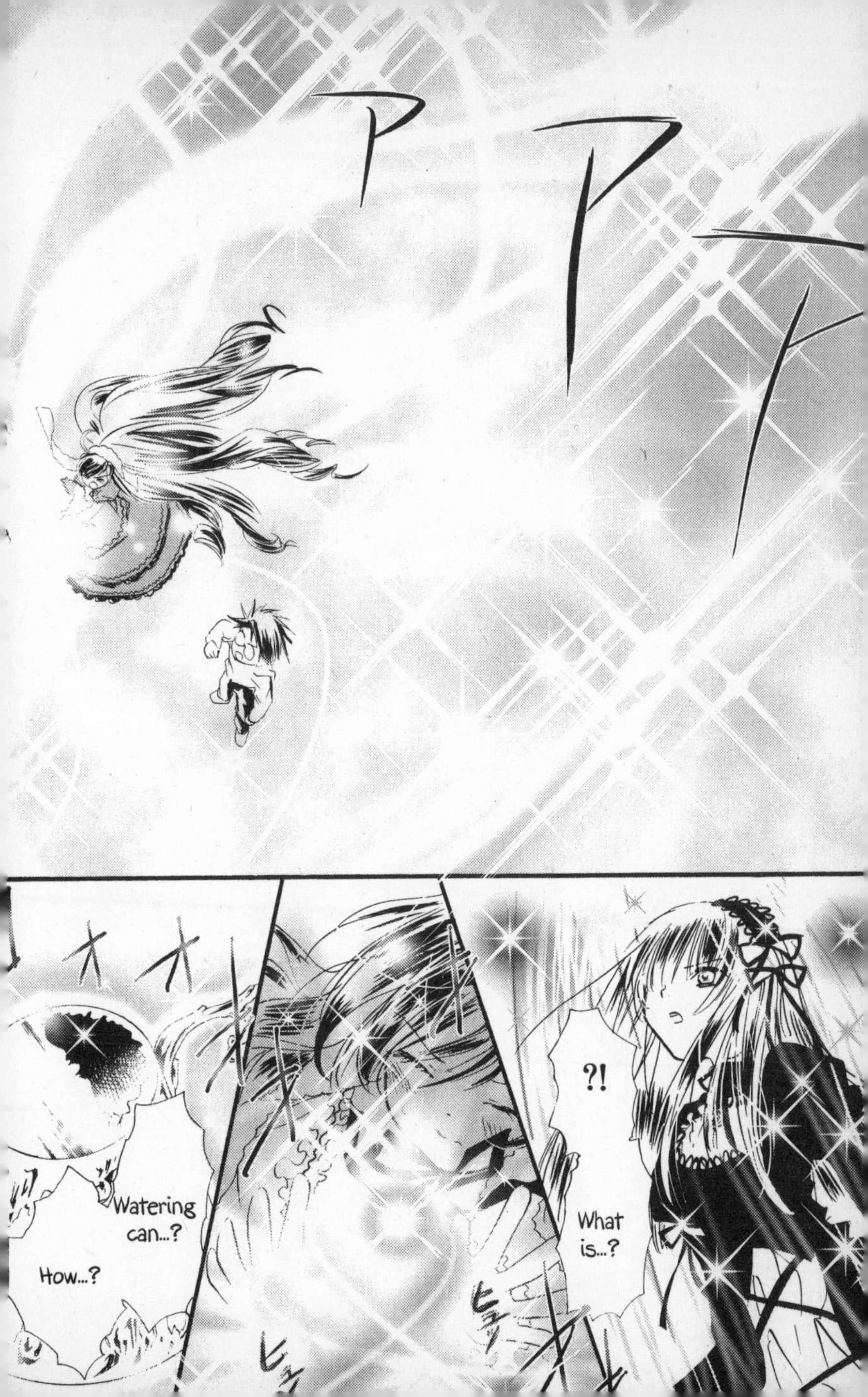

アアア
?!
What is...?
オオ
Watering can...?
How...?

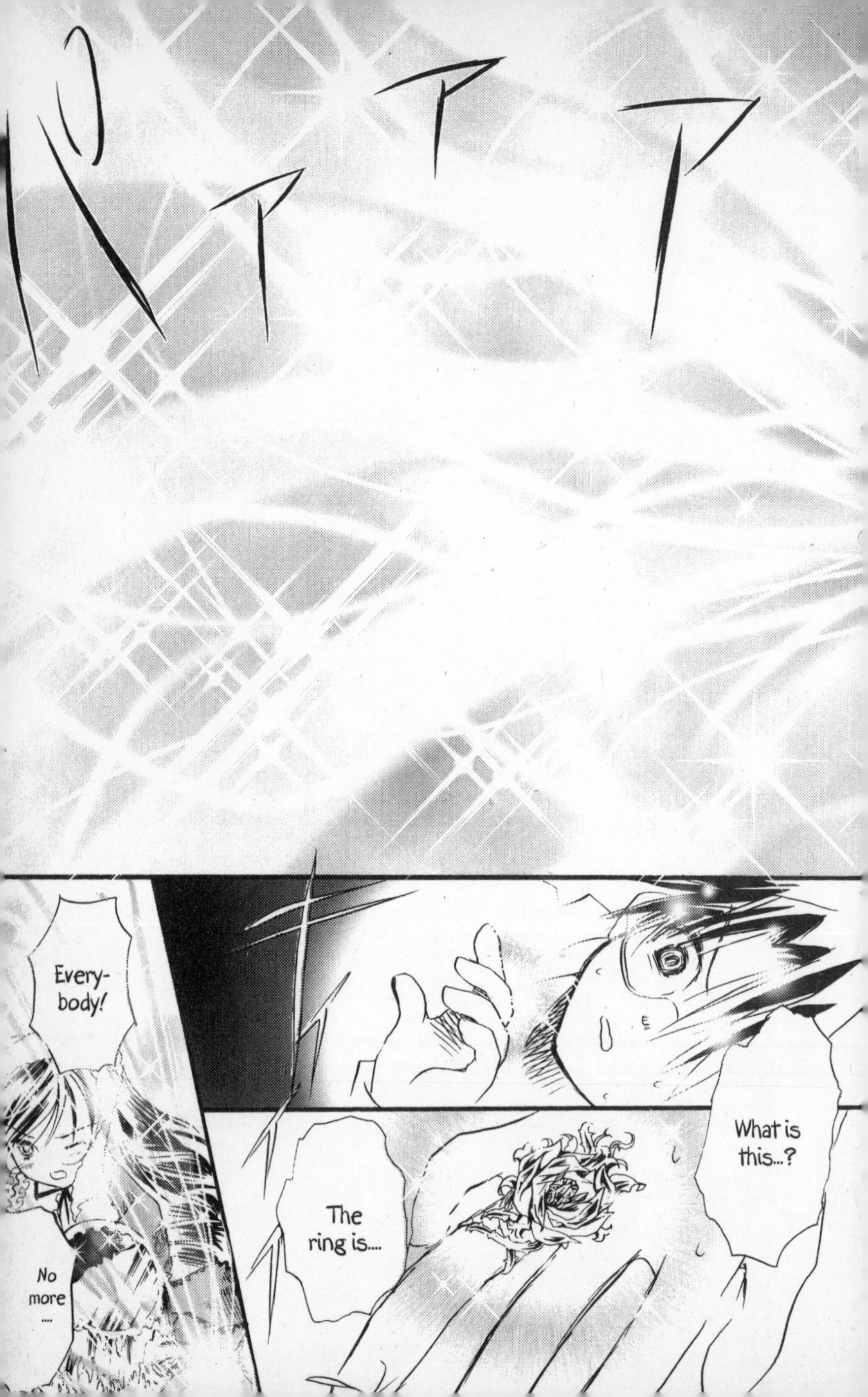
パァァァ
What is this...?
The ring is....
Every-body!
No more ....

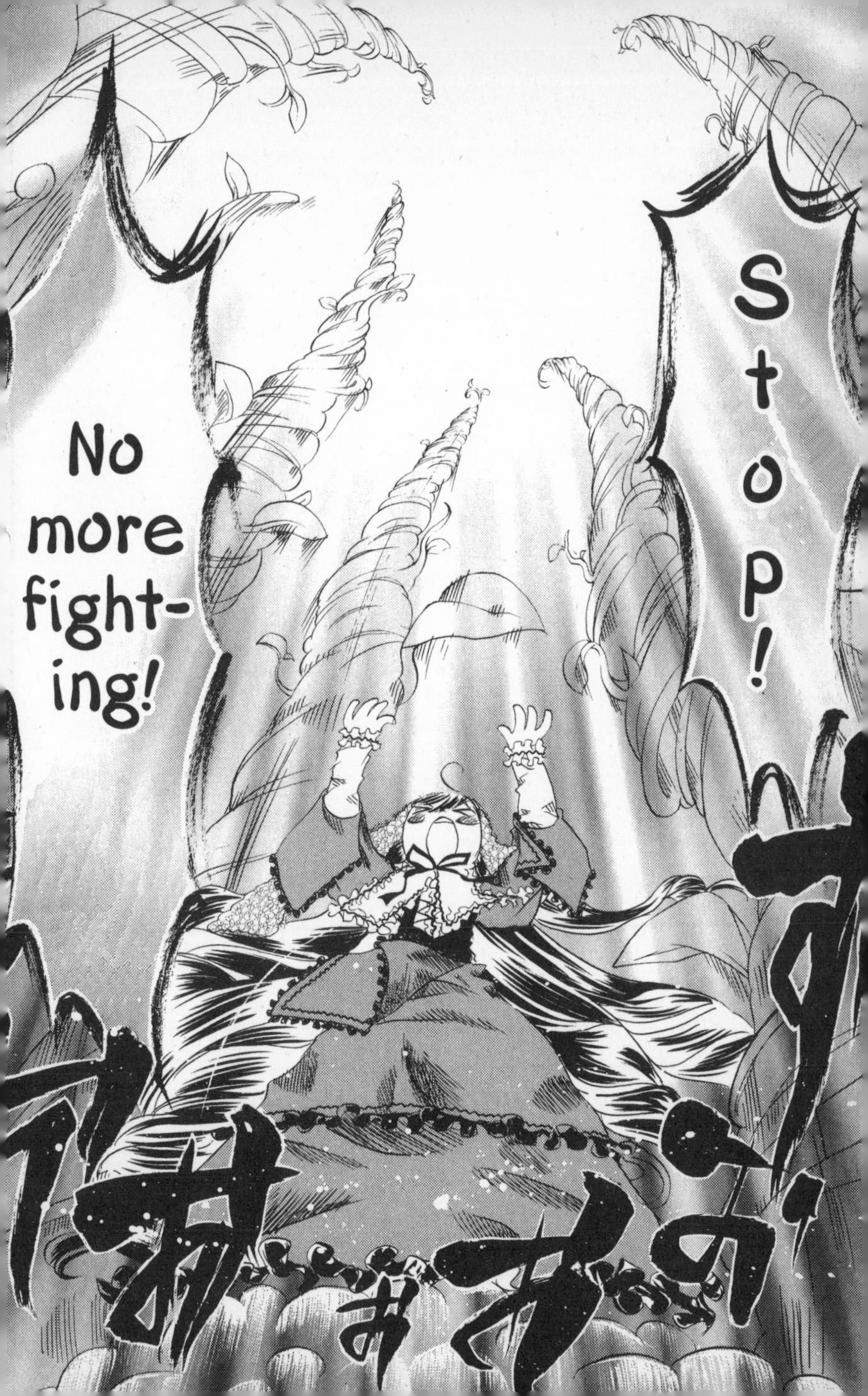
Stop!
No more fight-
ing!

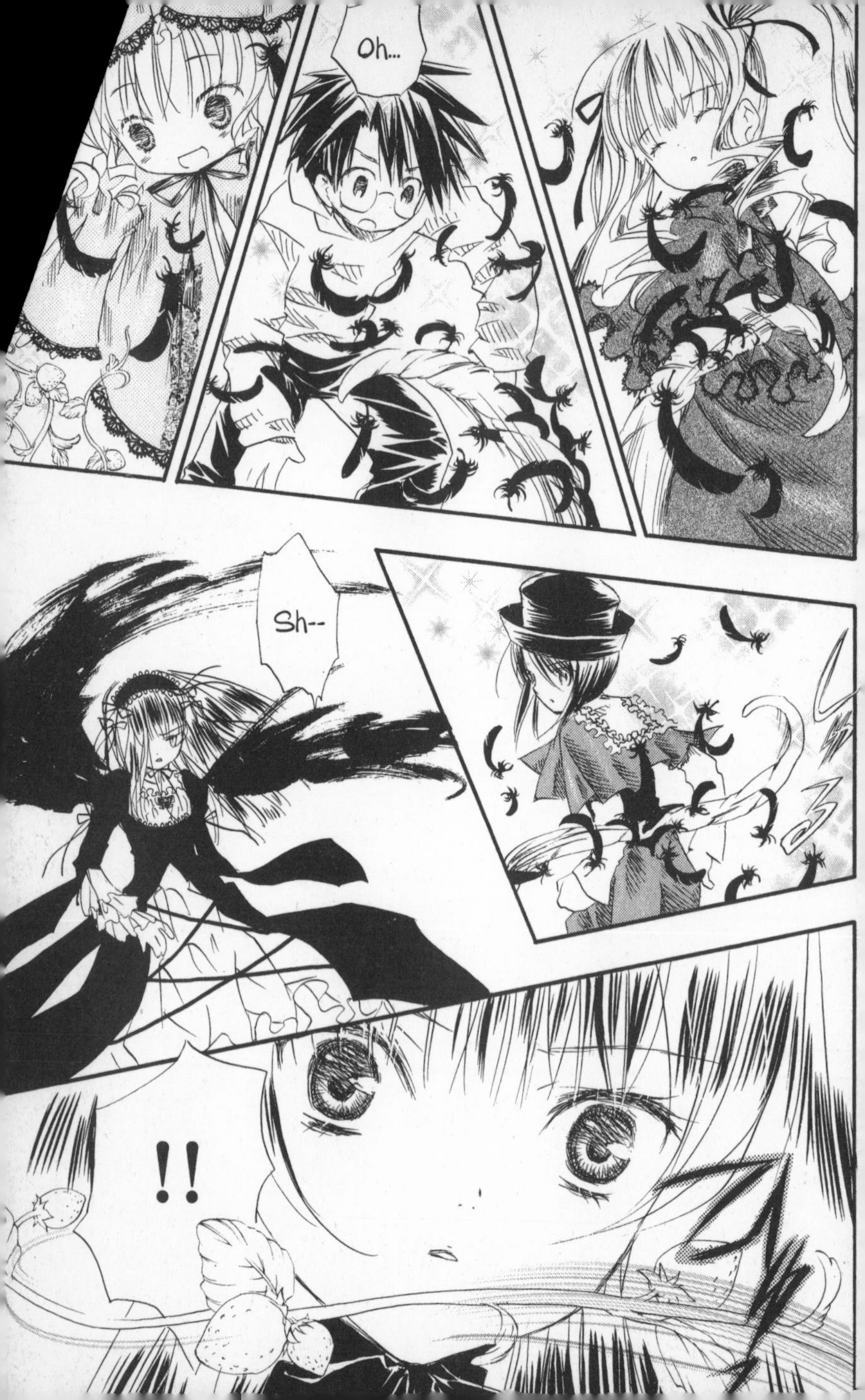
Oh...
Sh--
!!

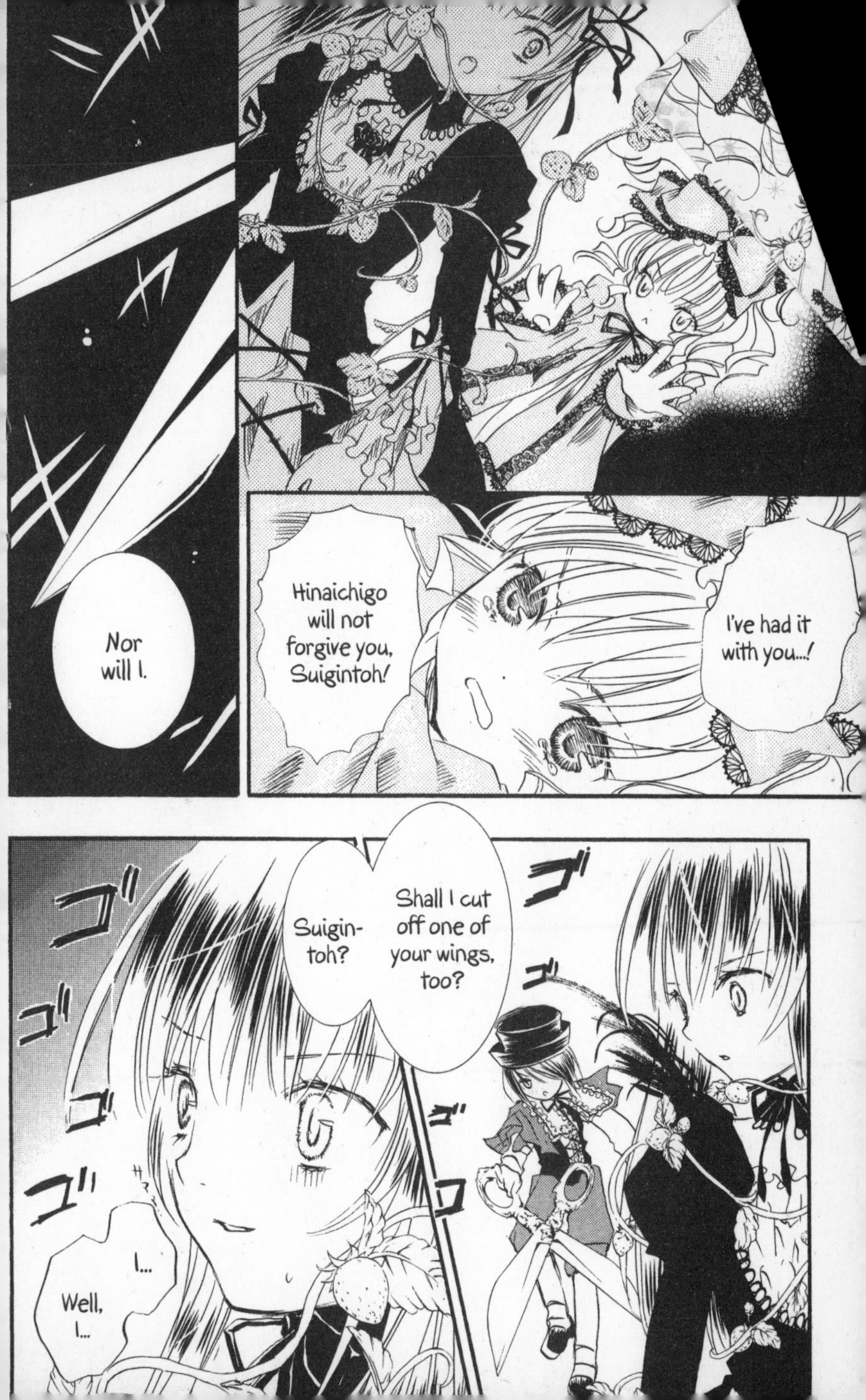

I've had it with you...!
Hinaichigo will not forgive you, Suigintoh!
Nor will I.
Shall I cut off one of your wings, too?
Suigin-toh?
I...
Well, I...

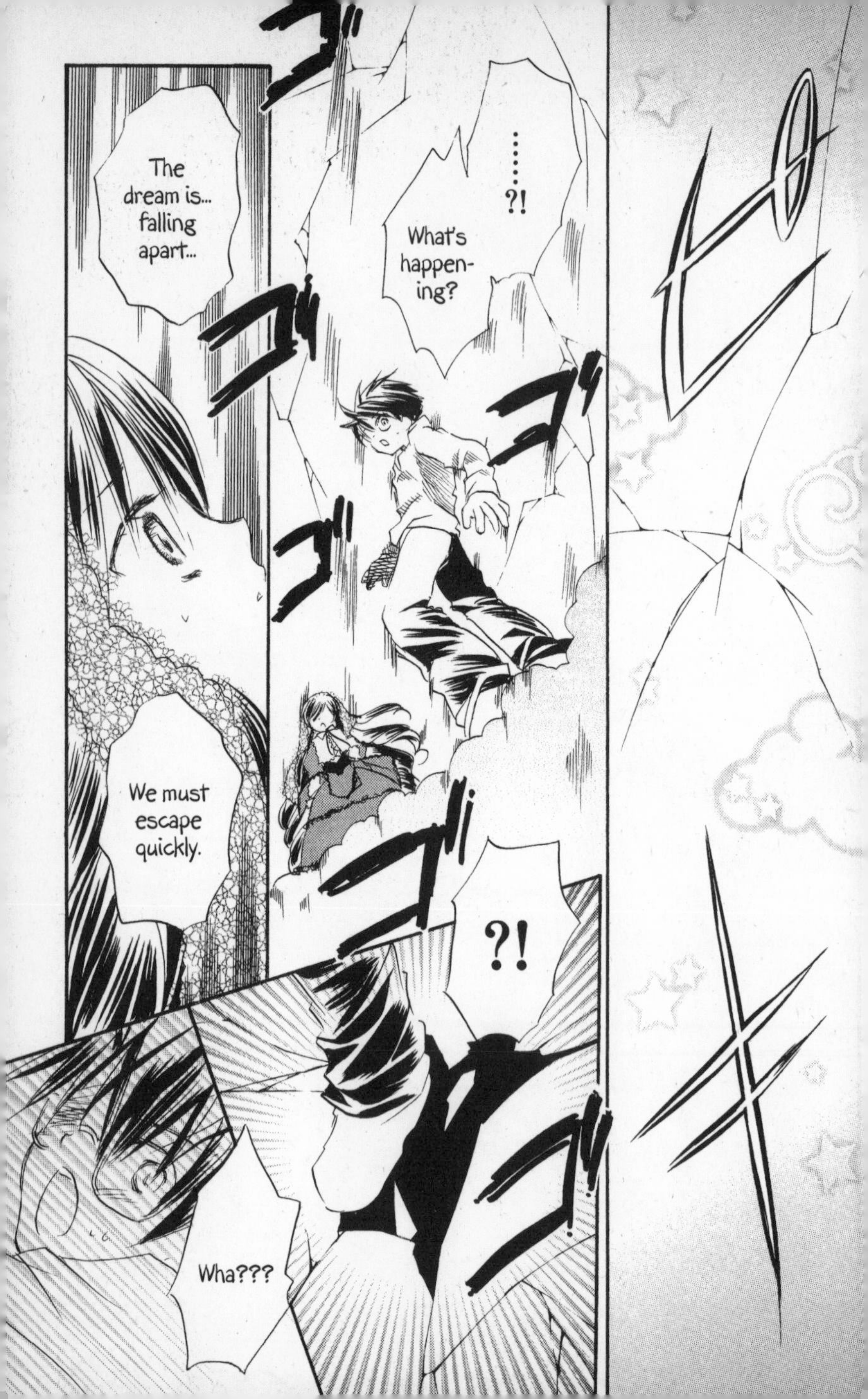

......?!
What's happening?
The dream is... falling apart...
We must escape quickly.
?!
Wha???

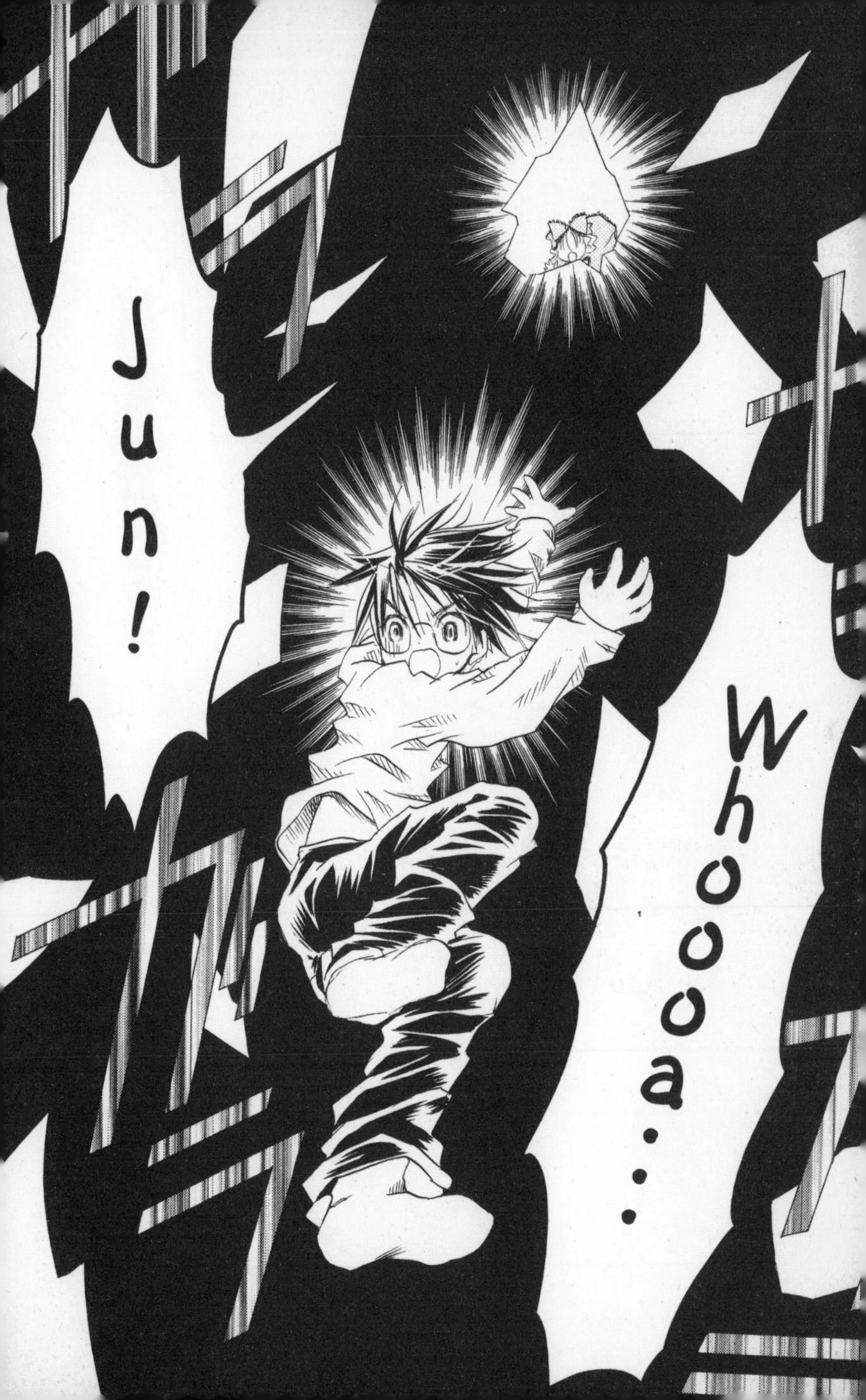
Jun!
Whoooa...

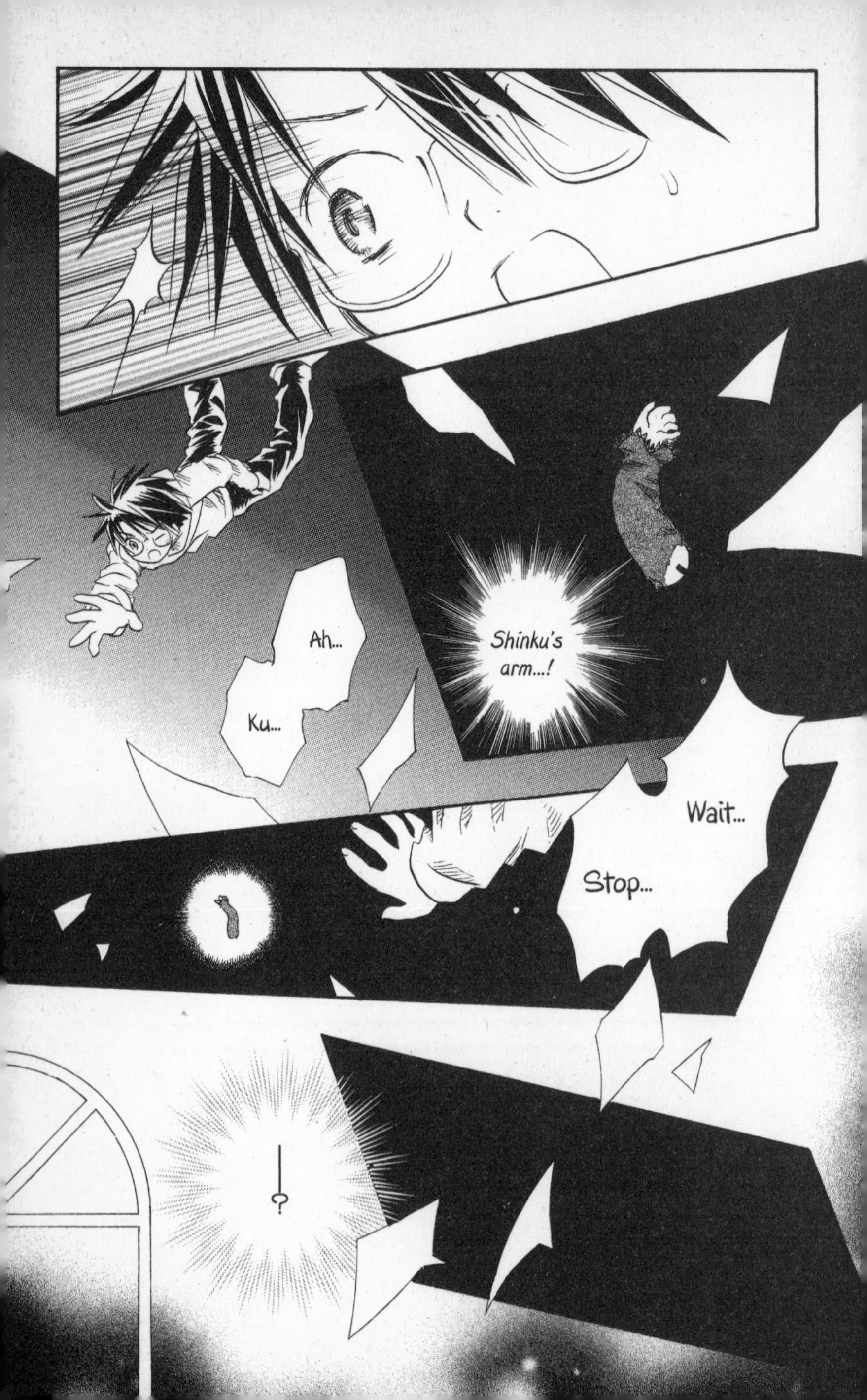
Shinku's arm...!
Ah...
Ku...
Wait...
Stop...
!?

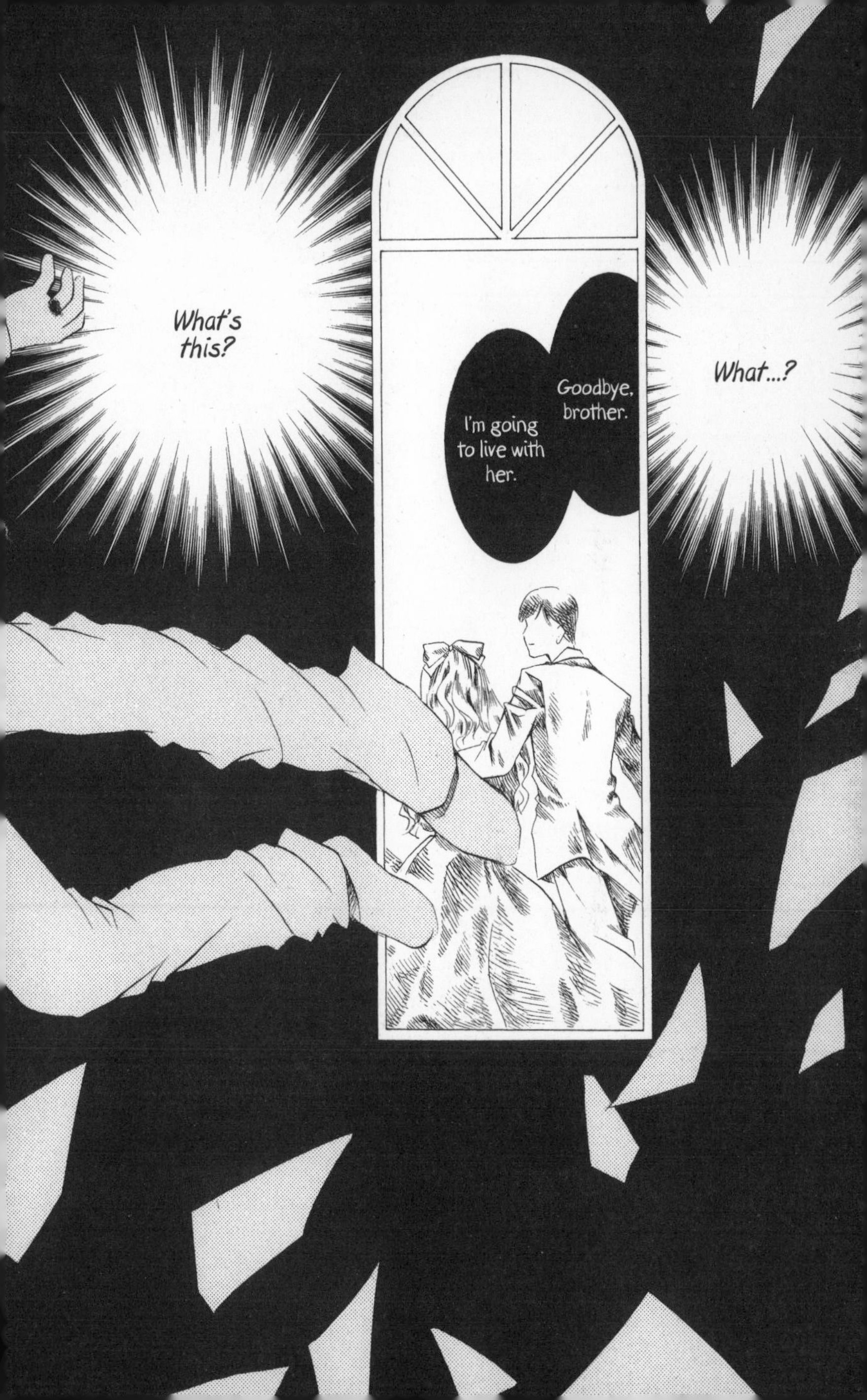
What...?
Goodbye, brother.
I'm going to live with her.
What's this?

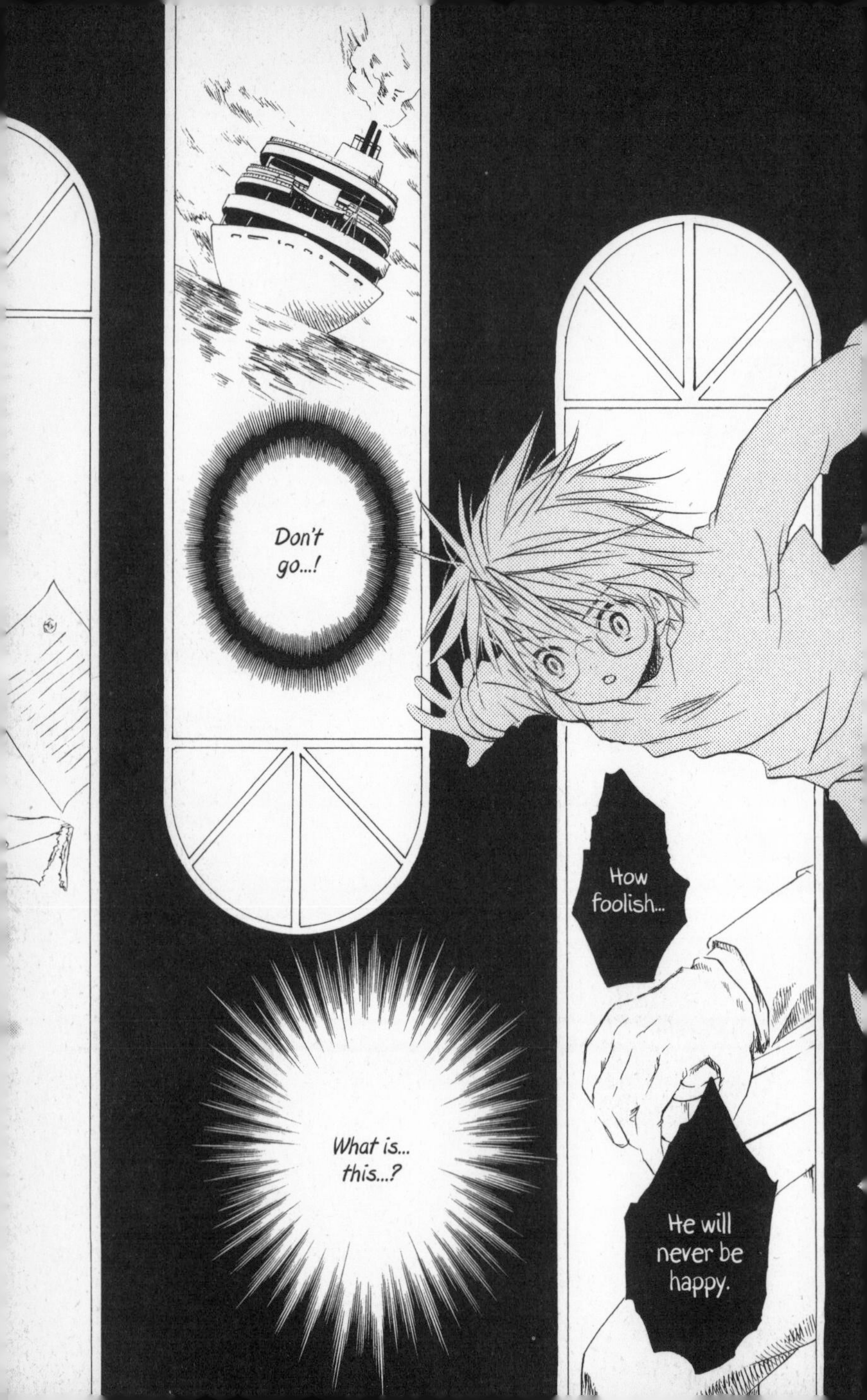
How foolish...
He will never be happy.
Don't go...!
What is... this...?

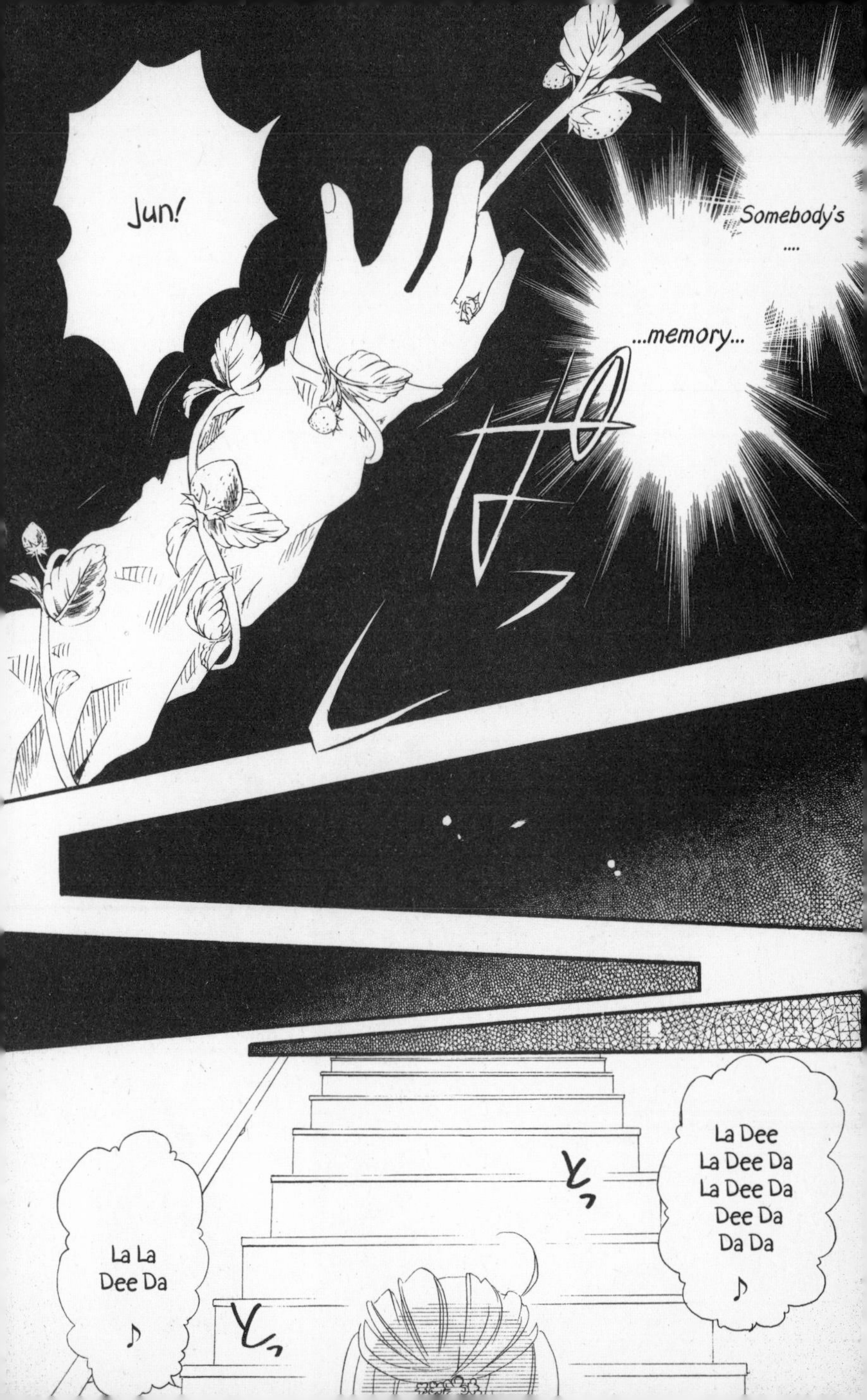

Somebody's ....
...memory...
Jun!
La Dee La Dee Da La Dee Da Dee Da Da Da ♪
La La Dee Da ♪

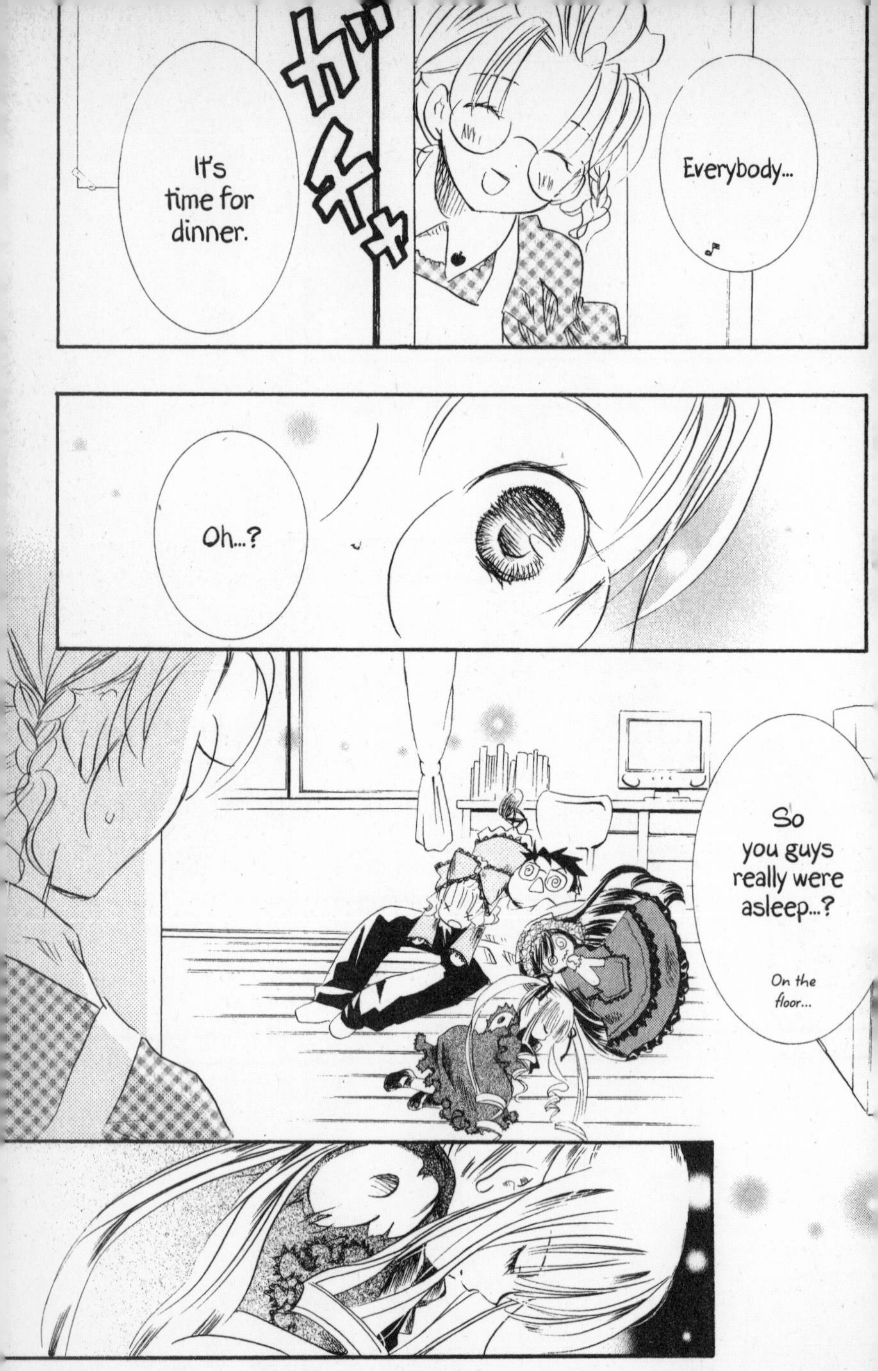
Everybody...
ガチャ
It's time for dinner.
Oh...?
So you guys really were asleep...?
On the floor...

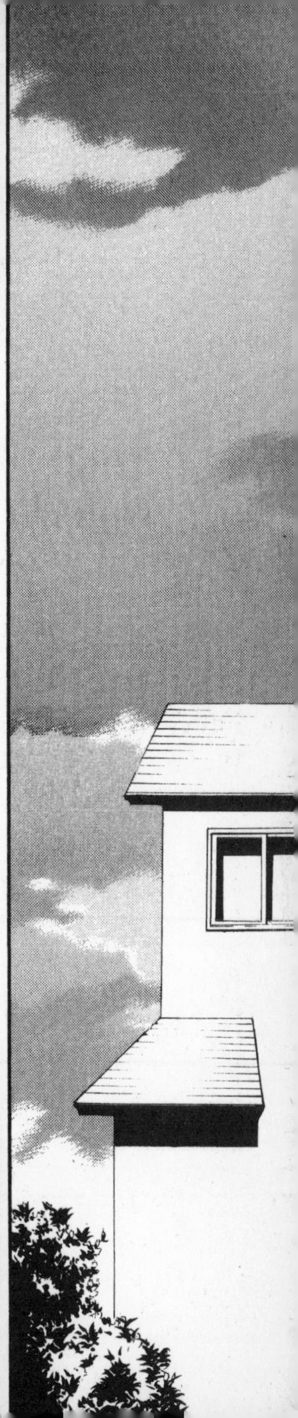

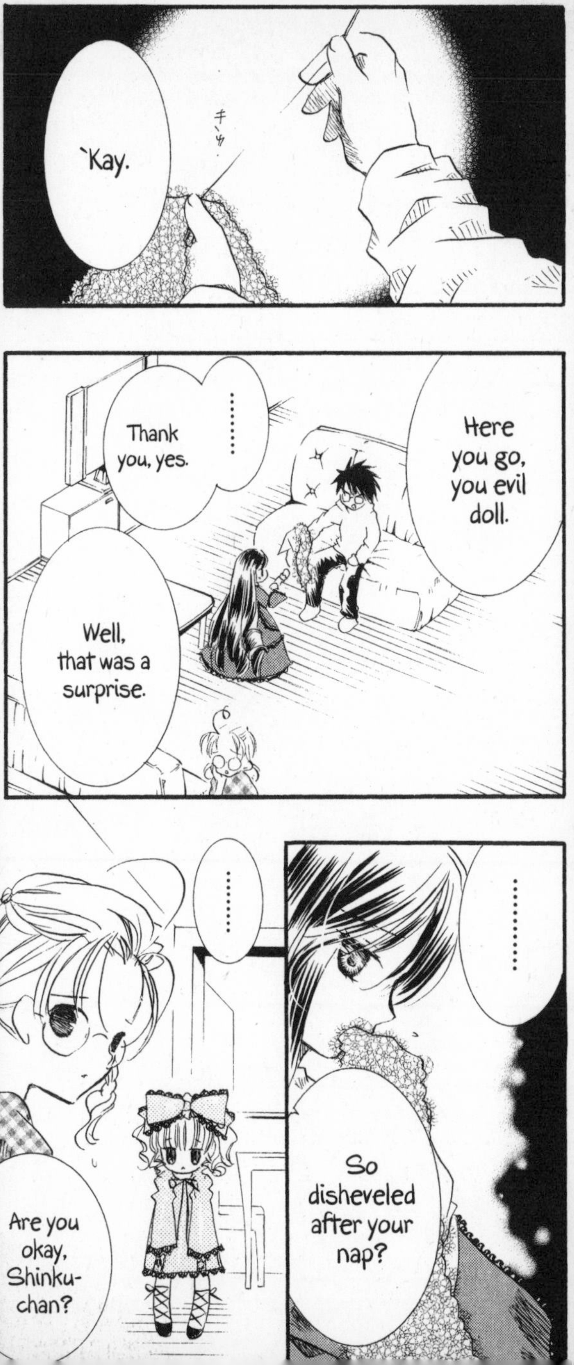
`Kay.
Here you go, you evil doll.
……
Thank you, yes.
Well, that was a surprise.
………
So disheveled after your nap?
………
Are you okay, Shinku-chan?

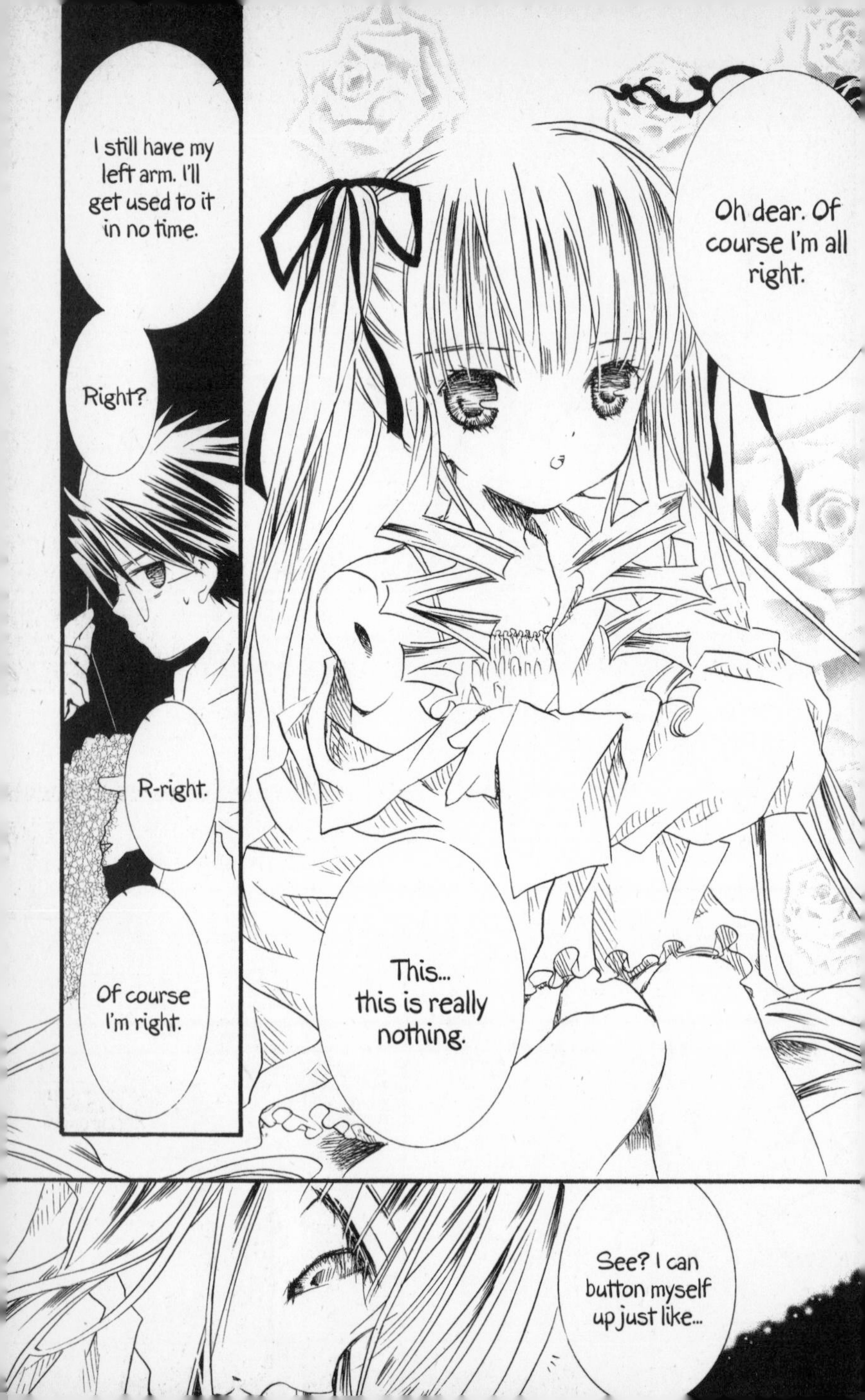
Oh dear. Of course I'm all right.
This... this is really nothing.
I still have my left arm. I'll get used to it in no time.
Right?
R-right.
Of course I'm right.
See? I can button myself up just like...

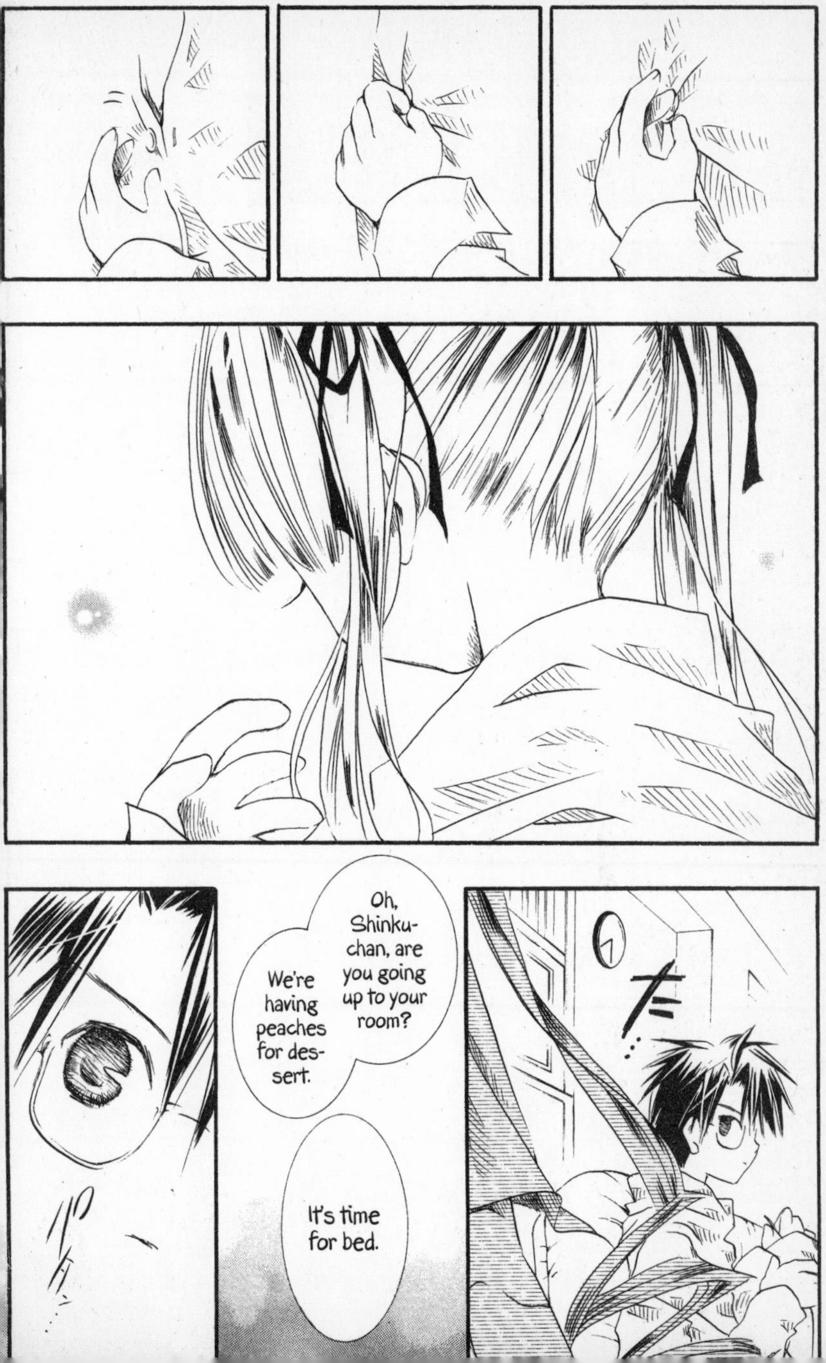
Oh, Shinku-chan, are you going up to your room?
We're having peaches for dessert.
It's time for bed.

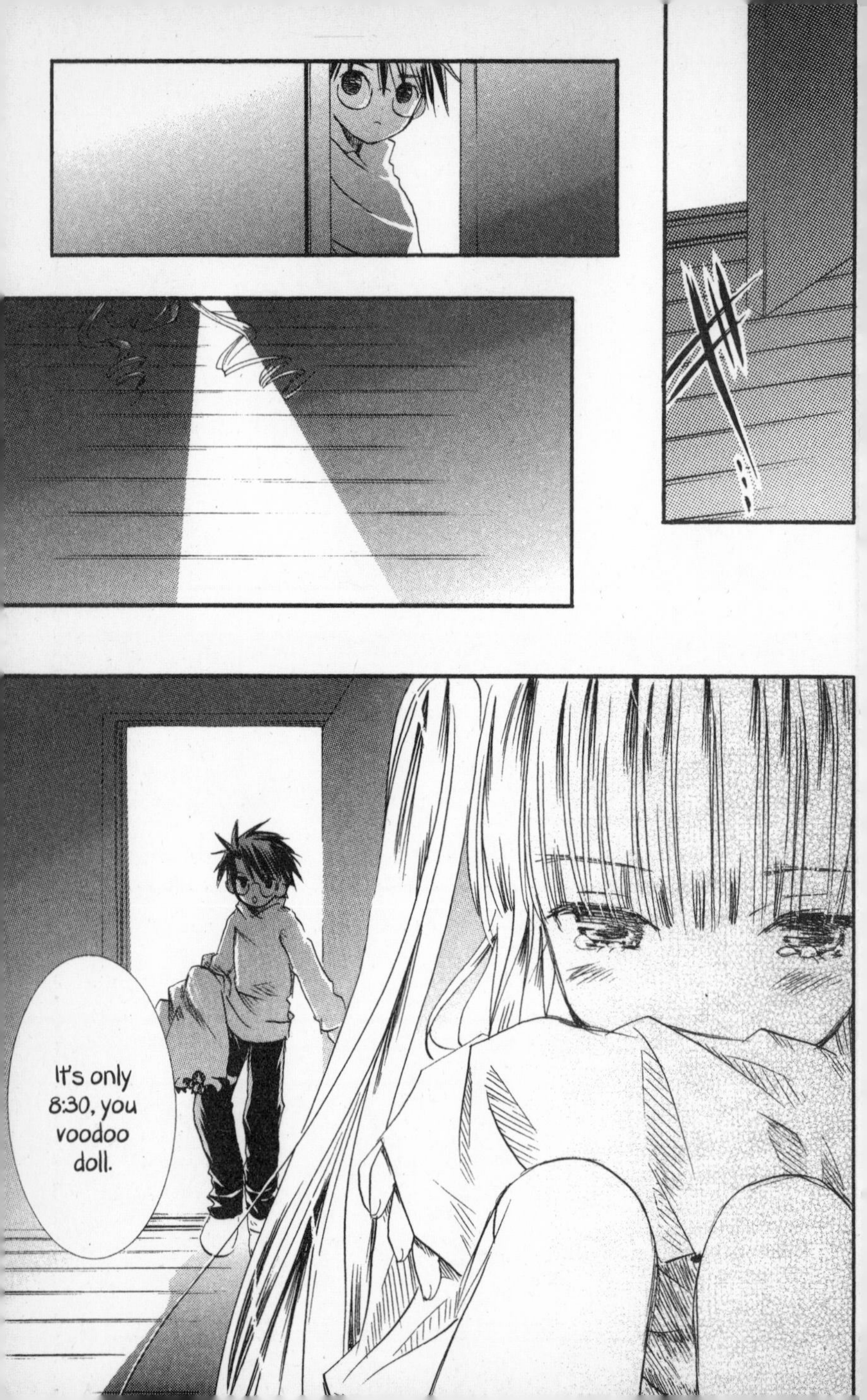
It's only 8:30, you voodoo doll.

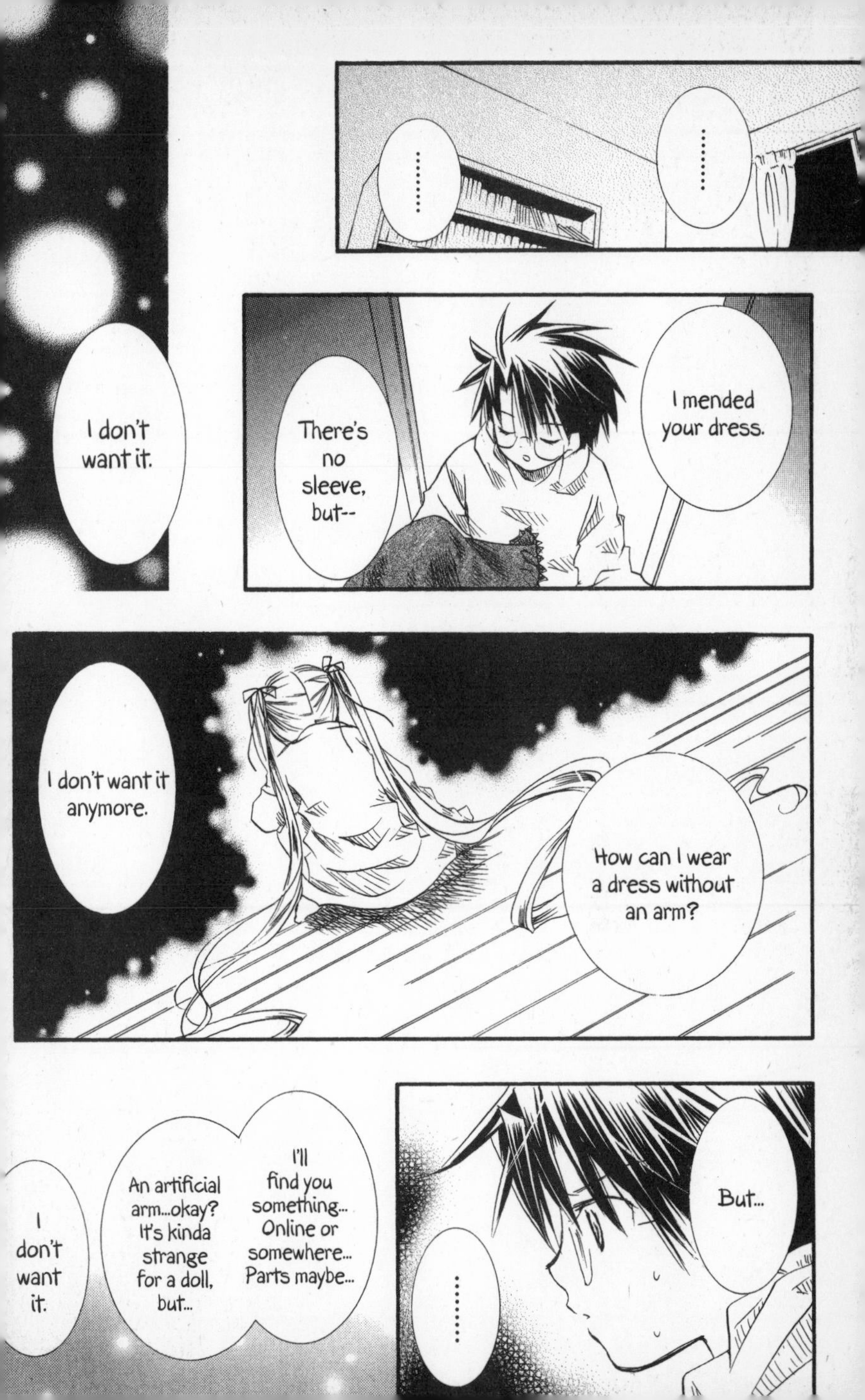
……
……
I mended your dress.
There's no sleeve, but--
I don't want it.
How can I wear a dress without an arm?
I don't want it anymore.
But...
……
I'll find you something... Online or somewhere... Parts maybe...
An artificial arm...okay? It's kinda strange for a doll, but...
I don't want it.

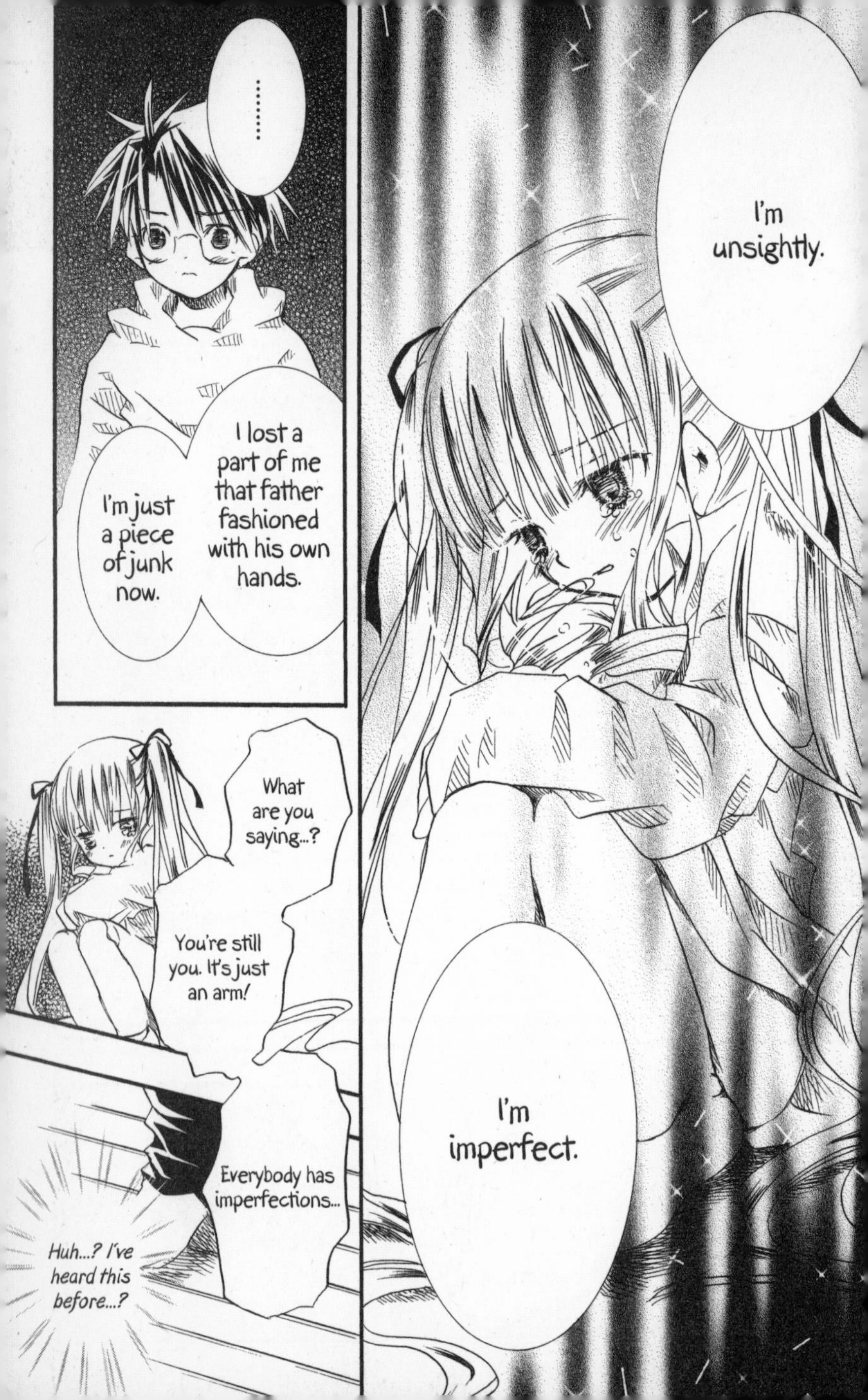
I'm unsightly.
I'm imperfect.
....
I lost a part of me that father fashioned with his own hands.
I'm just a piece of junk now.
What are you saying...?
You're still you. It's just an arm!
Everybody has imperfections...
Huh...? I've heard this before...?

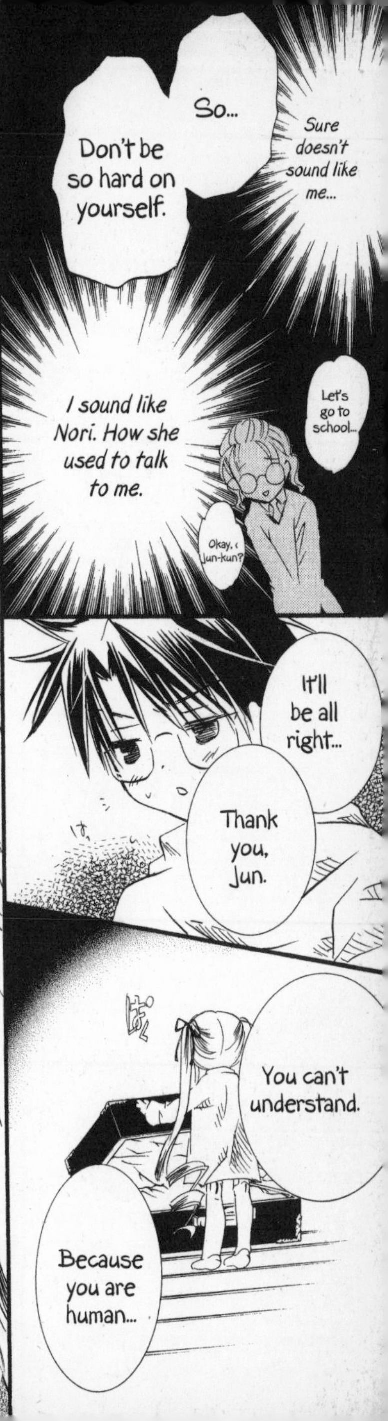
So...
Don't be so hard on yourself.
Sure doesn't sound like me...
I sound like Nori. How she used to talk to me.
Let's go to school...
Okay, Jun-kun?
It'll be all right...
Thank you, Jun.
You can't understand.
Because you are human...
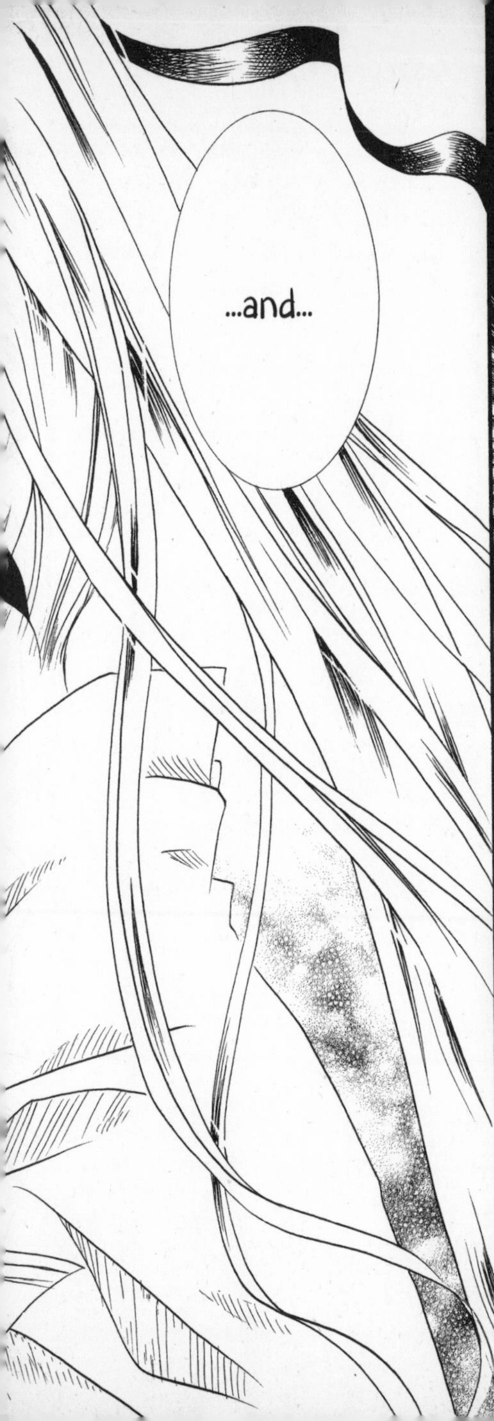
...and...

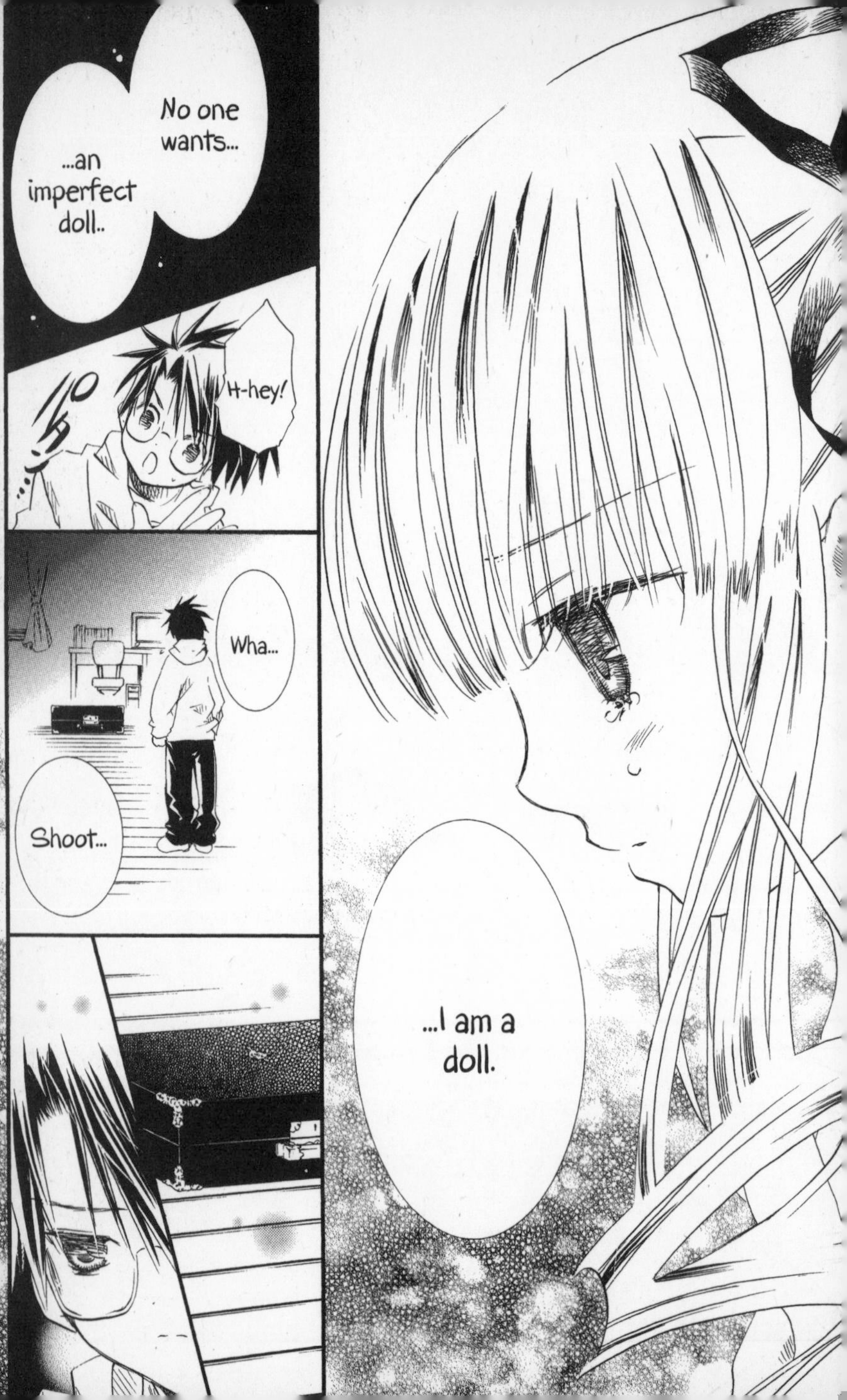
...I am a doll.
No one wants...
...an imperfect doll..
H-hey!
Wha...
Shoot...

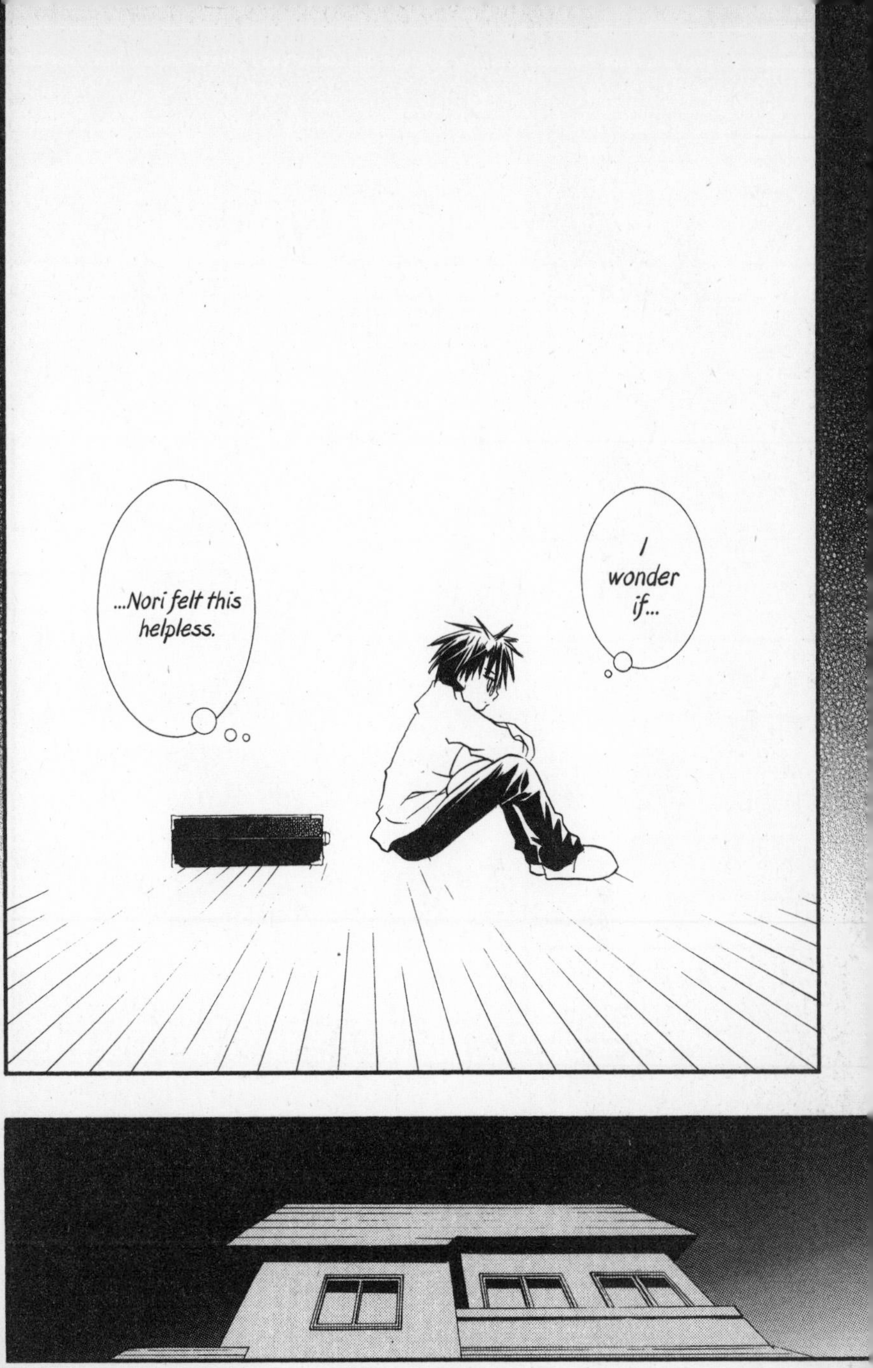
I wonder if...
...Nori felt this helpless.

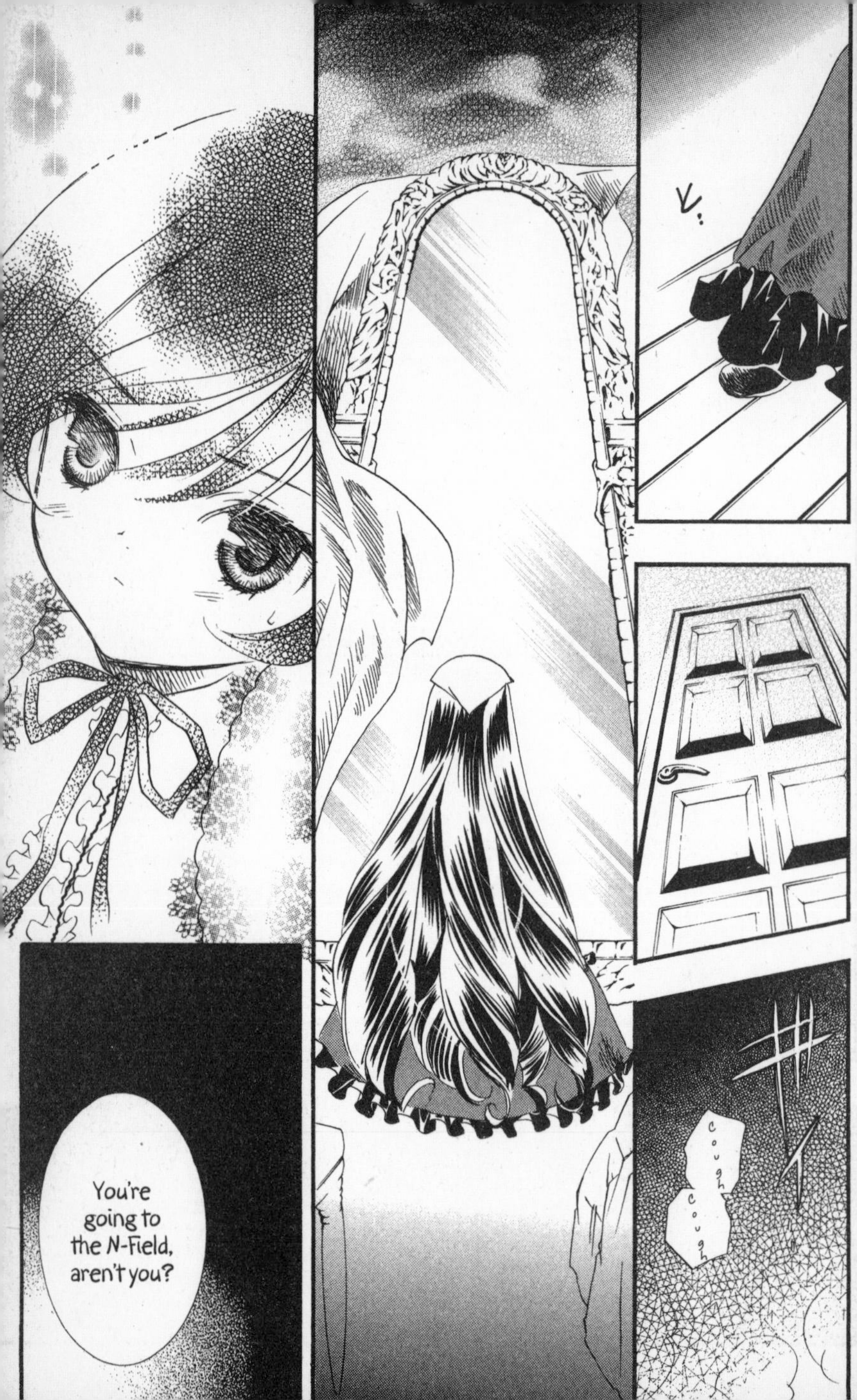
Cough
Cough
You're going to the N-Field, aren't you?

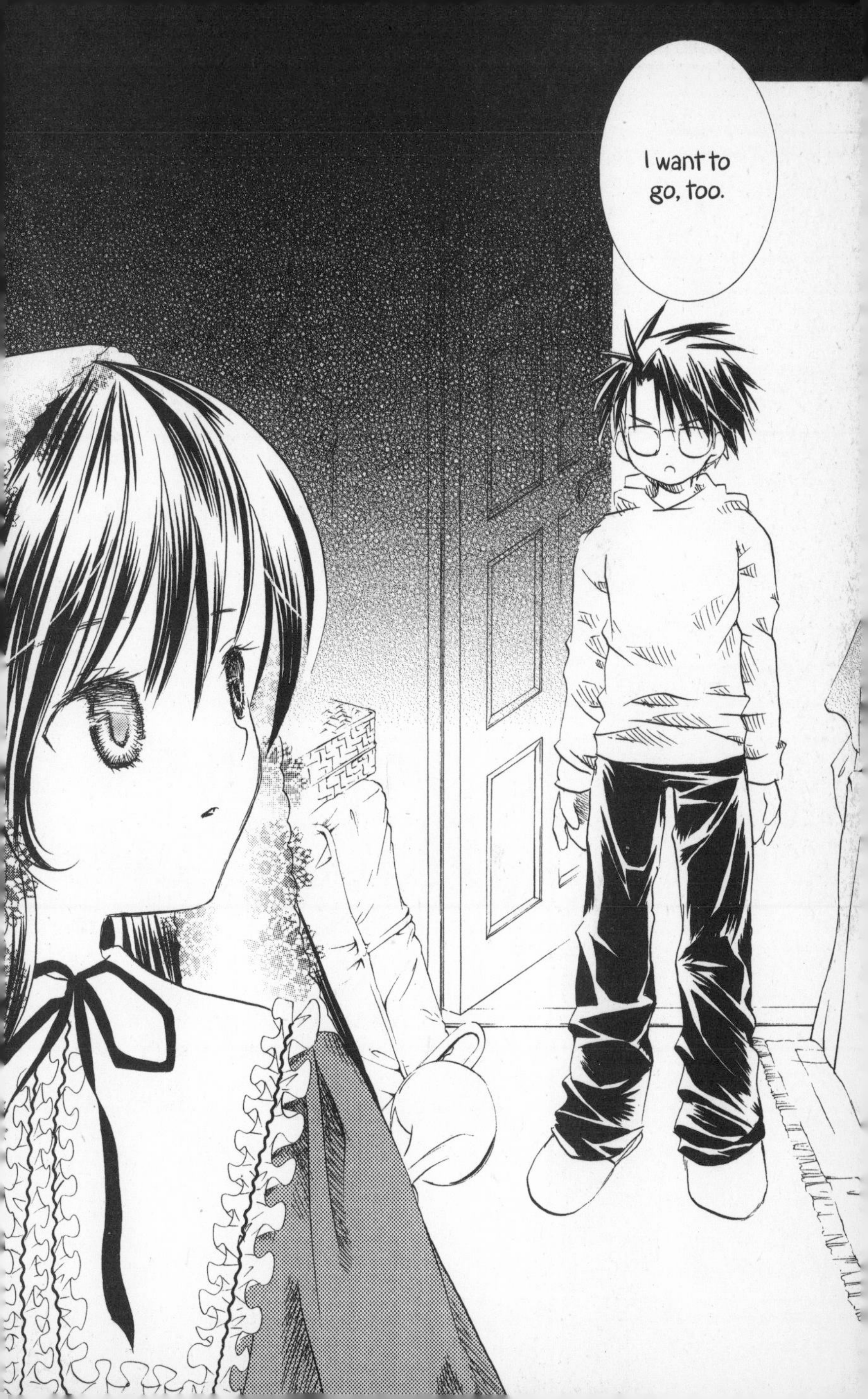
I want to go, too.

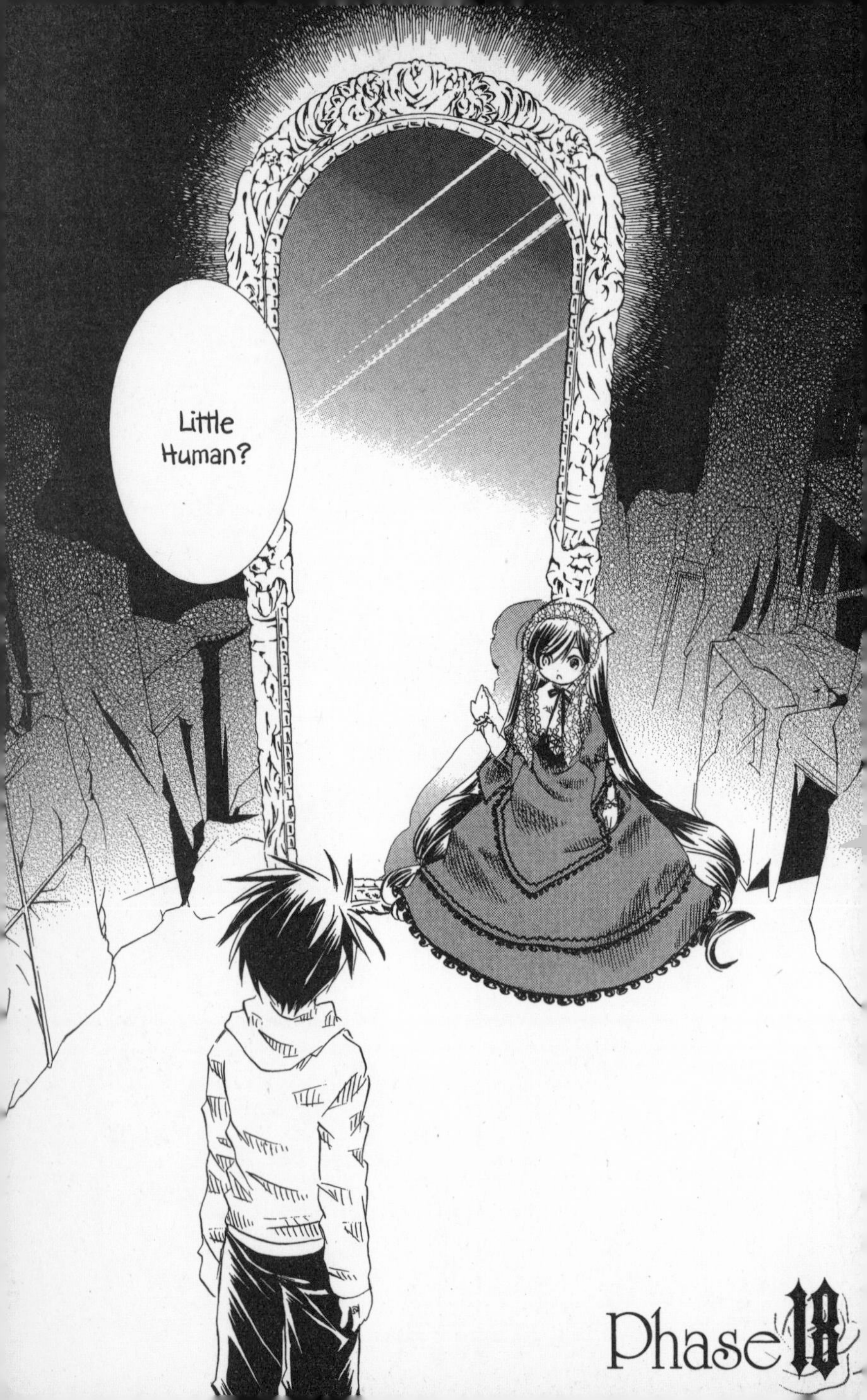
Little Human?
Phase 18

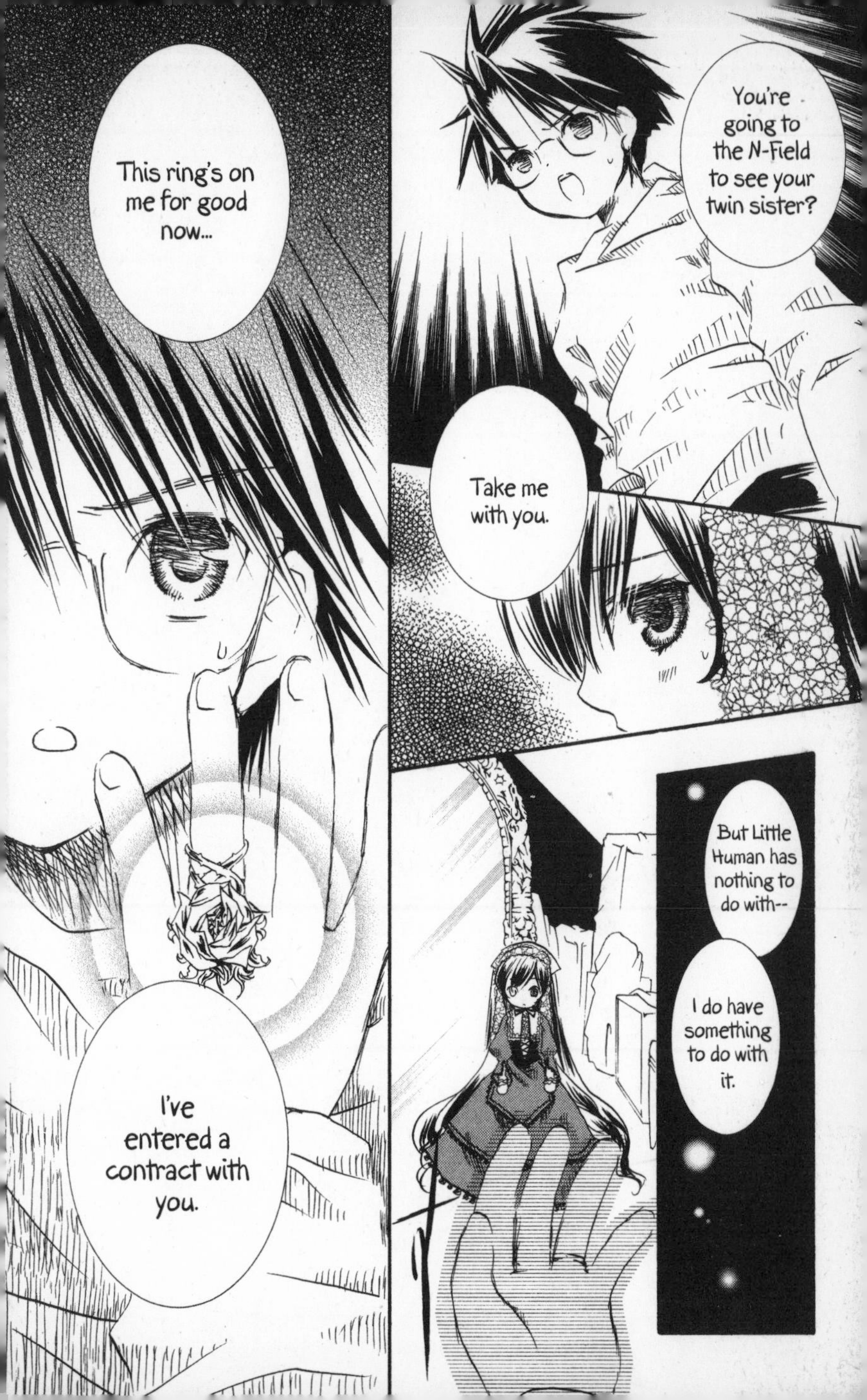
You're going to the N-Field to see your twin sister?
Take me with you.
But Little Human has nothing to do with--
I do have something to do with it.
This ring's on me for good now...
I've entered a contract with you.

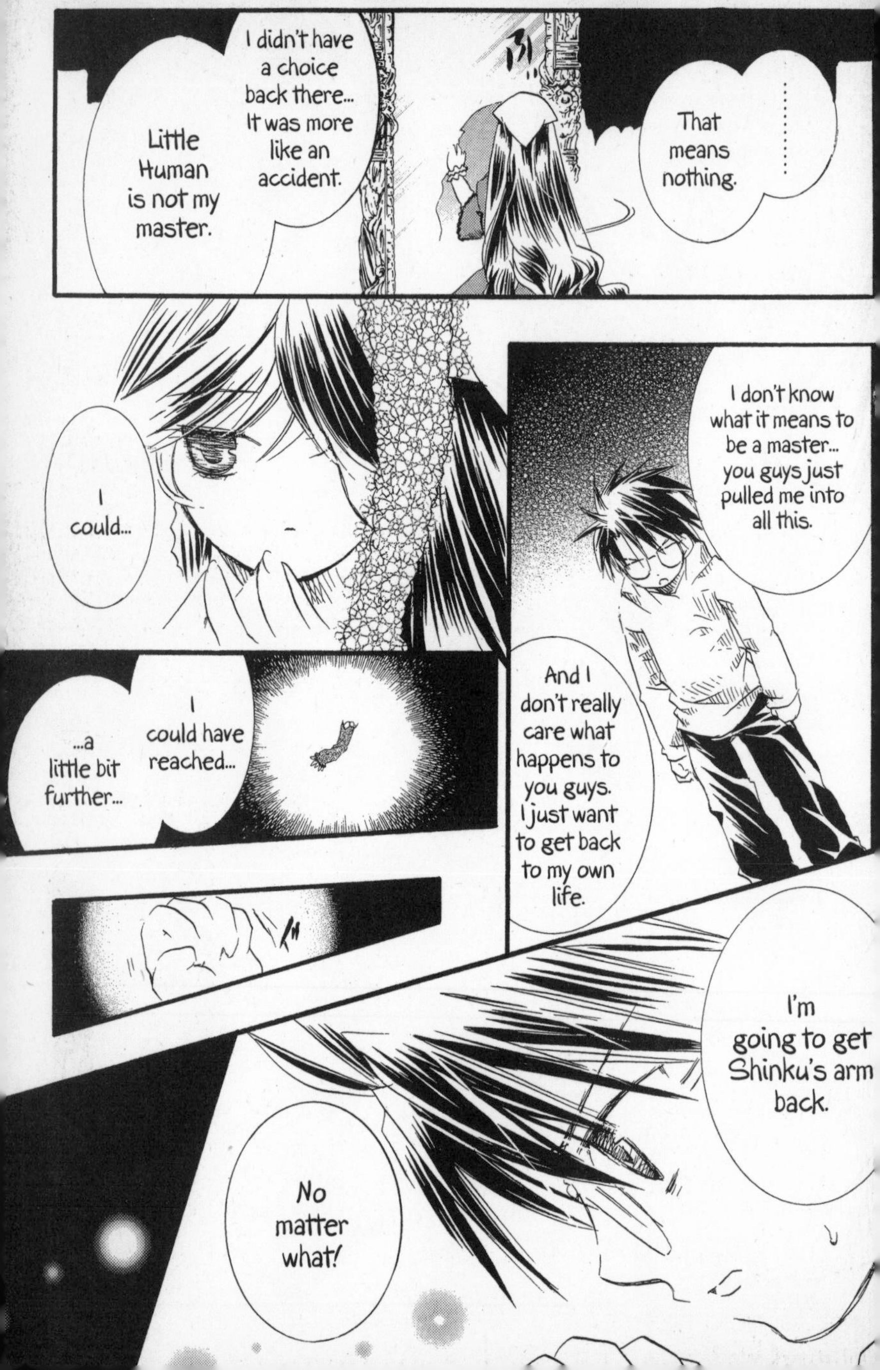
......
That means nothing.
I didn't have a choice back there... It was more like an accident.
Little Human is not my master.
I don't know what it means to be a master... you guys just pulled me into all this.
And I don't really care what happens to you guys. I just want to get back to my own life.
I could...
I could have reached...
...a little bit further...
I'm going to get Shinku's arm back.
No matter what!

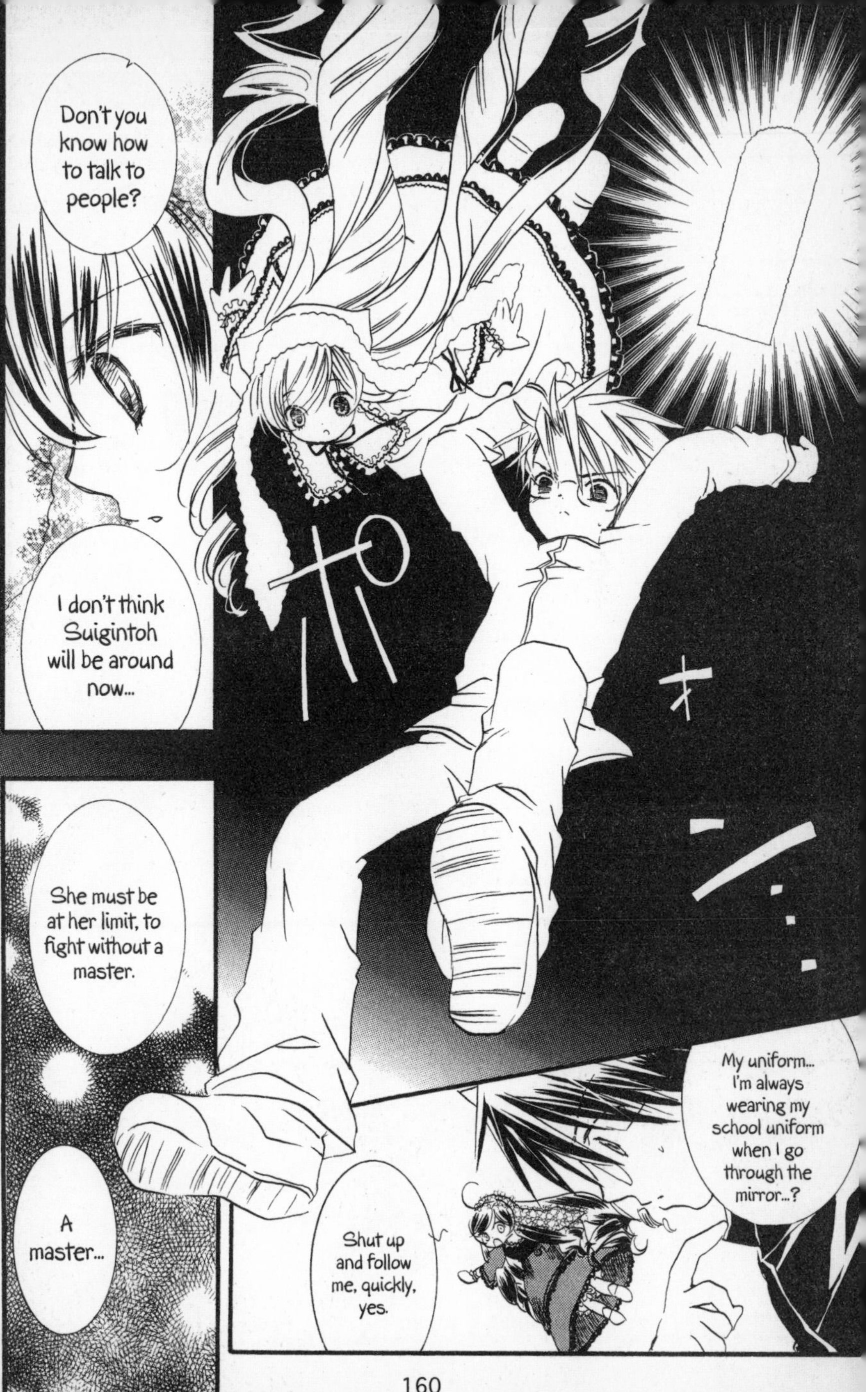
My uniform... I'm always wearing my school uniform when I go through the mirror...?
Shut up and follow me, quickly, yes.
Don't you know how to talk to people?
I don't think Suigintoh will be around now...
She must be at her limit, to fight without a master.
A master...

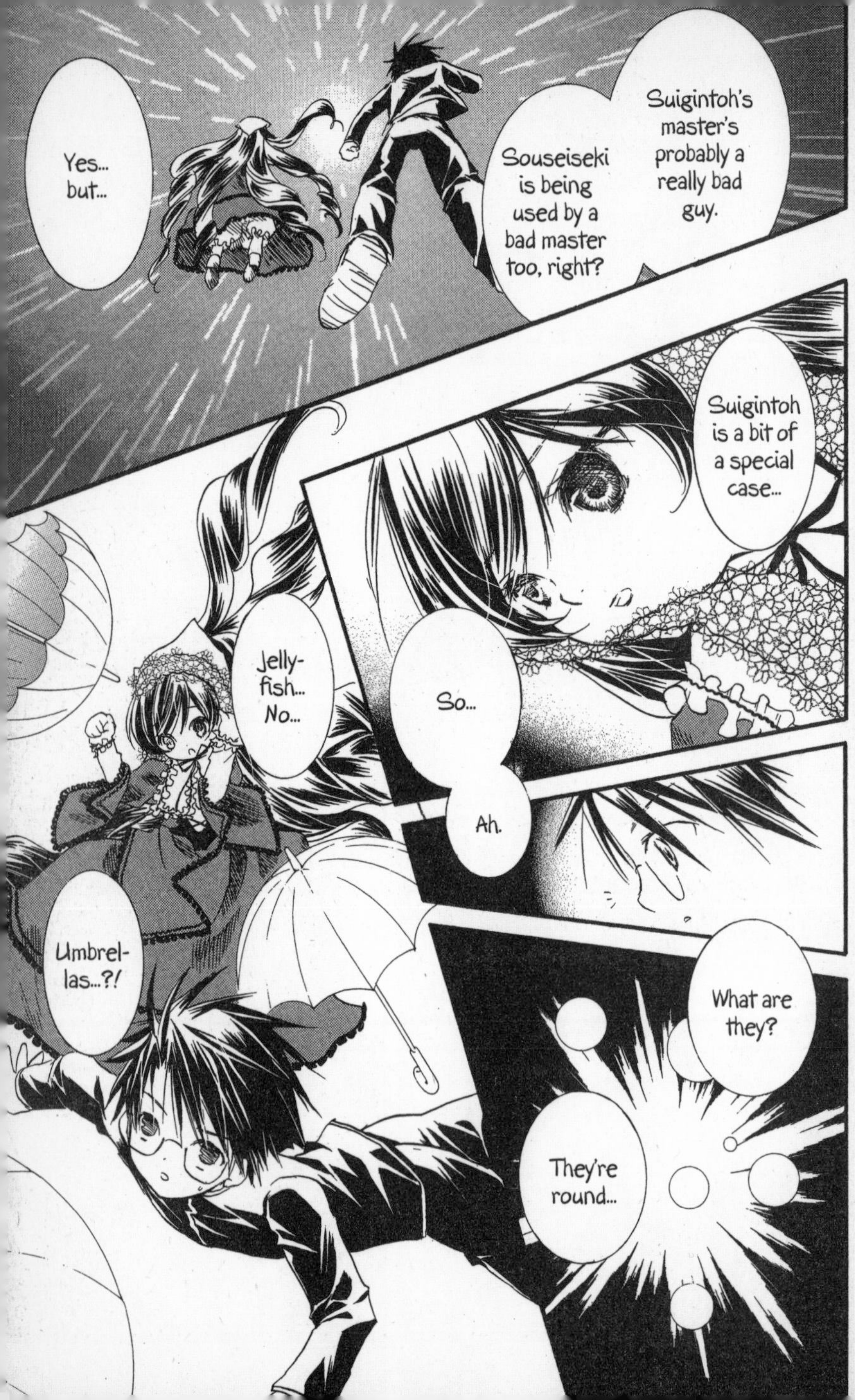
Suigintoh's master's probably a really bad guy.
Souseiseki is being used by a bad master too, right?
Yes... but...
Suigintoh is a bit of a special case...
So...
Ah.
What are they?
They're round...
Jelly-fish... No...
Umbrel-las...?!

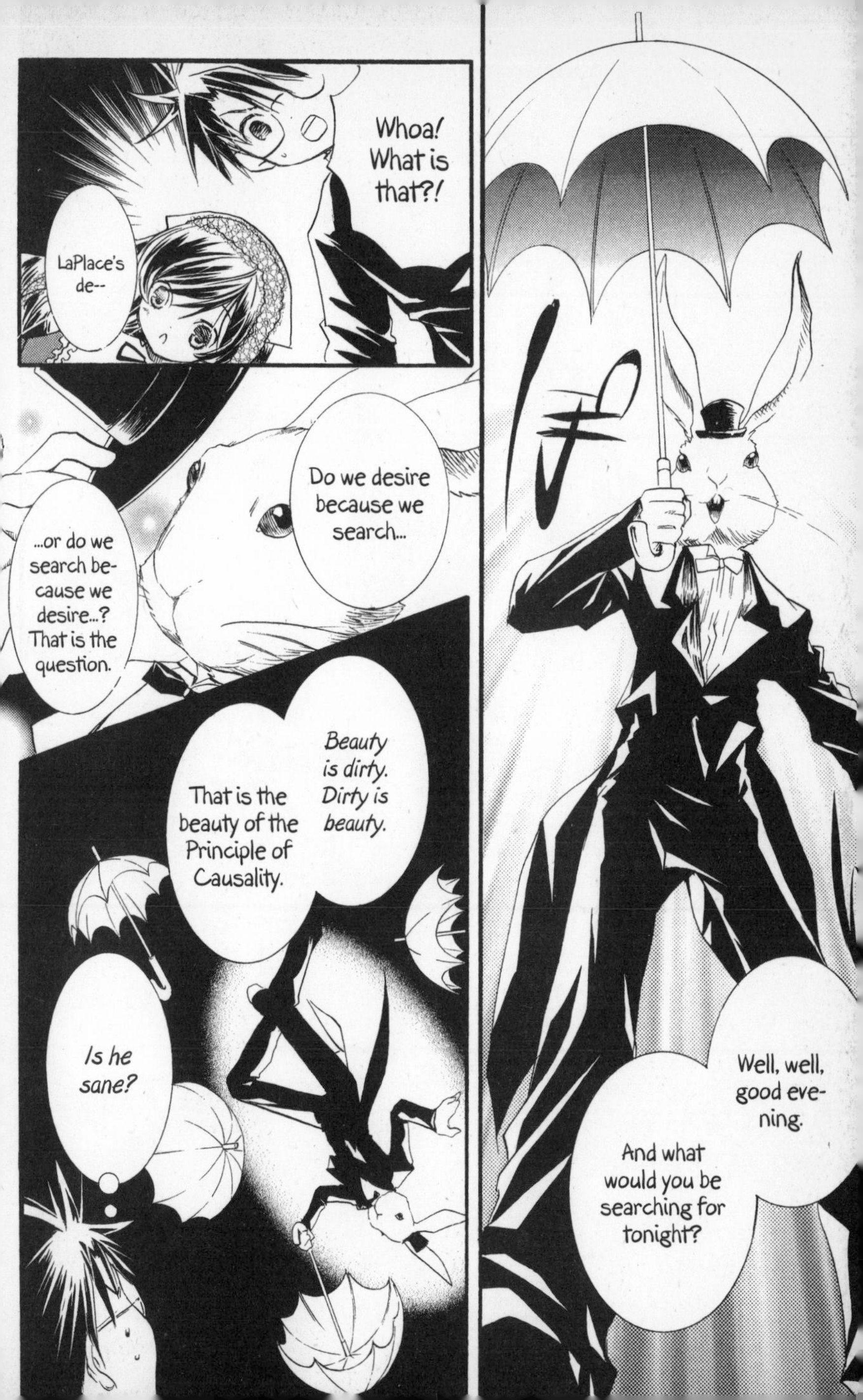
Well, well, good evening.
And what would you be searching for tonight?
Whoa! What is that?!
LaPlace's de--
Do we desire because we search...
...or do we search because we desire...? That is the question.
Beauty is dirty. Dirty is beauty.
That is the beauty of the Principle of Causality.
Is he sane?

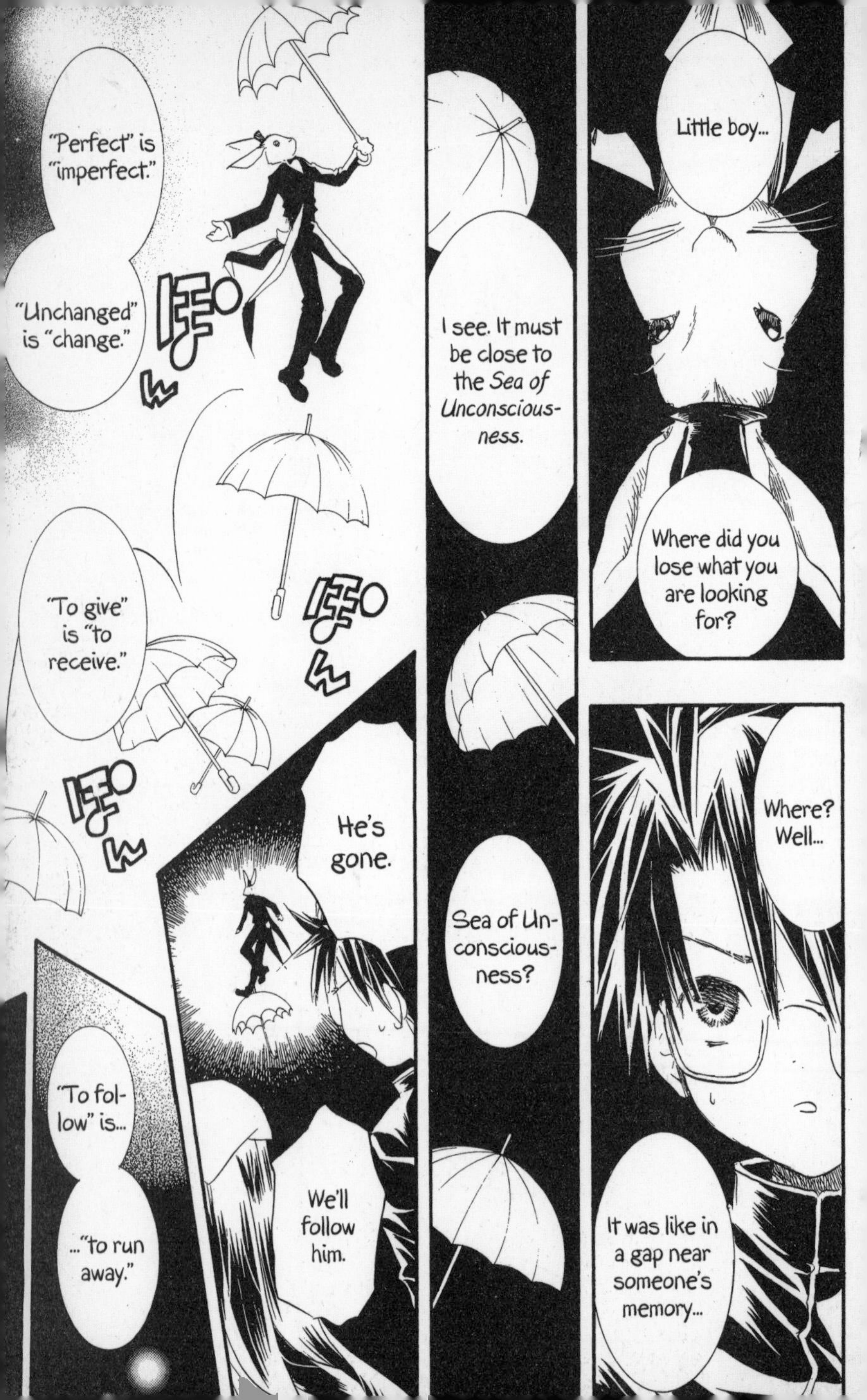
Little boy...
Where did you lose what you are looking for?
Where? Well...
It was like in a gap near someone's memory...
I see. It must be close to the *Sea of Unconsciousness.*
Sea of Unconsciousness?
"Perfect" is "imperfect."
"Unchanged" is "change."
"To give" is "to receive."
He's gone.
We'll follow him.
"To follow" is...
..."to run away."

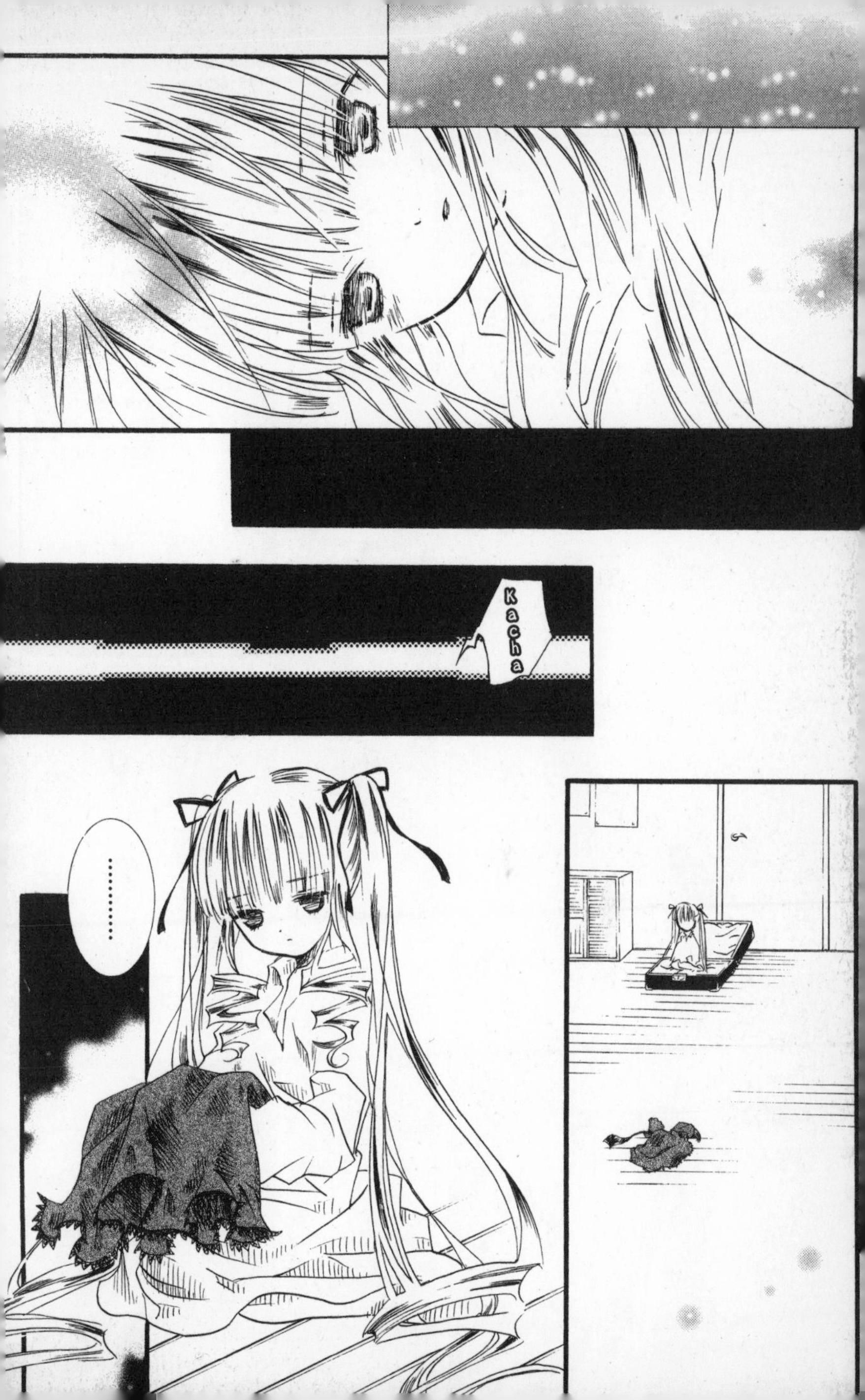
Kacha
......

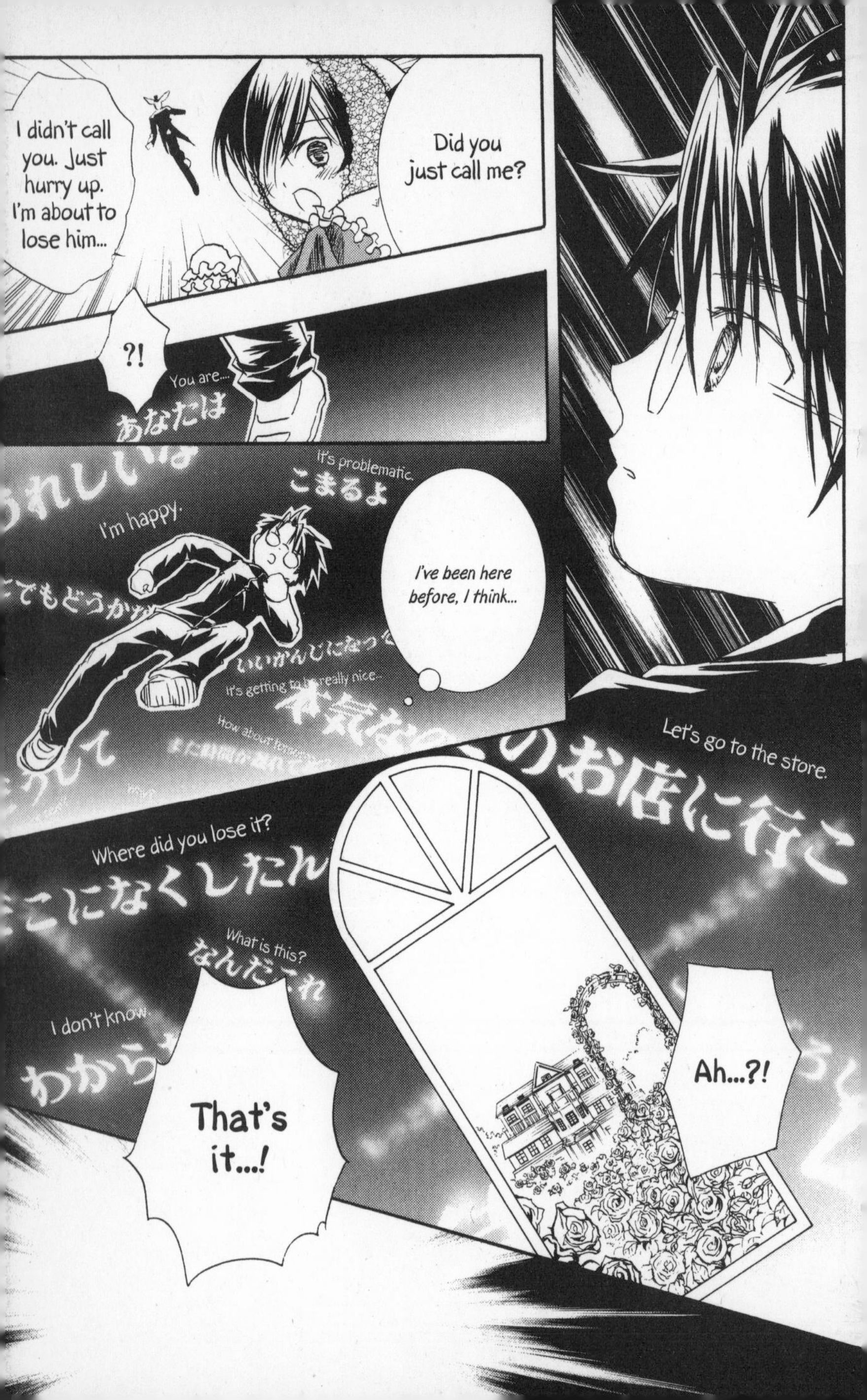
Did you just call me?
I didn't call you. Just hurry up. I'm about to lose him...
?!
You are...
あなたは
It's problematic.
こまるよ
I've been here before, I think...
I'm happy.
It's getting to be really nice.
Let's go to the store.
Ah...?!
Where did you lose it?
What is this?
That's it...!
I don't know.

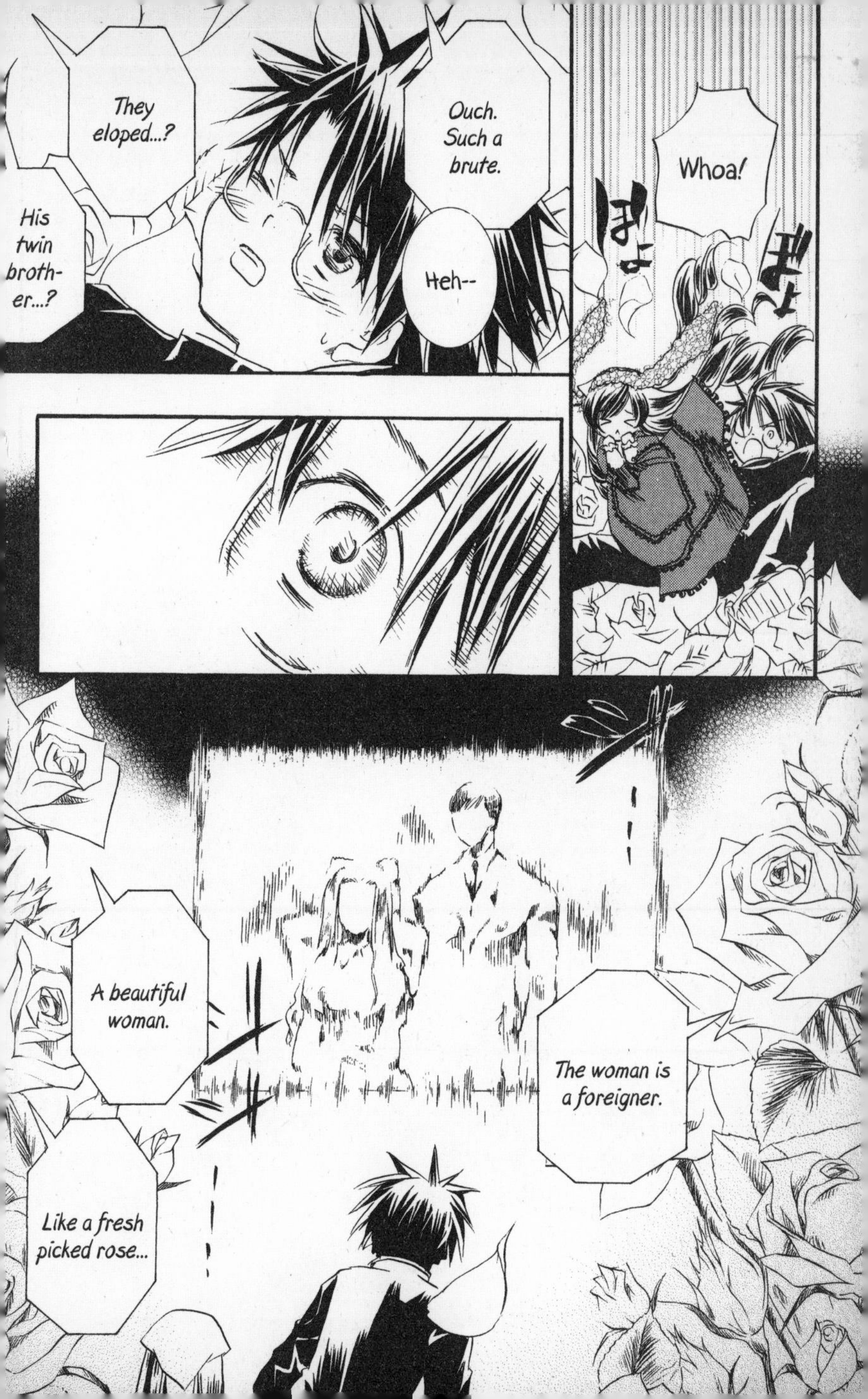
Whoa!
ぽよ
ぽよ
Ouch. Such a brute.
Heh--
They eloped...?
His twin brother...?
A beautiful woman.
The woman is a foreigner.
Like a fresh picked rose...

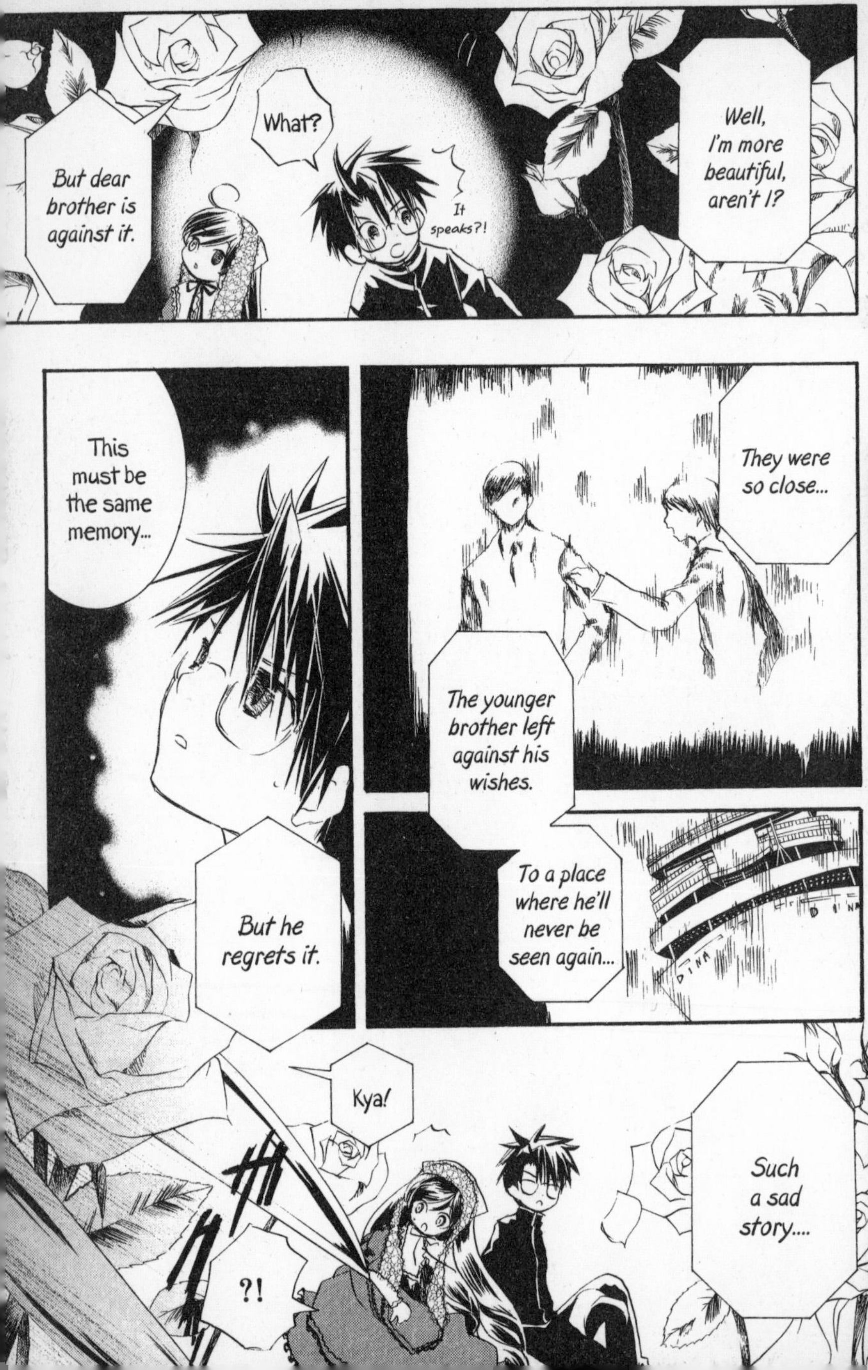
Well, I'm more beautiful, aren't I?
What?
It speaks?!
But dear brother is against it.
They were so close...
The younger brother left against his wishes.
To a place where he'll never be seen again...
This must be the same memory...
But he regrets it.
Such a sad story....
Kya!
?!

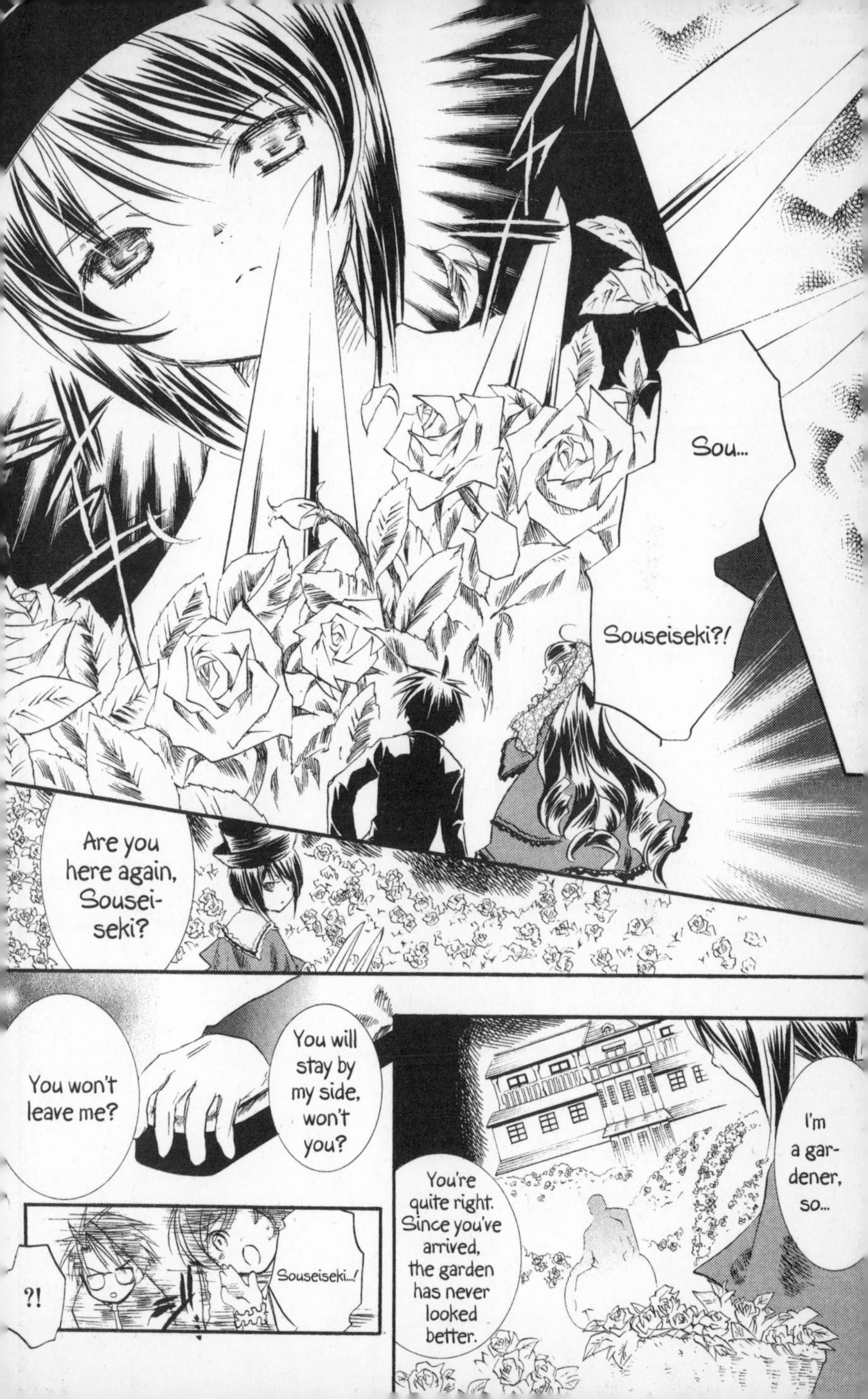
Sou...
Souseiseki?!
Are you here again, Sousei-seki?
I'm a gar-dener, so...
You're quite right. Since you've arrived, the garden has never looked better.
You will stay by my side, won't you?
You won't leave me?
Souseiseki...!
?!

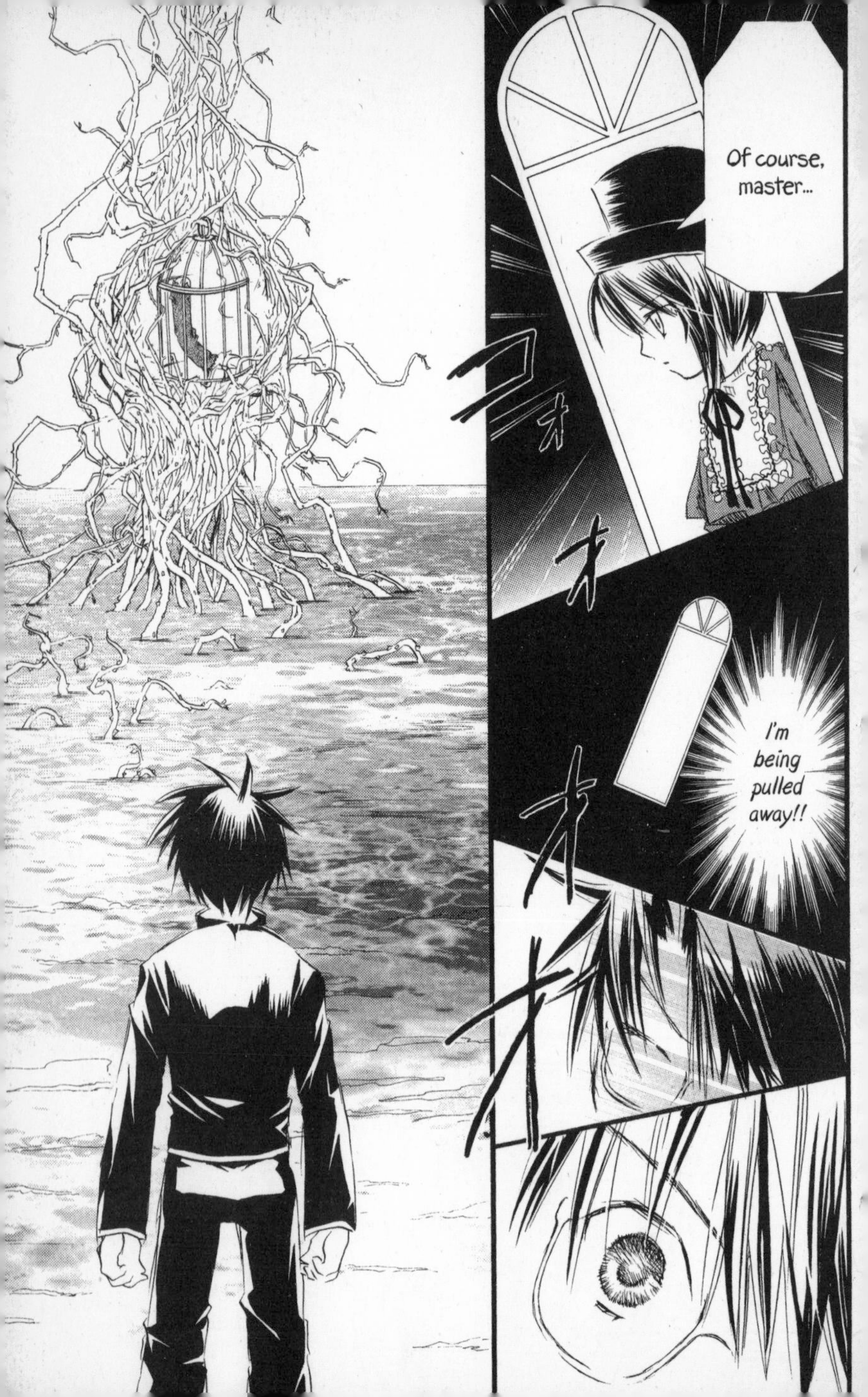
Of course, master...
I'm being pulled away!!

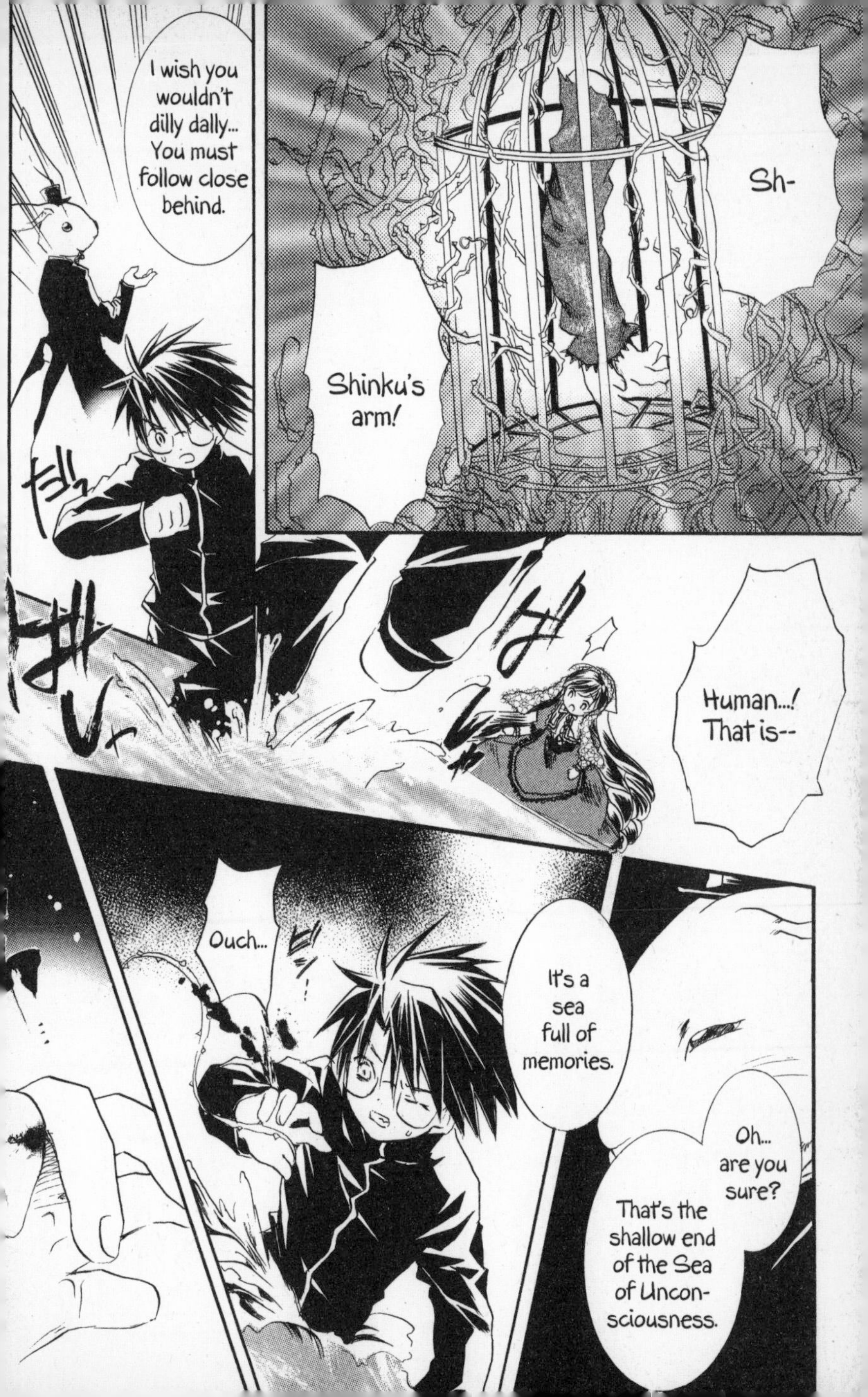
Sh-
Shinku's arm!
I wish you wouldn't dilly dally... You must follow close behind.
Human...! That is--
Oh... are you sure?
That's the shallow end of the Sea of Uncon-sciousness.
It's a sea full of memories.
Ouch...

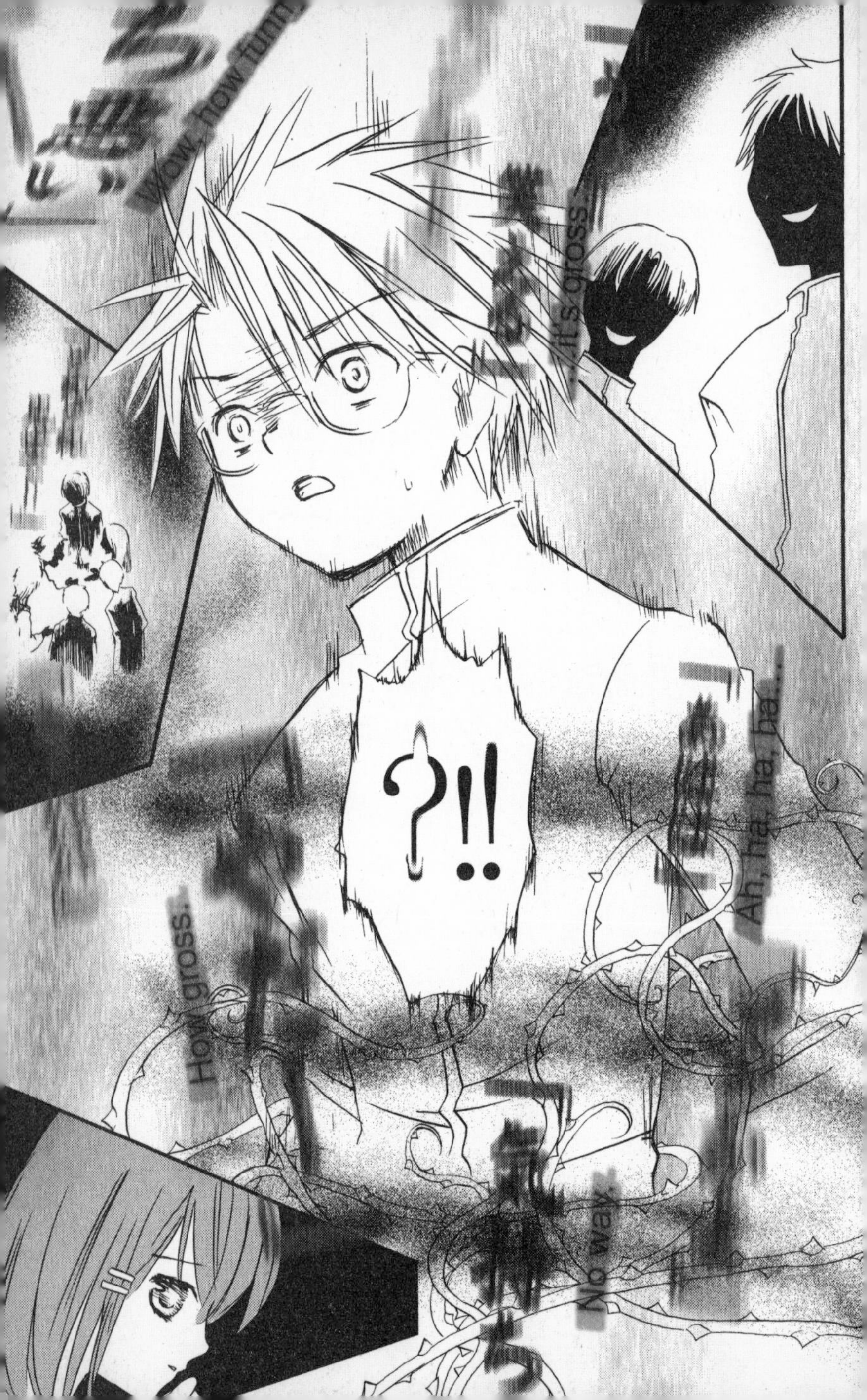
...It's gross...
Wow, how funn
?!!
Ah, ha, ha, ha...
How gross.
No way.

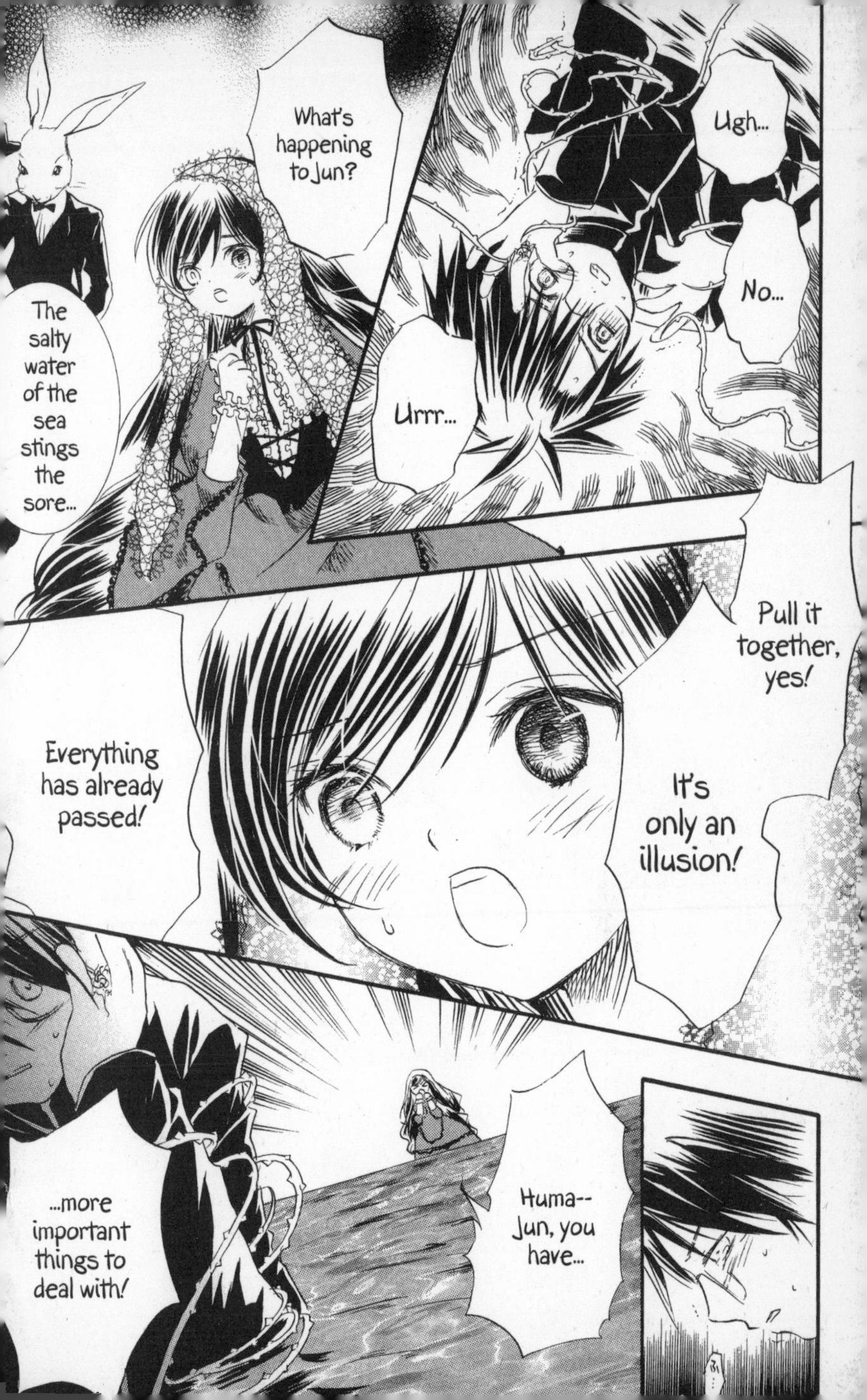
Ugh...
No...
Urrr...
What's happening to Jun?
The salty water of the sea stings the sore...
Pull it together, yes!
It's only an illusion!
Everything has already passed!
Huma-- Jun, you have...
...more important things to deal with!

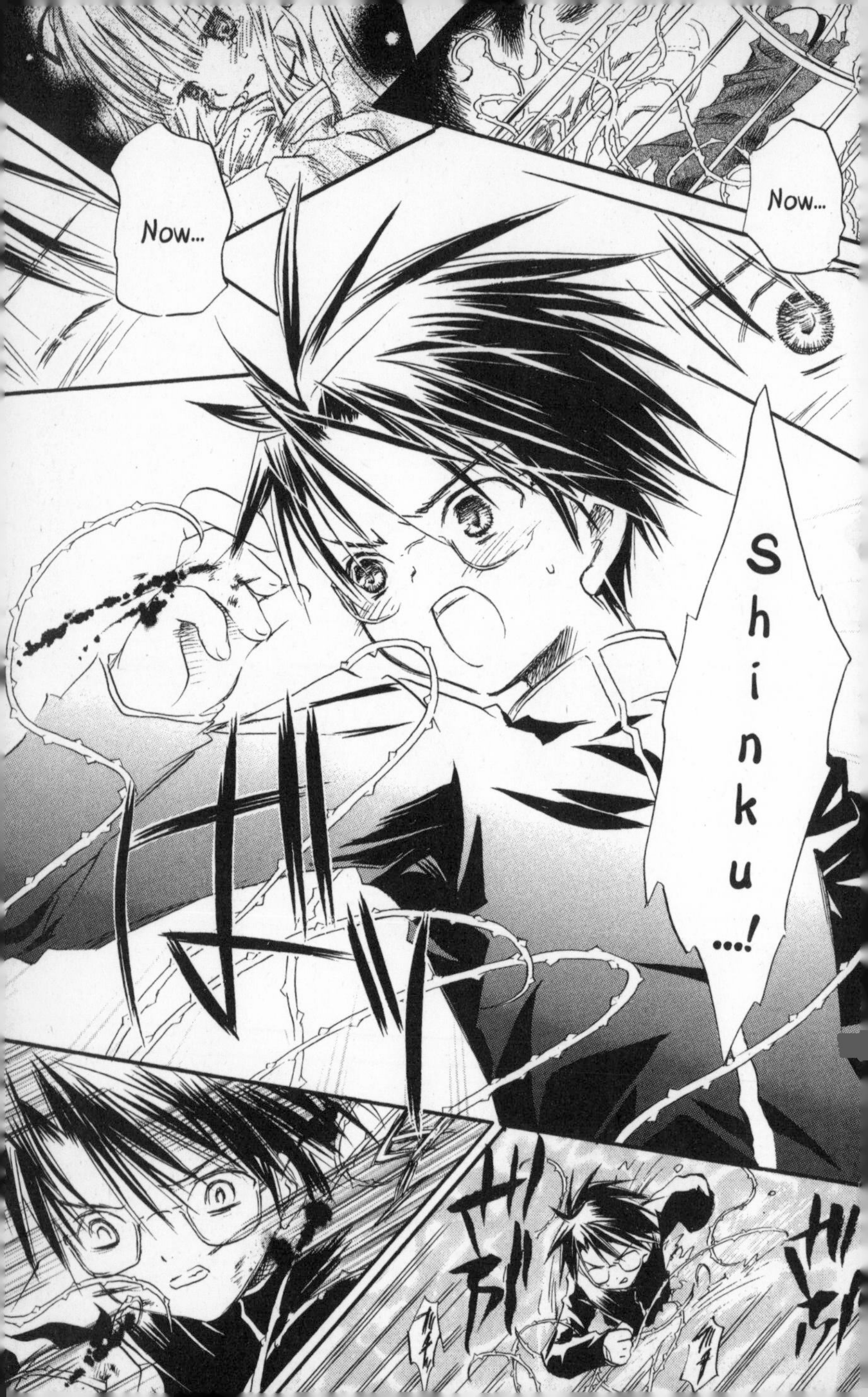
Now...
Now...
Shinku...!

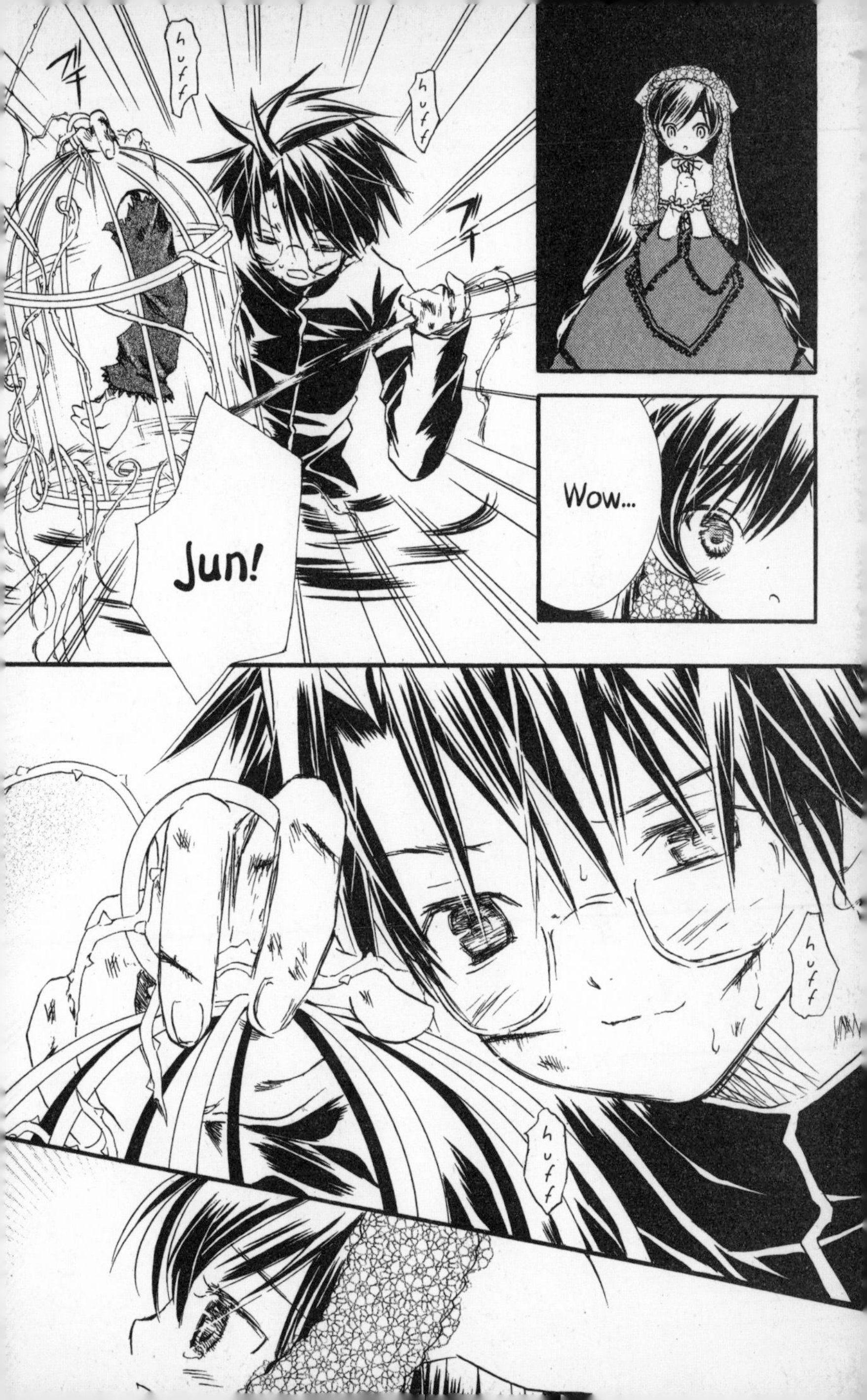
Wow...
huff
huff
Jun!
huff
huff

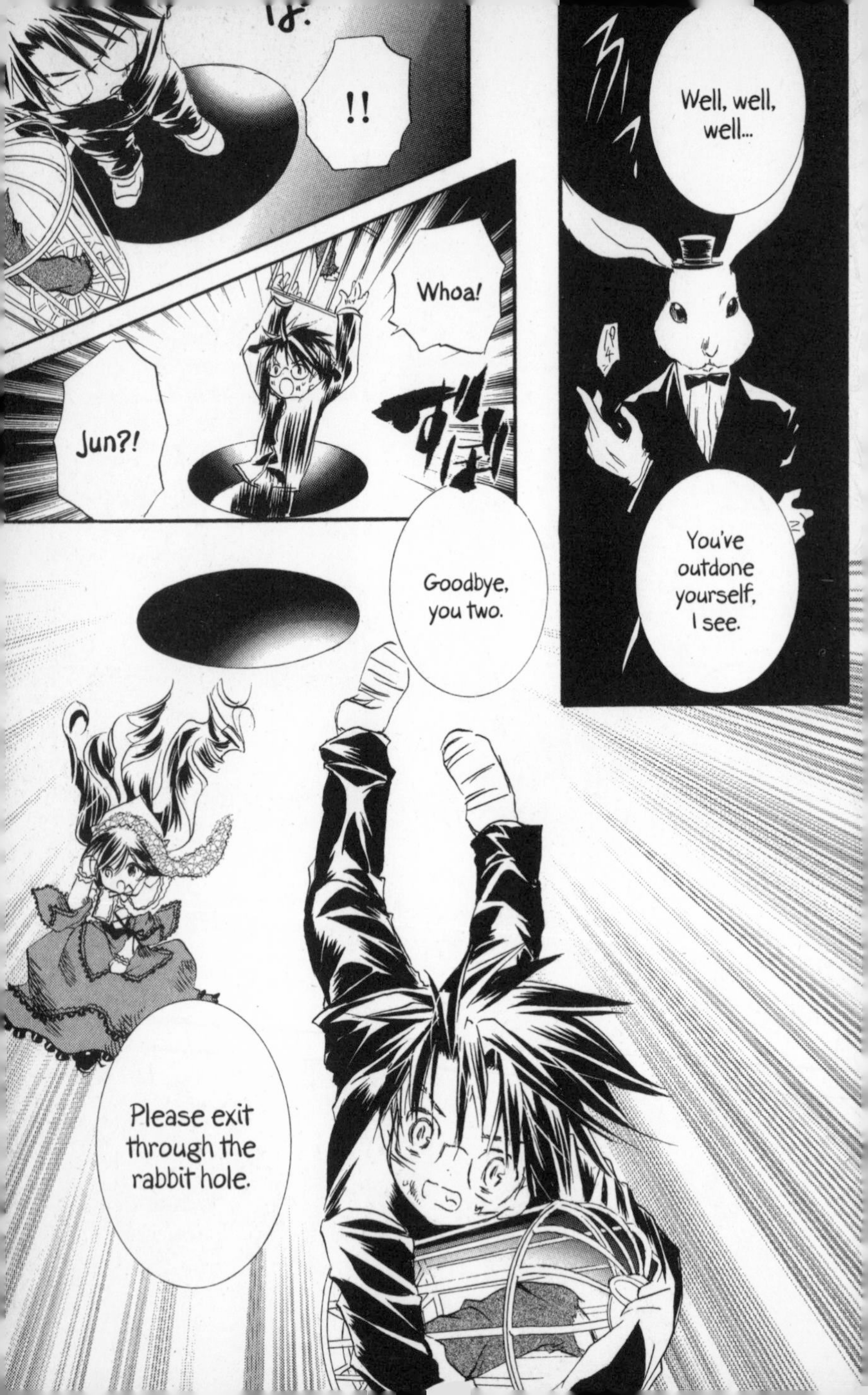
Well, well, well...
You've outdone yourself, I see.
!!
Whoa!
Jun?!
Goodbye, you two.
Please exit through the rabbit hole.

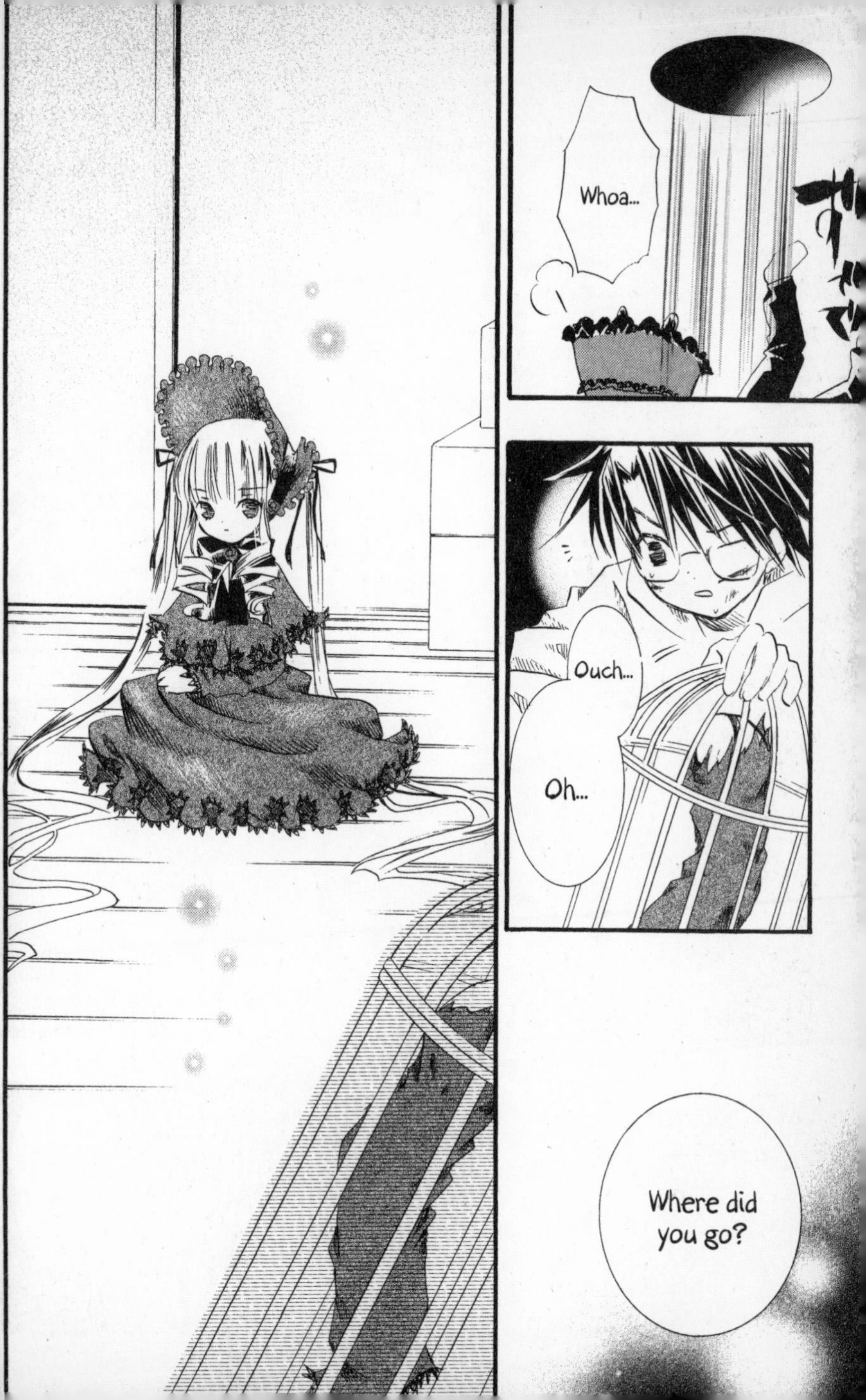
Whoa...
Ouch...
Oh...
Where did you go?

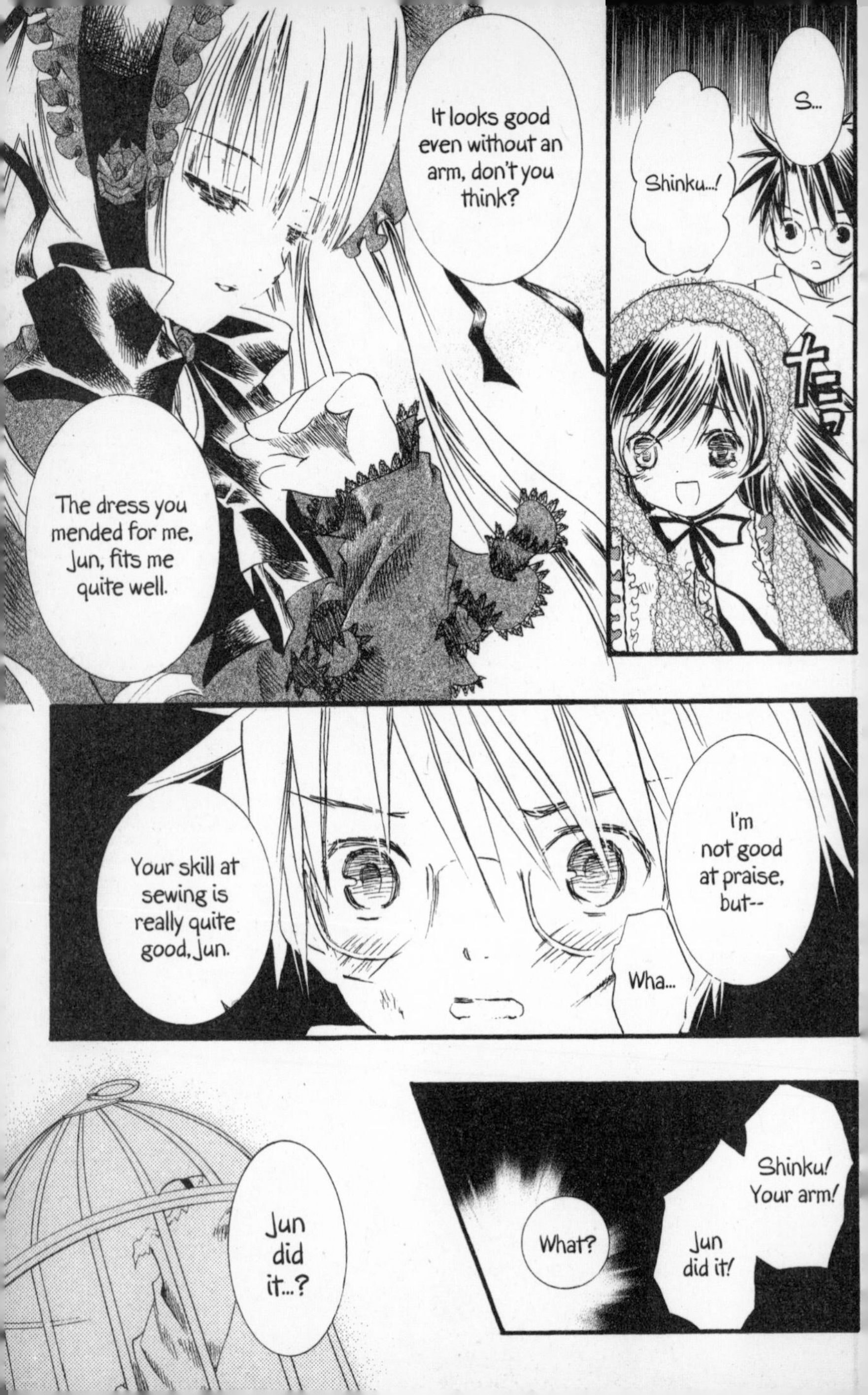
S...
Shinku...!
It looks good even without an arm, don't you think?
The dress you mended for me, Jun, fits me quite well.
I'm not good at praise, but--
Wha...
Your skill at sewing is really quite good, Jun.
Shinku! Your arm!
Jun did it!
What?
Jun did it...?

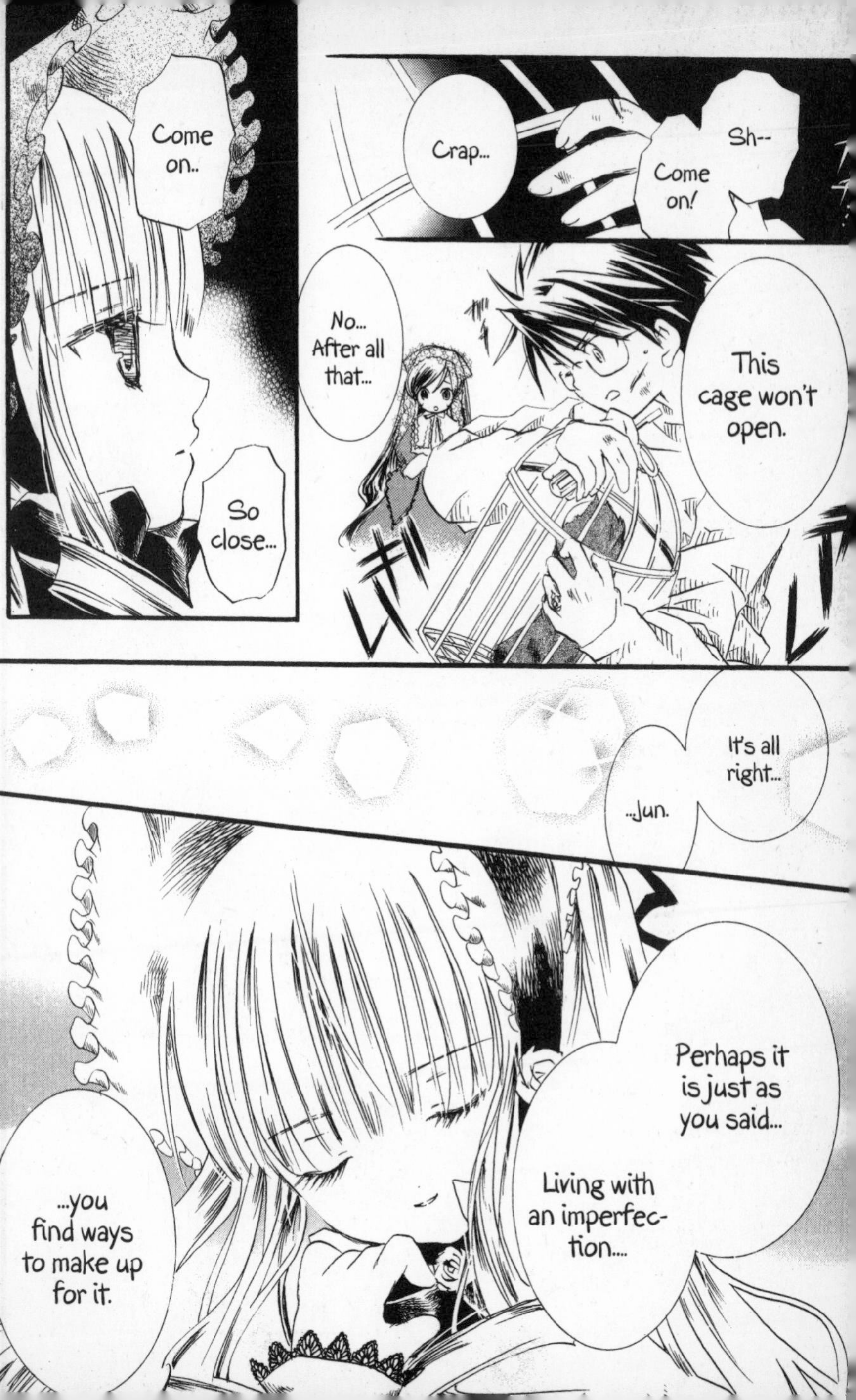
Sh--
Come on!
Crap...
This cage won't open.
No... After all that...
Come on..
So close...
It's all right...
...Jun.
Perhaps it is just as you said...
Living with an imperfection....
...you find ways to make up for it.

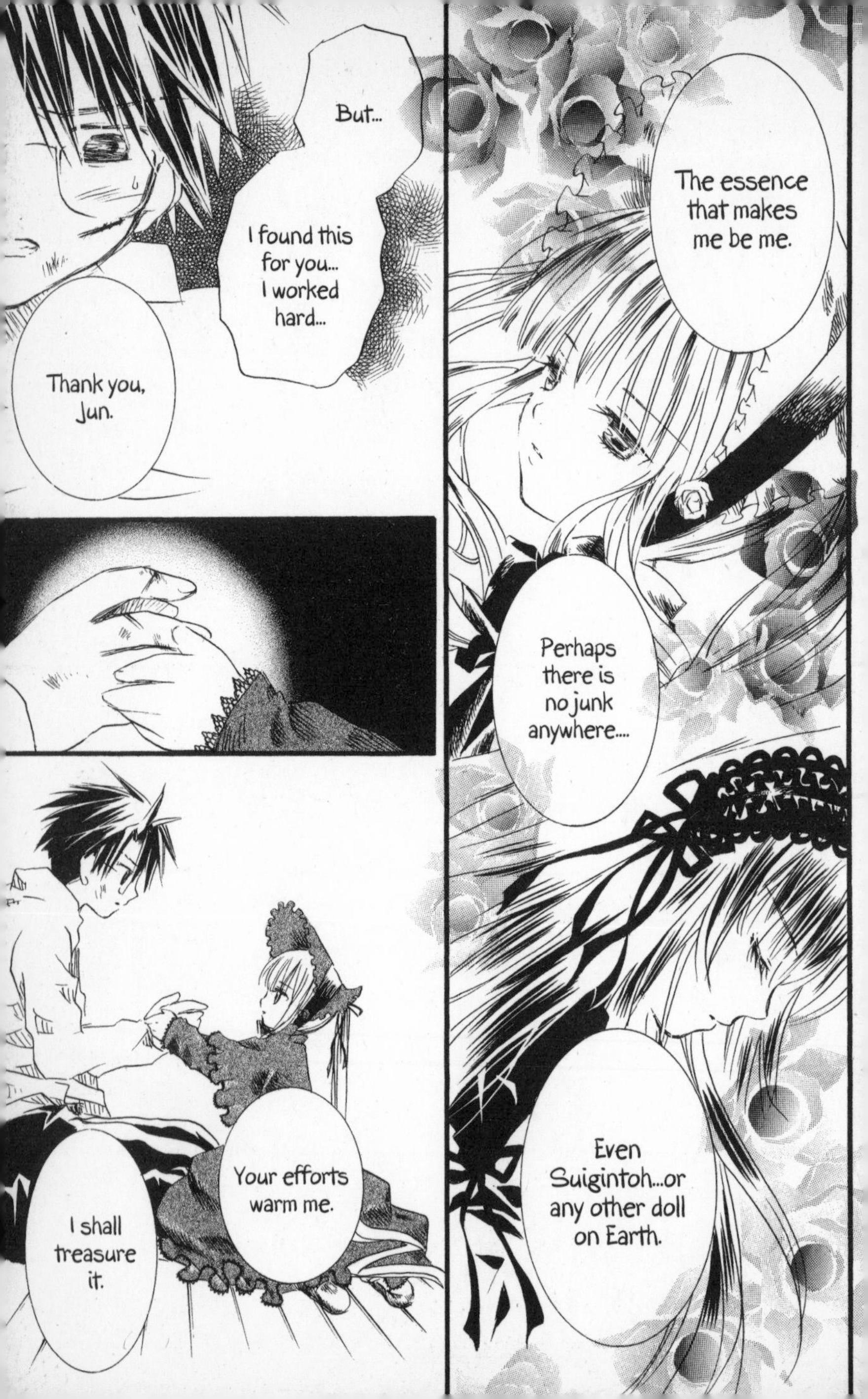
The essence that makes me be me.
Perhaps there is no junk anywhere....
Even Suigintoh...or any other doll on Earth.
But...
I found this for you... I worked hard...
Thank you, Jun.
Your efforts warm me.
I shall treasure it.

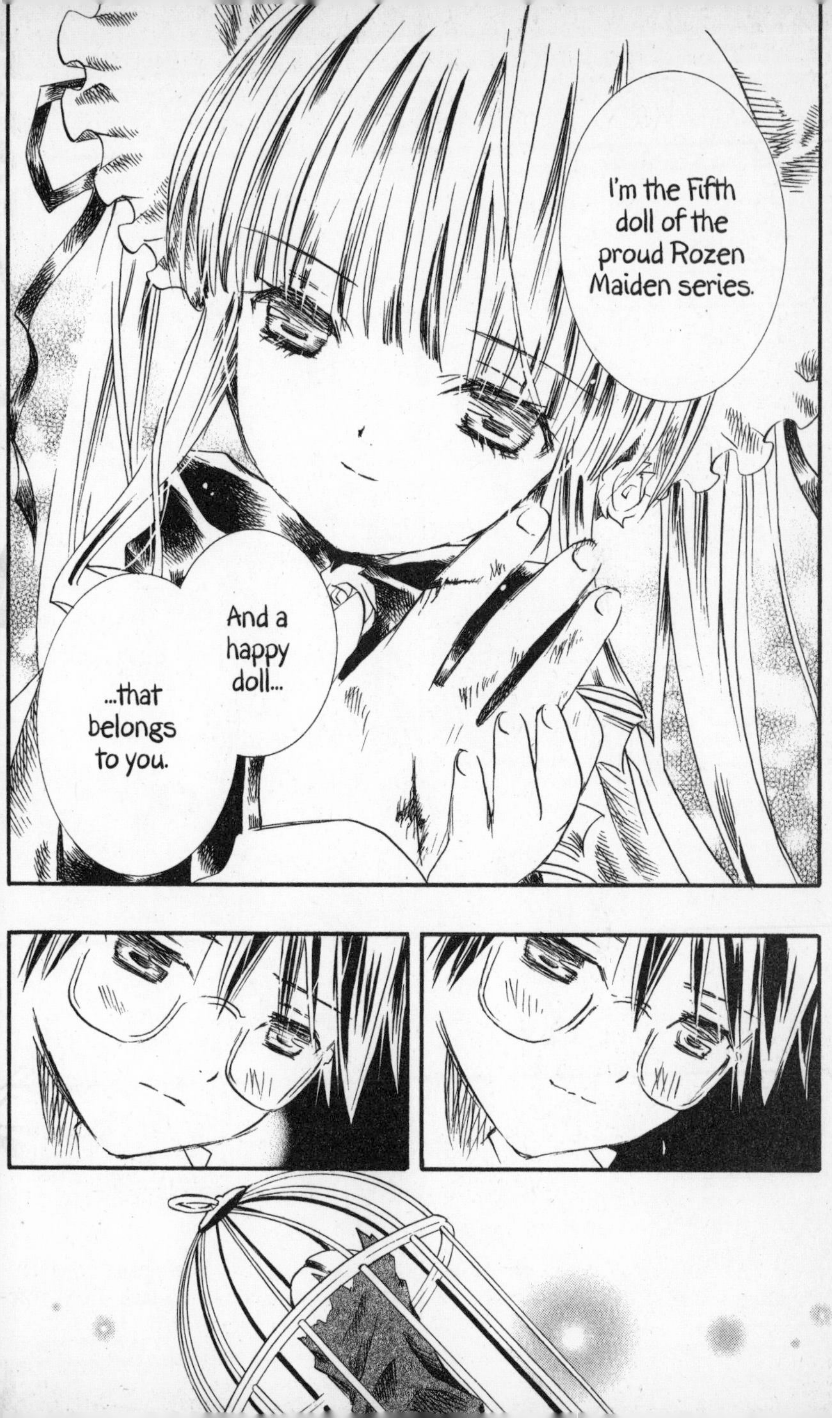
I'm the Fifth doll of the proud Rozen Maiden series.
And a happy doll...
...that belongs to you.

Three Titles Collaboration Comic

3作品コラボレーションコミック

RozenMaiden • ZOMBIE-LOAN • DearS

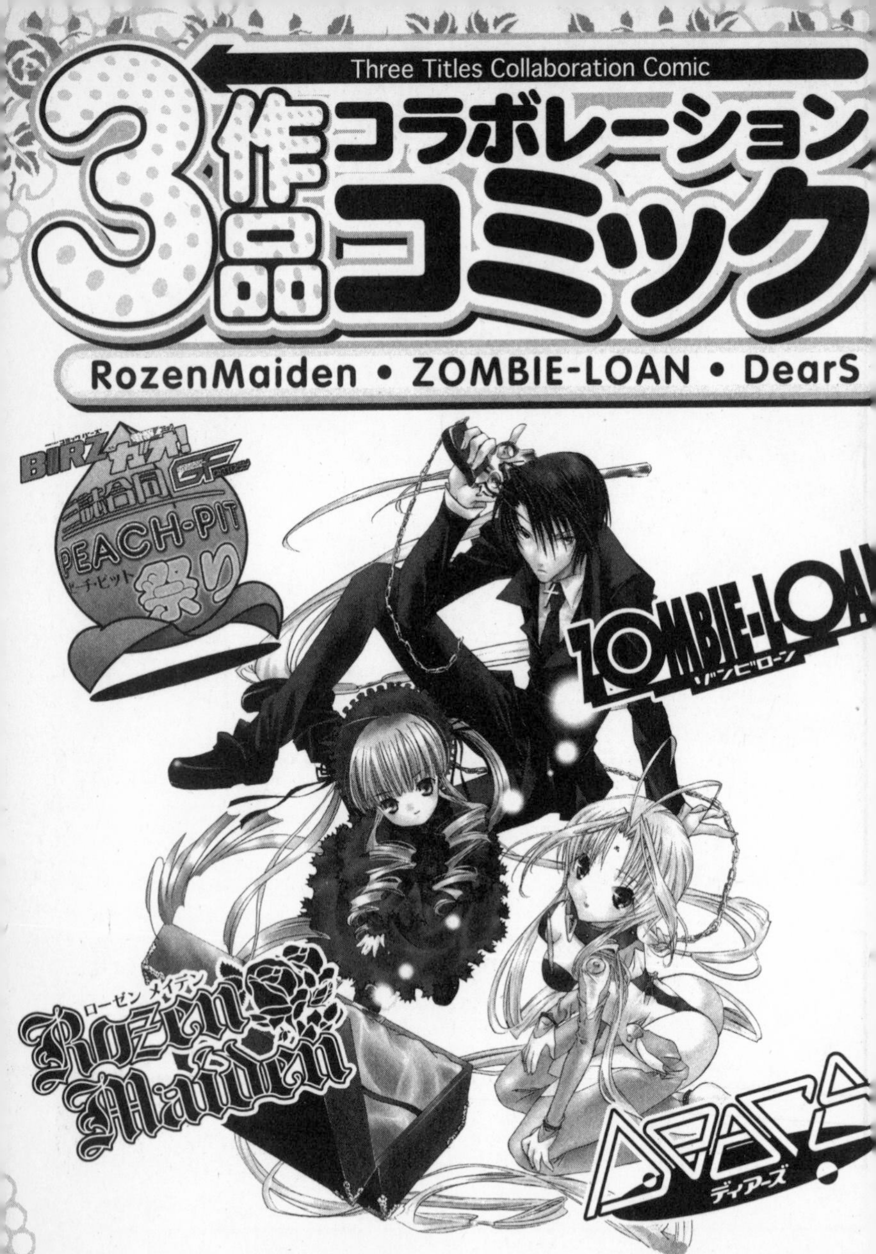
PEACH-PIT
ピーチ・ピット
祭り
ZOMBIE-LOAN
ゾンビローン
ローゼン メイデン
Rozen Maiden
ディアーズ

In the winter of 2003, a coordinated effort by three magazines, each of which carried one of the Peach-Pit titles, decided to create a comic in which the characters from the three titles all meet. We hope you enjoy!

Collaboration #1

RozenMaiden

First appeared on Comic Birz, Jan & Feb 2004 issue (Gentohsha Comics Publisher)

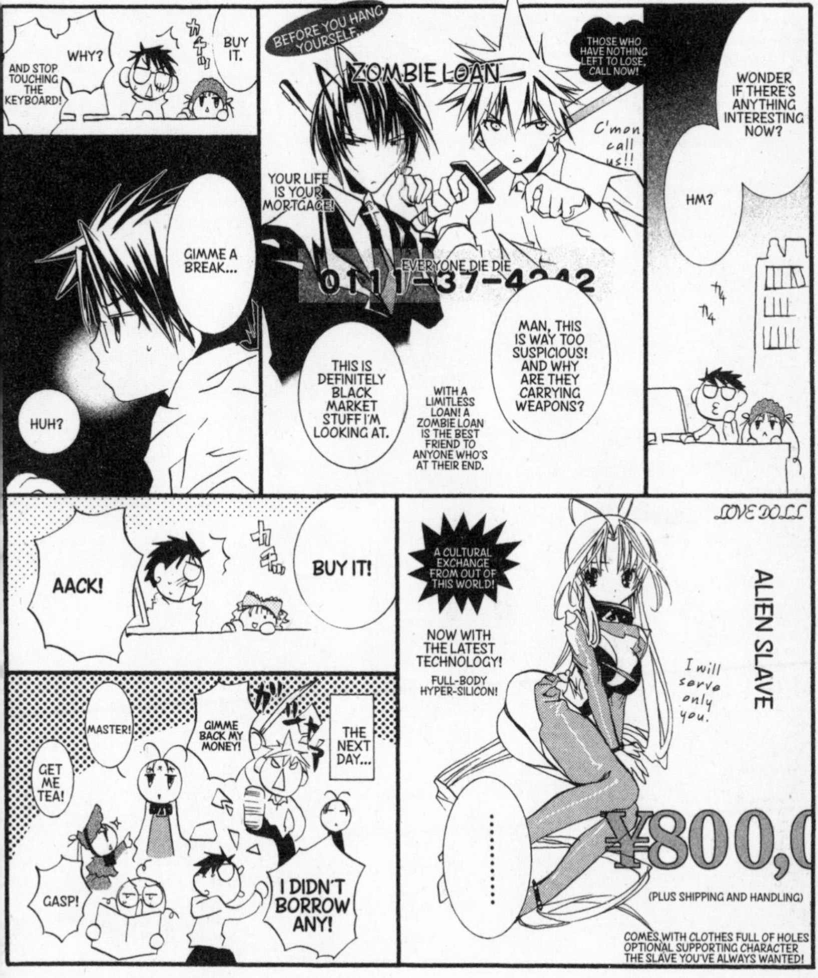

WONDER IF THERE'S ANYTHING INTERESTING NOW?
HM?
BEFORE YOU HANG YOURSELF...
THOSE WHO HAVE NOTHING LEFT TO LOSE, CALL NOW!
ZOMBIE LOAN
C'mon call us!!
YOUR LIFE IS YOUR MORTGAGE!
EVERYONE DIE DIE
0111-37-4242
MAN, THIS IS WAY TOO SUSPICIOUS! AND WHY ARE THEY CARRYING WEAPONS?
WITH A LIMITLESS LOAN! A ZOMBIE LOAN IS THE BEST FRIEND TO ANYONE WHO'S AT THEIR END.
THIS IS DEFINITELY BLACK MARKET STUFF I'M LOOKING AT.
BUY IT.
WHY?
AND STOP TOUCHING THE KEYBOARD!
GIMME A BREAK...
HUH?
LOVE DOLL
ALIEN SLAVE
A CULTURAL EXCHANGE FROM OUT OF THIS WORLD!
I will serve only you.
NOW WITH THE LATEST TECHNOLOGY!
FULL-BODY HYPER-SILICON!
¥800,0
......
(PLUS SHIPPING AND HANDLING)
COMES,WITH CLOTHES FULL OF HOLES
OPTIONAL SUPPORTING CHARACTER
THE SLAVE YOU'VE ALWAYS WANTED!
BUY IT!
AACK!
THE NEXT DAY...
GIMME BACK MY MONEY!
MASTER!
GET ME TEA!
I DIDN'T BORROW ANY!
GASP!

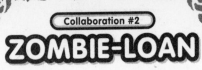

Collaboration #2

ZOMBIE-LOAN

First Published in Monthly G Fantasy, January 2004 issue (Square-Enix Publisher)

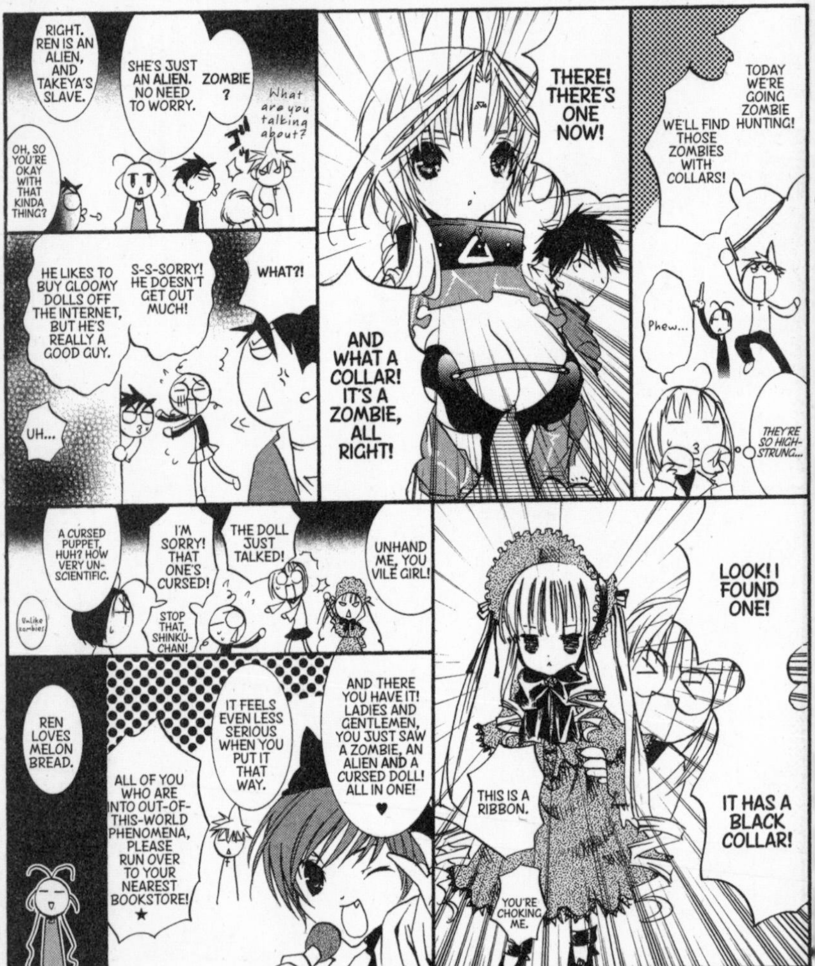
TODAY WE'RE GOING ZOMBIE HUNTING!
WE'LL FIND THOSE ZOMBIES WITH COLLARS!
Phew...
THEY'RE SO HIGH-STRUNG...
THERE! THERE'S ONE NOW!
AND WHAT A COLLAR! IT'S A ZOMBIE, ALL RIGHT!
What are you talking about?
ZOMBIE ?
SHE'S JUST AN ALIEN. NO NEED TO WORRY.
RIGHT. REN IS AN ALIEN, AND TAKEYA'S SLAVE.
OH, SO YOU'RE OKAY WITH THAT KINDA THING?
WHAT?!
S-S-SORRY! HE DOESN'T GET OUT MUCH!
HE LIKES TO BUY GLOOMY DOLLS OFF THE INTERNET, BUT HE'S REALLY A GOOD GUY.
UH...
LOOK! I FOUND ONE!
IT HAS A BLACK COLLAR!
THIS IS A RIBBON.
YOU'RE CHOKING ME.
UNHAND ME, YOU VILE GIRL!
THE DOLL JUST TALKED!
I'M SORRY! THAT ONE'S CURSED!
STOP THAT, SHINKU-CHAN!
A CURSED PUPPET, HUH? HOW VERY UN-SCIENTIFIC.
Unlike zombies
AND THERE YOU HAVE IT! LADIES AND GENTLEMEN, YOU JUST SAW A ZOMBIE, AN ALIEN AND A CURSED DOLL! ALL IN ONE! ♥
IT FEELS EVEN LESS SERIOUS WHEN YOU PUT IT THAT WAY.
ALL OF YOU WHO ARE INTO OUT-OF-THIS-WORLD PHENOMENA, PLEASE RUN OVER TO YOUR NEAREST BOOKSTORE! ★
REN LOVES MELON BREAD.

Collaboration #3

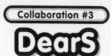

DearS

First Published in Gao! The Monthly Comic Magazine, Febuary 2004 issue (Media Works Publisher)

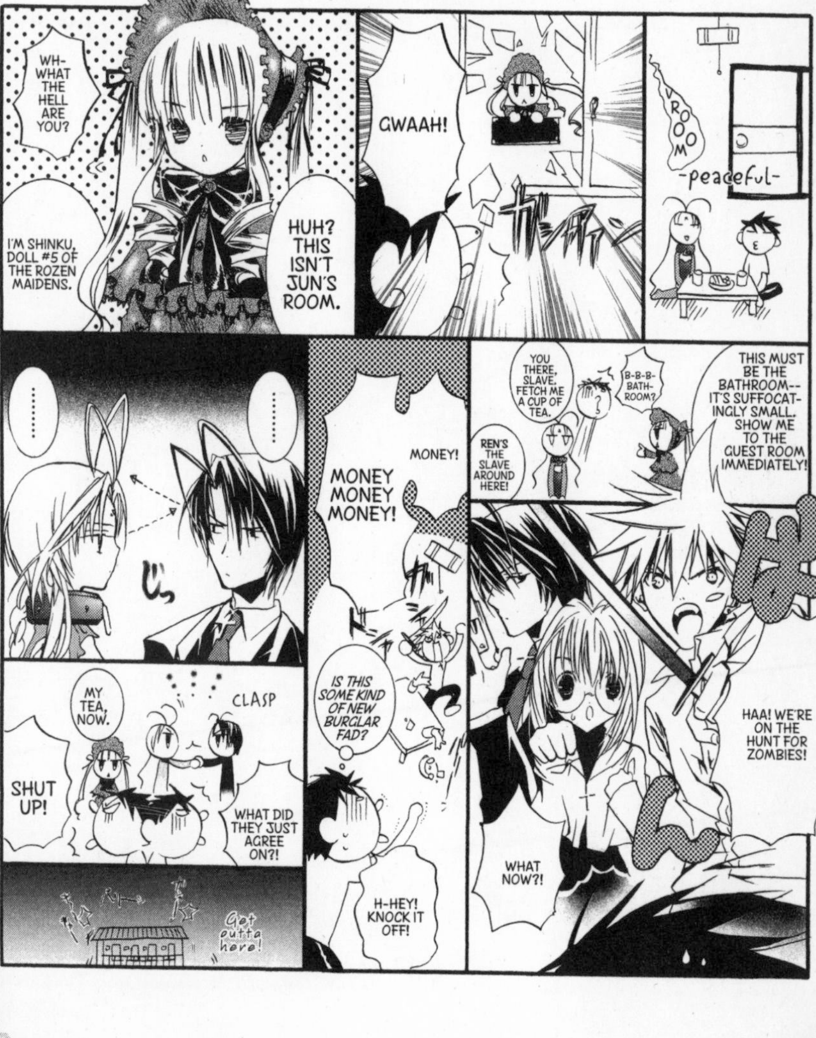
VROOOM
-peaceful-
GWAAH!
HUH? THIS ISN'T JUN'S ROOM.
WH- WHAT THE HELL ARE YOU?
I'M SHINKU, DOLL #5 OF THE ROZEN MAIDENS.
THIS MUST BE THE BATHROOM-- IT'S SUFFOCATINGLY SMALL. SHOW ME TO THE GUEST ROOM IMMEDIATELY!
B-B-B-BATHROOM?
YOU THERE, SLAVE, FETCH ME A CUP OF TEA.
REN'S THE SLAVE AROUND HERE!
HAA! WE'RE ON THE HUNT FOR ZOMBIES!
WHAT NOW?!
MONEY!
MONEY MONEY MONEY!
IS THIS SOME KIND OF NEW BURGLAR FAD?
H-HEY! KNOCK IT OFF!
......
......
MY TEA, NOW.
CLASP
SHUT UP!
WHAT DID THEY JUST AGREE ON?!
Get outta here!

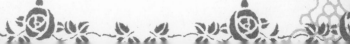

ローゼン メイデン
Rozen Maiden

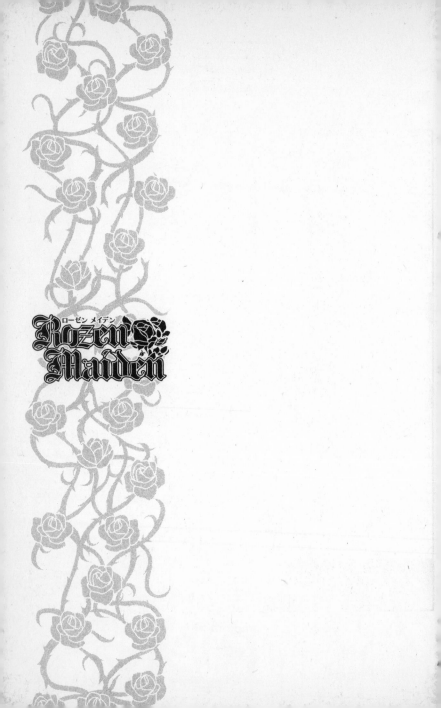

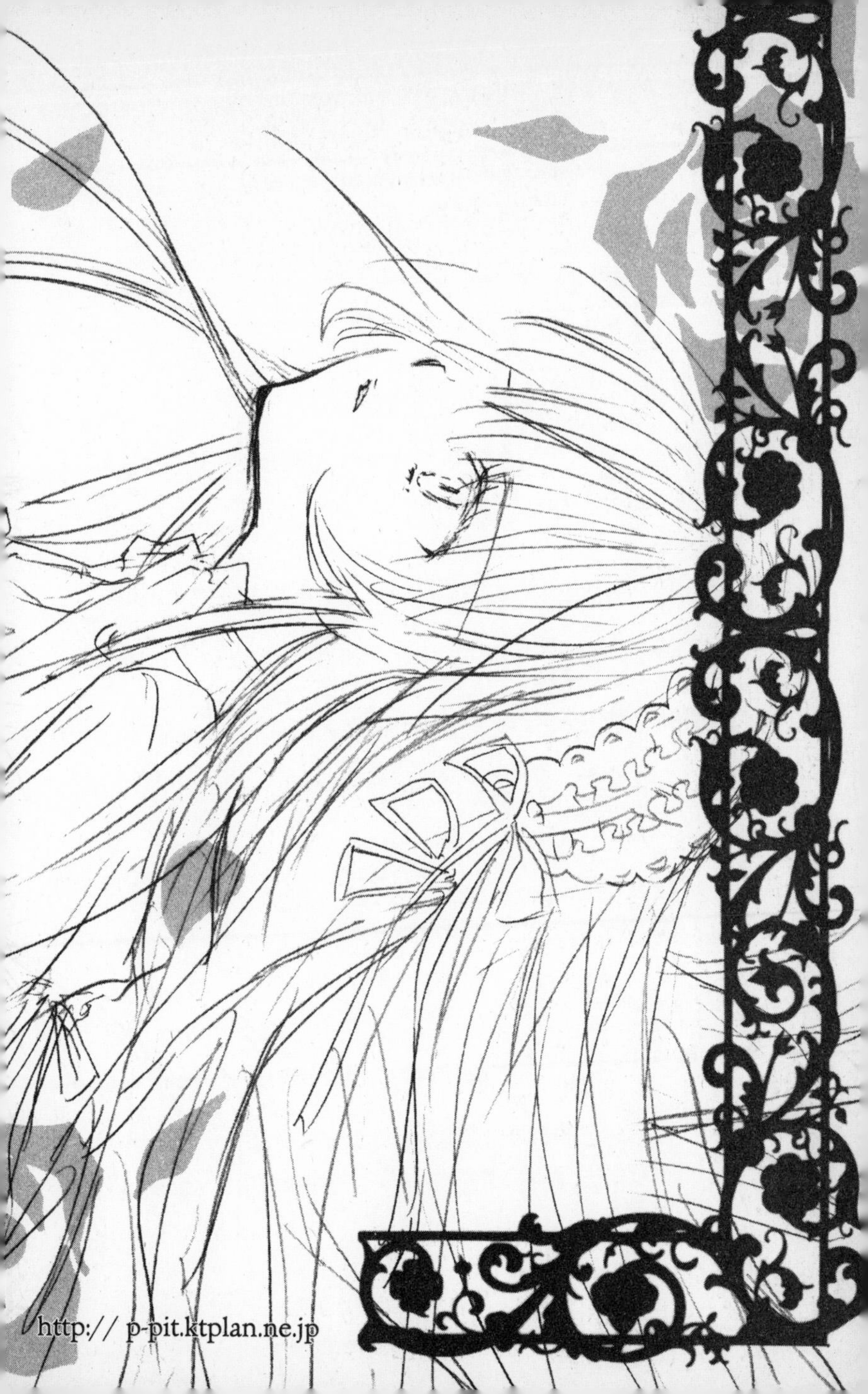

http:// p-pit.ktplan.ne.jp

Rozen Maiden

all produced by

PEACH·PIT

Shikniko Ebara *** Banri Sendou

MAIN STAFF
Nao
Zaki
Kiniming
Bunbun
Special thanks
T. Oda
Momiji Takako
...and your reading

Preview for Volume 4

Driven by what he saw in the dream world while retrieving Shinku's arm, Jun searches the internet for an explanation for it all, where he learns the identity of Souseiseki's dark and evil master...Kazuyo, one of the twin brothers he saw fighting in the sea of unconscious. And his thirst for revenge against the woman who took his brother Futaba away forever involves Souseiseki and Suiseiseki. But with Suiseiseki now bound to her new master Jun, another battle between siblings will begin.

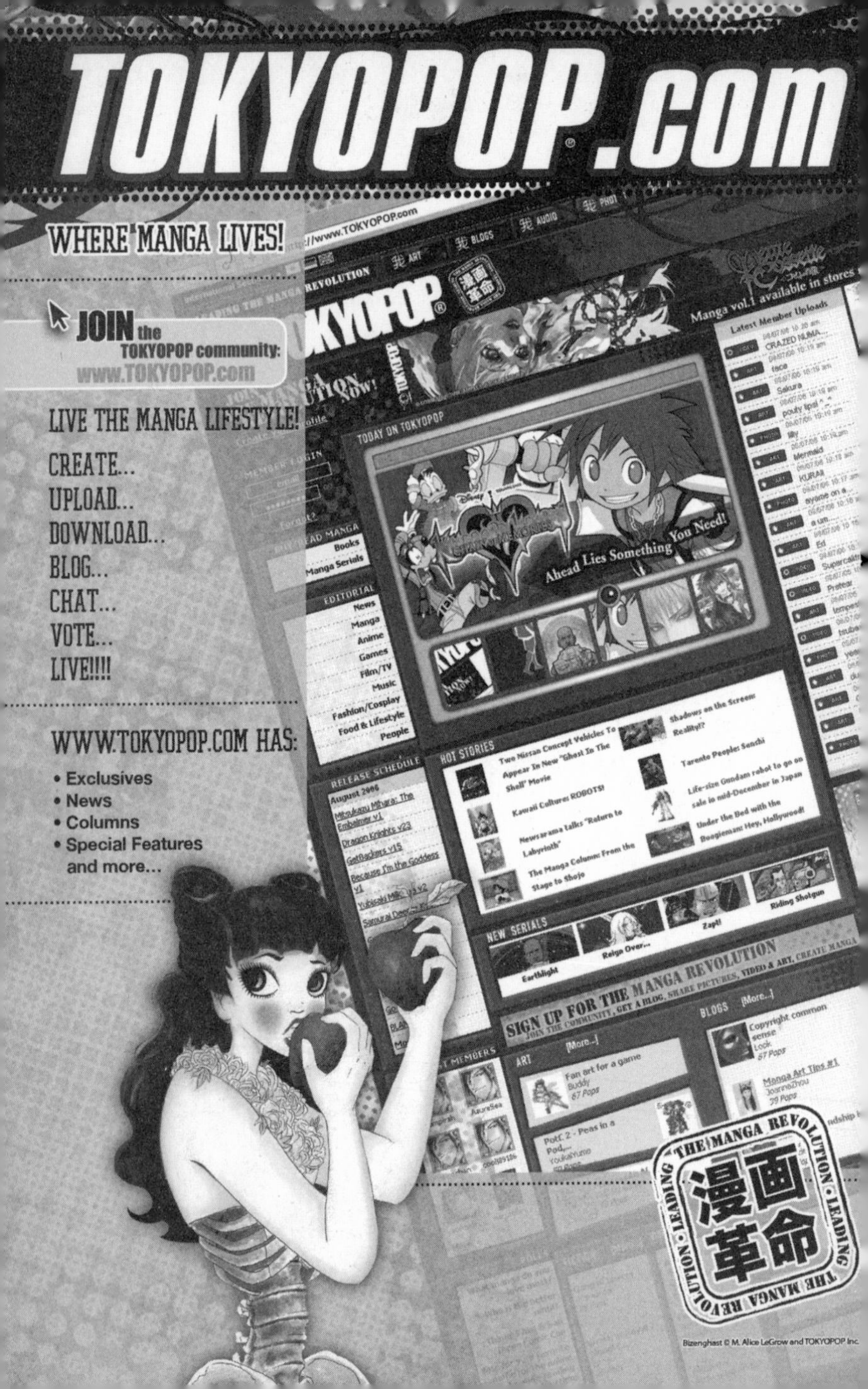
TOKYOPOP.com
WHERE MANGA LIVES!
JOIN the TOKYOPOP community: www.TOKYOPOP.com
LIVE THE MANGA LIFESTYLE!
CREATE...
UPLOAD...
DOWNLOAD...
BLOG...
CHAT...
VOTE...
LIVE!!!!
WWW.TOKYOPOP.COM HAS:
• Exclusives
• News
• Columns
• Special Features and more...
THE MANGA REVOLUTION • LEADING THE MANGA REVOLUTION • LEADING
漫画革命
Bizenghast © M. Alice LeGrow and TOKYOPOP Inc.

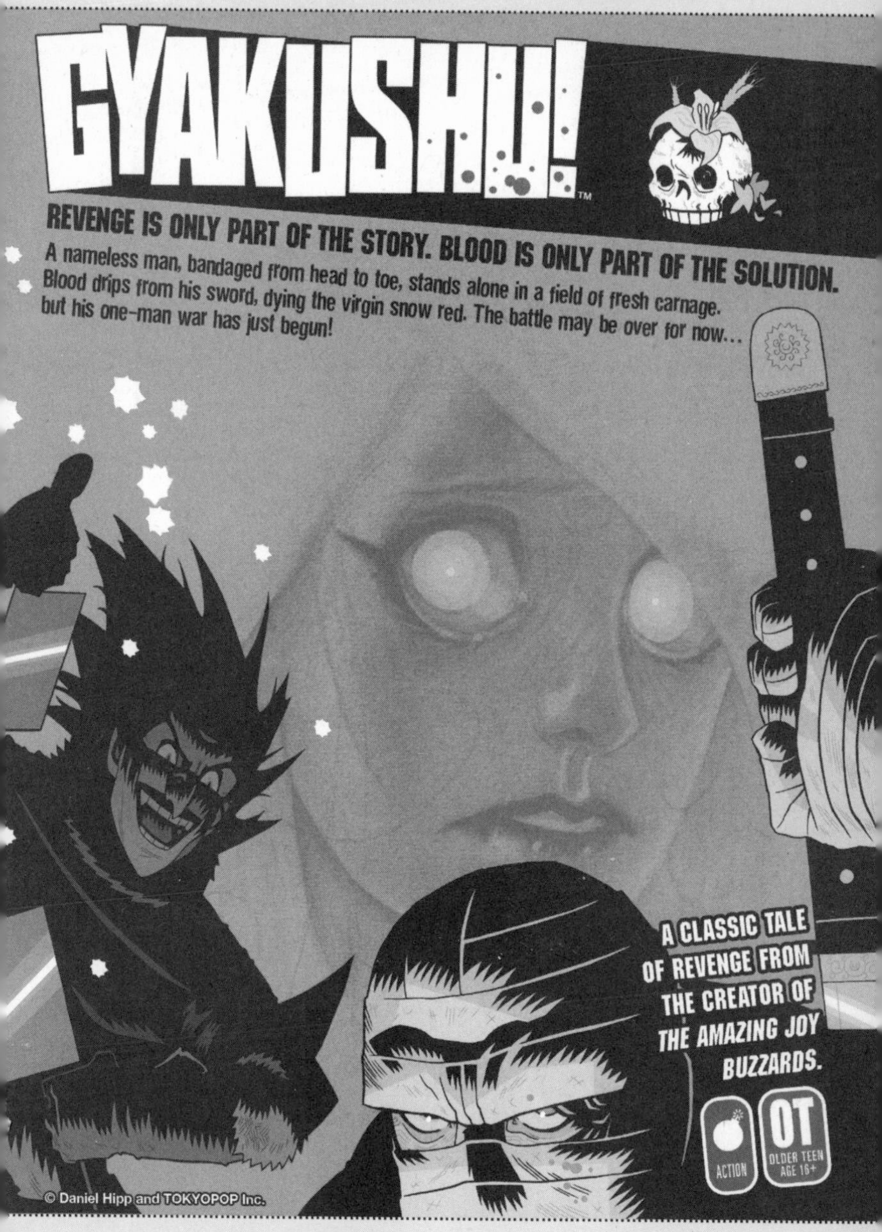
GYAKUSHU!™
REVENGE IS ONLY PART OF THE STORY. BLOOD IS ONLY PART OF THE SOLUTION.
A nameless man, bandaged from head to toe, stands alone in a field of fresh carnage. Blood drips from his sword, dying the virgin snow red. The battle may be over for now... but his one-man war has just begun!
A CLASSIC TALE OF REVENGE FROM THE CREATOR OF THE AMAZING JOY BUZZARDS.
ACTION
OT
OLDER TEEN AGE 16+
© Daniel Hipp and TOKYOPOP Inc.

STOP!

This is the back of the book.
You wouldn't want to spoil a great ending!

This book is printed "manga-style," in the authentic Japanese right-to-left format. Since none of the artwork has been flipped or altered, readers get to experience the story just as the creator intended. You've been asking for it, so TOKYOPOP® delivered: authentic, hot-off-the-press, and far more fun!

DIRECTIONS

1
2
3
4
5
6
7
8
9
10

If this is your first time reading manga-style, here's a quick guide to help you understand how it works.

It's easy... just start in the top right panel and follow the numbers. Have fun, and look for more 100% authentic manga from TOKYOPOP®!

THE MANGA REVOLUTION · LEADING
漫画革命
THE MANGA REVOLUTION · LEADING

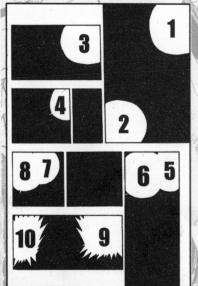

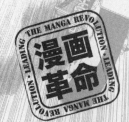